ENVIRONMENTAL LAW

FOURTH EDITION

Other books in the *Essentials of Canadian Law* Series

Immigration Law

International Trade Law

Family Law

Copyright Law

The Law of Sentencing

Administrative Law

Ethics and Canadian Criminal Law

Securities Law

Computer Law 2/e

Maritime Law

Insurance Law

International Human Rights Law

The Law of Trusts 2/e

Franchise Law

Pension Law

Legal Ethics and Professional Responsibility 2/e

Refugee Law

Statutory Interpretation 2/e

National Security Law: Canadian Practice in International Perspective

Remedies: The Law of Damages 2/e

Public International Law 2/e

Individual Employment Law 2/e

Bankruptcy and Insolvency Law

The Law of Partnerships and Corporations 3/e

Civil Litigation

International and Transnational Criminal Law

Conflict of Laws

Detention and Arrest

Canadian Telecommunications Law

The Law of Torts 4/e

Intellectual Property Law 2/e

The Law of Evidence 6/e

Animals and the Law

Income Tax Law 2/e

Fundamental Justice

Mergers, Acquisitions, and Other Changes of Corporate Control 2/e

Criminal Procedure 2/e

Criminal Law 5/e

Personal Property Security Law 2/e

The Law of Contracts 2/e

Youth Criminal Justice Law 3/e

Constitutional Law 4/e

Bank and Customer Law in Canada 2/e

The Law of Equitable Remedies 2/e

The Charter of Rights and Freedoms 5/e

ESSENTIALS OF
CANADIAN LAW

ENVIRONMENTAL LAW

FOURTH EDITION

JAMIE BENIDICKSON
Faculty of Law
University of Ottawa

Environmental Law, fourth edition
© Irwin Law Inc, 2013

Published in 2013 by

Irwin Law Inc
14 Duncan Street
Suite 206
Toronto, ON
M5H 3G8
www.irwinlaw.com

ISBN: 978-1-55221-345-2
e-book ISBN: 978-1-55221-346-9

Library and Archives Canada Cataloguing in Publication

Benidickson, Jamie, author
    Environmental law / Jamie Benidickson, Faculty of Law, University of Ottawa.—
Fourth edition.

(Essentials of Canadian law)
Includes bibliographical references and index.
Issued in print and electronic formats.
ISBN 978-1-55221-345-2 (pbk.).—ISBN 978-1-55221-346-9 (pdf)

    1. Environmental law—Canada. I. Title. II. Series: Essentials of Canadian law

| KE3619.B46 2013 | 344.7104'6 | C2013-904088-9 |
| KF3775.ZA2B46 2013 | | C2013-904089-7 |

The publisher acknowledges the financial support of the Government of Canada through the Canada Book Fund for its publishing activities.

We acknowledge the assistance of the OMDC Book Fund, an initiative of Ontario Media Development Corporation.

Printed and bound in Canada.

1 2 3 4 5   17 16 15 14 13

SUMMARY
TABLE OF CONTENTS

DETAILED
TABLE OF CONTENTS

FOREWORD
to the First Edition

When I graduated from law school in 1972, nowhere in the curriculum could one find a course called Environmental Law. To the extent that that subject matter was considered at all, it was through, at most, passing reference in courses such as Municipal Law, Torts, or International Law.

Twenty-five years later, the scene is remarkably changed. All Canadian law schools offer at least one such course. Many offer more. There are specialized law reports and journals, loose-leaf services, newsletters, casebooks, and national and provincial organizations devoted to research, education, and law reform. This flurry of activity reflects society's recognition of the importance of the environment. It also reflects the fact that law is one of the tools essential to environmental protection. Every day, courts and other tribunals in our country are called on to resolve disputes among parties such as governments, agencies, business, and private citizens, each of whom has a role to play in ensuring that our children will have a clean, healthy, and esthetically acceptable planet on which to reside.

As a judge, I appreciate the immense contribution made by my former academic colleagues to the clarification and explanation of law and legal systems. Academics are able to specialize in a way that most judges cannot. Judges must resolve specific cases; academics can take the long, wide view. I often turn to books and articles written by academic commentators to help me understand both the narrow and the broad aspects of a case that I have to decide.

That Professor Benidickson's book will play an integral role in informing readers like me is beyond doubt. It reflects the reality that legal problems about the environment arise in a myriad of settings from the common law to the *Charter*, from international law to statutory interpretation, from criminal liability to contractual arrangements — all these and many other legal areas provide the backdrop for environmental disputes. There are few other problems that require a decision maker to draw upon principles from such a vast array of legal doctrine. Equally important, environmental conflicts are rooted in a social, scientific, and economic context. This book will assist enormously in exposing that context, to, among others, law students, lawyers, regulators, scientists, business people, and judges.

The topics included in this book are broad and rich. Its explanations are clear, not only to those schooled in the law but to other affected professionals. It will help us understand the past. It will help point the way to the future. It will be an invaluable reference for legal professionals and the many others who are engaged in environmental protection endeavours.

Madam Justice Constance Hunt
Alberta Court of Appeal

ACKNOWLEDGMENTS

I would like to thank Elaine Borg, Barry Ditto, Suzanne Shreik, and Gil Yaron for research assistance on the first edition, and Maria Kotsoplous for her work in connection with the second. Carolyn Elliot Magwood, Sean Bawden, Anna Poliszot, and Michelle Jones made substantial contributions to the third edition. My work on revisions for the current edition has been greatly facilitated by the legal research expertise of Izabella Sowa.

Colleagues often provide helpful guidance on additions and improvements. In connection with the fourth edition, I am particularly appreciative of detailed suggestions from Martin Olszynski, who generously shared his experience as a teacher and practitioner of environmental law.

Financial support for research assistants has been provided by the Law Foundation of Ontario and the Foundation for Legal Research. I am very grateful for these valuable contributions.

INTRODUCTION

A. LAW AND THE ENVIRONMENT

In Canada and elsewhere, passionate advocates contend vigorously with resolute skeptics over many aspects of the environmental and sustainability agenda at the local, national, and global levels. And why would they not, given the significance of the issues facing the planet's 7 billion current human inhabitants and the more than 2 billion who are expected between now and 2050?

The Organization for Environmental Co-operation and Development recently re-examined four environmental challenges that are understood to be of some interest to the general population: climate change, biodiversity, water, and the impacts of pollution on human health. The results confirmed that prospects are "more alarming" than previously anticipated and called for further measures to be taken on an urgent basis to avoid the consequences—and costs—of inaction.[1]

The potential responses are diverse and often controversial. Means to promote environmental protection include public education, greater spending and investment to safeguard environmental functions, economic incentives and property rights to stimulate corporate and individual action, continued technological innovation, and a legal regime designed to prohibit environmentally detrimental activity and to encourage beneficial initiatives. Environmental law is thus a subject of

---

1 *Environmental Outlook to 2050: The Consequences of Inaction* (OECD, 2012).

1

profound importance to everyone whether they are concerned individuals, members of environmental public-interest groups, civil servants, corporate personnel and officials, technical and scientific experts, or part of the wide range of legal professionals whose practice is affected by environmental considerations.

Each of these constituencies may envisage the environmental legal regime from a somewhat different perspective. Not surprisingly, this results in considerable diversity of opinion whenever one contemplates the appropriateness, effectiveness, or utility of law as an instrument of environmental protection. Here it is sufficient to remark that, alongside essentially environmental concerns (safeguarding wildlife habitat, for example), general legal values have also influenced the evolution and operation of environmental law in Canada. By way of illustration, when environmental advocates urge resort to criminal law with the thought that the severity of possible penalties, even including imprisonment, may improve environmental protection, they simultaneously engage the attention of legal professionals with a deeply rooted appreciation of the procedural safeguards embedded in the overall relationship between the state's power as prosecutor and the accused's interest in liberty. Tensions such as these constantly reappear in environmental law. They are resolved on an ongoing basis through decision making at the legislative, administrative, judicial, and personal levels.

B. POLICY OBJECTIVES AND LEGAL TECHNIQUES FOR ENVIRONMENTAL PROTECTION

Environmental law, though continuing to evolve rapidly, is not new. However, its focus has clearly expanded beyond anti-pollution measures associated primarily with local public health and resource conservation. Ecosystem maintenance, biodiversity, and sustainability, concepts that are more thoroughly discussed in Chapter 1, now appear prominently on the list of environmental goals. The shift of attention towards these fundamental ideas reflects advances in scientific understanding of human impacts on the environment and the far greater scope of those impacts: where regional lumber operators were once concerned with the availability of pine timber to support their commercial activity, Canadians are now apprehensive about the maintenance of the boreal forest across the country in light of its role in the economy, its functions in relation to habitat and watersheds, and its contribution to planetary climatic conditions. Similarly, if local fisheries were once threatened by local sources of pollution, we are now aware, following the collapse of the Atlantic cod industry and contemporary threats to Pacific salmon, of the regional devastation that can result from over-harvesting.

The official objectives of environmental law are often embodied in legislation such as the *Canadian Environmental Protection Act, 1999 (CEPA 1999)*,[2] which declares that "the protection of the environment is essential to the well-being of Canada." Earlier federal legislation, the *Arctic Waters Pollution Prevention Act*,[3] contains an elaborate discussion of the various competing concerns underlying the scheme. On the one hand, the legislation "recognizes that recent developments in relation to the exploitation of the natural resources of Arctic areas, including the natural resources of the Canadian Arctic, and the transportation of those resources to the markets of the world are of potentially great significance to international trade and commerce and to the economy of Canada in particular." However, Parliament also expressed the determination "to fulfil its obligation to see that the natural resources of the Canadian arctic are developed and exploited and the arctic waters adjacent to the mainland and islands of the Canadian arctic are navigated only in a manner that takes cognizance of Canada's responsibility for the welfare of the Inuit and other inhabitants of the Canadian arctic." The legislation specifically insisted upon the importance of "the preservation of the peculiar ecological balance that now exists in the water, ice and land areas" of the Arctic region. This legislative objective, we are now undeniably aware, is being undermined on a daily basis by the impact of climate change on the region.

In the provincial realm, Ontario's *Environmental Protection Act*[4] is intended "to provide for the protection and conservation of the natural environment," while the same province's *Environmental Assessment Act* was enacted to promote "the betterment of the people of the whole or any part of Ontario by providing for the protection, conservation and wise management in Ontario of the environment."[5] Alberta's *Environmental Protection and Enhancement Act* of 1992[6] was amongst the first to set out an elaborate statement of purpose. The *AEPEA* is intended

---

2   SC 1999, c 33 [*CEPA 1999*]. *CEPA 1999* deals with the regulation of toxic substances, nutrients, ocean dumping, international air and water pollution, waste management, biotechnology, and the environmental management of federal government activity.

3   RSC 1985, c A-12.

4   RSO 1990, c E.19, s 3.

5   RSO 1990, c E.18, s 2.

6   SA 1992, c E-13.3 [*AEPEA*]. The revised Alberta legislation is noted elsewhere in this volume.

"to support and promote the protection, enhancement and wise use of the environment" in the context of a series of associated principles and sub-objectives:

- maintaining the integrity of ecosystems and human health and the well-being of society;
- promoting economic growth and prosperity in an environmentally responsible manner and integrating environmental protection and economic decisions in the earliest stages of planning;
- achieving sustainable development;
- preventing and mitigating the environmental impact of development and of government policies, programs, and decisions;
- ensuring opportunities for citizens to provide advice on decisions affecting the environment; and
- encouraging polluters to pay for the costs of their actions.

Manitoba's *Environment Act (MEA)* might be noted as well for expressly incorporating economic goals alongside environmental objectives. Specifically, the *MEA* seeks to "develop and maintain an environmental management system in Manitoba which will ensure that the environment is maintained in such a manner as to sustain a high quality of life, including social and economic development, recreation and leisure for this and future generations."[7] The Yukon *Environment Act* asserts the principle that "economic development and the health of the natural environment are inter-dependent."[8] In other cases, limitations that acknowledge that environmental protection measures must accommodate constraints faced by businesses are embodied in regulations such as those requiring the use of "practicable means" or the "best available technology economically achievable."

Such statutory formulations of the purposes of environmental law demonstrate that environmental protection regimes are not free-standing or autonomous. Rather, they have evolved alongside other economic, social, and legal considerations. As will be seen, various factors such as procedural fairness drawn from the realm of administrative law and constitutional considerations of proportionality, equitability, together with the economist's concern for efficiency, influence the design, implementation, and operation of environmental law regimes. Financial responsibility for the cleanup of contaminated lands is one area where these considerations have been subject to intense debate.[9]

---

7   *Environment Act*, CCSM c E125.
8   *Environment Act*, RSY 2002, c 76, s 5(2)(a) [YEA].
9   See Chapter 11.

Through law, a number of techniques may be employed to achieve the goals of environmental policy. Specified forms of conduct may be subject to clear prohibition, while other activities are permitted or regulated, often in connection with licensing controls where performance conditions may be set out. The law may also be used to create economic incentives, or as a means of more directly imposing advance planning and prevention programs to reduce the likelihood of environmental degradation. When damage occurs, however, legal principles and mechanisms regulate the distribution of costs and losses among those responsible, victims, and the general public. There are also situations where the legal regime may require some form of environmental restoration.

Jurisdictions differ with respect to the general style or orientation of their environmental regimes, with some favouring detailed legislative schemes and others preferring general statements of principle for administrative agencies or the courts to elaborate and refine. Similarly, some jurisdictions favour broad grants of discretionary authority to public officials, while others strive to prescribe rules or insist on close scrutiny of agencies to ensure conformity with overall policy.

Canadian environmental legislation has to a significant degree been enabling in nature rather than mandatory. That is, statutory powers authorizing designated officials to develop regulations for the protection of the environment are not generally construed as imposing upon those officials an obligation to do so. This principle governed an attempt by a public interest litigant to obtain a declaratory order compelling the lieutenant governor in council to enact regulations dealing with non-returnable beverage containers under legislation providing that such regulations "may" be made and stating that the regulations "shall" be filed by a specified date. In the opinion of the court, the authorization to make regulations was discretionary, and the obligation to file them was subject to the implied phrase "if enacted."[10] On the other hand when BC introduced a tire-recycling scheme on the basis of policy rather than by means of an existing regulation intended for this purpose, the validity of the scheme was undermined.[11]

---

10 Pim v Ontario (Minister of Environment) (1978), 23 OR (2d) 45.
11 Valley Rubber Resources Inc v British Columbia (Minister of Environment, Lands and Parks), [2001] BCJ No 629 (SC).

C. THE SCOPE OF ENVIRONMENTAL LAW

It is not a simple matter to determine the exact composition of a country's environmental regime. Some legal measures affecting the environment will be readily recognizable and agreed on, in that they were designed with environmental goals in mind and essentially operate for this purpose. Statute-based or regulatory standards governing allowable emissions or requiring environmental assessments might be examples of environmental law, narrowly defined. But it is misleading to presume that an inventory of "environmental standards" and "environmental enforcement practices" will identify the full range of issues falling within the ambit of environmental law. Traditional private law doctrines from fields such as tort and contract law have important environmental implications. Doctrines relating to the rights of riparian owners, nuisance, negligence, and strict liability are prominent examples. Through these long-standing common law claims, water-quality standards may be defended and various forms of pollution that threaten damage to individuals or property may be challenged in court, and so, in some sense, regulated.[12] Moreover, corporate law principles are also extremely relevant to the environmental regime. The same is true for the rules governing taxation, particularly in relation to the deductibility of expenses associated with environmental protection. Today, innovations such as carbon taxes and tradeable emission credits represent additional areas of intersection between taxation, finance and securities law, and environmental protection. Planning law and legislation affecting resource use and allocation in the agricultural, fisheries, forest, and mining sectors have important environmental implications, although none of these fields is extensively covered here.

Not all measures influencing the operation of an environmental regime take the form of substantive law. Some involve processes for environmental decision making. Application procedures relating to environmental licences and approvals for discharges, emissions, and waste management are typical illustrations. Even where such procedures do not actually prevent any particular activity, they are of vital interest in relation to timing, costs, appeals, and the right of other interested persons to participate or intervene in the application process. General statutory principles concerning the filing and disclosure of information also affect the operation of environmental measures.

---

12   Although the foregoing examples draw upon general principles from the common law, in Quebec, provisions of the *Civil Code of Québec* (*CCQ*) often have similar implications.

While some specific legal rules apply exclusively to environmental actions—the level of fines set for violating discharge standards, for example—other rules of significance to environmental protection may apply to several fields of law. Examples of the latter include rules for assessing damages in the context of personal injury that might equally arise in the context of medical malpractice claims or automobile accidents.[13] The rules of civil procedure in each jurisdiction and those governing standing to seek judicial review are of general application, but they are also of direct relevance to the conduct of environmental litigation. Specific standards and approaches to the proof of scientific causation might be applicable to environmental cases,[14] but general developments in the proof of causation may be equally significant. The availability of contingency fees and class action proceedings are further examples of legal rules that will clearly influence the frequency and character of environmental litigation. But these rules will rarely, if ever, have been adopted or designed with environmental actions specifically in mind.

D. THE INSTITUTIONAL FRAMEWORK FOR ENVIRONMENTAL RESPONSIBILITY

Several decades ago, governments in Canada began to establish departments formally charged with responsibility for environmental protection. Their functions, though prominent, tended to be carried out in a manner that was separate from, and generally subsequent to, the established processes of decision making. Considerable debate has since taken place about the appropriate design of institutions to promote timely and integrated attention to the environmental dimensions of projects, programs, and even policies in fields such as transportation, energy, housing, and so on. It was strongly argued by the World Commission on Environment and Development (WCED), for example, that environmental and economic considerations should be integrated

---

13   See, generally, SM Waddams, *The Law of Damages*, 5th ed (Toronto: Canada Law Book, 2012).

14   SE Gaines, "International Principles for Transnational Environmental Liability: Can Developments in Municipal Law Help Break the Impasse" (1989) 30 Harv Int'l LJ 311 at 336–37; LA Reynolds, "The Era of Juriscience: Investigating the Relationship between Science, Law and the Environment" (1995) 9 Can J Admin L & Prac 61; J Swaigen & AD Levy, "The Expert's Duty to the Tribunal: A Tool for Reducing Contradictions between Scientific Process and Legal Process" (1997–8) 11 Can J Admin L & Prac 277.

in decision making,[15] and as a consequence environmental units or branches often appeared within other governmental agencies. Departments of environment or equivalent exist today at the federal level and in all provinces, however, and remain the central source of policy making in the environmental field.

At the federal level, the *Government Organization Act, 1970* and the *Department of the Environment Act* set out the authority and responsibility of the DOE and departmental officials, including the minister.[16] The scope of departmental responsibility includes matters affecting the preservation and enhancement of the natural environment and resource conservation falling within Parliament's constitutional jurisdiction. Yet interdepartmental coordination and cooperation remain essential because of the wide-ranging nature of environmental issues. Thus, Health Canada and Transport Canada have important responsibilities in connection with some environmental matters, and, by way of an administrative agreement embodied in a memorandum of understanding (MoU), DOE assumed responsibilities for pollution-prevention aspects of the *Fisheries Act*, a statute otherwise under the authority of the Department of Fisheries and Oceans. Natural Resources is another federal department with extensive authority relating to federal environmental responsibilities.

Important contributions have been made to the development of the federal environmental framework by the House Standing Committee on Environment and Sustainable Development through a series of reports on legislative and policy initiatives, including recent studies of Blue-Green Algae, the role of the Commissioner of the Environment and Sustainable Development, and a five-year review of *CEPA 1999*.[17]

Provincial departments exercise corresponding responsibilities within the scope of their own constitutional powers. British Columbia's

---

15 World Commission on Environment and Development, *Our Common Future* (Oxford: Oxford UP, 1987).

16 A description of departmental organization may be found at www.ec.gc.ca/default.asp?lang=En&n=65D4D436-1.

17 *A Global Partnership: Canada and the Conventions of the United Nations Conference on Environment and Development* (1993); *It's About Our Health: Towards Pollution Prevention* (1995); *Harmonization of Environmental Protection: An Analysis of the Harmonization Initiative of the Canadian Council of Ministers of the Environment* (1997); *Enforcing Canada's Pollution Laws: The Public Interest Must Come First* (1998); *Pesticides: Making the Right Choice for the Protection of Health and the Environment* (2000); *Strengthening the Role of the Commissioner of the Environment and Sustainable Development* (2007); *Blue-Green Algae (Cyanobacteria) and their Toxins* (2008); *Study to Provide Recommendations Regarding the Development of a National Conservation Plan* (2012).

Environmental Management Act[18] provides an inventory of duties, powers, and functions of the provincial minister in relation to the management, protection, and enhancement of the environment:

- planning, research, and investigation with respect to the environment;
- development of policies for the management, protection, and use of the environment;
- planning, design, construction, operation, and maintenance of works and undertakings for the management, protection, or enhancement of the environment;
- providing information to the public about the quality and use of the environment;
- preparing and publishing policies, strategies, objectives, guidelines, and standards for the protection and management of the environment; and
- preparing and publishing environmental management plans for specific areas of British Columbia which may include, but need not be limited to, measures with respect to the following: flood control; drainage; soil conservation; water-resource management; fisheries and aquatic-life management; wildlife management; waste management; and air management.

In other provinces, corresponding functions are performed by the relevant ministry or ministries in conjunction with specialized agencies. An appendix to this volume lists website information for provincial environment ministries.

In addition to federal and provincial departments, the Canadian institutional framework for environmental matters includes several intergovernmental and international bodies such as the Canadian Council of Ministers of the Environment, the International Joint Commission, and the North American Commission on Environmental Co-operation.

E. OVERVIEW OF THE BOOK

This book begins with an examination of basic concepts in environmental law (Chapter 1) and a survey of constitutional (including the *Charter of Rights and Freedoms*) considerations (Chapters 2 and 3). The international legal context, including the growing significance of trade regulation, comes next (Chapter 4) and is followed by a review of the common law (Chapter 5) as it affects the environment and of the basic

---

18   SBC 2003, c 53, s 5.

regulatory regime governing approvals, permits, administrative supervision, offences, and penalties (Chapters 6 to 9). The volume then addresses a number of specific topics, including financial compensation for spills and the restoration of contaminated lands (Chapters 10 and 11), environmental assessment (Chapter 12), toxic substances (chapter 13), and protected spaces and species (Chapter 14). Afterwards, the text turns to other innovations, including emphasis on individual responsibility and consumer behaviour (Chapter 15), alternative dispute resolution (Chapter 16), and economic instruments (Chapter 17). Following a chapter on sources of environmental information (Chapter 18), is a specific discussion of climate change initiatives at the federal, provincial, and municipal levels (Chapter 19). The concluding chapter sets out some final reflections accompanied by a short review of Canada's sustainability performance.

The approach throughout emphasizes a description of representative examples from the range of Canadian jurisdictions rather than a comprehensive and detailed examination of any one province or the federal environmental regime. After an issue has been discussed in relation to selected jurisdictions, references for further reading are provided to assist readers to begin to identify some of the relevant provisions in the environmental legislation of other parts of Canada.

CHAPTER 1

BASIC CONCEPTS IN ENVIRONMENTAL LAW

A. ENVIRONMENT

"People," argued the authors of a report titled *The State of Canada's Environment* "have traditionally tended to view air, water, land, other organisms, and themselves as separate components that could each be understood in isolation from the whole."[1] This limiting assumption, although of diminished influence, asserts a residual effect in a variety of contexts, including the legal sphere where sectoral legislation governing forests, land use, and agriculture, for example, coexists alongside new frameworks oriented around environmental protection, ecosystem services, or sustainability.

The way the term *environment* is interpreted or understood in legal settings is directly linked to the scope of environmental protection: environmental protection legislation safeguards environment as defined in that legislation and as interpreted by the courts in the light of legal principles drawn from many different spheres. Thus interpreted, environment may, but frequently does not, correspond with professional, scientific, or popular understandings of the term. By way of example, those prosecuting the hypothetical offence of doing damage to the environment must establish that the damage was inflicted on environment as that term applies in the specific context of the offence. If the

---

1 Environment Canada, *The State of Canada's Environment* (Ottawa: Supply & Services, 1991) at 1–1.

damage was done to some man-made structure, and such structures are excluded from the courts' understanding of environment, then no offence has been committed under the Act.[2] Or, if environment is defined as "natural environment," excluding the indoors, them some other legal regime will be required to safeguard the indoor environment.

Courts have also considered the problem of contaminants moving through the natural environment and perhaps affecting private property in the process. One example concerned land situated between a farm and a lake:

> If the farmer uses excessive fertilizer, it could become a contaminant that seeps though the farm soil or runs into the abutting land or seeps into the soil of the abutting land, and through it into the lake. The intervening property owner would have no knowledge either of the contaminant or its location. The contaminant entered the natural environment on the farm and the owner of the in-between lands could not be said to be the owner of the source of contaminant. It would be an undue and improper strain upon the interpretation of the definition of a natural environment in s 1(1)(k) to read it as being disjunctive and to cover natural movements of contaminant from one part of the natural environment to another.[3]

Environmental impacts crossing jurisdictional boundaries or extending well beyond national territories are widespread. We know, for example, that agricultural and forest management practices—as well as domestic energy and transportation systems—can profoundly affect neighbouring jurisdictions, global atmospheric conditions, and ultimately climate systems. But these examples of harm to the environment have also been challenging to define and address.

Each environmental statute must nevertheless be carefully scrutinized to assess its operational scope. This need not alter anyone's personal inclination as to what environmental law should encompass, but it will serve to identify some of the practical legal limits of specific statutory initiatives. One need not dig too deeply to appreciate that the offence of operating a pit without a licence depends upon the legal interpretation of operating and on the law's understanding of a pit.[4]

---

2   *R v Enso Forest Products* (1992), 8 CELR (NS) 253 (BCSC), aff'd (1993), 12 CELR (NS) 221 (BCCA). See also *British Columbia (Minister of Environment Lands and Parks) v Alpha Manufacturing* (1996), 132 DLR (4th) 688 (BCSC), aff'd (1997), 150 DLR (4th) 193 (BCCA).

3   *Canadian National Railway v Ontario (Director appointed under the Environmental Protection Act)*, *(sub nom Re Canadian National Railway)* (1991), 3 OR (3d) 609 at 620 (Div Ct).

4   *R v Ontario Corp 311578*, 2012 ONCA 604.

The approach Alberta takes in section 1 of its *Environmental Protection and Enhancement Act* is typical of more recent drafting. There, environment "means the components of the earth and includes (i) air, land and water, (ii) all layers of the atmosphere, (iii) all organic and inorganic matter and living organisms, and (iv) the interacting natural systems that include components referred to in subclauses (i) to (iii)."[5] Saskatchewan, on the basis of 2002 amendments to its basic environmental legislation, elaborates the definition of environment to include "interacting natural systems and ecological and climatic interrelationships" among the range of components.[6]

For purposes of environmental assessment, Ontario lists plant and animal life, "including humans" and "the social, economic and cultural conditions that influence the life of humans or a community" as well as "any building, structure, machine or other device or thing made by humans," as components of the environment.[7] In its basic environmental protection statute, however, the same province defines natural environment as "the air, land and water, or any combination or part thereof, of the Province of Ontario."[8] In considering this definition and the purpose of the Ontario *Environmental Protection Act*, Gonthier J acknowledged that "the social importance of environmental protection is obvious, yet the nature of the environment does not lend itself to precise codification."[9]

Another judicial observer remarked: "To variably interpret the 'natural environment' according to the character of surrounding neighbourhoods would . . . create a multitude of natural environments . . . . This . . . appears contrary to . . . the Act, which refers to only one natural environment."[10] This observation was addressed, at least in part, to the risk that a polluter might avoid liability for causing adverse effects by adding contaminants to an already polluted environment. It is not unknown, however, for a single statute to embody more than one definition of environment, each applicable for particular purposes under the Act.[11]

Also noteworthy in connection with judicial understanding of environment are indications that the courts are sensitive to a range of objectives underlying environmental protection. In weighing the benefits of a municipal noise bylaw against the restrictive effects of the legisla-

---

5   *Environmental Protection and Enhancement Act*, RSA 2000, c E-12, s 1(t).

6   *Environmental Management and Protection Act, 2002*, SS 2002, c E-10.21, s 2(i).

7   *Environmental Assessment Act*, RSO 1990, c E.18, s 1.

8   *Environmental Protection Act*, RSO 1990, c E.19, s 1 [*OEPA*].

9   *R v Canadian Pacific Ltd*, [1995] 2 SCR 1028 at 1072.

10 *R v Commander Business Furniture Inc* (1992), 9 CELR (NS) 185 at 197–98 (Ont Prov Div), Hackett Prov J.

11 *Clean Environment Act*, RSNB 1973, c C-6.

tion on freedom of expression which is safeguarded in the *Canadian Charter of Rights and Freedoms*, the Supreme Court of Canada endorsed the following observation from the Quebec Court of Appeal: "the citizens of a city, even a city the size of Montreal, are entitled to a healthy environment. Noise control is unquestionably part of what must be done to improve the quality of this environment."[12] Even beyond this clear understanding of environment as a direct contributor to the well-being of the human population, are acknowledgements of the essential well-being of the environment independent of direct human interests. With reference to the toxic substance provisions of the *Canadian Environmental Protection Act*, Justices Lamer and Iacobucci remarked:

> Parliament's clear intention was to allow for federal intervention where the environment itself was at risk, whether or not the substances concerned posed a threat to human health and whether or not the aspect of the environment affected was one on which human life depended.[13]

B. POLLUTION

Anti-pollution measures are central features of environmental law, but their application has always been complicated by controversy about the nature of the conduct in question. What is meant by pollution, and particularly what constitutes prohibited levels of pollution, has varied depending on local conditions, scientific or professional analyses, and the judgments of observers, some of whom will be more tolerant than others of "acceptable" levels. Indeed, the argument has occasionally been made that pollution is a socially defined phenomenon, or even something constructed by enforcement officials:

> [P]ollution, in other words, is an administrative creation. The broad legal mandate of the agencies about water pollution control is transformed into policy by senior officials and given practical expression in the setting of pollution standards. . . . In this sense, the water authorities create pollution . . . by making the rules whose infraction constitutes pollution.[14]

---

12   Chamberland JA, quoted in translation in *Montreal (City)* v *2952-1366 Quebec Inc*, 2005 SCC 62 at para 99.
13   *R v Hydro Quebec*, [1997] 3 SCR 213 at para 42.
14   K Hawkins, *Environment and Enforcement: Regulation and the Social Definition of Pollution* (Oxford: Clarendon Press, 1984) at 23.

An apparent illustration of such an approach is found in Quebec's *Environment Quality Act* where a pollutant is defined as "a contaminant or a mixture of several contaminants present in the environment in a concentration or quantity greater than the permissible level determined by regulation of the government, or whose presence in the environment is prohibited by regulation."[15] Other statutory approaches to defining pollution include that of a British Columbia statute on waste management in which pollution is described as "the presence in the environment of substances or contaminants that substantially alter or impair the usefulness of the environment."[16]

A Saskatchewan statute set forth a more extended explanation in its definition of pollution as alteration of the physical, chemical, biological, or aesthetic properties of the environment, including the addition or removal of any substance that (1) will render the environment harmful to the public health; (2) is unsafe or harmful for domestic, municipal, industrial, agricultural, recreational, or other lawful uses of the environment; or (3) is harmful to wild animals, birds or aquatic life.[17] The explicit reference to aesthetic harm, something by no means found throughout environmental laws, is indicative of the potential for different conceptions of pollution in the minds of scientific experts and officials in the legal system.

Other jurisdictions, sometimes without reference to pollution as such, have employed the concepts of contaminant and adverse environmental effects to delineate the harms that anti-pollution legislation is intended to control. In Ontario's *Environmental Protection Act*, adverse effect is defined as one or more of: impairment of the quality of the natural environment for any use that can be made of it; injury or damage to property or to plant or animal life; harm or material discomfort to any person; an adverse effect on the health of any person; impairment of the safety of any person; rendering any property or plant or animal life unfit for human use; loss of enjoyment of normal use of property; and interference with the normal conduct of business.[18] Federal fisheries legisla-

---

15   RSQ c Q-2.

16   *Environmental Management Act*, SBC 2003, c 53, s 1(1).

17   *Environmental Management and Protection Act*, SS 1983–84, c E-10.2, s 2. Now see the *Environmental Management and Protection Act, 2002*, above note 6.

18   OEPA, above note 8, s 1(1). In *Ontario (Minister of the Environment) v Castonguay Blasting Ltd*, 2012 ONCA 165, leave to appeal to SCC granted, [2012] SCCA No 224, a majority of the Ontario Court of Appeal concluded that fly-rock from construction that landed on a house constituted a reportable adverse environmental effect notwithstanding that no more than trivial or minimal harm was caused to the natural environment defined as air, land, or water.

tion addresses related dimensions of environmental quality by means of a prohibition against the deposit of any "deleterious substance" in Canadian fisheries waters, with deleterious substance defined as: "any substance that, if added to any water, would degrade or alter or form part of a process of degradation or alteration of the quality of that water so that it is rendered or is likely to be rendered deleterious to fish or fish habitat or the use by man of fish that frequent that water."[19]

Although the legal concepts of pollution, adverse effects from contaminants, deleterious substances and so on may not appear to embody scientific precision, they should not be seen as arbitrary and subjective: they are utilized and applied in the context of relevant professional knowledge that is subject to ongoing evaluation and reassessment and are continually reviewable through formal judicial procedures. It should also be noted, however, that for these and other reasons, there are important interrelationships between legal responses to pollution and the concept of risk.

There are often limitations in our understanding of the nature or effects of polluting substances: perhaps they are more harmful than assumed. There are uncertainties associated with the presence of such substances in the environment: perhaps they persist longer or travel more broadly than we assume. There are unknown risks associated with environmental exposure to pollutants: perhaps more people will be exposed to a contaminant than we assume, or perhaps those people, children for example, are more susceptible to adverse effects than we assume. Managing risk and uncertainty has thus become an important element of the law's response to pollution.[20]

C. CONSERVATION

For earlier generations, the term *conservation* was used to describe an important social objective associated with maintaining resource stocks and capacity. The harm to be avoided in the minds of such conserva-

---

19   *Fisheries Act*, RSC 1985, c F-14, s 34.
20   Elizabeth Fisher observes that "it is now common for environmental problems to be characterized in terms of risk and the bulk of environmental regulatory law to be thought of as 'risk regulation'." E Fisher, "Risk and Environmental Law: A Beginner's Guide" in BJ Richardson & S Wood, eds, *Environmental Law for Sustainability* (Portland, OR: Hart Publishing, 2006) 97. See also, JD Fraiberg & MJ Trebilcock, "Risk Regulation: Technocratic and Democratic Tools for Regulatory Reform" (1998) 43 McGill LJ 835.

tionists might be described as resource depletion, for they certainly anticipated that resources would be fully utilized on an ongoing basis.[21]

Conservation remains an important element of environmental protection programs and can certainly be found as an objective in environmental and resource legislation. The federal *Fisheries Act*, for example, contains provisions associated with the objective of conservation; proposed revisions, which were never enacted, would have made it explicit that "the conservation of Canada's fisheries and their management on a sustainable basis are central to the economic viability of persons engaged in fishing and fish processors and the well-being of communities that are dependent on fisheries resources."[22] Conservation does, however, figure prominently in the *Oceans Act*.[23] Other legislation envisages conservation in terms of avoiding degradation of essential physical, chemical, and biological characteristics of the environment.[24]

Without defining conservation, the Canadian Council of Ministers of the Environment (CCME) explained conservation strategy as "a guide for the sustainable use of our resources and the environment,"[25] thereby signalling a transition from the historic conception of resource conservation to the current concern with sustainability, be it termed environmental sustainability or sustainable development. It is perhaps in this sense that a number of provinces continue to employ the term in relation to habitat restoration and wildlife protection measures. BC, for example, established a Habitat Conservation Trust Fund with responsibility for acquiring and maintaining parts of the province that contribute to wildlife preservation and for supporting community stewardship organizations and research initiatives oriented towards similar ends.[26] Another indication that the concept of conservation may now be interpreted broadly to correspond with the growing comprehensiveness of the contemporary environmental agenda is found in commentary from the Supreme Court of Canada. In *R v Sundown*, the

---

21   As used in the General Regulation under Ontario's *Environmental Assessment Act*, O Reg 334, s 8, to refer to the creation of shelter belts, erosion control, and soil and water conservation, the phrase "conservation services" is in this tradition. For historical background, see SP Hays, *Conservation and the Gospel of Efficiency: The Progressive Conservation Movement, 1890–1920* (Cambridge, MA: Harvard University Press, 1968).

22   Bill C-115, *An Act Respecting Fisheries*, 1st Sess, 35th Parl, 1995.

23   SC 1996, c 31, s 35.

24   *Environmental Protection and Enhancement Act*, SA 1992, c E-133, s 1.

25   Canadian Council of Ministers of the Environment, *Conservation Strategies: A Compendium of Canadian Experiences* (September 1989) at 7. For illustration, see *Conservation Authorities Act*, RSO 1990, c C.27, ss 20, 21.

26   Online: www.hctf.ca.

Court referred to the Crown's view that conservation extended no further than the scope of protective measures for fish, fur-bearing animals, and big game as possibly amounting to "an unnecessarily restrictive definition of conservation."[27] The judgment continued:

> . . . a requirement that cabins be built at least 150 feet away from the shore may be concerned with possible pollution of the lake, the erosion of the shoreline and the effects of that erosion on water quality. It may well be that . . . conservation laws . . . should be construed generously to refer not only to the conservation of game and fish but also to the environment they inhabit. Legislation aimed at preserving habitat and biodiversity, the water quality of ground water and lakes, rivers and streams, topsoil conservancy and the prevention of erosion may be laws in relation to conservation.[28]

Evidence from the international context also suggests that the historic concept of conservation remains sufficiently flexible to encompass emerging environmental challenges. In this vein, Achim Steiner, Director General of the International Union for Conservation of Nature and Natural Resources (IUCN), observed that "[c]onservation in the 21st Century will need to come to terms with a world that will increasingly struggle with the scale and complexity of our collective impact on the Earth's natural resources." He added in an explanation that:

> While species and ecosystems were once our departure points for protecting and restoring nature, we are today forced to recognize that we must redefine our work in terms of systems (e.g. economic, social, and political) and cycles (e.g. hydrological, climate, nutrient).[29]

D. SUSTAINABLE DEVELOPMENT

Popularized internationally through the report of the World Commission on Environment and Development (WCED) entitled *Our Common Future*, sustainable development has been widely endorsed within domestic environmental regimes. In Canada this process was initially en-

---

27 *R v Sundown*, [1999] 1 SCR 393 at para 45.
28 *Ibid*. For discussion that more sharply distinguishes between conservation and preservation, see Standing Committee on Environment and Sustainable Development, *Study to Provide Recommendations Regarding the Development of a National Conservation Plan* (June 2012).
29 A Steiner, Director General, World Conservation Union (IUCN), 22 December 2005.

couraged by the deliberations of a National Task Force on Environment and Economy, which preceded incorporation of sustainable development in several federal statutes.[30] Sustainability is now widely regarded as a criterion or performance standard against which various developmental initiatives should be assessed. Indeed, the promotion of sustainable development is among the stated objectives of the *North American Free Trade Agreement (NAFTA)* and its environmental side agreement (see Chapter 4). Sustainable development has also been acknowledged in international law as the "need to reconcile economic development with protection of the environment."[31]

The WCED's formulation of sustainable development as development that "meets the needs of the present without compromising the ability of future generations to meet their own needs" is not without controversy and has been subject to fairly open-ended interpretation. In the words of the National Task Force on Environment and Economy, "Long-term economic growth depends on a healthy environment. It also affects the environment in many ways. Ensuring environmentally sound and sustainable economic development requires the technology and wealth that is generated by continued economic growth."[32] Such an approach suggests the importance of integrating economic and environmental decision making, although the manner in which this is to be accomplished remains to be determined.

In the words of one experienced observer of the policy process from both the domestic and international perspectives:

> Sustainable development is an approach to decision making that takes a long-term focus, . . . and recognizes the interdependence of domestic and global activities. It is an ethical principle that incorporates a commitment to equity between the current generation and those that will follow; and between the poor and the more affluent. It means working to ensure a fair distribution of the costs and benefits of development between the nations of the developed and developing worlds. Sustainable development is also about ensuring that choices we make as citizens, consumers, producers, and investors are com-

---

30 See, for example, the *Canadian Environmental Assessment Act*, SC 1992, c 37; and the *Department of Forestry Act*, SC 1989, c 27.

31 *Case Concerning the Gabčíkovo-Nagymaros Project* (Hungary/Slovakia), [1997] ICJ Rep 3.

32 National Task Force on Environment and Economy, *Report of the National Task Force on Environment and Economy: submitted to the Canadian Council of Resource and Environmental Ministers, September 24, 1987*, G Lecuyer, Chair (Downsview, ON: National Task Force on Environment and Economy, 1987) at 2.

patible with an excellent quality of life for all Canadians and the global community, now and in the future.[33]

Legislative elaboration of sustainability incorporates increasing detail without often appearing to specify legally enforceable standards. As discussed in the federal *Auditor General Act*, for example, sustainable development is "a continually evolving concept based on the integration of social, economic and environmental concerns." It may be achieved, according to the statute, in various ways. These include:

(a) the integration of the environment and the economy;

(b) protecting the health of Canadians;

(c) protecting ecosystems;

(d) meeting international obligations;

(e) promoting equity;

(f) an integrated approach to planning and making decisions that takes into account the environmental and natural resource costs of different economic options and the economic costs of different environmental and natural resource options;

(g) preventing pollution; and

(h) respect for nature and the needs of future generations.[34]

For purposes of forest management, British Columbia set out to codify sustainable use as:

a) managing forests to meet present needs without compromising the needs of future generations;

b) providing stewardship of forests based on an ethic of respect for the land;

c) balancing productive, spiritual, ecological, and recreational values of forests to meet the economic and cultural needs of peoples and communities, including First Nations;

d) conserving biological diversity, soil, water, fish, wild life, scenic diversity, and other forest resources; and

e) restoring damaged ecologies.[35]

33 R Ballhorn, "The Role of Government and Policy in Sustainable Development" (2005) 1 Journal of Sustainable Development Law and Policy 19.

34 *Auditor General Act*, RSC 1985, c A-17, s 21.1. *Canadian Environmental Protection Act, 1999*, SC 1999, c 33, s 54 [*CEPA 1999*] requires the federal minister of the environment to issue objectives, guidelines, and codes of practice addressing sustainable development among other factors. See also the *Environmental Trust Fund Act*, SNB 1990, c E-9.3, s.3; the *Environment Act*, RSNS 1994–95, c 1, s 2.

35 *Forest Practices Code of British Columbia Act*, RSBC 1996, c 159. Aspects of the Code were subsequently replaced by the *Forest and Range Practices Act*, SBC 2002, c 69.

Similarly, in Ontario, forest management legislation calls for the use of enforceable indicators of sustainability to replace a prior regime oriented around guidelines and policy statements.[36] Manitoba has also taken steps to recognize the importance of sustainability in provincial decision making. Legislation in that province set out principles and guidelines for sustainable development and called for the development of sustainability indicators.[37]

E. BIODIVERSITY AND ECOLOGICAL INTEGRITY

The international *Convention on Biological Diversity* defined an ecosystem as "a dynamic complex of plant, animal and micro-organism communities and their non-living environment interacting as a functional unit."[38] Thus, reference to ecosystems acknowledges the interconnectedness of biological communities and the surrounding environmental complex of which they are a part. The contrast between an ecosystem approach and a purely sectoral or media-based approach emphasizing air, land, and water in isolation is seen in *CEPA 1999*'s definition of environment as the components of the Earth including air, land, and water, together with all layers of the atmosphere, all organic and inorganic matter and living organisms, as well as the interacting natural systems that comprise any of these components.[39] As explained by the House of Commons Standing Committee on Environment and Sustainable Development, "the key insight of the ecosystem approach is that it is the integration and interaction among the living and non-living elements of an ecosystem that enable it to function as a unit. If one part is harmed, the entire ecosystem itself may be affected. Sustained life is a property of ecosystem integrity. Individual species can-

---

36 *Crown Forest Sustainability Act*, SO 1994, c 25; *Algonquin Wildlands League v Ontario (Minister of Natural Resources)* (1998), 26 CELR (NS) 163 (Ont Div Ct), additional reasons at (1998), 27 CELR (NS) 218 (Ont Div Ct), aff'd in relation to sustainability indicators (1998), 29 CELR (NS) 31 (Ont CA), additional reasons at (2000), 32 CELR (NS) 233 (Ont CA).

37 *Sustainable Development and Consequential Amendments Act*, SM 1997, c 61. See also the *Waste Reduction and Prevention Act*, CCSM c W40. For commentary on the federal experience, see F Bregha, "A Decade of Sustainable Development Strategies" in G Toner, ed, *Innovation, Science and Environment, 2008–2009* (McGill-Queen's UP, 2008).

38 *Convention on Biological Diversity*, 5 June 1992, 31 ILM 818, art 2.

39 Above note 34.

not exist on their own."[40] Arguably then, adoption of the ecosystem focus represents a broadening of the objectives of environmental protection regimes.[41]

The concept of *biological diversity* gives prominence to the importance of variety in terms of life on Earth, with variety including ecological diversity, species diversity, and genetic diversity. "Genetic diversity comprehends variability within a species, measured by variation in genes within a particular variety, subspecies, or breed; species diversity relates to the range of terrestrial living organisms; ecological diversity concerns the variety of habitats, biotic communities, and ecological processes found in the biosphere and the great variety within ecosystems in terms of difference in habitat and ecological processes."[42] As an objective for environmental legislation, biodiversity is increasingly common in Canadian statutes. Thus, for example, the Northwest Territories' *Environmental Rights Act* is intended to further the "integrity, biological diversity and productivity of the ecosystems."[43]

Following consideration by an expert panel, the concept of *ecological integrity* was introduced to national parks legislation in 2000. For purposes of the *Canada National Parks Act*, ecological integrity means "a condition that is determined to be characteristic of its natural region and likely to persist, including abiotic components and the composition and abundance of native species and biological communities, rates of change and supporting processes."[44]

---

40   *Report of the House of Commons Standing Committee on Environment and Sustainable Development: It's About Our Health! Towards Pollution Prevention* (Ottawa: Canadian Communication Group, 1995) at 50. See also, T Mosquin, "The Roles of Biodiversity in Creating and Maintaining the Ecosphere" in S Bocking, ed, *Biodiversity in Canada: Ecology, Ideas, and Action* (Broadview Press, 2000) at 112–13.

41   For a judicial endorsement of an ecosystem focus in environmental legislation, see *R v Inco Ltd* (2001), 54 OR (3d) 495 (CA). For comprehensive international insights into policy making for ecosystems and biodiversity, see the work of the Economics of Ecosystems and Biodiversity initiative online at: www.teebweb. org.

42   PW Birnie & AE Boyle, *International Law and the Environment* (Oxford: Clarendon Press, 1992) at 483.

43   RSNWT 1988 (Supp), c 83. For implementation of biodiversity goals in the NWT, see *Northwest Territories Biodiversity Action Plan: Major Initiatives on Biodiversity* (2004), online: www.enr.gov.nt.ca/_live/documents/content/NWT%20 BAP%20Report%201_Complete.pdf. See also *Environmental Bill of Rights, 1993*, SO 1993, c 28, s 2(2)2; *Environment Act*, SY 1991, c 5, s 5.5(1)(a); *Environment Act*, SNS 1994–95, c 1, s 2 [*NSEA*]; *CEPA 1999*, above note 34, s 3.

44   *Canada National Parks Act*, SC 2000, c 32, s 2.

F. THE POLLUTER-PAYS PRINCIPLE

The "polluter-pays" principle emphasizes the responsibility of those who engage in environmentally harmful conduct (either as producers or consumers) for the costs associated with their activity. They should not be directly subsidized by public expenditures, nor should they enjoy indirect advantages from damaging the environment in ways that are not attributed back to them but are instead borne by others. This concept enjoys international recognition[45] and constitutional status within the European Union[46] and has begun to influence penalty regimes, the design of economic instruments and incentives, and the nature of environmental restoration programs in Canada.

Recognition of the polluter-pays principle is one of the goals of Nova Scotia's *Environment Act* where this concept is explained as "confirming the responsibility of anyone who creates an adverse effect on the environment to take remedial action and pay for the costs of that action."[47] As explained by the Supreme Court of Canada:

> To encourage sustainable development, that principle assigns polluters the responsibility for remedying contamination for which they are responsible and imposes on them the direct and immediate costs of pollution. At the same time, polluters are asked to pay more attention to the need to protect ecosystems in the course of their economic activities.[48]

The extent of liability under the polluter-pays principle and how responsibility might be apportioned remain complex and difficult issues in many circumstances. By general implication from the Supreme Court commentary, it would be necessary to distinguish pollution costs of a direct and immediate nature from those that would not be so described. These matters are occasionally addressed in the particularities of statutory regimes.[49] In the absence of precise statutory guidance, courts and

---

45 *1992 Rio Declaration on Environment and Development*, 14 June 1992, 31 ILM 874, Principle 16.

46 *Single European Act*, 1986, art 25, 1992 adding art 130R2.

47 NSEA, above note 43, s 2(c).

48 *Imperial Oil Ltd v Quebec (Minister of the Environment)*, [2003] 2 SCR 624 at para 24. See also *Nova Scotia (Attorney General) v Marriott*, 2008 NSSC 160.

49 For an inventory of federal and provincial legislation where the principle of polluter pays is incorporated either explicitly or by implication, see *Imperial Oil Ltd v Quebec (Minister of the Environment)*, above note 48 at para 23. Recent amendments to federal environmental legislation are intended to strengthen the polluter-pays principle in sentencing. See *Environmental Enforcement Act*, SC 2009, c 14.

tribunals appear reluctant to apply the polluter-pays principle as a generalized norm.[50]

G. THE PRECAUTIONARY PRINCIPLE AND POLLUTION PREVENTION

From its German origins in relation to good household management, the *precautionary principle* has evolved to encompass a cluster of basic principles with both substantive and procedural implications. It includes, for example, the proposition that early preventive action is appropriate even in the absence of scientifically documented need when delay would impose increased costs and greater risks of environmental harm. Precaution also entails recognition of the importance of leaving wide margins of tolerance or room for manoeuvre to permit natural adaptation to human interference. In addition, the precautionary principle implies a shift in the onus of proof to those who propose initiatives, innovations, and activities whose environmental impact is not fully understood.[51] The precautionary principle accordingly offers guidance on managing the relationships between scientific uncertainty, the potential for adverse effects, and the legal or administrative decision-making process. Scientific uncertainty as it affects decision making about adverse environmental impacts may take several forms. These include conceptual uncertainty or shortcomings in our understanding of causation, as well as limitations in our ability to sample and take measurements, or deficiencies in modelling procedures.[52]

The principle of precaution has been formulated in a number of ways and enjoys varying degrees of acceptance. In international law, the *Rio Declaration on Environment and Development* clearly raised the visibility of precautionary claims in stating that "[w]here there are threats of serious or irreversible damage, lack of full scientific certainty shall not be used as a reason for postponing cost-effective measures to prevent environmental degradation."[53]

---

50 *EnviroGun Ltd v Saskatchewan (Minister of the Environment)*, 2012 SKCA 73 at para 27.

51 T O'Riordan, A Jordan, & J Cameron, eds, *Reinterpreting the Precautionary Principle* (London: Cameron May, 2001). For illustration of the precautionary approach in Canada, see *Dillon v Ontario (Director, Ministry of the Environment)* (2001), 36 CELR (NS) 141 (OEAB).

52 VR Walker, "The Siren Song of Science: Toward a Taxonomy of Scientific Uncertainty for Decisionmakers" (1991) 23 Conn L Rev 567.

53 *Rio Declaration of the United Nations Conference on Environment and Development*, 14 June 1992, 31 ILM 874, Principle 15.

There are growing indications of formal recognition of the pre-cautionary idea in Canada, in *CEPA 1999*, for example, or in the *Oceans Act* where reference is made to "erring on the side of caution." The use of the precautionary principle in decision making is also a goal associated with sustainable development in Nova Scotia's environmental legisla-tion so that "where there are threats of serious or irreversible damage, the lack of full scientific certainty shall not be used as a reason for postponing measures to prevent environmental degradation."[54] In con-firming the authority of a Quebec town to regulate pesticide use within its municipal boundaries, a majority of the Supreme Court of Canada suggested that the legitimacy of the bylaw was enhanced insofar as the bylaw's preventive approach respected the precautionary principle in international law.[55] Precaution has recently been described as a "guid-ing" principle for interpreting environmental assessment legislation.[56]

In consideration of the challenges of implementing precaution-ary decision making in a consistent manner across the wide range of circumstances for which it is responsible, the government of Canada formulated a set of guiding principles.[57] As summarized below, these suggest some of the factors relevant to putting precaution into operation:

1) The precautionary approach is a legitimate and distinctive deci-sion-making tool within risk management.

2) It is legitimate for decisions to be guided by society's chosen level of protection against risk.

3) Sound scientific information and its evaluation must be the basis for applying the precautionary approach, particularly with regard to (i) the decision to act or not to act (i.e., to implement precaution-ary measures or not), and (ii) the measures taken once a decision is made.

4) The scientific evidence required should be established relative to the chosen level of protection. Further, the responsibility for pro-ducing the information base (burden of proof) may be assigned. It is recognized that the scientific information base and responsibility for producing it may shift as the knowledge evolves.

---

54 *NSEA*, above note 43, s 2(b)(ii). See also *Endangered Species Act*, SNS 1998, c 11, ss 2(1)(h) and 11(1).

55 *114957 Canada Ltée (Spraytech, Société d'arrosage) v Hudson (Town)*, 2001 SCC 40 at paras 31–32.

56 *Pembina Institute for Appropriate Development. v Canada (Attorney General)*, 2008 FC 302.

57 Government of Canada, *A Canadian Perspective on the Precautionary Approach* (Discussion Document, September 2001).

5) Mechanisms should exist for re-evaluating the basis for the decisions and for providing a transparent process for further consultation.

6) A greater degree of transparency, clearer accountability, and increased public involvement are appropriate.

7) Precautionary measures should be subject to reconsideration, on the basis of the evolution of science, technology, and society's chosen level of protection.

8) Precautionary measures should be proportional to the potential severity of the risk being addressed and to society's chosen level of protection.

9) Precautionary measures should be non-discriminatory and consistent with measures taken in similar circumstances.

10) Precautionary measures should be cost-effective, with the goal of generating (i) an overall net benefit for society at least cost, and (ii) efficiency in the choice of measures.

11) Where more than one option reasonably meets the above characteristics, then the least trade-restrictive measure should be applied.

There has also been extensive discussion of *pollution prevention*, often known simply as "P2."[58] Pollution prevention is envisaged as a reorientation of environmental protection efforts so as to reduce or avoid the creation of environmental contaminants in the first instance rather than trying to control and contain their impact later. The federal government's working definition of pollution prevention is "the use of processes, practices, materials, products, substances or energy that avoid or minimize the creation of pollutants and waste, and reduce the overall risk to the environment or human health."[59]

Nova Scotia is among those jurisdictions that have explicitly embraced the principle of pollution prevention, describing it, along with waste reduction, as "the foundation for long-term environmental protection." Specifically, the Nova Scotia statute provides that pollution prevention includes: "the conservation and efficient use of resources . . . the promotion of the development and use of sustainable, scientific and technological innovations and management systems, and . . . the importance of reducing, reusing, recycling and recovering the products of our society."[60]

---

58 Canadian Council of Ministers of the Environment, *National Commitment to Pollution Prevention* (Canadian Council of Ministers of the Environment, 1993).

59 *CEPA 1999*, above note 34, s 3(1). For discussion and examples, see online: www.ec.gc.ca/planp2-p2plan.

60 *NSEA*, above note 43, s 2(b)(iii).

H. ADAPTIVE MANAGEMENT

Adaptive management might be described as a process of continuous learning grounded upon the acceptance of uncertainty. The concept originated in efforts to address two persistent challenges in environmental management: "how one deals with the uncertain, and how lessons learned from management experiences are communicated and incorporated into future management policies and practices."[61]

Key characteristics of adaptive management are that it favours action that is experimental and exploratory while accepting the existence of uncertainty and acknowledging benefits in the form of learning from unexpected consequences. Evans J of the Federal Court of Appeal captured the significance of this approach in a decision concerning environmental assessment and park management:

> The concept of "adaptive management" responds to the difficulty, or impossibility, of predicting all the environmental consequences of a project on the basis of existing knowledge. It counters the potentially paralysing effects of the precautionary principle on otherwise socially and economically useful projects. The precautionary principle states that a project should not be undertaken if it *may* have serious adverse environmental consequences, even if it is not possible to prove with any degree of certainty that these consequences will in fact materialise. Adaptive management techniques and the precautionary principle are important tools for maintaining ecological integrity.[62]

Adaptive management is flexible and discretionary in relation to means, while directed toward general and longer-term goals. Monitoring and evaluation are vital components of ongoing institutional learning, integration, and adjustment. The concept appears in several legislative and policy contexts. In the Canada-Ontario Agreement on Great Lakes Water Quality, it was described as "openness, continuous learning, innovation and improvement [to ensure] effective and efficient management."[63] In British Columbia, adaptive management has been described as "a sys-

---

61 BF Noble, "Applying Adaptive Environmental Management," in B Mitchell, ed, *Resource and Environmental Management in Canada: Addressing Conflict and Uncertainty*, 3d ed (Oxford UP, 2004) 445.

62 *Canadian Parks and Wilderness Society v Canada (Minister of Canadian Heritage)*, 2003 FCA 197 at para 24 (emphasis added).

63 *Canada-Ontario Agreement Respecting the Great Lakes Basin Ecosystem*, 22 March 2002, online: www.ec.gc.ca/Publications/A30508E0-1CAB-4236-890B-7CEB2AEF068A%5C2002-2007-Canada-Ontario-Agreement.pdf.

tematic process for continually improving management policies and practices by learning from the outcomes of operational programs."[64] Until 2012, opportunities for adaptive management were included in federal environmental assessment legislation.[65]

I. CONCLUSION

Individual decisions within the overall realm of environmental law are generally influenced—whether explicitly or implicitly—by underlying concepts and principles such as those introduced here. The list might certainly be extended to include, for example, intergenerational equity or adaptive management,[66] but the concepts reviewed above are certainly the most prominent. Their dynamic character or recent vintage have significantly contributed to the pace of change in the environmental law field.

Insofar as the concepts introduced here constitute norms, they may be considered to be objectives or standards against which the performance of an environmental protection regime may be assessed. Indeed, there are indications that biodiversity and sustainability have begun to assume such a status in the minds of many observers.[67] It should be noted, however, that there is considerable room for debate about whether such goals are being effectively pursued. Some of the other concepts, such as the polluter-pays principle or that of precaution, are more likely to perform instrumental functions; that is, rather than being ends in themselves, they may be useful in reaching other objectives.

---

64   Online: www.for.gov.bc.ca/hfp/amhome/Admin/index.htm.

65   *Canadian Environmental Assessment Act*, above note 30, s 38(5), as repealed by SC 2012, c 19, s 66.

66   C Walters, *Adaptive Management of Renewable Resources* (New York: McMillan, 1986); BC Karkkainen, "Adaptive Ecosystem Management and Regulatory Penalty Defaults: Toward a Bounded Pragmatism" (2003) 87 Minn L Rev 943; J Benidickson *et al*, *Practicing Precaution and Adaptive Management: Legal, Institutional and Procedural Dimensions of Scientific Uncertainty* (Report to the Law Commission of Canada, Ottawa, June 2005); AJ Kwasniak, "Use and Abuse of Adaptive Management in Environmental Assessment Law and Practice: A Canadian Example and General Lessons" (2010) 12 Journal of Environmental Assessment Policy and Management 425.

67   RB Keiter, "Conservation Biology and the Law: Assessing the Challenges Ahead" (1994) 69 Chicago-Kent L Rev 911; Richardson & Wood, *Environmental Law for Sustainability*, above note 20.

FURTHER READINGS

ABOUCHAR, J, "Implementation of the Precautionary Principle in Canada" in T O'Riordan, J Cameron, & A Jordan, eds, *Reinterpreting the Precautionary Principle* (London: Cameron May, 2001) 235

ATTRIDGE, I, ed, *Biodiversity Law and Policy in Canada: Review and Recommendations* (Toronto: Canadian Institute for Environmental Law and Policy, 1996)

BALLHORN, R, "The Role of Government and Policy in Sustainable Development" (2005) 1 Journal of Sustainable Development Law and Policy 19

CORDONIER SEGGER, M-C, ed, *Sustainable Justice: Reconciling Economic, Social and Environmental Law* (Boston: Martinus Nijhoff, 2005)

DeMARCO, JV, "Building a Strong Foundation for Action: A Review of Twelve Fundamental Principles of Environmental and Resource Management Legislation" (2008) 19 J Env L & Prac 59

FISHER, E, "Shifting Environmental Law: A Beginner's Guide" in BJ Richardson & S Wood, eds, *Environmental Law for Sustainability* (Portland: Hart Publishing, 2006) 97

JARDINE, CG, "Risk and Risk Management Frameworks for Human Health and Environmental Risks" (2003) 6 Journal of Toxicology and Environmental Health 569

KWASNIAK, AJ, "Use and Abuse of Adaptive Management in Environmental Law and Practice: A Canadian Example and General Lessons" (2010) 12 Journal of Environmental Assessment Policy and Management 425

LEVY, AD, & J SWAIGEN, "The Expert's Duty to the Tribunal: A Tool for Reducing Contradictions between Scientific Process and Legal Process" (1998) 11 CJALP 277

MULDOON, P, A LUCAS, RB GIBSON, & P PICKFIELD, *An Introduction to Environmental Law and Policy in Canada* (Toronto: Emond Montgomery, 2009)

Report of the House of Commons Standing Committee on Environment and Sustainable Development: It's About Our Health! Towards Pollution Prevention (Ottawa: Canadian Communication Group, 1995)

REYNOLDS, LA, "The Era of Juriscience: Investigating the Relationship Between Science, Law and the Environment" (1995) 9 Can J Admin L & Prac 61

SCOTT, DN, "The Burden of Proof: The Precautionary Principle and Its Potential for the 'Democratization of Risk'" in Law Commission of Canada, *Law and Risk* (Vancouver: UBC Press, 2005) 50

TRUDEAU, H, "Du droit international au droit interne: l'émergence du principe de précaution en droit de l'environnement" (2003) 28 Queen's LJ 455

VANDER ZWAAG, D, "The Precautionary Principle in Environmental Law and Policy" (1999) 8 J Envtl L & Prac 355

WOOD, S, G TANNER, & BJ RICHARDSON, "What Ever Happened to Canadian Environmental Law?" (2011) 37 Ecology LQ 981

THE CONSTITUTIONAL ALLOCATION OF ENVIRONMENTAL RESPONSIBILITIES AND INTERJURISDICTIONAL COORDINATION

A. INTRODUCTION

Although pollution of Canada's lakes and rivers was actively under discussion in the Confederation era, environment is not specifically mentioned in the documentation that formally established the constitutional framework. There was therefore no assignment of responsibility for the environment as such to either the provinces or the federal government. Accordingly, constitutional authority over the environment is divided on the basis of a number of heads of power, essentially as formulated at the time of Confederation in what is now known as the *Constitution Act, 1867*. In *Friends of the Oldman River Society v Canada (Minister of Transport)*[1] Justice La Forest of the Supreme Court of Canada discussed the difficulty these arrangements present for those who seek to identify and allocate responsibility for environmental matters in the Canadian process of constitutional adjudication:

> The environment, as understood in its generic sense, encompasses the physical, economic and social environment touching several of the heads of power assigned to the respective levels of government. . . .
>
> It must be recognized that the environment is not an independent matter of legislation under the *Constitution Act, 1867* and that it is a constitutionally abstruse matter which does not comfortably fit

---

1   [1992] 1 SCR 3.

within the existing division of powers without considerable overlap and uncertainty.[2]

La Forest J then emphasized the necessity of linking environmental initiatives at either the federal or the provincial level to an existing head of power, under the *Constitution Act*, further noting that "the extent to which environmental concerns may be taken into account in the exercise of a power may vary from one power to another." As an example he indicated that the federal government's environmental authority in relation to the management of fisheries, a resource, will not necessarily correspond with the environmental role permitted in association with federal constitutional power over such activities as navigation or railways.

The foregoing confirms that responsibility for important environmental questions has not been allocated with the level of constitutional certainty often thought to be desirable from the perspective of legislators, policy makers, and anyone seeking to ensure governmental accountability in this field. This is partly a consequence of the original omission dating from 1867, but it is also a result of the processes of constitutional interpretation and of the changing perceptions of the nature of environmental problems and appropriate policy responses. Al Lucas writes, for example, that it is "constitutionally meaningless" to attempt to determine conclusively whether the federal or the provincial government has jurisdiction over air pollution. An answer to the question would, he explains, "depend not only on factual matters such as the source, nature and consequences of particular air pollution, but also on the precise form and scope of any law aimed at it."[3]

This is a useful reminder that constitutional analysis in Canada requires one to determine or specify the subject of the allocation or the specific matter one wishes a particular level of government to regulate.[4] One might be concerned with the availability of a particular instrument or technique of environmental control such as criminal law, general regulatory schemes, or licensing controls such as quotas and emission standards. Alternative instruments might include zoning and land-use restrictions, positive programs with respect to wilderness protection,

---

2   *Ibid* at para 86.
3   AR Lucas, "Harmonization of Federal and Provincial Environmental Policies: The Changing Legal and Policy Framework" in JO Saunders, ed, *Managing Natural Resources in a Federal State: Essays from the Second Banff Conference on Natural Resources Law* (Toronto: Carswell, 1986) 33 at 34.
4   D Gibson, "Environmental Protection and Enhancement under a New Constitution" in SM Beck & I Bernier, eds, *Canada and the New Constitution: The Unfinished Agenda*, vol 2 (Montreal: Institute for Research on Public Policy, 1983) 113 at 117–23.

or cleanup initiatives directed towards the rehabilitation of contaminated sites. The potential utility of each of these forms of legal intervention often induces people to focus on the availability of such powers as justification for environmental protection measures by the level of government entitled to use them. But most of these general techniques are applicable in relation to subjects other than the environment.

The risk in focusing on legal instruments can be that the government with the interest in safeguarding the environment may not be the government with the most effective tools. This difficulty partly explains the persistence of analysis centred on so-called environmental media or sectors: air, land, water. Yet this sectoral approach is also problematic because administrative measures frequently involve interrelationships outside the subject being regulated. A third model sometimes put forward associates constitutional authority with the territory to be affected. Thus, national parks, Indian reserves, coastal waters, or federal lands are sometimes identified as zones within which environmental responsibility might be neatly allocated.[5] However, the interrelationship between activity within and without any areas of this type demonstrates the limitations of geographic demarcation schemes as a basis for assigning legislative responsibilities.

The potential for overlapping or shared environmental responsibility was highlighted in litigation that emerged from controversy over environmental assessment procedures applicable to resource development in northern Quebec:

> There is no doubt that a vanadium mining project, considered in isolation, falls within provincial jurisdiction under s 92A of the *Constitution Act, 1867* over natural resources. There is also no doubt that ordinarily a mining project anywhere in Canada that puts at risk fish habitat could not proceed without a permit from the federal Fisheries Minister, which he or she could not issue except after compliance with *CEAA*. The mining of non-renewable mineral resources aspect falls within provincial jurisdiction, but the fisheries aspect is federal.[6]

Before describing some non-constitutional mechanisms of intergovernmental coordination, we will consider the bases on which claims about the allocation of constitutional authority are typically formulated.

---

5   *Canadian Environmental Protection Act, 1999*, SC 1999, c 33 [*CEPA 1999*]. Part 9 addresses environmental issues on "federal lands."

6   *Quebec (AG) v Moses*, 2010 SCC 17 at para 36.

B. SOURCES OF FEDERAL ENVIRONMENTAL AUTHORITY

Certain specific heads of constitutional power provide the federal government with legislative authority encompassing associated environmental measures. Powers concerning the regulation of trade and commerce (section 91[2]), navigation and shipping (section 91[10]), seacoast and inland fisheries (section 91[12]), federal works and undertakings (section 91[29] and section 92[10]), and Indians and lands reserved for the Indians (section 91[24]) are notable examples. However, the scope of environmental measures linked to the exercise of such powers is not unlimited. The courts remain sensitive to the existence of provincial powers and have formulated procedures for resolving conflicts.

In *R v Northwest Falling Contractors Ltd*[7] the Supreme Court of Canada upheld a federal *Fisheries Act* provision prohibiting the deposit of deleterious substances into water frequented by fish, despite arguments that this measure invaded the realm of provincial responsibility for property and civil rights under section 92(13) of the *Constitution Act*. The validity of the federal measure rested on the close linkage between the prohibition and the potential for harm to fish, a connection based on the definition of *deleterious substance* as one posing the prospect of harm to fish or their habitat. On the other hand, the fate of another, more broadly worded *Fisheries Act* provision illustrated that the scope of the fisheries' power to support federal environmental initiatives is subject to constraints. When the federal government declared that "[n]o person engaging in logging, lumbering, land clearing or other operations, shall put or knowingly permit to be put, any slash, stumps or other debris into any water frequented by fish or that flows into such water, or on the ice over either such water, or at a place from which it is likely to be carried into either such water," the legislation was struck down for its failure to link the prohibited conduct to actual or potential harm to the fishery.[8] The existence or threat of such harm was thus determined to be an essential precondition of federal jurisdiction in this area.

Federal authority in connection with trade and commerce, and in connection with international agreements, has also failed to provide broad support for federal initiatives in the environmental area. The

---

7   [1980] 2 SCR 292.
8   *R v Fowler*, [1980] 2 SCR 213. See also *Ward v Canada (Attorney General)*, 2002 SCC 17 at paras 41 & 42. Recent legislative changes to the *Fisheries Act* are discussed in Chapter 8, Section C.

courts have historically interpreted the trade and commerce power in a restrictive manner, so that it permits federal regulation of international and interprovincial but not intraprovincial trade.[9] To fall within the federal trade and commerce power, the matter to be regulated must be genuinely national in scope, broader than a particular industry or commodity, and beyond the capacity of local provincial regulation to address effectively.[10] And it has long been established that the federal government cannot, simply by entering into international agreements, extend the scope of its domestic jurisdiction over a matter that would otherwise fall within provincial jurisdiction.[11] In situations where pollution originating in one province will have an external impact on neighbouring provinces or internationally, however, the federal government can assert jurisdiction resulting from the lack of extraterritorial competence on the part of the provinces.[12]

Potentially more expansive sources of federal authority in relation to environmental matters include the general or residual power for the peace, order, and good government of Canada (POGG) and the criminal law power (section 91[27]). The POGG power, and in particular its "national concern" branch, has been considered for some time as a promising foundation for extensive federal jurisdiction in the environmental field. In R v Crown Zellerbach Canada Ltd, the constitutionality of federal provisions dealing with dumping in coastal waters was challenged by a company charged for activity in a British Columbia bay.[13] After determining that provisions of the federal Ocean Dumping Control Act[14] could not be upheld constitutionally under any of the specific powers listed in section 91, Justice Le Dain assessed the statutory scheme against the "national concern" doctrine relating to the federal POGG power. To satisfy the "national concern" test, the subject matter of the statute must have "a singleness, distinctiveness, and indivisibility that clearly distinguishes it from matters of provincial concern and a scale of impact on provincial jurisdiction that is reconcilable with the fundamental distribution of legislative power under the Constitution."[15]

---

9   *Labatt Breweries v Canada (AG)*, [1980] 1 SCR 914.
10 *General Motors of Canada Ltd v City National Leasing Ltd*, [1989] 1 SCR 641; *Reference re Securities Act*, 2011 SCC 66.
11 *Canada (AG) v Ontario (AG)*, [1937] AC 326 (PC).
12 *Interprovincial Co-operative v R*, [1976] 1 SCR 477 [*Interprovincial Co-operative*]; PW Hogg, *Constitutional Law of Canada*, 2d ed (Toronto: Carswell, 1985) at 598.
13 [1988] 1 SCR 401 [*Crown Zellerbach*].
14 Provisions originally found within ocean dumping legislation are now found in *CEPA 1999*, above note 5, Part 7.
15 *Crown Zellerbach*, above note 13 at 432.

Taking account of a series of considerations, including the implications of provincial inaction or inability to address the problems of ocean dumping, the extent to which the federal measures affected provincial jurisdiction, and the nature of marine pollution itself, Justice Le Dain concluded that such pollution, given its "predominantly extra-provincial as well as international character and implications" qualified as a matter of national concern.

But there was apprehension that the breadth of the authority potentially available under the "national concern" test might threaten the essential and underlying balance of the federation. The tension was in fact apparent in the dissenting judgment of Justice La Forest in *Crown Zellerbach*:

> All physical activities have some environmental impact. Possible legislative responses to such activities cover a large number of the enumerated legislative powers, federal and provincial. To allocate the broad subject-matter of environmental control to the federal government under its general power would effectively gut provincial legislative jurisdiction.[16]

The challenge for the courts, he concluded, "will be to allow the federal Parliament sufficient scope to acquit itself of its duties to deal with national and international problems while respecting the scheme of federalism provided by the Constitution."

Commentators had speculated, however, that in addition to securing the foundations of the ocean-dumping provisions of *CEPA*, the "national concern" test as applied in *Crown Zellerbach* might offer constitutional support for other matters addressed in the federal legislation, including toxic substances.[17] When, in fact, the constitutionality of *CEPA*'s toxic substance provisions was judicially examined, the national concern branch of the POGG power was not the basis on which the legislation was upheld.

In *Canada (AG) v Hydro-Québec*, the Quebec Court of Appeal ruled that environmental protection, as a subject which is itself an aggregate of other matters falling within both federal and provincial competence, lacks the "singleness, distinctiveness and indivisibility" necessary to satisfy the national concern as formulated in *Crown Zellerbach*.[18] A majority of the Supreme Court subsequently upheld the toxic substance provisions of *CEPA* on the basis of the federal criminal power.[19]

---

16   *Ibid* at 455.
17   Lucas, above note 3 at 366.
18   *Canada (AG) v Hydro-Québec* (1995), 17 CELR (NS) 34 at 52–53 (Que CA).
19   *Canada (AG) v Hydro-Québec*, [1997] 3 SCR 213.

In attempting to prevent the conception of the criminal law power from becoming too all-encompassing, courts have generally looked for the characteristic of blameworthiness in the relevant conduct and a formal prohibition against it. In consequence, federal legislation of a regulatory nature not amounting to actual prohibition of blameworthy conduct has not found constitutional shelter under the criminal law power. "Criminal sanctions designed to prohibit certain wrongful conduct are constitutional," explained Paul Emond, "whereas sanctions used to regulate conduct are not."[20] Jurisprudence—even before the Supreme Court's *Hydro-Québec* decision—suggested some softening in the rigidity of such traditional constraints on the criminal power.[21]

When Hydro-Quebec was charged in 1990 with dumping PCBs (polychlorinated biphenyls) contrary to interim regulations made pursuant to sections 34 and 35 of *CEPA*'s toxic substance provisions, the utility defended on the grounds that neither the statutory provisions nor the regulations were within the constitutional scope of federal law-making authority. Briefly stated, section 34 provided for the regulation of toxic substances as determined under *CEPA*. Toxic substances were those that had been shown to have potential for harmful effects on the environment or constituted a danger to the environment on which human life depends or represented a danger in Canada to human life or health. As itemized in section 34, the list of considerations specifically subject to the regulation of toxic substances ran from (a) to (x) where (x) authorized "any other matter necessary to carry out the purposes of this Part" of *CEPA*. Section 35 allowed temporary orders equivalent to regulations under section 34 to be made when the ministers of health and environment believed immediate action was required. The *Chlorobiphenyls Interim Order* was one of these.

In the deliberations of the Supreme Court, the legitimacy of the various impugned provisions under the criminal law power became central. In the forcefully expressed view of four dissenting judges:

> While the protection of the environment is a legitimate public purpose which could support the enactment of criminal legislation, we believe the impugned provisions of the Act are more an attempt to regulate environmental pollution than to prohibit or proscribe it. As

---

20   P Emond, "The Case for a Greater Federal Role in the Environmental Protection Field: An Examination of the Pollution Problem and the Constitution" (1972) 10 Osgoode Hall LJ 647 at 664.

21   *RJR-MacDonald Inc v Canada (AG)*, [1995] 3 SCR 199.

such, they extend beyond the purview of criminal law and cannot be justified under s 91(27).[22]

The majority opinion, written by La Forest J, took a more generous approach to the criminal law power as "plenary in nature." With respect to the validity of the underlying objective, La Forest identified environmental protection as "a public purpose of superordinate importance."[23] He found *CEPA*'s toxic substance provisions to be consistent with established judicial understanding of criminal law: "These listed substances, toxic in the ordinary sense, are those whose use in a manner contrary to the regulations the Act ultimately prohibits. This is a limited prohibition applicable to a limited number of substances. The prohibition is enforced by a penal sanction and is undergirded by a valid criminal objective, and so is valid criminal legislation."[24]

C. SOURCES OF PROVINCIAL ENVIRONMENTAL JURISDICTION

Provincial authority to enact environmental protection measures derives principally from power in relation to "Property and Civil Rights in the Province" (92[13]) and "Generally all Matters of a merely local or private Nature in the Province" (92[16]). Further potentially relevant sources of provincial constitutional authority include: the management and sale of public lands and timber (92[5]); municipal institutions (92[8]); licensing for local, municipal, and provincial revenue (92[9]); local works and undertakings [92[10]]; and the enforcement powers enumerated in section 92(15). In addition, section 92A of the *Constitution Act, 1982*, known as the natural resources amendment, is relevant to environmental law-making insofar as it confers on each provincial legislature exclusive authority to make laws in relation to the

> development, conservation and management of non-renewable natural resources and forestry resources in the province, including laws in relation to the rate of primary production therefrom; and . . . development, conservation and management of sites and facilities in the province for the generation and production of electrical energy.

Apart from these enumerated powers, the courts have recognized provincial legislative authority deriving from rights of ownership or pro-

---

22   *Canada (AG) v Hydro-Québec*, above note 19 at 246.
23   *Ibid* at 266.
24   *Ibid* at 308.

prietary rights over natural resources.[25] Collectively, these sources of legislative power provide the provinces with a strong constitutional basis for the extensive range of regulatory initiatives each has taken in relation to environmental protection. Yet certain constraints must be acknowledged, beginning with the geographic restriction of provincial authority within provincial boundaries. In *Interprovincial Cooperative*, an attempt by Manitoba to create a statutory right of action against pollution that originated upstream in the neighbouring provinces of Saskatchewan and Ontario was found unconstitutional.[26] In a complex decision, a plurality of the judges determined that the extraterritorial origin of the pollution removed it from the legislative reach of Manitoba, despite the acknowledged fact of injury to that province's fishery. The delimitation of provincial boundaries is therefore of considerable importance to the applicability of environmental regulatory regimes,[27] although there are recent indications that provinces are anxious to extend the protective reach of their environmental laws.

From the perspective of those industries that face actual compliance obligations, shared or overlapping environmental jurisdiction may entail inconvenience, uncertainty, additional expense, or still more serious consequences, including prosecution. Some of those facing prosecution, especially in such federally regulated industries as interprovincial transportation, have argued that on this basis they are not subject to provincial environmental requirements and that, somewhat like the federal Crown and its agents, they enjoy a form of interjurisdictional immunity.

It has been confirmed that federally regulated industries enjoy no such immunity.[28] In *R v Canadian Pacific Ltd*, the company was charged under the Ontario *EPA* in connection with the adverse environmental effects of smoke, a contaminant, which resulted from a controlled burn of weeds along the railway right of way. The railway's claim that the *EPA* unconstitutionally interfered with the management of a federally regulated undertaking was rejected. The statute was one of general application in the province, not directed at the management of the railway; and, though it affected the railway's clearing operations, it did not have an impermissible impact on CP's essential functions. Similarly, it

---

25   *Constitution Act, 1867* (UK), 30 & 31 Vict, c 3, s 109.
26   *Interprovincial Co-operative*, above note 12. See also *Mathias Colomb Band of Indians v Saskatchewan Power Corp* (1994), 13 CELR (NS) 245 (Man CA).
27   *Reference Re Offshore Mineral Rights (British Columbia)*, [1967] SCR 792; *Canada (AG) v British Columbia (AG)*, [1984] 1 SCR 388; *Reference Re Seabed & Subsoil of Continental Shelf Offshore Newfoundland*, [1984] 1 SCR 86.
28   *R v Canadian Pacific Ltd*, [1995] 2 SCR 1028.

was determined that an interprovincial trucking company was subject to provincial PCB transport regulation. As Mackinnon ACJO explained:

> In the same way that the province can regulate speed limits and the mechanical conditions of vehicles on the roads of the province for the protection and safety of other highway users, it can set conditions for the carriage of particular toxic substances within the province, provided that the conditions do not interfere in any substantial way with the carrier's general or particular carriage of goods, and are not in conflict either directly or indirectly with federal legislation in the field.[29]

D. MUNICIPAL GOVERNMENT AND THE ENVIRONMENT

As "creatures of the provinces" for constitutional purposes, municipal and local governments lack constitutional autonomy. Their executive and legislative powers are exercised on the basis of delegation, primarily by means of provincial legislation. But once conferred, such powers include the capacity to enact fully enforceable bylaws reflecting the decisions of municipal or local officials. As subordinate instruments, such bylaws cannot exceed the scope or contradict the intent of corresponding provincial legislation. Thus, in *Superior Propane Inc v York (City)*, a municipal bylaw designed to regulate propane storage and distribution in the interests of public safety was struck down. The Ontario Court of Appeal concluded that the municipal initiative was in conflict with a comprehensive scheme of regulations under the provincial *Energy Act*.[30]

It is evident nevertheless that municipal authority in the environmental context is both vital and extensive. Local authority to regulate and manage the environment has been classified in relation to six sets of powers: environment powers; public health powers; planning and zoning powers; business licensing and regulation powers; dangerous

---

29   *R v TNT Canada Inc* (1986), 37 DLR (4th) 297. In *Canadian Western Bank v Alberta*, 2007 SCC 22 at para 77, the Supreme Court emphasizes that interjurisdictional immunity is of limited application.

30   (1995), 23 OR (3d) 161 (CA), leave to appeal to SCC refused (1996), 19 CELR (NS) 270 (SCC). For a more recent example of conflict between a municipal bylaw and provincial regulation, see *Peacock v Norfolk (County)* (2006), 81 OR (3d) 530 (CA).

substances powers; and plenary powers.[31] This range of responsibility requires some further consideration, even if the limited scope of this text precludes detailed discussion of local environmental protection regimes.[32]

Judicial consideration of municipal decision making in the environmental area suggests a willingness to acknowledge the importance of action at the local government level. This is true both in relation to the treatment of the scope of municipal authority and in relation to judicial review of the exercise of that authority.[33]

When the town of Hudson, Quebec, enacted a pesticide bylaw without specific legislative authority to do so, it became necessary to ascertain whether such authority could be found within a general provision of the province's *Cities and Towns Act*.[34] This provision, similar to that found in other jurisdictions, stated simply: "The Council may make bylaws to secure peace, order, good government, health and general welfare in the territory of the municipality, provided such bylaws are not contrary to the laws of Canada, or of Quebec, nor inconsistent with any special provision of this act or of the *Charter*."

The court's finding that the bylaw in question was within the scope of this general authority is widely regarded as enhancing the role of municipalities in relation to environmental, health, and other matters.

In an earlier decision, *Rascal Trucking*,[35] after the court had concluded that a specific *Municipal Act* provision dealing with nuisance applied to a municipal resolution that had been challenged, Justice Major endorsed the following observation:

> Courts must respect the responsibility of elected municipal bodies to serve the people who elected them and exercise caution to avoid substituting their views of what is best for the citizens for those of municipal councils. Barring clear demonstration that a municipal decision was beyond its powers, courts should not so hold.

---

31   LA Reynolds, "Environmental Regulation and Management by Local Public Authorities in Canada" (1993) 3 J Envtl L & Prac 41.

32   See SM Makuch, N Craik, & SB Leisk, *Canadian Municipal and Planning Law*, 2d ed (Toronto: Thomson Carswell, 2004); MV MacLean & JR Tomlinson, *A User's Guide to Municipal By-Laws*, 2d ed (Markham: LexisNexis, 2008).

33   See, for example, *Wallot c Québec (Ville de)*, 2011 QCCA 1773, where the court found not only municipal authority to require riparian owners to restore shorelines alongside a water supply source, but a responsibility to do so.

34   *114957 Canada Ltée (Spraytech, Société d'arrosage) v Hudson (Town)*, 2001 SCC 40.

35   *Nanaimo (City) v Rascal Trucking Ltd*, 2000 SCC 13. Subsequent developments have once again altered the Supreme Court of Canada's approach to the standard of review of administrative decisions See *Dunsmuir v New Brunswick*, 2008 SCC 9.

Thus, the court concluded as a matter of administrative law that judicial review of municipal decisions should be conducted according to a deferential standard.

In relation to judicial respect for the environmental responsibilities of municipal government and, of course, for the significance of environmental considerations themselves, it is equally noteworthy that a Montreal bylaw regulating noise survived a challenge grounded on the constitutional right to freedom of expression.[36]

Municipal environmental efforts require supporting resources that are not always available. Even major cities and large metropolitan areas have lamented financial limitations that have restricted their capacity to pursue desirable initiatives. Some level of assistance, at least in terms of research, information, and policy guidance is available through the Federation of Canadian Municipalities, which has taken steps to encourage local government action in relation to waste management, water quality, air pollution, climate change, toxics, and other issues.[37]

E. ABORIGINAL RIGHTS, RESOURCES, AND THE ENVIRONMENT

The constitutional framework governing environmental and resource issues extends beyond the allocation of powers between the federal and provincial governments to encompass the relationship between those governments and the Aboriginal peoples of Canada, including the Indian, Inuit, and Metis communities. This observation is grounded in section 35(1) of the *Constitution Act, 1982*, which asserts that "[t]he existing aboriginal and treaty rights of the aboriginal peoples of Canada are hereby recognized and affirmed."[38]

The importance of section 35 for resource management and the environment was demonstrated in the *Sparrow* decision, where the Supreme Court of Canada established a strict test for the extinguishment of Aboriginal rights, that is, inherent rights associated with Aboriginal

---

36   *Montreal (City)* v *2952-1366 Quebec Inc*, 2005 SCC 62.

37   For an illustration of significant municipal actions, see the pesticides discussion in Chapter 13. See also the City of Toronto sewer bylaw No. 457-2000 introducing pollution prevention requirements and Edmonton's "Toward a Cleaner River" initiative.

38   On the importance of describing or characterizing the scope and nature of the right being asserted, see *Lax kw'alaams Indian Band v Canada (Attorney General)*, 2011 SCC 56.

occupancy preceding European settlement.[39] "The test of extinguishment to be adopted, in our opinion, is that the Sovereign's intention must be clear and plain if it is to extinguish an aboriginal right."[40] Legislation or regulation affecting Aboriginal rights is not precluded, for "[r]ights that are recognized and affirmed are not absolute," but regulation must be enacted "according to a valid objective" such as "conservation and resource management." In other words, legislative authority in areas associated with Aboriginal rights is subject to close judicial scrutiny under section 35: moreover, courts have repeatedly underlined the significance of the Crown's honour and fiduciary duties in relation to Aboriginal peoples.

In *Sparrow*, a Musqueam Indian was charged for fishing salmon illegally with a net whose dimensions exceeded those established in the Musqueam Band Indian Food Fishing Licence, which had been issued in accordance with regulations under the federal *Fisheries Act*. The defence put forward by the accused was that he enjoyed an Aboriginal right to fish that overrode the licence restrictions. As explained by the court, the initial step in cases of this kind is for the party asserting an Aboriginal right to demonstrate its existence and to show that its exercise has been interfered with by the regulation being challenged.[41] It then falls to the Crown to justify the interference. This exercise will require the Crown to show a valid legislative objective, pursued through means that are consistent with or respectful of the existence of the Aboriginal right and that interfere as little as possible with that right.[42]

In subsequent decisions, the SCC returned to the question of limitations on section 35 rights concerning resource use and conservation. In *Nikal*, the relationship between Aboriginal fishing rights and resource conservation programs was explicitly addressed:

> The aboriginal right to fish must be balanced against the need to conserve the fishery stock. This right cannot automatically deny the ability of the government to set up a licensing scheme or program as part of a conservation program since the right's exercise depends on the continued existence of the resource.[43]

---

39   *R v Sparrow*, [1990] 1 SCR 1075 [*Sparrow*].
40   *Ibid* at para 37.
41   As discussed below, certain protections now extend to Aboriginal rights that are claimed or asserted rather than established.
42   *Sparrow*, above note 39.
43   *R v Nikal*, [1996] 1 SCR 1013 at para 94.

In *Gladstone*,[44] in the context of charges of selling herring spawn on kelp without a licence against Heiltsuk Indians who asserted an Aboriginal right to fish commercially, the SCC observed:

> Where the aboriginal right is one that has no internal limitation [so that it is clear when that right has been satisfied and other users can be allowed to participate in the fishery] . . . the doctrine of priority requires that the government demonstrate that, in allocating the resource, it has taken account of the existence of aboriginal rights and allocated the resource in a manner respectful of the fact that those rights have priority over the exploitation of the fishery by other users.[45]

In connection with the distribution of the fisheries resource after conservation goals and Aboriginal uses have been satisfied, the Court identified several relevant criteria or appropriate objectives including "the pursuit of economic and regional fairness, and the recognition of the historical reliance upon, and participation in, the fishery by non-Aboriginal groups."[46]

In a subsequent decision, the SCC again elaborated on the range of legislative objectives that might justify infringement of Aboriginal rights Protection of the environment or endangered species was specifically listed among such objectives, along with resource development, the building of infrastructure, and settlement.[47]

The existence of constitutionally required safeguards is no longer confined to Aboriginal rights whose existence has been established. Thus, in two cases from British Columbia where extensive land claims remain unresolved, the SCC, with reference to section 35, insisted upon a duty of consultation (and of appropriate accommodation).[48] It is also noteworthy that Metis Aboriginal rights in relation to hunting have been recognized.[49]

Although the scope of Aboriginal rights remains to be determined in many parts of the country, especially in relation to self-government, acknowledged and asserted Aboriginal interests in land and resources

---

44   *R v Gladstone*, [1996] 2 SCR 723.
45   *Ibid* at para 62.
46   *Ibid* at 187.
47   *Delgamuukw v British Columbia*, [1997] 3 SCR 1011 at 1111.
48   *Haida Nation v British Columbia (Minister of Forests)*, [2004] 3 SCR 511; *Taku River Tlingit First Nation v British Columbia (Project Assessment Director)*, [2004] 3 SCR 550. The nature of Aboriginal consultation requirements is discussed in Chapter 16.
49   *R v Powley* (2001), 53 OR (3d) 35 (CA), appeal and cross-appeal dismissed, 2003 SCC 43.

will have an important influence on the design and operation of re-source management and environmental protection regimes in various parts of Canada.[50]

Treaty rights and land-claim agreements, that is, governing docu-ments derived from negotiation and mutual consent, also affect the nature and extent of Aboriginal participation in resource and environ-mental management.[51] Modern treaties typically address, sometimes in great detail, issues associated with decision making over land use, environmental assessment and approvals, and the relationship of these processes to traditional Aboriginal interests. Historic treaties, even when largely silent on such matters, may also be of significance as the first *Marshall* decision demonstrates.[52]

In a situation not unlike that in *Sparrow*, in *Marshall*, a Mi'kmaq Indian was charged with catching eels by means of a prohibited net dur-ing the close season and then selling these without holding a commer-cial licence to do so. The accused's defence rested on an interpretation of treaties dating from the mid-eighteenth century, and specifically a *Treaty of Peace and Friendship (1860)* in which a Mi'kmaq chief agreed "not to traffick, barter or exchange any commodities in any manner but with such persons or the managers of such truck houses as shall be ap-pointed or established by His Majesty's governor." A majority of the SCC concluded that the treaty preserved "a treaty right to continue to ob-tain necessaries through hunting and fishing by trading the products of those traditional activities subject to restrictions,"[53] stating further that "necessaries" was equivalent to "a moderate livelihood."[54] Marshall, not being subject to the close season rule or the licence requirement, was ac-quitted. The court subsequently clarified its initial *Marshall* judgment by emphasizing that, like Aboriginal rights, the treaty right that had been recognized could be subject to both regulation and licensing where such measures are justified. Justification requires a valid legislative object-ive, appropriate consultation, minimal infringement of the right affected, and consideration of the special trust relationship of the government toward Aboriginal peoples.[55]

---

50 *Canada (AG) v Inuvialuit Regional Corp.* (1994), 119 DLR (4th) 373 (FCA); *Que-bec (AG) v Canada (National Energy Board)*, [1994] 1 SCR 159.

51 *Cree Regional Authority v Canada (Federal Administrator)*, [1992] 1 FC 440 (TD); *Eastmain Band v Canada (Federal Administrator)*, [1993] 1 FC 501 (TD).

52 *R v Marshall* (1999), 138 CCC (3d) 97 (SCC).

53 *Ibid* at 129.

54 *Ibid* at 107.

55 *R v Marshall* (1999), 139 CCC (3d) 391 (SCC).

F. INTERGOVERNMENTAL COORDINATION AND ENVIRONMENTAL PROTECTION

Overlap and ambiguity in the scope of federal and provincial constitutional authority respecting the environment present challenges of coordination in the interests of reducing costly duplication, avoiding gaps, and generally promoting consistency. In the face of increasingly urgent and wide-ranging environmental challenges such as those presented by climate change and biodiversity loss, the costs of dysfunctional constitutional arrangements are incalculable. To minimize the impact of this ambiguity and dysfunction, numerous mechanisms—both informal and statutorily prescribed—have been employed to enhance intergovernmental coordination. These include simple information exchange and ongoing consultations, negotiation of formal agreements—on a bilateral or multilateral basis—concerning environmental responsibilities, the delegation of authority from one government to another, and the development of joint-decision-making bodies and procedures whereby one government can adopt the outcome of another's processes.

1) Intergovernmental Consultation

In addition to ongoing communication between environmental officials in one jurisdiction and their counterparts elsewhere, several institutions facilitate coordination of policy and decision making. In the 1980s a national task force consisting of government, industry, and representatives of environmental groups contributed to the formation of multistakeholder "round tables" in many jurisdictions.[56] One of these, the National Round Table on the Environment and the Economy (NRTEE), included participants from the federal and a number of provincial governments.[57]

Certain pieces of federal legislation also provide for mechanisms to encourage coordination by means of consultation. Section 6 of the *CEPA 1999*, for example, calls for the creation of a National Advisory Committee (formerly the Federal-Provincial Advisory Committee) "[f]or the purpose of enabling national action to be carried out and taking

---

56   *Report of the National Task Force on Environment and Economy* (Downsview: Canadian Council of Resource and Environment Ministers, 1987).

57   The NRTEE contributed productively to national debate on a wide range of environmental and sustainability issues from its origins in 1988 until the closure of its operations in 2013.

co-operative action in matters affecting the environment and for the purpose of avoiding duplication in regulatory activity among governments." Consisting of representatives from the federal departments of environment and health, from each of the provincial governments, and from Aboriginal government representatives, the National Advisory Committee provides a forum for discussion of a range of issues.

The most important institution today in terms of intergovernmental consultation on environmental matters is the Canadian Council of Ministers of the Environment (CCME). To address the problem of regulatory costs on Canadian business in the environmental field, the CCME has undertaken several examinations of regulatory arrangements with a view to promoting increased harmonization. In 1993, the CCME's *Statement of Interjurisdictional Cooperation on Environmental Matters* argued that "[t]he increased complexity of environmental issues, particularly their interjurisdictional impacts, requires coordinated responses from both orders of government; and . . . [e]ffective interjurisdictional cooperation leads to certainty and predictability of environmental regulation, and promotes public confidence and sound economic planning."[58] This statement was one of the antecedents of the harmonization accord discussed later in this chapter.

2) Intergovernmental Bilateral Agreements

The federal government has occasionally negotiated bilateral agreements with specific provinces concerning the administration of particular features of the environmental law regime. Over thirty years ago, all provinces but Newfoundland, Quebec, and British Columbia signed federal-provincial "Accords" for the protection and enhancement of environmental quality. Renewals updated and extended the life of some of these agreements, and arrangements have been negotiated in relation to other matters.[59]

---

58   Canadian Council of Ministers of the Environment, *Statement of Interjurisdictional Cooperation on Environmental Matters* (1993). For further information on the history and contribution of the CCME, see online: www.ccme.ca.

59   For one of the early examples, see *Canada-Alberta Accord for the Protection and Enhancement of Environmental Quality*, 8 October 1991, quoted in D Tingley, "Conflict and Cooperation on the Environment" in DM Brown, ed, *Canada: The State of the Federation 1991* (Kingston: Queen's University Institute of Intergovernmental Relations, 1991) 131 at 135–36. For background in the context of fisheries, see Department of Fisheries and Oceans, *Freshwater Initiative Discussion Document* (Ottawa, 1999).

CEPA 1999 section 9 authorizes federal-provincial agreements concerning the administration of the Act. Administrative agreements are described as "working arrangements" between governments to streamline the administration of regulations. The *Canada-Saskatchewan Administrative Agreement* (15 September 1994) addresses the administration of seven federal regulations within the province.[60] The *Canada-Quebec Pulp and Paper Administrative Agreement* (13 June 2009) establishes a joint committee and provides for reporting procedures and information exchange in relation to federal regulation of the pulp and paper sector under *CEPA 1999* and the *Fisheries Act*.[61]

Pursuant to *CEPA 1999* section 10, when the federal minister of the environment and a provincial government agree that provincial law is equivalent to *CEPA 1999* regulations on toxic substances and that citizens' rights to require investigation of an alleged offence are similar to those established under *CEPA 1999*, the federal government may declare that the federal regulations do not apply in that province other than to federal works, undertakings, and lands. In 1994, the first federal-provincial equivalency agreement dealing with four federal regulations was concluded with Alberta.[62]

3) The Harmonization Accord and the Agreement on Internal Trade

In January 1998, following half a decade of discussion under the general auspices of the CCME, the federal, provincial, and territorial governments (excluding Quebec) signed a Canada-wide Accord on Environmental Harmonization.[63] The stated objectives of the harmonization initiative are to enhance environmental protection, to promote sustainable development, and to improve environmental management from the perspective of effectiveness, efficiency, accountability, predictability, and clarity. These goals are to be accomplished by means

60   Online: www.ec.gc.ca/ee-ue/default.asp?lang=En&n=91B094B6-1.
61   Online: www.gazette.gc.ca/rp-pr/p1/2009/2009-06-13/html/notice-avis-eng.html#d101.
62   *Agreement on the Equivalency of Federal and Alberta Regulations for the Control of Toxic Substances in Alberta* (June 1994), available as *Alberta Equivalency Order*, SOR/94-752, C Gaz 1994.II.4056. For discussion of this and other federal-provincial agreements, see Canada, House of Commons, Standing Committee on Environment and Sustainable Development, "Enforcing Canada's Pollution Laws: The Public Interest Must Come First" at c 3 (1998); and Commissioner of the Environment and Sustainable Development, *Annual Report 1999* at c 5, "Streamlining Environmental Protection Through Federal-Provincial Agreements."
63   Online: www.ccme.ca.

of cooperation and the delineation of governmental roles and responsibilities. Overlapping environmental management of activities is to be prevented; gaps and weaknesses are to be filled. Thirteen principles, set out as follows, were incorporated within the accord:

1) those who generate pollution and waste should bear the cost of prevention, containment, cleanup, or abatement (polluter-pays principle);

2) where there are threats of serious or irreversible environmental damage, lack of full scientific certainty shall not be used as a reason for postponing cost-effective measures to prevent environmental degradation (precautionary principle);

3) pollution prevention is the preferred approach to environmental protection;

4) environmental measures should be performance-based, results-oriented, and science-based;

5) openness, transparency, accountability, and the effective participation of stakeholders and the public in environmental decision making is necessary for an effective environmental management regime;

6) working cooperatively with Aboriginal people and their structures of governance is necessary for an effective environmental management regime;

7) Canada-wide approaches on how to meet the objectives of this accord will allow for flexible implementation required to reflect variations in ecosystems and local, regional, provincial, and territorial conditions;

8) decisions pursuant to the accord will be consensus-based and driven by the commitment to achieve the highest level of environmental quality within the context of sustainable development;

9) nothing in this accord alters the legislative or other authority of the governments or the rights of any of them with respect to the exercise of their legislative or other authorities under the Constitution of Canada;

10) legislation, regulations, policies, and existing agreements should accommodate the implementation of this accord;

11) the environmental measures established and implemented in accordance with this Accord will not prevent a government from introducing more stringent environmental measures to reflect specific circumstances or to protect environments or environmental values located within its jurisdiction;

12) this Accord and sub-agreements do not affect Aboriginal or treaty rights;

13) all Canadians should be confident that their environment is respected by neighbouring Canadian jurisdictions.

A number of sub-agreements have been formulated to implement the principles of the Accord in a series of designated subject areas. To date, sub-agreements have been developed with respect to environmental standards, environmental inspections and enforcement, and environmental assessment. Other specific initiatives within the framework address dioxin and furan emissions from incinerators, coastal pulp and paper boilers, iron sintering plants, steel manufacturing, electric arc furnaces, and conical waste combustion, mercury-containing lamps, mercury in dental amalgam wastes, mercury from incineration, benzene, and petroleum hydrocarbons in soil.[64]

The Canadian Environmental Law Association (CELA) unsuccessfully sought judicial review of the decision of the federal minister of environment to sign the Accord and accompanying sub-agreements.[65] CELA had argued that any proposed realignment of federal and provincial roles and responsibilities for environmental management pursuant to the Accord was beyond the authority of the minister under existing federal legislation. Alternatively, CELA had argued that insofar as the agreements constituted an undertaking to not act in certain circumstances, the minister's authority was unlawfully fettered.

In the context of interprovincial trade, other efforts have been made to address the problems of inconsistent and conflicting environmental standards within Canada's comparatively small domestic market. Thus, the *Agreement on Internal Trade (AIT)* addresses environmental protection and extends general rules of entry, non-discrimination, transparency, and so on to this area while simultaneously calling on all parties to maintain high standards.[66] Chapter 15 of the *AIT*, which deals with environmental protection, has remained largely intact since implementation in 1995. Under Chapter 15, provinces are called upon to "take into account the need to restore, maintain and enhance the environment"

---

64   For commentary and assessment, see M Winfield and D Macdonald, "The Harmonization Accord and Climate Change Policy: Two Case Studies in Federal-Provincial Environmental Policy," in H Bakvis and G Skogstad, eds, *Canadian Federalism: Performance, Effectiveness, and Legitimacy*, 2d ed (Oxford UP, 2008) c 13.

65   *Canadian Environmental Law Assn v Canada (Minister of the Environment)* (1999), 34 CELR 159.

66   B Schwartz, "Assessing the Agreement on Internal Trade: The Case for a 'More Perfect Union'" in DM Brown & JW Rose, eds, *Canada: The State of the Federation 1995* (Kingston: Queen's University Institute of Intergovernmental Relations, 1995) 189.

when dealing with internal trade matters. Current negotiations concerning a proposed Energy Chapter within the *AIT* include consideration of energy conservation and energy efficiency objectives.

FURTHER READINGS

BANKES, N, "*Delgamuukw*, Division of Powers and Provincial Land and Resource Laws: Some Implications for Provincial Resource Rights" (1998) 32 UBC L Rev 317

CASTRILLI, J, "*R v Hydro Québec*: The Criminal Law Power May Hinder the Future of Federal Protection of the Environment" (1997) 9 CR (5th) 312

CURRAN, D, & M M'GONIGLE, "Aboriginal Forestry: Community Management as Opportunity and Imperative" (1999) 37 Osgoode Hall LJ 711

DONIHEE, J, & P. KENNEDY, *Wildlife and the Canadian Constitution: Wildlife Paper #4* (Calgary: Canadian Institute of Resources Law, 2006)

HARRISON, K, *Passing the Buck: Federalism and Canadian Environmental Policy* (Vancouver: University of British Columbia Press, 1996)

LECLAIR, J, "Aperçu de virtualités de la compétence fédérale en droit criminel dans le contexte de la protection de l'environnement" (1996) 27 RGD 137

LUCAS, A, & J YEARSLEY, "The Constitutionality of Federal Climate Change Legislation" (2012) 23 J Envtl L & Prac 205

MAINVILLE, ROBERT, BA CRANE, & MW MASON, *First Nations Governance Law* (Markham, ON: LexisNexis Canada, 2006)

RICHARDSON, BJ, S IMAI, & K MCNEIL, "The Ties that Bind: Indigenous Peoples and the Environmental Governance" in BJ Richardson, S Imai, & K McNeil, eds, *Indigenous Peoples and the Law: Comparative and Critical Perspectives* (Oxford: Hart Publishing, 2009)

CHAPTER 3

ENVIRONMENTAL RIGHTS

A. HUMAN AND CONSTITUTIONAL RIGHTS TO ENVIRONMENTAL QUALITY

The attraction of human rights or constitutional safeguards for environmental interests lies in the improved position of environment in the legal hierarchy in both practical and symbolic ways. Proponents envisage environmental rights as a philosophical and practical advance that would not only acknowledge the fundamental importance of environmental quality as a public value, but also facilitate enforceability by helping to overcome existing obstacles to environmental protection. These obstacles include constraints on opportunities for participation in judicial and administrative decision making, broad delegations of discretion conferred upon government officials, and the significant weight or priority accorded to property or similar competing interests in cases of conflict with other values of the community.

While discussion of environmental rights has not been prominent in Canada, the subject has certainly not been ignored. In the words of the Law Reform Commission of Canada, for example, "a fundamental and widely shared value is indeed seriously contravened by some environmental pollution, a value which we will refer to as the *right to a safe environment*."[1] Recently, in discussing a provision of Quebec's *En-*

---

1   Law Reform Commission of Canada, *Crimes Against the Environment* (Ottawa: The Commission, 1985) at 8.

vironment Quality Act dealing with a statutory entitlement to a healthy environment and to which we will shortly refer, the Supreme Court of Canada stated:

> To ensure that this right may be effectively exercised, and that the duties created to give effect to it are executed, the Act provides for a variety of mechanisms for taking action. Various schemes are established for authorizing and monitoring activities that could threaten the environment. Others prohibit or restrict the emission of contaminants and impose obligations to decontaminate.[2]

Environmental rights are sometimes further classified on the basis of a distinction between procedural and substantive rights. The former encompass safeguards for effective participation in environmental decision making while the latter imply some acknowledged change in priorities and therefore in the expected outcome of environmentally significant decisions. The distinction is aptly summarized in an early Canadian commentary on environmental rights:

> Those who search for a right to environmental quality hope it will confer more than a right to participate or some requirement of due process or natural justice before environmentally harmful decisions are taken. They want a right which will dictate a decision in favour of environmental protection in difficult cases. They hope this right will be equivalent to a civil liberty, on the one hand, constraining government actions harmful to the environment, and, on the other, equivalent to a property right, restraining the use of private property in ways that are incompatible with sound ecological management.[3]

A more recent synthesis of the continuing debate pulls together some of the uncertain ingredients of environmental rights while it also identifies direct linkages between environmental rights and the essentials of ecological management. With regard to matters of scope and design associated with environmental rights, questions along these lines arise:

> Is such a right individual or collective? Is it a positive or a negative right? Can we conceptualize such rights as anthropocentric (i.e., human rights to environmental quality) or ecocentric (animal rights, species' rights or rights for nature)? Do these rights extend to future generations? Are there duties that accompany the rights . . . ?[4]

2   *Imperial Oil Ltd v Quebec (Minister of the Environment)*, [2003] 2 SCR 624 at 640.
3   J Swaigen & RE Woods, "A Substantive Right to Environmental Quality" in J Swaigen, ed, *Environmental Rights in Canada* (Toronto: Butterworths, 1981) 195 at 200.
4   E Hughes & D Iyalomhe, "Substantive Environmental Rights in Canada" (1998–

The extent to which positive measures must be contemplated to ensure simple survival is set out in relation to essential ecological functions:

> to supply the essentials of life, it is necessary to maintain essential biological processes. Thus, for example, humans need to have photosynthesis continue to supply atmospheric oxygen, and to maintain hydrological cycles to supply fresh water. Second, the only known way to maintain essential biological processes is to maintain functioning ecosystems . . . . To maintain functioning ecosystems (i.e., natural processes) scientific consensus tells us to do things such as: preserve biological diversity; maintain soil fertility and the productive capacity of the land; protect the oceans; receive sunlight only at wavelengths to which the planet's biology is accustomed; maintain climatic stability; and protect ourselves and our environment from toxic contamination.[5]

Before examining Canadian developments in the law in this area, it is worthwhile to note related initiatives in other jurisdictions and to touch on international considerations.

Attempts have been made in a number of jurisdictions around the world to confer constitutional status on environmental interests or to establish environmental rights on a legislative basis. By way of example, the South African *Bill of Rights* states that:

> Everyone has the right . . . to an environment that is not harmful to their health or well-being; and to have the environment protected for the benefit of present and future generations, through reasonable legislative and other measures that prevent pollution and ecological degradation, promote conservation, and secure ecologically sustainable development and use of natural resources while promoting justifiable economic and social development.[6]

Provisions of the treaty arrangements under which the European Union is constituted establish that European community policy on the environment will contribute to pursuit of the following objectives:

- preserving, protecting, and improving the quality of the environment;
- protecting human health;

1999) 30 Ottawa L Rev 229 at 232. For an exploration of tentative answers to some of these questions, see E Eacott, "A Clean and Healthy Environment: The Barriers and Limitations of this Emerging Right" (2001) 10 Dal J Leg Stud 74 at 89–94.

5   Hughes & Iyalomhe, above note 4 at 236.

6   *Constitution of the Republic of South Africa 1996*, No 108 of 1996, c 2, s 24.

- utilizing natural resources prudently and rationally; and
- promoting measures at the international level to deal with regional or worldwide environmental problems.[7]

Moreover, the treaty requires that "Community policy on the environment shall aim at a high level of protection taking into account the diversity of situations in the various regions of the Community."[8] In fact, Europe's constitutional framework incorporates several fundamental principles of environmental law by requiring that policy:

> shall be based on the precautionary principle and on the principles that preventive action should be taken, that environmental damage should as a priority be rectified at source and that the polluter should pay. Environmental protection requirements must be integrated into the definition and implementation of other Community policies.[9]

Several US state constitutions also incorporate environmental rights. Under Pennsylvania's constitution, for example, "[t]he people have a right to clean air, pure water, and to the preservation of the natural, scenic, historic, and esthetic values of the environment." Public natural resources in the state are "the common property of all the people, including generations yet to come." Moreover, the state is expected to conserve and maintain these resources for the benefit of all the people in its capacity as trustee.[10]

Statements supporting the principle of a human right to environmental quality may also be found in the international context. In the words of the *Stockholm Declaration, 1972*, "[m]an has the fundamental right to freedom, equality and adequate conditions of life, in an environment of a quality that permits a life of dignity and well-being, and he bears a solemn responsibility to protect and improve the environment for present and future generations."[11] Legal principles for environmental protection proposed in conjunction with the work of the WCED articulate as a fundamental human right that "[a]ll human beings have

---

7   *Treaty Establishing the European Community*, art 174, [2002] OJ C 325/33. The treaty is now known as the *Treaty on the Functioning of the European Union.*
8   *Ibid.*
9   *Treaty on European Union*, 7 February 1992, 31 ILM 247, art 130 R.
10 Pa Const art I, § 27, cl 1, quoted in E Brandl & H Bungert, "Constitutional Entrenchment of Environmental Protection: A Comparative Analysis of Experiences Abroad" (1992) 16 Harv Envtl L Rev 1 at 15–16. For an updated review of environmental rights, see DR Boyd, *The Environmental Rights Revolution* (UBC Press, 2012).
11 *Declaration of the United Nations Conference on the Human Environment*, 16 June 1972, 11 ILM 1416, principle 1.

the fundamental right to an environment adequate for their health and well-being."[12]

It has been generally understood, however, that although environmental rights may be derived from existing treaty rights such as the right to life, health, and property, international law has not yet effectively incorporated an independent right to environmental quality.[13] Ongoing developments, including some at the regional level, nevertheless suggest directions for further discussion and elaboration. In 1994, a Special Rapporteur operating under the auspices of the United Nations Sub-Commission on Prevention of Discrimination and Protection of Minorities, presented a *Draft Declaration of Principles on Human Rights and the Environment* as an appendix to her report.[14] In 1998, the *Aarhus Convention* on access to information and public participation, in particular, referred in the statement of its objective to "the right of every person of present and future generations to live in an environment adequate to his or her health and well-being."[15] In the following year, the *Protocol of San Salvador* to a human rights convention previously developed by the Organization of American States entered into force. It declared that "[e]veryone shall have the right to live in a healthy environment" and called upon State Parties to "promote the protection, preservation and improvement of the environment."[16] Despite such developments, the rights-based approach to environmental protection has advanced only modestly and remains subject to persistent criticisms and reservations.[17]

---

12   Quoted in World Commission on Environment and Development, *Our Common Future* (Oxford UP, 1987) at 348.

13   PW Birnie, AE Boyle, & C Redgwell, *International Law and the Environment*, 3d ed (Oxford UP, 2009) at 303–11.

14   KA Wolfe, "Greening the International Human Rights Sphere? An Examination of Environmental Rights and the Draft Declaration of Principles on Human Rights and the Environment" (2003) 13 J Envtl L & Prac 109.

15   *Convention on Access to Information, Public Participation in Decision-Making and Access to Justice in Environmental Matters*, 25 June 1998, 2161 UNTS 447, (adopted at Aarhus, Denmark; entered into force 30 October 2001).

16   *Additional Protocol to the American Convention on Human Rights in the Area of Economic, Social, and Cultural Rights "Protocol of San Salvador,"* 14 November 1988, San Salvador, 28 ILM 156, art 11.

17   Wolfe, above note 14.

B. THE *CHARTER* AND ENVIRONMENTAL LAW

No express recognition of a right to environmental quality or protection exists in Canadian constitutional instruments. Yet the absence of an explicit reference to the environment has not precluded argument that environmental rights exist implicitly within other constitutional provisions.

Since the time of its enactment as Part 1 of the *Constitution Act, 1982*, the *Canadian Charter of Rights and Freedoms* has profoundly influenced judicial decision making and legislative development in many fields. This is so because the rights and freedoms articulated in the *Charter* are applicable to the Parliament of Canada, the provincial legislatures, and the federal and provincial governments in relation to all matters within the constitutional authority of each and are enforceable through judicial proceedings.[18] Not surprisingly, the implications of *Charter* jurisprudence for environmental matters have attracted considerable attention.

Sections 7 and 15 initially appeared most promising to those seeking to ground substantive environmental rights within the *Charter*. The former confirms that "[e]veryone has the right to life, liberty and security of the person and the right not to be deprived thereof except in accordance with the principles of fundamental justice," while the latter provides that "[e]very individual is equal before and under the law and has the right to the equal protection and equal benefit of the law without discrimination" on the basis of a non-comprehensive listing of prohibited grounds.

The scope of interests protected under the phrase "life, liberty and security of the person" is still under consideration. It encompasses freedom from threats to one's physical integrity, including risks to health,[19] but excludes property and economic interests.[20] Accordingly, people whose property or perhaps livelihoods suffer because of environmental contamination or degradation resulting from the decisions of an institution subject to the *Charter*'s application will have limited recourse under the *Charter*, whereas those exposed to health risks in the same circumstances might envisage a *Charter* claim. The prospects of success in each case are dependent on satisfactory proof of a causal connection between the injury alleged and the impugned decision or official action.

---

18   *Canadian Charter of Rights and Freedoms*, Part I of the *Constitution Act, 1982*, being Schedule B to the *Canada Act 1982* (UK), 1982, c 11, s 32 [*Charter*].
19   *R v Morgentaler*, [1988] 1 SCR 30.
20   *Reference Re Criminal Code ss 193 & 195.1(1)(c)*, [1990] 1 SCR 1123.

In *Operation Dismantle*, where a public interest group challenged a decision of cabinet to allow cruise missile tests in northern Canada on the grounds that this increased the risk of nuclear war, the SCC found that there was an insufficient link between the decision to permit the testing and the alleged harm.[21] In *Manicom v Oxford*[22] resident landowners in the vicinity of a site that had been approved by the Ontario Cabinet for waste disposal challenged the decision on several grounds, including the assertion that the approval violated their interest in life, liberty, and security of the person and was not made in accordance with the "principles of fundamental justice" as required by section 7. The Divisional Court rejected the plaintiffs' claim on the grounds that property interests were not protected under section 7 of the *Charter*. In a dissenting opinion, one member of the court concluded that the matter should have been left to the trial judge to determine whether the allegations made, including allegations of adverse health effects, could be substantiated:

> The landowners' claim that the provincial Cabinet decision to permit the construction of the waste disposal site poses a direct threat to them, a specific segment of the population . . . . Moreover, the landowners do not claim only that their right to life, liberty and security will be violated by the Cabinet decision; they also claim that the decision to violate these rights was not made in accordance with the principles of fundamental justice.[23]

Two subsequent cases concerning alleged health risks related to municipal water treatment also suggest that a genuine health hazard resulting from a decision of government could constitute a violation of constitutionally protected interests within the scope of section 7.[24]

It must be borne in mind that the concept of fundamental justice is central to proceedings under section 7. As underlined by the Supreme Court of Canada: "Claimants whose life, liberty or security of the person is put at risk are entitled to relief only to the extent that their complaint arises from a breach of an identifiable principle of fundamental justice."[25] A section 7 claim asserted by residents of a First Nation Reserve seeking redress for the effects of toxic mould in reserve

---

21   *Operation Dismantle Inc v R*, [1985] 1 SCR 441.

22   (1985), 52 OR (2d) 137 (Div Ct).

23   *Ibid* at 155–56.

24   *Locke v Calgary (City)* (1993), 15 Alta LR (3d) 70 (QB); *Millership v Kamloops (City)*, 2003 BCSC 82.

25   *Chaoulli v Quebec (AG)* (2005), 254 DLR (4th) 577 at para 199 (SCC).

housing which had been located, designed, and constructed under the supervision of the Crown foundered on precisely this ground.[26]

Moreover, even where infringement of section 7 interests can be shown to have taken place in a manner contrary to "principles of fundamental justice," the government will have the opportunity to justify that infringement under section 1 of the *Charter* as being a "reasonable limit prescribed by law as can be demonstrably justified in a free and democratic society." In *Reference Re S 94(2) of the Motor Vehicle Act (British Columbia)*, Lamer J concluded that an offence imposing absolute liability on the accused will violate section 7 if and to the extent that it has the potential for depriving life, liberty, or security of the person.[27] In response to some observations by the British Columbia Court of Appeal about the importance of environmental legislation, he remarked that the public interest might be a justification under section 1 for absolute liability offences, depending on the specific circumstances:

> I think the balancing under section 1 of the public interest against the financial interests of a corporation [charged with an absolute liability offence, and if entitled to claim section 7 protection] would give very different results from that of balancing public interest and the liberty and security of the person of a human being.
>
> Indeed, the public interest as regards "air and water pollution offences" requires that the guilty be dealt with firmly, but the seriousness of the offence does not in my respectful view support the proposition that the innocent *human* person be open to conviction, quite the contrary.[28]

It is thus of great interest to imagine (for that is all that one can do) a constitution that had been amended after the Brundtland Report to include a different justification test for *Charter* infringement applicable to a free, democratic, and *sustainable* society.

The equality rights provisions in section 15 of the *Charter* have also proven difficult to apply in relation to environmental matters. For example, the applicability of section 15 to environmental claims was once considered to involve claims of discrimination based on differential treatment according to jurisdiction, geography, economic activity, and so on. In *Aluminum Co of Canada Ltd v Ontario (Minister of the Environment)*, a case arising in connection with refillable container regulations, the aluminum can manufacturer contended that the regu-

---

26   *Grant v Canada (AG)* (2005), 77 OR (3d) 481 (SCJ).
27   [1985] 2 SCR 486.
28   *Ibid* at 518.

lations discriminated to the economic advantage of steel manufacturers and imposed economic detriment on the aluminum industry. After concluding that the protection afforded by the *Charter*'s equality provisions was not available to corporations, the court further observed that economic discrimination was not a prohibited form of discrimination.[29] Subsequent judicial interpretation restricted the scope of section 15 by insisting upon reference to the enumerated or analogous grounds, not including territory:

> A complainant under section 15(1) must establish that he or she is a member of a discrete and insular minority group, that the group is defined by characteristics analogous to the enumerated grounds of discrimination set out in section 15(1), and that the law has a negative impact.[30]

Section 7 and section 15 claims were combined prominently in litigation over the constitutionality of certain provisions of the federal *Nuclear Liability Act*, which established a compensation scheme for victims of nuclear accidents while limiting the liability of a nuclear plant operator to $75 million for any particular incident. Plaintiffs in the case[31] argued that the effect of limited liability was to increase the exposure of the public to risk of nuclear accident by encouraging the proliferation of nuclear reactors and by reducing the operator's incentive to take appropriate care and safety measures. This, it was alleged, infringes the public's constitutionally protected interest in security of the person under section 7. With regard to section 15, plaintiffs argued that those in closest proximity to nuclear reactors were most exposed to physical risk and thereby suffered discrimination, and that all victims of a nuclear incident—being limited in their total damage claims—suffered discrimination in comparison with victims of other accidents who are not similarly limited in their ability to seek financial compensation.

At trial, Wright J of the Ontario Court of Justice (General Division) rejected both lines of analysis. Citing regulatory controls on the nuclear industry, he concluded that the required link between the *Nuclear Liability Act* and reduced levels of safety that would increase the likelihood of a nuclear incident had not been established. In relation to section 15,

---

29 *Aluminum Co of Canada v Ontario (Minister of the Environment)* (1986), 55 OR (2d) 522 (Div Ct).

30 *Haig v Canada (Chief Electoral Officer)*, [1993] 2 SCR 995 at 1043–44, L'Heureux-Dubé J.

31 *Energy Probe v Canada (AG)* (1994), 17 OR (3d) 717 (Gen Div).

Wright J observed that the *Nuclear Liability Act* does not discriminate as that concept is understood within the meaning of the section.

Section 7 and 15 claims were again combined by members of the Aamjiwmaag First Nation in an application for judicial review challenging an environmental authorization respecting sulphur at an industrial plant in Sarnia. The applicants assert that because of existing pollution surrounding their reserve community, which has suffered significant health impacts, the failure of the decision maker in the approval process to consider cumulative effects of all pollution violates their life, liberty, and security rights and the equality provisions of the *Charter.*[32]

Although the jurisprudence will continue to evolve in this area, one experienced environmental lawyer provided a frank summary of the limitations presented by or the obstacles facing the rights paradigm in the context of environmental protection. First, insofar as human rights are generally perceived to involve safeguards from state interference (so-called negative rights), it is not clear how this applies to environmental protection, which will rarely take the form of a contest between government and the individual. State action appears to be an essential component of environmental protection, for the right to a healthy environment is a classic illustration of a right that must be enjoyed collectively or not at all. Moreover, human rights safeguards have generally operated in the context of relatively immediate and relatively severe threats to the individual, while the adverse effects of environmental degradation are frequently gradual, cumulative, and often difficult to link causally to individual victims, sometimes including members of future generations. There are additional limitations in the sense that the appropriate scope of environmental rights remains unresolved. Fundamentally, however, "the mere assertion of a right fails to give sufficient guidance in making the hard choices of pollution control."[33]

Hard choices will also arise in relation to the allocation of limited environmental resources rather than their direct degradation. Such a situation arose in *R v Kapp* where commercial fishermen—mainly non-Aboriginal—in British Columbia challenged communal fishing licences issued to Aboriginal bands to allow them exclusive, short-term access to salmon in the mouth of the Fraser River. An equality rights challenge to those licences under section 15(1) failed. In the view of the Supreme Court of Canada, the communal fishing licences constituted

---

32   *Lockridge v Ontario (Director, Ministry of the Environment)*, 2012 ONSC 2316.
33   D Saxe, *Environmental Offences: Corporate Responsibility and Executive Liability* (Aurora, ON: Canada Law Book, 1990) at 18–20.

a "law, program, or activity" within the meaning of section 15(2) which "has as its object the amelioration of conditions of disadvantaged individuals or groups." A distinction between groups such as the preference embodied in the communal fishing licences will not constitute unlawful discrimination where it serves an ameliorative or remedial purpose in favour of a disadvantaged group.[34]

Somewhat ironically perhaps, constitutional safeguards also serve to constrain the ability of government to intrude into private decision making or to coerce and punish individuals accused of wrongdoing, including environmentally harmful conduct. Thus, in the environmental context, claims about *Charter* rights are used simultaneously to promote and to check environmental protection measures. One common form of attack by defendants has been to suggest that, where individual liberty is in question as a consequence of the prospect of imprisonment for conviction, the entitlement to "fundamental justice" includes prohibition against vague or uncertain offence provisions. The test for assessing vagueness claims under section 7 is that "a law will be found unconstitutionally vague if it so lacks in precision as not to give sufficient guidance for legal debate."[35]

In *R v Canadian Pacific Ltd*, the railway was charged with a violation of section 13 of Ontario's *Environmental Protection Act* which stated that:

> . . . no person shall deposit, add, emit or discharge a contaminant or cause or permit the deposit, addition, emission or discharge of a contaminant into the natural environment that, (a) causes or is likely to cause impairment of the quality of the natural environment for any use that can be made of it.[36]

The railway alleged that aspects of the section were so vague and broad that they failed to establish a standard of sufficient intelligibility to allow citizens to regulate their conduct. CP challenged the provision in its entirety and specifically criticized the concepts of contaminant, impairment, natural environment, and the expression "for any use that can be made of it."

Writing for six members of the Supreme Court of Canada, Gonthier J was fully satisfied that the legislative language under attack survived the vagueness challenge. General observations accompanying the decision are equally, if not more, significant. Gonthier J remarked that, in the environmental protection context, "a strict requirement of drafting

34   *R v Kapp*, 2008 SCC 41.
35   *R v Nova Scotia Pharmaceutical Society*, [1992] 2 SCR 606.
36   *Environmental Protection Act*, RSO 1980, c 141, s 13(1)(a). Now see RSO 1990, c E-19, s 14.

precision might well undermine the ability of the legislature to provide for a comprehensive and flexible regime."[37] Precise legislative codification of environmental hazards, he added, might even impede rather than promote understanding of the prohibited conduct. Having examined environmental legislation from several provinces, and after noting that virtually all of the regimes in place might have been vulnerable to challenge if the grounds on which the Ontario provision was criticized for vagueness were valid, Gonthier J explained his view of the options available to legislators:

> They may enact detailed provisions which prohibit the release of particular quantities of enumerated substances into the natural environment. Alternatively, they may choose a more general prohibition of "pollution" and rely on the courts to determine whether, in a particular case, the release of a substance into the natural environment is of sufficient magnitude to attract legislative sanction. The latter option is, of course, more flexible and better able to accommodate developments in our knowledge about environmental protection. However, a general enactment may be challenged . . . for failing to provide adequate notice to citizens of prohibited conduct.[38]

This does not necessarily mean that detailed technical provisions are therefore the best means of alerting citizens about prohibited conduct. "If a citizen requires a chemistry degree to figure out whether an activity releases a particular contaminant in sufficient quantities to trigger a statutory prohibition," Gonthier J continued, "then that prohibition provides no better fair notice than a more general enactment." The court concluded that an objective approach is applicable to the notice aspect of the vagueness analysis. "[W]ould the average citizen, with an average understanding of the subject matter of the prohibition, receive adequate notice of prohibited conduct?"[39]

C. THE LEGISLATIVE BASIS OF ENVIRONMENTAL RIGHTS

Several provinces and territories have established environmental rights through legislation. Though lacking the authority of constitutional entrenchment, such measures embody a number of crucial principles,

---

37   R v Canadian Pacific Ltd, [1995] 2 SCR 1028 at 1073.
38   Ibid at 1073–74.
39   Ibid at 1074.

including, on occasion, formal recognition of human entitlements to environmental security or a healthy environment.

Quebec's *Environment Quality Act* (*EQA*), as previously noted, affirms that "[e]very person has a right to a healthy environment and to its protection, and to the protection of the living species inhabiting it, to the extent provided for by this act and the regulations, orders, approvals, and authorizations issued under any section of this act."[40] In *Calvé v Gestion Serge Lafrenière inc*, riparian owners secured an interlocutory injunction limiting fish production and the phosphorous discharge level of an aquaculture plant that had been operating pursuant to provincial approvals. Plaintiffs, also invoking protections embodied in the *Civil Code of Quebec*, had argued that the approvals were unreasonable in the circumstances of a lake already known to be experiencing eutrophication and were contrary to the letter and spirit of the *EQA*. A unanimous Court of Appeal, in upholding (with modifications) the interlocutory injunction issued at the trial level, remarked that in order for the statutory right to environmental quality to be respected, some judicial remedy was required.[41]

In 2006 Quebec enhanced environmental rights at the provincial level by means of amendments to the Quebec *Charter of human rights and freedoms*. This "quasi-constitutional" instrument now provides that "[e]very person has a right to live in a healthful environment in which biodiversity is preserved, to the extent and according to the standards provided by law."[42] While the contents of the new right are circumscribed by the state of the law, this right offers reinforcement to the existing legal framework by providing potentially forceful remedies to those whose right has been violated.

Pursuant to the *Environmental Rights Act* of 1990, "the people of the Northwest Territories have the right to a healthy environment and a right to protect the integrity, biological diversity and productivity of the ecosystems in the Northwest Territories."[43] The legislation more specifically confirms the right of any person resident in the territories "to protect the environment and the public trust from the release of contaminants" thus granting standing to private individuals to seek injunctive relief, a remedial order, or compensation for breaches of the

---

40   *Environment Quality Act*, RSQ 1977, c Q-2, s 19, as am by SQ 1978, c 64, s 4.

41   [1999] RJQ 1313.

42   RSQ c C-12, s 46.1. See *Carrier v Québec* (*Procureur général*), 2011 QCCA 1231 at paras 32 and 59.

43   *Environmental Rights Act*, RSNWT 1988 (Supp), c 83, as am by SNWT 1999, c 21. Provision is made in the *Nunavut Act* for the applicability of legislation from the former jurisdiction.

law. The statute also ensures that such a plaintiff be provided with relevant information. With reference to the public trust as embodied in the *Environmental Rights Act*, territorial courts have observed that:

> Wildlife management, indeed environmental policy in general takes on a special significance in the Northwest Territories. The legislature has deemed the collective interest of the people of the Territories in the quality of the environment and the protection of the environment for future generations to be a "public trust."[44]

The Yukon *Environment Act* asserts the right of the people of the Yukon to "a healthful natural environment" and that it is "in the public interest to provide every resident in the Yukon with a remedy adequate to protect the natural environment."[45] Saskatchewan had also initiated discussion on legislation concerning a *Charter of Environmental Rights and Responsibilities*, which in its initial form was less explicit on the issue of rights. The draft legislation simply affirmed that "the health and integrity of the environment is of paramount concern to Saskatchewan residents" and that "the health and integrity of the environment must be sustained for the benefit of present and future generations of Saskatchewan citizens."[46]

A somewhat different approach was taken in Ontario where the *Environmental Bill of Rights, 1993 (OEBR)* noted "the inherent value of the natural environment" and the people's "right to a healthful environment." In the protection, conservation, and restoration of the environment, the *OEBR* distinguished between government and individual roles; the former was acknowledged to have primary responsibility, but the people should have means to ensure that these goals are realized in "an effective, timely, open and fair manner."[47] Yet, because these assertions are made in the preamble to the *OEBR* rather than in the substantive provisions of the legislation itself, they lack the full authority of actual legislative provisions.

However, the *OEBR*'s purposes as enunciated in section 2 do encompass environmental protection, conservation, and "where reasonable," restoration as well as sustainability and protection for "the right to a healthful environment," all to be accomplished "by the means provided

---

44 *R v Ram Head Outfitters*, [1995] NWTR 298.
45 RSY 2002, c 76, ss 6 & 7. See *Western Copper Corp v Yukon Water Board*, 2010 YKSC 61.
46 Bill 48, *An Act to Provide a Charter of Environmental Rights and Responsibilities*, 2d Sess, 22nd Leg, Saskatchewan, 1992.
47 *Environmental Bill of Rights, 1993*, SO 1993, c 28.

in this Act."[48] Those means include a requirement for designated Ontario ministries to prepare a statement of environmental values (SEV) explaining how the OEBR's purposes will be applied when the ministry makes decisions that might significantly affect the environment. Designated ministries must also explain how they propose to integrate objectives of the OEBR with "other considerations, including social, economic and scientific considerations, that are part of decision making in the ministry."[49] Other provisions confirm or establish a variety of public rights to participate in environmental decision making in Ontario:

- the right to get notice of, and to comment on, proposed policies, Acts, regulations, and instruments that may affect the environment;
- the right to seek leave to appeal certain ministry decisions;
- the right to ask a minister to change or eliminate existing environmental policies, Acts, regulations, and instruments;
- the right to ask a ministry to consider the need for new policies, Acts, and regulations;
- the right to ask a ministry to investigate contraventions of environmental Acts, regulations, and instruments;
- the right to sue those responsible for harming a public resource; and
- the right to sue for damages in the case of direct economic or personal loss resulting from an environmentally harmful public nuisance.

In addition, the OEBR facilitates access to information and public accountability through the creation of an environmental registry[50] and the appointment of an environmental commissioner for the province as an officer of the Legislative Assembly.[51] The commissioner's operations encompass responsibilities for:

- reviewing implementation of the OEBR;
- reviewing ministerial compliance with the OEBR;
- providing guidance on request to ministries concerning compliance with the OEBR;
- providing assistance on request concerning public educational programs regarding the OEBR;
- providing advice and assistance to the public concerning opportunities for participating in decision making as provided for in the OEBR;

---

48   *Ibid*, s 2.
49   *Ibid*, s 7. The Statement of Environmental Values may be found online: www.ebr. gov.on.ca/ERS-WEB-External/content/sev.jsp?pageName=sevList&subPageName= 10001.
50   Above note 47, s 5. See online: www.ebr.gov.on.ca.
51   *Ibid*, ss 49 and 57.

- reviewing the use of the environmental registry;
- reviewing the exercise of ministerial discretion under the *OEBR*; and
- reviewing the public's use of rights of participation provided under the *OEBR*.

The environmental commissioner enjoys extensive powers of inquiry in connection with the performance of these responsibilities[52] and reports annually to the speaker of the legislature.[53]

In conjunction with a ten-year review of the *OEBR*, the commissioner, in 2003–2004, formulated a series of recommendations intended to update and strengthen environmental rights in Ontario.[54] These call for explicit recognition of emerging environmental principles such as polluter pay, more regular revision and stricter adherence to Ministry Statements of Environmental Values, and greater accountability for decisions to exempt decisions from disclosure on the EBR Registry. According to a 2012 report of the ECO, during the period from 1 April 2000 to 31 March 2010, residents of Ontario submitted 312 applications for review and investigation under the *Environmental Bill of Rights, 1993*. Most of the applications were submitted to the Ministry of the Environment or the Ministry of Natural Resources with concerns related to water quality, land-use planning, and fish and wildlife management.[55] At the federal level, *CEPA 1999* also addressed a number of issues relating to public participation and provided for an environmental registry relating to matters under the Act.[56] In addition, pursuant to earlier federal legislation, designated federal departments are required to prepare sustainable development strategies for presentation to the House of Commons. To monitor and report on departmental progress towards sustainable development, the office of federal commissioner of the environment and sustainable development (CESD) was created to work with the auditor general of Canada, whose responsibilities include bringing to the attention of the House of Commons

---

52   *Ibid*, s 60.
53   *Ibid*, s 58; The Environmental Commissioner of Ontario's annual reports may be found online at: www.eco.on.ca/index.php/en_US/pubs/annual-reports-and-supplements.
54   *Looking Forward: The Environmental Bill of Rights* (Toronto: Environmental Commissioner of Ontario, 2004).
55   Environmental Commissioner of Ontario, *Ministries' Handling of EBR Applications: A Ten-Year Statistical Retrospective (2000–2010)* (Toronto: Government of Ontario, 2012).
56   *Canadian Environmental Protection Act, 1999*, SC 1999, c 33, Part 2 [*CEPA 1999*]. A number of these public participation provisions are noted and discussed elsewhere in this volume.

any cases where "money has been expended without due regard to the environmental effects of those expenditures in the context of sustainable development."[57] A resident of Canada may petition the auditor general about an environmental matter associated with the sustainable development responsibilities of designated departments. Within fifteen days such inquiries are to be forwarded to the appropriate minister who must acknowledge the petition and then prepare a reply, generally within 120 days of receiving the petition from the auditor general.[58]

The CESD reports annually on the use that is being made of the federal environmental petition process and conducts audits on selected responses. According to the most recent CESD report on the environmental petition process, during the reporting period 1 July 2010 to 30 June 2011, the Office of the Auditor General of Canada received 25 environmental petitions, compared with 18 in 2009–2010 and 28 in 2008–2009.[59]

FURTHER READINGS

ANDREWS, W, "The Environment and the *Canadian Charter of Rights and Freedoms*" in N. Duplé, ed., *Le droit à la qualité de l'Environnement: un droit en devenir, un droit à définir* (Montreal, Québec/ Amérique, 1988)

BIRNIE, PW, AE Boyle, & K Redgwell, *International Law and the Environment*, 3d ed (Oxford University Press, 2009)

BOYLE, AE, & MR Anderson, eds, *Human Rights Approaches to Environmental Protection* (New York: Clarendon Press, 1996)

CHALIFOUR, NJ, & G SMITH, "The Pursuit of Environmental Justice in the McLachlin Court" in S Rogers & S McIntyre, eds, *The Supreme Court of Canada and Social Justice: Commitment, Retrenchment or Retreat* (Markham: LexisNexis, 2010)

COLLINS, LM, "An Ecologically Literate Reading of the *Canadian Charter of Rights and Freedoms*" (2009) 26 Windsor Rev Legal Soc Issues 7

GAGE, A, "Public Health Hazards and Section 7 of the *Charter*" (2003) 13 J Envtl L & Prac 1

---

57   *Auditor General Act*, RSC 1985, c A-17, s 7(2)(f).
58   *Ibid*, s 22.
59   *2011 December Report of the Commissioner of the Environment and Sustainable Development* (Ottawa: Office of the Auditor General, 2011).

GIBSON, N, "The Right to a Clean Environment" (1990) Sask L Rev 54

HUGHES, E, & D IYALOMHE, "Substantive Environmental Rights in Canada" (1998–1999) 30 Ottawa L Rev 229

LINDGREN, R, & P MULDOON, *The* Environmental Bill of Rights: *A Practical Guide* (Toronto: Emond Montgomery, 1995)

SWAIGEN, J, & RE WOODS, "A Substantive Right to Environmental Quality" in J Swaigen, ed, *Environmental Rights in Canada* (Toronto: Butterworths, 1981) 195

THÉRIAULT, S, & D ROBITAILLE, "Les droits environnementaux dans la *Charte des droits et libertés de la personne* du Québec: Pistes de réflexion" (2011) 57:2 McGill LJ 211

WINFIELD, MS, "A Political and Legal Analysis of Ontario's *Environmental Bill of Rights*" (1998) 47 UNBLJ 325

WINFIELD, MS, *Blue-Green Province: The Environment and the Political Economy of Ontario* (UBC Press, 2012)

CHAPTER 4

THE INTERNATIONAL CONTEXT OF CANADIAN ENVIRONMENTAL LAW

A. INTERNATIONAL ENVIRONMENTAL LAW AND ORGANIZATIONS

Nations around the world have had long-standing concerns about the impact on their domestic environments of transboundary air and water pollution, as well as about offshore tanker spills inflicting economic and ecological damage on their coastal regions and resources. In addition, indications of environmental deterioration in areas of common interest outside national boundaries such as the oceans, the Antarctic, and the atmosphere sheltering the planet have encouraged efforts to identify effective international responses, including legal measures. To some degree, pressure in this direction is even increased by awareness that environmental deterioration constitutes a threat to both peace and security.[1]

The United Nations Conference on the Human Environment (Stockholm, 1972), the report of the World Commission on Environment and Development, *Our Common Future* (1987), the UN Conference on Environment and Development in Rio de Janeiro (1992) and the *Johannesburg Declaration* following the World Summit on Sustain-

---

1   A Daniel, "Environmental Threats to International Peace and Security: Combatting Common Security Threats Through Promotion of Compliance with International Environmental Agreements" (1994) Canadian Council for International Law 134–46.

able Development (2002) have been landmarks in the development of principles of international environmental law.[2] Principle 21 from the Stockholm Convention is a particularly prominent example of attempts to formulate environmental norms:

> States have, in accordance with the Charter of the United Nations and the principles of international law, the sovereign right to exploit their own resources pursuant to their own environmental policies, and the responsibility to ensure that the activities within their jurisdiction or control do not cause damage to the environment of other states or of areas beyond the limits of national jurisdiction.

The evolution of international law affecting the environment is ongoing (see table 4.1). As explained by the international legal scholar Alexandre Kiss, evolution of "environmental governance" involves the interrelated emergence of legal norms and management institutions:

> The two sides of governance interact: different forms of international co-operation, conferences or permanent institutions create international legal norms the implementation of which needs new forms of international organisms. The co-operation is to be undertaken at a world-wide level as well as in regional frameworks. Such forms can be considered as the world Constitution governing environmental matters.[3]

The latest global deliberations, the United Nations Conference on Sustainable Development (Rio+20) took place in 2012. Political outcomes offering guidance for continuing implementation of sustainability were captured in a conference statement — The Future We Want, a document that identifies gaps and opportunities for action at the local, regional, and international levels.[4]

Public international law, that is, the principles governing relations between and among nations, derives from several sources — agreement, customary international law, and general principles of law. All are independent sources of international obligations. For example, over seventy years ago, in connection with an arbitration between Canada and the United States concerning liability for damage from air pollution from smelting facilities in Trail, British Columbia, an international

2   *Johannesburg Declaration on Sustainable Development*, online: www.un.org/esa/sustdev/documents/Johannesburg%20Declaration.doc.
3   A Kiss, "The Legal Ordering of Environmental Protection" in R MacDonald & D Johnston, eds, *Towards World Constitutionalism: Issues in the Legal Ordering of the World Community* (Boston: Martinus Nijhoff, 2005) 567.
4   Online: www.uncsd2012.org/thefuturewewant.html.

tribunal stated that "no State has the right to use or permit the use of its territory in such a manner as to cause injury by fumes in or to the territory of another or the persons or property therein, when the case is of serious consequence and the injury is established by clear and convincing evidence."[5] Here one can discern some indication of the origins of Stockholm Principle 21 quoted above.[6]

Today, however, treaties or conventions as they are also known are increasingly used to embody the text of environmental agreements between states. Such agreements may be reached on a bilateral basis—between neighbouring countries, for example—or they may involve many signatories. Formal agreements of this nature dealing with such subjects as the law of the sea, the protection of endangered species, transboundary movement of hazardous wastes, prevention of pollution from ships, and so on are the primary forms of international environmental law. These agreements will often directly influence the shape of domestic environmental regimes. Indeed, some commentators have speculated about a process of "internationalization" of environmental regulation.[7] This is in part a consequence of various forms of recognition in the international context of a range of fundamental environmental principles: intergenerational equity, common heritage of humankind, prevention, precaution, polluter pays, common but differentiated responsibilities, and prior notification, among others.[8]

The process for incorporating international law into Canada's domestic legal regime varies as between customary and treaty law; the former is presumed to apply automatically in the absence of conflict with statute or judicial precedent, while treaty obligations are implemented by means of legislative enactment.[9] Consistent with the division of powers under the *Constitution Act, 1867*, domestic Canadian responsibility

---

5   *Trail Smelter Arbitration* (1941), 3 UN Rep Int Arb Awards 1908 at 1965.
6   See RM Bratspies & RA Miller, *Transboundary Harm in International Law: Lessons from the Trail Smelter Arbitration* (New York: Cambridge University Press, 2006).
7   RW Hahn & KR Richards, "The Internationalization of Environmental Regulation" (1989) 30 Harv Int'l LJ 421.
8   D Bodansky, J Brunnée, & E Hey, *The Oxford Handbook of International Environmental Law* (Oxford UP, 2007).
9   For judicial suggestion of the possible relevance of international environmental law developments to the legal powers of Canadian municipalities, see *114957 Canada Ltée (Spraytech) v Hudson (Town)*, 2001 SCC 40 at paras. 31–32. See also JV DeMarco & ML Campbell, "The Supreme Court of Canada's Progressive Use of International Environmental Law and Policy in Interpreting Domestic Legislation" (2004) 13 RECIEL 320.

for treaty implementation is divided between the federal government and the provinces depending on the subject matter in question.[10]

Although nation states remain the principal players in international environmental matters, intergovernmental and non-governmental organizations have a significant and influential role in fostering cooperation between states in relation to discussion and research on environmental issues. Some of these bodies, such as the International Maritime Organization and the World Meteorological Organization, are associated with the United Nations. These and other institutional mechanisms provide research, technical support, and monitoring, or facilitate dispute resolution and enforcement, or contribute to continuing refinement of the legal regime itself.

The United Nations Environment Program (UNEP), whose secretariat is located in Nairobi, Kenya, was created following the 1972 Stockholm Conference. UNEP was intended to serve as "a focal point for environmental action" by offering coordination, advice, and policy guidance within the UN system of agencies and institutions and by promoting international environmental cooperation.[11]

Outside the United Nations framework, various international bodies with regional focus or otherwise concerned with the common interests of their members have incorporated environmental considerations within their mandates. In the case of the Organisation for Economic Co-operation and Development (OECD), in which Canada participates along with some two dozen other industrialized nations, environmental matters are addressed under the auspices of an environment committee. A certain amount of policy advice is provided alongside research initiatives and valuable detailed analyses of environmental conditions in the member states.[12]

The involvement of environmental non-governmental organizations (ENGOs) in international environmental law and policy should also be noted. Organizations such as Greenpeace International, Friends of the Earth, and the World Wildlife Fund have participated actively in research, public information, and awareness campaigns to promote both domestic and international responses to environmental issues such as species protection and resource conservation. ENGO representatives quite frequently have observer status or some other formal

---

10 *Canada (AG) v Ontario (AG)*, [1937] AC 326 (PC). For information on Canadian participation in international environmental agreements, see online: www.ec.gc. ca/international/default.asp?lang=En&n=0E5CED79-1.

11 PW Birnie, AE Boyle, & C Redgwell, *International Law and the Environment*, 3d ed (Oxford UP, 2009) at 48-58.

12 *Ibid* at 83; see *Environmental Performance Reviews: Canada* (Paris: OECD, 2004).

affiliation with intergovernmental organizations. The long-established International Union for Conservation of Nature and Natural Resources (IUCN), has been particularly important for its ongoing contributions to international law-making.[13]

B. INTERNATIONAL INSTITUTIONS AND ENVIRONMENTAL PROTECTION IN CANADA

Many examples of the influence of international considerations on Canadian environmental law and policy could be identified.[14] The following are important illustrations.

1) Great Lakes Water Quality, Diversion, and Exports

For the roughly fifty million North Americans living on either side of the Great Lakes, the condition of the region is a paradigm test of the effectiveness of contemporary responses to environmental protection. The experience of the Great Lakes region contributed significantly to North American understanding of the complexity of environmental challenges. Thus, cross-media effects (those that transfer from one media—air, land, or water—to another), the role of non-point (generalized) sources of pollution such as pesticide use in forest management and agriculture, acid rain, and long-range transport of airborne pollutants, persistent toxicity, invasive species and sustainability are on the broader agenda to some degree because they were encountered in the Great Lakes Region and in part were brought to public attention through work associated with the International Joint Commission (IJC).

The IJC is the creation of Article VII of the *Treaty Between the United States and Great Britain Relating to Boundary Waters, and Questions Arising Between the United States and Canada [Boundary Waters Treaty]* of 1909, an agreement reached in response to significant Canada–US border irritants, including proposals by civic officials from Chicago to divert water south from the Great Lakes for sewage disposal[15] and disputed access to the hydroelectric power potential at Niagara Falls. It

---

13 B Lausche, *Weaving a Web of Environmental Law: Contributions of the IUCN Environmental Law Programme* (Bonn: IUCN/ICEL, 2008).

14 See discussion below of *CITES*, transboundary waste, etc.

15 J Benidickson, *The Culture of Flushing: A Social and Legal History of Sewage* (Vancouver: UBC Press, 2007) c. 8.

operates as a binational panel or administrative agency consisting of three commissioners from Canada and three from the United States whose responsibilities centre on water-related conflicts between the two North American countries that—one way or another—share some three hundred rivers.

The IJC's functions have been classified as quasi-judicial, investigative, and arbitral. In relation to the assessment and approval of works that might affect the natural level and flow of boundary waters, the commission exercises quasi-judicial authority. Decisions are to reflect a commitment to the "equal and similar rights" of the parties and an established hierarchy of uses. The IJC was also authorized to undertake investigative work on the basis of a reference from the parties and to make recommendations to the two national governments. In addition, and subject to the advice and consent of the US Senate, which has never been given, the IJC has an arbitration function for the resolution of disputes connected with its jurisdiction.

Until comparatively recently, the IJC's work emphasized flooding and diversions. Concerns about water quality tended to be of secondary importance through to the 1960s even though the *Boundary Waters Treaty* of 1909 explicitly addressed pollution. Article IV embodies the agreement of the parties "that . . . waters . . . defined as boundary waters and waters flowing across the boundary shall not be polluted on either side to the injury of health or property on the other."

Since 1964, when the Canadian and US governments referred issues of pollution of Lake Erie, Lake Ontario, and the international section of the St. Lawrence River to the IJC for investigation, the commission has become increasingly active in relation to the Great Lakes environment. The study's finding that "grave deterioration of water quality on each side of the boundary" was "causing injury to health and property on the other side"[16] led to the *Great Lakes Water Quality Agreement* (GLWQA) of 1972.

In outline, this original agreement enumerated both general and specific water-quality objectives, identified a series of programs to be undertaken for preventive and remedial purposes, authorized the parties to proceed with implementation according to their own legislative regimes, and accorded to the IJC certain functions relating to information gathering and exchange, coordination, monitoring of progress, and making recommendations.

According to the general water-quality objectives, the waters were to be made:

---

16   *Great Lakes Water Quality Agreement*, 15 April 1972, TIAS No 7312.

a) free from substances that enter the waters as a result of human activity and that will settle to form putrescent or otherwise objectionable sludge deposits, or that will adversely affect aquatic life or waterfowl;

b) free from floating debris, oil, scum, and other floating materials entering the waters as a result of human activity in amounts sufficient to be unsightly or deleterious;

c) free from materials entering the waters as a result of human activity producing colour, odour, or other conditions in such a degree as to create a nuisance;

d) free from substances entering the waters as a result of human activity in concentrations that are toxic or harmful to human, animal, or aquatic life;

e) free from nutrients entering the waters as a result of human activity in concentrations that create nuisance growths of aquatic weeds and algae.[17]

In 1978 a revised agreement reaffirmed the basic objectives but added important elements. First, although the 1972 agreement had broadened the scope of operation beyond the narrowly defined 1909 definition of boundary waters to encompass tributary waters of the Great Lakes system, the 1978 agreement further extended the challenge to what was known as the "Great Lakes Basin Ecosystem," defined as "the interacting components of air, land, water and living organisms, including man, within the drainage basin of the St. Lawrence River."[18] Second, by 1978, with measures taking hold to deal with phosphates and municipal sewage, the parties singled out toxics for more elaborate attention.[19] The 1978 agreement recognized a toxic substance as "a substance which can cause death, disease, behavioural abnormalities, cancer, genetic mutations, physiological or reproductive malfunctions or physical deformities in any organism or its offspring, or which can become poisonous after concentration in the food chain or in combination with other substances."[20] Early candidates included mercury, DDT, mirex, PCBs, and dioxin.[21]

Moreover, by 1978, the parties had adopted an overall statement of purpose: "to restore and maintain the chemical, physical, and biologic-

17 Ibid, art II.
18 Great Lakes Water Quality Agreement of 1978, 22 Nov 1978, Can TS 1978 No 20, art I(g).
19 Ibid.
20 Ibid, art I(v).
21 Ibid.

al integrity of the waters of the Great Lakes Basin Ecosystem." To that end they adopted as a policy the principle that "[t]he discharge of toxic substances in toxic amounts be prohibited and the discharge of any or all persistent toxic substances be virtually eliminated."[22]

In 1987 the *GLWQA* was amended by a protocol setting out a process for rehabilitating the overall ecosystem by means of more localized remediation mechanisms.[23] Further changes to Great Lakes water quality management were recently incorporated in the *2012 Great Lakes Water Quality Agreement*. The new protocol seeks to promote operational effectiveness through a series of procedural and institutional commitments and innovations: clear and achievable goals, accountability, binational coordination, adaptive management, research, monitoring and surveillance, and regular reporting. From a program perspective, annexes to the 2012 agreement highlight priority objectives and new initiatives: clean up of severely contaminated locations; development of an integrated nearshore water quality framework; elimination or reduction of chemicals; managing phosphorus concentrations and loadings; prevention of harmful vessel discharges; conservation of native species and their habitat; controls on the introduction and spread of aquatic invasive species; prevention of groundwater contamination; coordination of science, strategies, and actions to address climate change impacts within the basin.[24]

Concern about water quantity issues has also arisen in connection with a series of export and diversion proposals.[25] In its February 2000 report, *Protection of the Waters of the Great Lakes*,[26] the IJC responded to a reference from the governments of Canada and the United States requesting an examination of the way in which the levels and flows of waters within the boundary and transboundary basins and in relation to shared aquifers might be affected by:

- existing and potential consumptive uses of water;
- existing and potential diversions of water in and out of the transboundary basins, including withdrawals of water for export;
- the cumulative effects of existing and potential diversions, and removals of water, including removals in bulk for export;

22   *Ibid*, art. II.
23   For further discussion, see Chapter 11.
24   Online: www.ec.gc.ca/grandslacs-greatlakes/default.asp?lang=En&n=A1C62826.
25   P Annin, *The Great Lakes Water Wars* (Washington, DC: Island Press, 2006).
26   *Protection of the Waters of the Great Lakes: Final Report to the Governments of Canada and the United States* (Ottawa: International Joint Commission, 2000).

- the current laws and policies as may affect the sustainability of the water resources in boundary and transboundary basins.

Following investigation by binational interdisciplinary study teams and an extensive program of public consultation, the IJC published findings and recommendations. With regard to water removals, the commission recommended that the governments of the US states bordering the Great Lakes and the Canadian provinces of Ontario and Quebec should not permit a proposed water removal from the Great Lakes to proceed unless the project proponent is able to demonstrate that the integrity of the Great Lakes ecosystem would not be endangered by the removal and that

- there are no practical alternatives for obtaining the water;
- full consideration has been given to the potential cumulative impacts of the proposed removal, taking into account the possibility of similar proposals in the foreseeable future;
- effective conservation practices will be implemented in the place to which the water would be sent;
- sound planning practices will be applied with respect to the proposed removal;
- there is no net loss to the area from which the water is taken and, in any event, there is no greater than a 5 percent loss; and
- the water is returned in a condition that, using the best available technology, protects the quality of and prevents the introduction of alien invasive species into the waters of the Great Lakes.

On the basis of extensive discussion involving the Great Lakes states and provinces, arrangements have been put in place to govern water-taking and diversion proposals in the basin. In 2005, eight Great Lakes states and the provinces of Ontario and Quebec signed the *Great Lakes–St. Lawrence River Basin Sustainable Water Resources Agreement*.[27] In 2007, Ontario passed the *Safeguarding and Sustaining Ontario's Water Act*, and Quebec amended its *Environment Quality Act* to embody the terms of the agreement. The following year, the eight Great Lakes states (Illinois, Indiana, Michigan, Minnesota, New York, Ohio, Pennsylvania, and Wisconsin) completed ratification of the companion *Great Lakes–St. Lawrence River Basin Water Resources Compact*, which was approved by the US Congress.

---

27   *Great Lakes–St. Lawrence River Basin Sustainable Water Resources Agreement* (13 December 2005).

2) The Arctic Circumpolar Environment

The Arctic and its inhabitants are particularly vulnerable or susceptible to certain forms of environmental damage and contamination. As was explained by the House of Commons Standing Committee on Environment and Sustainable Development some time ago:

> One reason for this vulnerability is that contaminants persist longer in the Arctic because cold temperatures, persistent ice cover and low levels of solar radiation retard natural degradation processes. Another reason is that organisms at the top of the food chain tend to have long lifespans and, as a result, more time to accumulate contaminants they ingest in their tissues.[28]

In addition, the location of the Arctic region exposes it to particularly disruptive impacts from climate change and atmospheric damage:

> [C]limate models . . . imply that the effects of global warming will be most pronounced at higher latitudes. Furthermore, because polar regions receive more ultraviolet radiation due to a naturally thin ozone layer, emission of chlorofluorocarbons (CFCs) have always had the greatest effect in these areas.[29]

Concern about the impact of climate change in the Arctic has continued to intensify on the basis of actual northern experience and scientific study.[30] To address some issues associated with environmental contamination, the *Arctic Waters Pollution Prevention Act* (*AWPPA*) was specifically enacted with a view to "the preservation of the peculiar ecological balance that now exists in the water, ice and land areas of the Canadian arctic."[31] Through regulations on the construction and operation of ships and on their cargo, as well as by means of controls on deposits of waste in the Arctic, the *AWPPA* establishes a framework safeguarding the fragile environment of Canada's northern waters. Canada has also pursued a program on northern contaminants and other measures associated with wildlife protection and habitat preservation which derive, at least in part, from international undertakings.[32]

---

28 Canada, House of Commons, Standing Committee on Environment and Sustainable Development, *It's About Our Health! Towards Pollution Prevention* (Ottawa: Canada Communication Group, 1995) at 191–92. See also A. Saunders, *For Generations to Come: Contaminants, the Environment and Human Health in the Arctic* (Conference Report) (Ottawa: Canadian Polar Commission, 1997).
29 *Ibid.*
30 *Arctic Climate Impact Assessment*, online: www.acia.uaf.edu.
31 RSC 1985, c A-12.
32 For a detailed review of implementation measures, see Commissioner of the

Canada has also collaborated with other northern countries in signing the *Arctic Environmental Protection Strategy*.[33] In connection with this initiative, Canada, the Russian Federation, the United States, Denmark, Sweden, Finland, Iceland, and Norway agreed in 1996 to form an Arctic Council.[34] The Council's objectives include coordination of northern environmental monitoring, wildlife preservation and management, and emergency response programs. Specific programs or initiatives, sometimes circumpolar in extent and sometimes focused on particular northern regions such as that of the Russian Federation have targeted PCB wastes, offshore oil and gas operations, atmospheric mercury releases, and biodiversity monitoring.

The Arctic Council has now joined the chorus of voices calling attention to climate change. At its 2004 meeting in Iceland, the organization adopted the *Reykjavik Declaration* in which it encouraged its member states "to take effective measures to adapt and manage the environmental, economic and social impact of climate change and ultraviolet radiation, *inter alia* through enhancing the access of Arctic residents to information, decision makers and institutional capacity-building."[35] In light of the Arctic's distinctive regional features, including the extensive presence of indigenous populations, some legal researchers have begun to directly address the possibility that—in a manner roughly analogous to previous developments in the Antarctic—a dedicated international Arctic environmental treaty might be desirable.[36]

3) Controlling Acid Rain

Acid rain, more formally known as acid deposition, which derives from the reaction of sulphur dioxide and nitrogen oxides with atmospheric water vapour, has been acknowledged as an environmental concern for

---

Environment and Sustainable Development, *2004 October Report*, c 1, online: www.oag-bvg.gc.ca/internet/English/parl_cesd_200410_e_1125.html. On the vulnerability of the Arctic to chemical contaminants, see L Downey & T Fenge, eds, *Northern Lights Against POPs: Combatting Toxic Threats in the Arctic* (Montreal: McGill-Queen's University Press, 2003).

33   14 June 1991, 30 ILM 1624.

34   *Declaration on the Establishment of the Arctic Council*, 19 September 1996, 35 ILM 1382. See T Koivurova & D VanderZwaag, "The Arctic Council at 10 Years: Retrospect and Prospects" (2007) 40 UBC L Rev 121.

35   *The Reykjavik Declaration on the occasion of the Fourth Ministerial Meeting of the Arctic Council* (24 November 2004), online: http://arctic-council.org/filearchive/ Reykjavik_Declaration.pdf [*Reykjavik Declaration*].

36   L Nowlan, *Arctic Legal Regime for Environmental Protection*, IUCN Environmental Law and Policy Papers No 44 (Bonn: IUCN, 2001).

a long time. Legal responses to the problem were greatly complicated by the interjurisdictional diffusion of responsibility and by diplomatic considerations.

European scientific initiatives demonstrated long ago that the transmission of air pollutants associated with acid rain occurs over great distances. This understanding helped to lay the foundations for a 1979 *Convention on Long Range Transboundary Air Pollution* (LRTAP) to which Canada and the United States were signatories along with some thirty European nations. On the basis of this framework agreement to reduce air pollution in general, several more detailed protocols were negotiated in relation to specific substances: sulphur (Helsinki Protocol, 1985, and Oslo Protocol, 1994); nitrogen oxides (Sophia Protocol, 1988); and volatile organic compounds (Geneva Protocol, 1991); further sulphur reductions (Oslo Protocol, 1994); heavy metals (Aarhus Protocol, 1998); more rigorous sulphur, NOx, VOCs, and ammonia controls (Gothenburg Protocol, 1999).

When bilateral discussions between Canada and the United States produced only limited substantive progress, the government of Canada and the seven provincial governments eastward from and including Manitoba reached agreement in 1985 on a schedule to reduce SO_2 emissions. The initiative involved significant public spending to support modernization of smelters and power production facilities that were the principal source of emissions.[37] Inco, Falconbridge, Algoma Steel, and Ontario Hydro accounted for over 70 percent of Ontario's total emissions in 1983, and these operations became the subject of specific regulatory emission limits under Ontario's Countdown Acid Rain Program.[38]

The success of the Ontario program by no means marked the end of major efforts directed towards the problem of acid rain. In October 1998, energy and environment ministers from the federal, provincial, and territorial governments signed the *Canada-Wide Acid Rain Strategy for Post-2000* with a view to "meet the environmental threshold of critical loads for acid deposition across Canada." As outlined in table 4.2, Ontario, Quebec, New Brunswick, and Nova Scotia adopted new reduction targets.

---

37   GB Doern & T Conway, *The Greening of Canada: Federal Institutions and Decisions* (University of Toronto Press, 1994) at 158–63.

38   *Inco Regulation*, O Reg 660/85; *Algoma Regulation*, O Reg 663/85; *Ontario Hydro Regulation*, RRO 1990, Reg 355; *Falconbridge Regulation*, O Reg 661/85.

82   ENVIRONMENTAL LAW

Table 4.2   SO₂ reduction targets for Ontario, Quebec, New
Brunswick, and Nova Scotia

	Eastern Canada Acid Rain Program Cap	New Target under *The Canada-Wide Acid Rain Strategy*	Timeline for New Target
Ontario	885 kt	442.5 kt (50% reduction) announced January 2000	2015
Quebec	500 kt	300 kt (40% reduction) announced November 1997	2002
		250 kt (50% reduction) announced April 2001	2010
New Brunswick	175 kt	122.5 kt (30% reduction)	2005
		85 kt (50% reduction) announced March 2001	2010
Nova Scotia	189 kt	142 kt (25% reduction)	2005
		94.5 kt (50% cumulative reduction total)	2010

Source: online: www.ccme.ca/ourwork/air.html?category_id=31.

In view of the important transboundary dimensions of the acid rain problem, Canada and the United States concluded a bilateral *Air Quality Agreement* in 1991.[39] This agreement required Canada and the United States to set objectives and to pursue the implementation of air pollution reduction measures, including measures directed towards sulphur dioxide and nitrogen oxides. Domestic activities are now to be assessed from the perspective of potential transboundary air pollution, and—alongside notification and consultation requirements—mitigative measures are required. The agreement established an air quality committee and designated the International Joint Commission as the body responsible for making progress reports available for public comment. Disputes not resolved through negotiations may be referred to the IJC.[40]

Pursuant to the *Canadian Environmental Protection Act*, the federal government consulted with the provinces to reach a series of federal–provincial agreements on sulphur dioxide and nitrogen oxides reductions, and the provinces affected, for their part, took steps to fulfil their

---

39   *Agreement Between the Government of Canada and the Government of the United States on Air Quality*, 13 March 1991, 30 ILM 678, online: www.ijc.org/en_/ Air_Quality__Agreement.

40   *Ibid.*

obligations. SO_2 emissions have fallen dramatically, and thus acid rain may be regarded as an example of a comprehensive regulatory response to a serious cause of environmental deterioration. However, on the basis of scientific research, it is far less clear that recovery is proceeding at satisfactory rates. Indeed, water, soil, and forest damage from acid rain appears to be far more persistent than earlier, more optimistic predictions had anticipated.[41]

CEPA Part V provided a mechanism for the federal government to regulate (in relation to Canadian sources of international air pollution, or anticipated violations of international agreements to control or abate pollution) in cases where attempts to have the situation addressed by provincial action have been unsuccessful.[42] CEPA, 1999 preserves such authority.[43] There are a number of international air agreements that might lead to the power being used: the Canada–US Air Quality Agreement, 1991; the Climate Change Convention, 1992; the Montreal Protocol, 1987, and the Geneva Convention on Long-Range Transboundary Air Pollution, 1979.

4) Protecting the Ozone Layer

The ozone layer, an atmospheric band some nine to fifty kilometres above the Earth's surface, provides a protective filter against harmful ultraviolet radiation. This layer is vulnerable to deterioration brought about by the decomposition at high altitudes of certain substances, notably chlorofluorocarbons and halons. Through further chemical interaction, these substances deplete the protective ozone shield.[44]

Ozone depleting substances (ODSs) were widely used in a variety of important economic applications such as refrigeration and fire suppression, especially within industrialized economies. The detrimental impact of ozone depletion on human health and the environment is global in nature, a situation that highlights the importance of a comprehensive international response.

The environmental regime to protect the ozone layer derives from the 1985 Vienna Convention for the Protection of the Ozone Layer. Although essentially a framework agreement creating no concrete remedial agenda, the convention stimulated ongoing research and established

---

41   For descriptive information, see online: www.ec.gc.ca/Air/default.asp?lang=En&n=AA1521C2-1.
42   Canadian Environmental Protection Act, RSC 1985 (4th Supp), c 16 [CEPA].
43   Canadian Environmental Protection Act, 1999, SC 1999, c 33, part 7, division 6.
44   For descriptive information on the stratospheric ozone situation, see online: www.ec.gc.ca/ozone/default.asp?lang=En&n=9090CC46-1.

a conference of the parties and a secretariat for the purpose of gathering and disseminating research and with responsibility for refining the convention through protocols, annexes, and amendments. Given the limitations of scientific knowledge at the time, the convention heralded the precautionary era at the international level. As well, with its formulation of adverse effects as "changes in the physical environment or biota, including changes in climate, which have significant deleterious effects on human health or on the composition, resilience and productivity of natural and managed ecosystems, or on materials useful to mankind," the convention's commitment to a broadly conceived ecosystem approach is notable.[45]

The *Montreal Protocol on Substances that Deplete the Ozone Layer* was signed in 1987 and entered into force on 1 January 1989.[46] It established targets for reducing the production and consumption of specified groups of ODSs and subjected these substances to a control regime accompanied by reporting obligations, a commitment to research on ODS containment techniques, and alternatives to controlled substances. In addition, the Montreal Protocol addressed the risk that non-parties posed to the integrity and effectiveness of the arrangements by banning trade between parties and non-parties in relation to controlled substances shipped in bulk and products containing controlled substances, as well as to goods produced with controlled substances. To encourage the participation of developing nations, many of whom wished to increase rather than lower levels of ODS use and production, the Montreal Protocol offered delayed compliance along with financial and technical incentives to facilitate implementation.

Amendments to the protocol at London in 1990 and again at Copenhagen in 1992 accelerated (subject to an exception for "essential uses") the phasing-out of substances on the original ODS list and extended coverage to new substances on the basis of evolving scientific understanding about the rate of ozone depletion.[47] The protocol has been either ratified or approved by 197 parties.[48] UNEP, while acknowledging continuing challenges, reports significant improvements attributable to the agreement:

---

45 *Vienna Convention for the Protection of the Ozone Layer*, 22 March 1985, 26 ILM 1529, art 1(2).
46 16 September 1987, 26 ILM 1550 [Montreal Protocol].
47 29 June 1990, 30 ILM 541; 23–25 November 1992, 32 ILM 874.
48 A progress report on the Protocol may be found online: http://ozone.unep.org/Publications/MP_Acheivements-E.pdf.

Without the Protocol, by the year 2050 ozone depletion would have risen to at least 50% in the northern hemisphere's mid latitudes and 70% in the southern mid latitudes, about 10 times worse than current levels. . . . The amount of ozone-depleting chemicals in the atmosphere would have been five times greater. The implications of this would have been horrendous and have been estimated to include: 19 million more cases of non-melanoma cancer, 1.5 million more cases of melanoma cancer.[49]

Within Canada, initiatives pursuant to the Montreal Protocol have included both federal and provincial legislation and regulations intended to eliminate certain uses of ODSs, to control imports and exports, and to govern the handling and maintenance of various forms of equipment where ODSs have historically been used.[50]

5) Climate Change, Global Warming, and the Kyoto Protocol

As atmospheric concentrations of greenhouse gases (GHG) (including carbon dioxide (CO_2), methane (CH_4), and nitrous oxide (N_2O)) have increased since the pre-industrial era, climate change has been observed. Prominent initial indications included global warming or a general rise in average temperatures around the planet. Other indications of climate change include the increasing frequency of extreme weather occurrences, floods and droughts, alpine and polar melting, and shifts in ocean currents. Despite some uncertainty about the pace and nature

---

49 UNEP, Ozone Secretariat, "Basic Facts and Data on the Science and Politics of Ozone Protection" (Backgrounder) (9 September 2010), online: http://ozone. unep.org/Events/ozone_day_2010/press-backgrounder-2010-update.pdf. See also Donald Kaniaru, ed, *The Montreal Protocol: Celebrating 20 Years of Environmental Progress* (London: Cameron May, 2007).

50 *CEPA Regulations*: SOR/89-351, SOR/90-127, SOR/90-583, SOR/90-584, SOR/93-214, consolidated and revised in *Ozone-Depleting Substances Regulations, 1998*, SOR/99-7. See online: www.ec.gc.ca/ozone/default.asp?lang=En&n=9F5687EF-1; *Ozone-depleting Substances and Halocarbons Regulation*, Alta Reg 181/2000; *Ozone Depleting Substances and Other Halocarbons Regulation*, BC Reg 387/99; *The Ozone Depleting Substances Act*, CCSM c O80; *Ozone Depleting Substances and Other Halocarbons Regulation*, Man Reg 103/94; *Ozone Depleting Substances and Other Halocarbons Regulation*, O Reg 463/10; *Ozone Layer Protection Regulations*, NS Reg 54/95; *Ozone Depleting Substances and Other Halocarbons Regulation*, NB Reg 97-132; *Ozone Layer Protection Regulations*, PEI Reg EC 619/94; and *Ozone Depleting Substances and Other Halocarbons Regulation*, YOIC 2000/127. For an unsuccessful prosecution of a CFC importer, see *R v Haas* (1993), 139 AR 180 (Prov Ct). More recently, a number of convictions have been secured.

of future developments, particularly at the regional level, global climate change is expected to continue as a consequence of discernable human influence. As expressed in the Fourth Assessment Report of the Intergovernmental Panel on Climate Change, "[c]ontinued greenhouse gas emissions at or above current rates would cause further warming and induce many changes in the global climate system during the 21st century that would *very likely* be larger than those observed during the 20th century."[51] The social, economic, and ecological impact of global warming and climate change is not precisely understood, but the immensity of the risk and challenge is such that international attempts to promote legal, institutional, and behavioural responses have been intense.

In 1988 the United Nations General Assembly identified climate change as a "common concern of mankind,"[52] and in the same year the World Meteorological Society and UNEP established an intergovernmental panel on climate change (IPCC) to undertake an assessment of available evidence. In the 1992 meetings of the UN Conference on Environment and Development at Rio de Janeiro, a *Framework Convention on Climate Change (FCCC)* was opened for signature. The *FCCC*, which entered into force in 1994, articulated as an international objective the "stabilization of greenhouse gas concentrations in the atmosphere at a level that would prevent dangerous anthropogenic interference with the climate system." The desired level is to be achieved in a timeframe "sufficient to allow ecosystems to adapt naturally to climate change, to ensure that food production is not threatened and to enable economic development to proceed in a sustainable manner."[53]

The *FCCC* set out a series of commitments on information exchange, technical and scientific cooperation, and education and training applicable to all parties, and specified additional undertakings for developed and developing country parties. Developed country parties, including Canada, are specifically committed to "adopt national policies and take corresponding measures on the mitigation of climate change, by limiting . . . anthropogenic emissions of greenhouse gases and protecting and enhancing . . . greenhouse gas sinks and reservoirs."[54]

---

51   Intergovernmental Panel on Climate Change, *Climate Change 2007: The Physical Science Basis-Summary for Policymakers* (Geneva: Intergovernmental Panel on Climate Change Secretariat, 2007) at 13.

52   UNGA 43/53.

53   *Framework Convention on Climate Change*, 9 May 1992, 31 ILM 849, art 2.

54   *Ibid*, art 4(2)(a).

Within the context of the *FCCC*, further negotiations were pursued through the mechanism of Conference of the Parties (COP).[55] On 11 December 1997, the Kyoto Protocol was agreed to at COP-3. The most prominent innovation of the Kyoto Protocol was the adoption of quantitative objectives for greenhouse gas (GHG) reductions by developed nations. Specifically, on the basis of varying individual commitments, those countries undertook to reduce their overall GHG emissions by 5.2 percent below 1990 levels in the period from 2008 to 2012. For its part, Canada committed to a 6 percent reduction from the 1990 baseline, and ratified the Protocol in 2002.

The Protocol does not require the adoption of any particular policy in connection with the emissions reduction goal, although all efforts to implement commitments should be designed to minimize adverse social, environmental, and economic impacts on developing nations. The Kyoto agreement, however, did provide for several flexible mechanisms including an emissions trading system and cooperative arrangements involving developed nations (joint implementation) or involving developed and developing nations (clean development mechanism).

The formula for entry into force of the Kyoto Protocol required ratification by fifty-five parties so long as the developed countries that have ratified account for at least 55 percent of 1990 emissions by developed countries. These requirements were met on 16 February 2005.[56] International negotiations concerning future commitments to GHG emissions reductions are ongoing.[57]

With the first Kyoto commitment period (2008–2012) scheduled to end, thirty-five developed countries, notably members of the EU, accepted a second round of emission reduction commitments at the 17th Conference of the Parties to the UNFCCC in Durban, South Africa. There was general agreement on a Platform for Enhanced Action, the details of which are under negotiation. Shortly following the Durban meeting, Canada announced its intention to withdraw from the Kyoto Protocol with the effect that Canada is no longer subject to enforceable emission reduction commitments. Notice of withdrawal, authorized by Order in Council (6 December 2011), became effective one year later pursuant to

---

55 For ongoing coverage of the negotiations process, see the Earth Negotiations Bulletin, online: www.iisd.ca/enbvol/enb-background.htm.
56 M Doelle, "The Cat Came Back, or the Nine Lives of the Kyoto Protocol" (2006) 16 J Envtl L & Pol'y 261.
57 S Bernstein *et al*, eds, *A Globally Integrated Climate Policy for Canada* (University of Toronto Press, 2008).

section 27(2) of the Kyoto Protocol. A judicial review challenge to the decision to withdraw was dismissed.[58]

Canada's response to climate change at the federal, provincial, and municipal levels is more fully discussed in Chapter 19.

C. INTERNATIONAL TRADE AND THE ENVIRONMENT

The promotion of international trade raises difficult issues for the design and operation of domestic environmental protection regimes. Strong divergences of opinion have separated certain advocates of environmental protection from others committed to trade liberalization, with adherents to each perspective frequently assuming that the two interests are antithetical. Others argue that the free trade and environmentalist communities share the common objective of minimizing waste and maximizing the efficient use of resources. "The trade approach," it is sometimes argued, "seeks to do so through control of the end product and its consumption—that is, the 'finished' end of the production cycle—while the more apparently environmental perspective focuses on the conservation of the 'raw' end of the production cycle."[59]

With general acceptance of the legitimacy of environmental imperatives and trade policy goals, especially in relation to development, attention has been more positively directed towards reconciliation of environmental and trade promotion regimes and on mechanisms to ensure the benefits of each.[60] Environmentalists, for example, often see important advantages in being able to utilize powerful trade sanctions to enforce environmental standards, while those committed to trade liberalization industriously pursue their efforts to ensure that environmental protection measures do not interfere unduly with international

---

58   *Turp v Canada (Minister of Justice)*, 2012 FC 893.

59   ML McConnell, "International Trade and Environmental Law" in G Thompson, ML McConnell, & LB Huestis, eds, *Environmental Law and Business in Canada* (Aurora, ON: Canada Law Book, 1993) 343 at 345. See also Canada, Department of Foreign Affairs and International Trade, *Framework for Conducting Environmental Assessments of Trade Agreements* (Ottawa: Department of Foreign Affairs and International Trade, 2001); D McRae, "Trade and the Environment: Competition, Cooperation or Confusion?" (2003) 41 Alta L Rev 745.

60   Canada is among the group of nations that endeavours systematically to evaluate trade agreements from an environmental perspective. See Canada, Department of Foreign Affairs and International Trade, *Handbook for Conducting Environmental Assessments of Trade Negotiations* (Ottawa: Foreign Affairs Canada, 2004).

trade. The underlying challenge then becomes the need for institutions and processes to resolve conflicts when they arise.

1) The *General Agreement on Tariffs and Trade (GATT)* and the World Trade Organization (WTO)

The sophistication of decision-making and dispute-resolution institutions in international trade law, in comparison with more recently developed international efforts to address environmental concerns, resulted in a situation in which trade-environment reconciliation was often attempted in the context of trade regimes. Of the latter, the most notable is the 1947 *General Agreement on Tariffs and Trade (GATT)*, encompassed as of January 1995 within the framework of the World Trade Organization (WTO). Other agreements have been reached within the WTO framework, and multilateral negotiations continue.

GATT and several subsequent rounds of multilateral negotiations elaborated a set of rules to regulate tariffs and non-tariff barriers to trade, (import quotas, for example) among contracting parties. Subject to specified exceptions, a *most-favoured nation* rule was implemented, meaning that trade restrictions had to operate on a *non-discriminatory* basis as between one *GATT* member and another.[61] Products imported by a *GATT* contracting party were to be accorded *national treatment*; that is, imports could be treated no less favourably in relation to taxes and regulations than goods produced domestically by the importing nation.[62] In addition, Article XI provided that "[n]o prohibitions or restrictions other than duties, taxes or other charges, whether made effective through quotas, import or export licences or other measures, shall be instituted or maintained by any contracting party on the importation of any product of the territory of any other contracting party or on the exportation or sale for export of any product destined for the territory of any other contracting party." However, *GATT* itself provided certain exceptions which came to be regarded as providing some scope for environmental measures within the overall framework. In particular, in Article XX, *GATT* itself identified exceptions in the case of measures "necessary to protect human, animal or plant life or health"; and measures "relating to the conservation of exhaustible natural resources if such measures are made effective in conjunction with restrictions on domestic production or consumption," so long as the measures did not in the words of Article XX's "chapeau" constitute a "disguised restric-

---

61   *General Agreement on Tariffs and Trade*, 30 October 1947, Can TS 1947 No 27, art I.
62   *Ibid*, art III.

tion on international trade" or an "arbitrary or unjustifiable discrimination between countries where the same conditions prevail."

Interpretation of Article XX initially suggested comparatively limited scope for these provisions as mechanisms with which to defend environmental measures. Interpretation of "necessary," for example, directed decision making towards the least trade restrictive alternative. That is, given two or more equally effective mechanisms for protecting human life or health, only the approach involving the least restrictions on trade will be considered "necessary" in the context of the GATT exceptions.[63] It was also understood that measures defended on the grounds that they "relate to" conservation must meet the test of being "primarily aimed at" conservation.[64] At the time, commentators observed that the determination to restrict exemptions to measures that are least restrictive of international trade has produced "a very rigorous kind of test that may result in measures taken for genuinely environmental purposes being nevertheless found to violate the GATT . . . ."[65]

Apprehension that interpretation of the Article XX exemptions might tilt overwhelmingly towards trade objectives was reinforced in 1998. In a decision concerning a challenge to US legislation seeking to protect endangered species of sea turtles from dangerous shrimp harvesting practices, the Shrimp-Turtle panel reported that:

> If an interpretation of the chapeau of Article XX were to be followed which would allow a member to adopt measures conditioning access to its market for a given product upon the adoption by the exporting members of certain policies, including conservation policies, GATT 1994 and the WTO Agreement could no longer serve as a multilateral framework for trade among members as security and predictability of trade relations under these agreements would be threatened.[66]

In addition, proceedings under GATT established the scope of measures "necessary to protect human, animal or plant life or health" as confined to measures intended to safeguard these interests within the jurisdiction of the importing state. Thus, measures intended to

---

63   Thailand: Restrictions on Importation of and Internal Taxes on Cigarettes, BISD (1990) 37th Supp 200.

64   In the Matter of Canada's Landing Requirement for Pacific Coast Salmon and Herring, 16 October 1989, 2 TCT 7163.

65   MJ Trebilcock & R Howse, The Regulation of International Trade (London: Routledge, 1995) at 338.

66   United States — Import Prohibition of Certain Shrimp and Shrimp Products WT/DS58/R, 15 May 1998 (Panel Report) at para 7.45. This decision is often referred to as Shrimp-Turtle.

safeguard species outside the enacting jurisdiction—on the high seas, for example—could not be saved by the Article XX(b) exemption. This was the decision reached in the controversial *Tuna-Dolphin* decision when a *GATT* panel concluded that US legislation could not be saved by the exemption. The United States had introduced an embargo against tuna from Mexico on the grounds that that country's fishing practices led to the killing of excessive numbers of dolphins contrary to the US *Marine Mammal Protection Act*.[67] A subsequent *GATT* panel decision arising from European concerns about other provisions in the same US legislation suggested a greater degree of tolerance for extraterritorial environmental protection.[68] It did so on the basis that there were no prohibitions in "general international law" against measures relating to matters located outside a country's own territory, and because there were no indications in the *GATT*'s background documentation to suggest the framers had intended to exclude extraterritorial environmental initiatives from the scope of Article XX.

More recent indications suggest that application of Article XX principles in the WTO context will ease or eliminate certain highly restrictive interpretations and thus permit greater scope for the justification of environmental and conservation measures. This increased flexibility results from procedural changes and the evolution of the jurisprudence effected by the WTO Appellate Body (WTOAB). Procedurally, the WTOAB has indicated a willingness in appropriate circumstances to receive *amicus curiae* briefs from environmental NGOs. This may permit panel access to a wider range of relevant perspectives on trade and environmental relationships than disputing parties are able to provide.

In a report that severely criticized the panel in *Shrimp-Turtle* quoted above, the WTOAB emphasized the legitimate nature of the policies and interests embodied in Article XX.[69] Accordingly, "the right to invoke one of those exceptions is not to be rendered illusory." The goal of interpretation would be to strike a balance between "the right of a member to invoke an exception under Article XX and the duty of that same member to respect the treaty rights of the other members."[70]

The appropriate approach to the Article XX exceptions, reflecting "the fundamental structure and logic" of the Article is now said to be two-tiered. First, provisional justification by reason of characterization

67   *United States—Restrictions on Imports of Tuna*, 16 August 1991, 30 ILM 1594.
68   *Dispute Settlement Panel Report on United States Restrictions on Imports of Tuna* (July 1994), 33 ILM 839.
69   *United States—Import Prohibition of Certain Shrimp and Shrimp Products* WT/DS58/AB/R, 12 October 1998 [*Shrimp-Turtle*, Appellate Body].
70   *Ibid* at para 156.

of the measure under Article XX(g) is called for. Second, further appraisal of the same measure will be undertaken with reference to the introductory clauses of Article XX.[71]

With respect to Article XX(g) in *Shrimp-Turtle* itself, the WTOAB provided several indications that the tests for provisional justification would be more accommodating to environmental considerations than the preceding *GATT* approach. In connection with "exhaustible natural resources" these may be either living or non-living and with respect to the former, it is enough that migratory species migrate or pass through the waters of a state for there to be a "sufficient nexus" to support protective measures. Insofar as those measures must "relate to" conservation, "a close and genuine relationship of ends and means" replaced the more restricted "primarily aimed at" requirement.[72]

Article XX(b) — "necessary to protect human, animal or plant life or health" — may also be more liberally viewed in light of the WTOAB's discussion of "necessary" in the *Asbestos* report of 12 March 2001. When Canada argued against a French decree banning asbestos on the ground, amongst others, that controlled use was a "reasonably available" alternative to the prohibition, the WTOAB noted the undisputed right of members of the WTO to determine the level of health protection they consider appropriate. France, having chosen to halt the spread of asbestos-related health risks, "could not reasonably be expected to employ any alternative measure if that measure would involve a continuation of the very risk that the Decree seeks to halt."[73]

Where a measure otherwise inconsistent with *GATT* principles is provisionally justified under either Article XX(b) or (g) exemptions, a second tier analysis must still be conducted under the "chapeau." In this regard, the three factors to be addressed are: (a) the existence of discrimination; (b) the arbitrary or unjustifiable character of such discrimination; and (c) whether the discrimination occurs between countries where the same conditions prevail.[74]

In addition to disputes that might arise between parties to the WTO framework on the basis of the domestic environmental measures of one that might be challenged as trade-restricting by another, there may be situations in which conflicts arise between the terms of multilateral environmental agreements such as the Montreal Protocol and obligations associated with the WTO regime. General rules of international law,

---

71   *Ibid* at paras 118–19.
72   *Ibid* at para 136.
73   *European Communities — Measures Affecting Asbestos and Asbestos-Containing Products* WT/DS135/AB/R, 12 March 2001 at paras 168 and 174.
74   *Shrimp-Turtle*, Appellate Body, above note 69 at para 150.

notably in relation to treaty interpretation, would be brought to bear in such circumstances. A training manual prepared by UNEP outlines some possible outcomes:

> Applying these rules, it would follow that the trade restrictions established under post-1994 agreements, such as the 2000 Biosafety Protocol and the 2001 POPs Convention, would prevail over inconsistent obligations established under the 1994 GATT (to the extent that they are inconsistent) when the states involved are parties to both the MEA as well as the GATT. In the case when a state is not a party to the relevant MEA, the obligations of the GATT might prevail, to the extent that the GATT obligations are inconsistent. The situation is slightly more complex in the case of pre-1994 MEAs, such as the Montreal Protocol. . . . With the GATT 1947 being re-adopted as the GATT 1994 at the Uruguay Round of trade negotiations, the trade agreement is at least technically, the *lex posterior*. However, the ruling of the WTO Appellate Body in the Shrimp/Turtle dispute suggests that trade restrictions in most MEAs, like the 1987 Montreal Protocol . . . are unlikely to fall afoul of the GATT 1994 requirements. Moreover, some MEAs may also be seen as *lex specialis* rules (i.e., more specific rules) than those embodied in the GATT.[75]

Just as conflict between trade law and environmental principles generated extensive discussion and debate, the potential for tension between the goals of investor protection and environmental law have attracted attention. The fear has been expressed that investor protection measures, typically found in Bilateral Investment Treaties (BIT) might undermine domestic environmental regimes. This debate is less advanced than the trade and environment relationship, but has already resulted in some adjudicated disputes. Several of these arising in the context of North American Free Trade are discussed below.

2) The Canada–United States and North American Free Trade Agreements

The *Canada–United States Free Trade Agreement*, covering bilateral trade in goods and services, came into force in January 1989. It incorporated *GATT* principles, including Article XX, but otherwise provided little

---

75   L Kurukulasuriya & NA Robinson, eds, *Training Manual on International Environmental Law* (Nairobi: Division of Policy Development and Law, UNEP, 2006) at 334–35.

explicit direction concerning environmental protection measures.[76] However, when Canada, the United States, and Mexico embarked on negotiations for a North American free trade pact in 1991, environmental considerations figured prominently. This high level of interest and attention may be explained by a combination of factors. For their part, environmentalists were anxious to try to avoid some of the limitations that had emerged under the *GATT* regime and were concerned that existing environmental safeguards might be undermined if trade provisions and economic integration measures promoted a "race to the bottom," that is, a competitive lowering of environmental standards. At the same time, free trade advocates were apprehensive that, by manipulating environmental standards or enforcement practices, a party to *NAFTA* might gain an advantage over other trading partners that could lower export prices unfairly or induce investors to migrate to a perceived "pollution haven" in order to avoid the costs of environmental protection. Their interest in environmental measures was thus part of a wider preoccupation with maintaining a "level playing field" in relation to trade matters and investment decisions.

NAFTA[77] addresses these fears in several provisions, including the preamble where the parties express their commitment to pursuing the commercial and economic objectives of the agreement in a manner that is consistent with environmental protection and conservation, sustainable development, and a strengthened development and enforcement of environmental law and regulations. Detailed provisions deal with other aspects of the relationship between environmental measures and trade and investment.

NAFTA establishes that, to the extent that inconsistency exists between the specific trade obligations set out in a number of specified international environmental agreements and *NAFTA*, the terms of the environmental agreements shall take precedence.[78] Where such agreements allow a choice among equally effective and reasonably available options, however, a party intending to rely on this provision must select the alternative that involves the least level of inconsistency with

---

76   Arguably, article 904 of the *Canada–United States Free Trade Agreement*, 22 December 1987, 27 ILM 281, dealing with energy goods, could be construed as environmental in nature.

77   *North American Free Trade Agreement*, Can TS 1994 No 2 [*NAFTA*].

78   *Convention on International Trade in Endangered Species of Wild Fauna and Flora*, 3 March 1973, 12 ILM 1085 [*CITES*]; *Basel Convention on the Control of Transboundary Movements of Hazardous Wastes and Their Disposal*, 22 March 1989, 28 ILM 657; Montreal Protocol, above note 46.

NAFTA.[79] *NAFTA* also acknowledges the possibility that a party to the agreement might wish to adopt sanitary or phytosanitary measures that are more stringent than established international standards, guidelines, or recommendations in order to protect human, animal, or plant life or health in its territory. Circumstances in which such action would be permissible under *NAFTA* are set out.[80]

Environmental considerations are also discussed in relation to investment in the agreement, which confirms the understanding of the parties that "it is inappropriate to encourage investment by relaxing domestic health, safety or environmental measures." Thus, in the words of the agreement itself: "[a] Party should not waive or otherwise derogate from, or offer to waive or otherwise derogate from, such measures as an encouragement for the establishment, acquisition, expansion or retention in its territory of an investment of an investor."[81]

Another provision of *NAFTA*'s investment chapter has already raised significant controversy from the perspective of environmental law and regulation. Except when employed for a public purpose, on a non-discriminatory basis, and in accordance with due process of law, and where compensation is provided, Article 1110 prohibits *NAFTA* parties from taking measures that are "tantamount to expropriation." An investor-state dispute-resolution process permits aggrieved companies to sue member states for redress. The particular controversy associated with Article 1110 relates to the uncertain ambit of measures "tantamount to expropriation." Although state confiscation of physical property is readily understood as expropriation, it is less clear within the *NAFTA* context that other forms of government action such as regulation making or contractual behaviour are encompassed. In the US, however, a strong tradition of concern for the status of contracts as a form of property and with "regulatory takings" supports the expectation that companies that suffer losses when contracts are interfered with or regulations altered may be entitled to compensation. On the other hand, environmentalist concern has been expressed that a "regulatory chill" may be created by the prospect that any alteration of the regulatory framework could give rise to compensation claims.

When the Canadian government banned trade in the fuel additive MMT, the exclusive North American producer, Ethyl Corporation of Richmond, Virginia, claimed on behalf of its Canadian subsidiary that its assets had been "indirectly expropriated." In other words, ending

---

79   *NAFTA*, above note 77, art 104.
80   *Ibid*, arts 712 & 713.
81   *Ibid*, art 1114.

the MMT business was equivalent to an expropriation. This dispute was settled on the basis of a $19-million payment for costs and lost profits and repeal of the MMT ban.[82] In another case, SD Myers, an Ohio-based company involved in PCB disposal, challenged Canadian regulations prohibiting the transborder shipment of PCB wastes for treatment in the United States.[83] A subsequent dispute between an American investor and Mexico, *Metalclad v United Mexican States*, resulted in the first successful claim against a host jurisdiction under Chapter 11, accompanied by a comparatively broad interpretation of the scope of compensable expropriation.[84]

The *NAFTA* tribunal decision in *Chemtura v Canada* provides guidance and encouragement for environmental protection measures that are consistent with Article 1110 criteria. In a challenge by a lindane manufacturer against a Canadian ban on the use of this substance as a pesticide, the arbitral panel noted bans and restrictions in numerous other countries and in several international environmental agreements as indications of the legitimate intent of Canadian regulatory review of the chemical.[85] Importantly, the tribunal concluded on the issue of expropriation that:

> Irrespective of the existence of a contractual deprivation . . . the measures challenged . . . constituted a valid exercise of . . . police powers . . . . [T]he PMRA took measures within its mandate, in a non-discriminatory manner, motivated by the increasing awareness of the dangers presented by lindane for human health and the environment. A measure adopted under such circumstances is a valid exercise of the State's police powers and, as a result, does not constitute an expropriation.[86]

---

82   J Soloway, "Environmental Regulation as Expropriation: The Case of NAFTA's Chapter 11" (2000) 33 Can Bus LJ 92 at 114–19; and G Dufour, "L'impact du chapitre 11 de l'aléna sur la capacité de l'état d'adopter des mesures protégeant de l'environnement et de la santé publique" (2013) 90 Can Bar Rev 653.

83   Soloway, above note 82.

84   Award, Case No ARB (AF)/97/1 (30 August 2000), online: www.naftaclaims.com. The decision was ultimately subject to judicial review in British Columbia, *United Mexican States v Metalclad Corp* (2001), 89 BCLR (3d) 359. See C Tollefson, "*Metalclad v United Mexican States* Revisited: Judicial Oversight of NAFTA's Chapter Eleven Investor-State Claim Process" (2002) 11 Minn J Global Trade 183.

85   *Chemtura Corporation (formerly Crompton Corporation) v Canada* (Permanent Court of Arbitration), 2 August 2010, at paras 135–38.

86   *Ibid* at para 266.

Disputes between *NAFTA* parties, including disagreements about the operation of environmental measures, are to be resolved by a dispute-settlement mechanism established under the agreement. The influence of other jurisprudence relating to trade and environment conflicts—including decisions under *GATT*—will continue to be felt. Nevertheless, *NAFTA*'s assigning of the burden of proof to the challenging party, as well as its allowing of the use of scientific experts on panels,[87] suggests that environmental protection measures could be less vulnerable to trade-based challenges under *NAFTA* than they had been under *GATT*.

In addition to *NAFTA* itself, a side agreement was concluded between Canada, the United States, and Mexico in 1993. The stated objectives of the *North American Agreement on Environmental Cooperation* (*NAAEC*) are to

a) foster the protection and improvement of the environment in the territories of the Parties for the well-being of present and future generations;

b) promote sustainable development based on cooperation and mutually supportive environmental and economic policies;

c) increase cooperation between the Parties to better conserve, protect, and enhance the environment, including wild flora and fauna;

d) support the environmental goals and objectives of the *NAFTA*;

e) avoid creating trade distortions or new trade barriers;

f) strengthen cooperation on the development and improvement of environmental laws, regulations, procedures, policies, and practices;

g) enhance compliance with, and enforcement of, environmental laws and regulations;

h) promote transparency and public participation in the development of environmental laws, regulations, and policies;

i) promote economically efficient and effective environmental measures; and

j) promote pollution prevention policies and practices.

NAAEC, in addition to establishing the Commission for Environmental Cooperation (located in Montreal), articulates a series of obligations. Of particular interest is Article 3, which recognizes each party's right "to establish its own levels of domestic environmental protection and environmental development policies and priorities" while indicating that each "shall ensure that its laws and regulations provide for high levels of environmental protection and shall strive to continue to

---

87   *NAFTA*, above note 77, arts 2014 & 2015.

improve those laws and regulations." The parties have also agreed to environmental research, reporting, and educational initiatives, to appropriate environmental impact assessment, and to promotion of economic instruments for achieving environmental goals efficiently.[88]

Enforcement obligations also figure prominently in the side agreement. Thus, each party is to ensure "appropriate access" to "fair, open and equitable" administrative, quasi-judicial, or judicial proceedings where those with recognized legal interests can pursue their claims.[89] Moreover, in pursuit of effective environmental enforcement and compliance, the parties are committed to appropriate governmental action[90] although nothing in the agreement authorizes a party to undertake environmental law enforcement activities in another's territory.[91] The *NAFTA* environmental side agreement now makes a party's "persistent pattern of failure . . . to effectively enforce its environmental law" the basis for invoking a dispute-settlement mechanism leading potentially to significant sanctions. However, critics of environmental enforcement practices will be discouraged from advancing their complaints by broadly crafted exceptions to the notion of failing to enforce effectively. Specifically, a party will not fail the standard where the conduct of officials in a particular case "reflects a reasonable exercise of their discretion in respect of investigatory, prosecutorial, regulatory or compliance matters" or where action or inaction "results from *bona fide* decisions to allocate resources to enforcement in respect of other environmental matters determined to have higher priorities."[92] In addition, a complaints process allows individuals and non-governmental organizations to make submissions to the secretariat concerning the alleged failure of a party to enforce its environmental law effectively.[93]

In order to facilitate the application of *NAAEC* in Canada, the federal government entered into negotiations with the provinces for an

88   *North American Agreement on Environmental Cooperation*, 12 and 14 September 1993, 32 ILM 1480, art 2. Now see *Ten Years of North American Environmental Cooperation: Report of the Ten-year Review and Assessment Committee to the Council of the Commission for Environmental Cooperation* (15 June 2004).

89   *North American Agreement on Environmental Cooperation*, above note 88, arts 6 & 7.

90   *Ibid*, art. 5.

91   *Ibid*, art. 37.

92   *Ibid*, art. 45.

93   *Ibid*. For further discussion of the complaints process, see *Bringing the Facts to Light: A Guide to Articles 14 and 15 of the North American Agreement on Environmental Cooperation* (CEC, 2000). For an example of a "factual record" relating to Canada, see *BC Hydro Final Factual Record* (CEC, 2000). These and other materials are available online: www.cec.org.

intergovernmental agreement on *NAAEC*. The first such agreement was concluded with Alberta on 15 August 1995, thereby providing for that province's involvement in implementing and further elaborating *NAAEC*. Quebec (26 December 1996) and Manitoba (21 January 1997) subsequently signed the *Canadian Intergovernmental Agreement*.

FURTHER READINGS

ARBOUR, J-M, S LAVALLÉE, & H TRUDEAU, *Droit international de l'environnement*, 2d ed (Cowansville: Éditions Yvon Blais, 2012)

BERNSTEIN, S, *et al*, eds, *A Globally Integrated Climate Policy For Canada* (University Of Toronto Press, 2008)

BIRNIE, PW, & AE BOYLE, *International Law and the Environment*, 2d ed (Oxford UP, 2002)

BRUNNÉE, J, *Acid Rain and Ozone Layer Depletion: International Law and Regulation* (Dobbs Ferry, NY: Transnational Publishers, 1988)

BRUNNÉE, J, "From Bali to Copenhagen: Towards a Shared Vision for a Post-2012 Climate Regime?" (2010) 25 Maryland Journal of International Law 86

COOPER, EWT, & N CHALIFOUR, *CITES, Eh? A Review of Canada's Implementation of CITES under WAPPRIITA* (Toronto: WWF Canada, 2004)

CORDONIER SEGGER, M-C, & CG WEERAMANTRY, *Sustainable Justice: Reconciling Economic, Social and Environmental Law* (Boston: Martinus Nijhoff, 2005)

NOWLAN, L, & C ROLFE, *Kyoto, POPs and Straddling Stocks: Understanding Environmental Treaties* (Vancouver: West Coast Environmental Law, 2003)

PEREZ, O, *Ecological Sensitivity and Global Legal Pluralism: Rethinking the Trade and Environment Conflict* (Oxford: Hart Publishing, 2004)

SANDS, P, *Principles of International Environmental Law*, 2d ed (New York: Cambridge University Press, 2003)

SMITH, DA, "The Implementation of Canadian Policies to Protect the Ozone Layer" in GB Doern, ed, *Getting It Green: Case Studies in Canadian Environmental Regulation* (Toronto: CD Howe Institute, 1990) 111–28

TREBILCOCK, MJ, R HOWSE, & A ELIASON, *The Regulation of International Trade*, 4th ed (London: Routledge, 2013)

VANDERZWAAG, DL, "The Precautionary Approach and the International Control of Toxic Chemicals: Beacon of Hope, Sea of Confusion and Dilution" (2011) 23:3 Houston J Int'l L 605

VOGEL, D, & AM RUGMAN, "Environmentally Related Trade Disputes between the United States and Canada" (1997) American Review of Canadian Studies 271

WOLD, C, *et al*, *Trade and the Environment: Law and Policy* (Durham, NC: Carolina Academic Press, 2005)

ZAELKE, D, D KANIARU, & E KRUZIKOVA, *Making Law Work: Environmental Compliance and Sustainable Development* (London: Cameron May, 2005)

CHAPTER 5

CIVIL LIABILITY FOR ENVIRONMENTAL HARM

The civil courts have a long history of dealing with disputes that would readily be acknowledged today as environmental in nature. Nuisance claims, along with negligence, strict liability, trespass, and riparian rights have all been asserted—occasionally in combination—on behalf of those seeking judicial protection from the effects of conduct that has resulted, or that may result in the future, in some form of environmental damage.[1] Intermittently, courts have provided strong encouragement for private claims of this nature. Justice Rinfret remarked, for example, that "[p]ollution is always unlawful and, in itself, constitutes a nuisance."[2] Nevertheless, private litigants have faced significant obstacles in pursuing environmental claims. The challenges naturally include specific doctrinal requirements, but encompass as well complex evidentiary burdens, and the costs of litigation, possibly including responsibility for defendants' costs where environmental claims ultimately fail. Some of the constraints—notably in connection with class actions—have recently been addressed through statutory reforms.

---

1 Analogous claims arise under the *Civil Code of Québec* (*CCQ*). See, for example, c III, s III, arts 980, 981, & 982 concerning riparian rights and water quality. For discussion of no-fault liability under art 976 respecting environmental disturbances, see *St Lawrence Cement Inc v Barrette*, 2008 SCC 64.
2 *Groat v Edmonton (City)*, [1928] SCR 522 at 532.

A. COMMON LAW CAUSES OF ACTION

1) Nuisance

The common law doctrine of nuisance affords some protection to persons whose use and enjoyment of land is unreasonably interfered with by the actions of another, typically though not exclusively a neighbour. The cause of the plaintiff's complaint might be toxic fumes, chemicals or smoke, unpleasant odours, or excessive light or noise, while the interference experienced might involve actual physical damage to property, personal injury or risk to health and safety, or discomfort or inconvenience. A significant distinction has been drawn between nuisance entailing physical damage and interference described as amenity nuisance.[3]

The courts' central concern in nuisance is to determine whether the activity complained of substantially and unreasonably interferes with the plaintiff's own reasonable use of the land:

> [I]t is the impact of the defendant's activity on the plaintiff's interest which is the focus of attention and not the nature of the defendant's conduct. The interference must be unreasonable in the sense that the plaintiff should not be required to suffer it, not that the defendant failed to take appropriate care. By the same token, if the level of interference is unreasonable, it is irrelevant that the defendant was taking all possible care. Furthermore, it makes no difference that in his mind he was making reasonable use of his land, or that his operation was beneficial to the community. The plaintiff satisfies the substantive requirement of the tort if he can point to tangible damage resulting from the defendant's activity or a significant degree of discomfort or inconvenience.[4]

A judicial formulation of the requirements drawing upon a scholarly synthesis indicates that actionable nuisance

> must be such as to be real interference with the comfort or convenience of living according to the standards of the average man. . . . Moreover, the discomfort must be substantial and not merely with reference to the plaintiff; it must be of such a degree that it would be substantial to any person occupying the plaintiff's premises, irrespective of his position in life, age, or state of health; it must be

---

3   *Smith v Inco Ltd*, 2011 ONCA 628 at paras 39–67 (*Smith v Inco*), leave to appeal to SCC refused, [2011] SCCA No. 539.

4   JPS McLaren, "Annotation" (1976) 1 CCLT 29 at 300.

an "inconvenience materially interfering with the ordinary comfort physically of human existence, not merely according to elegant or dainty modes and habits of living, but according to plain and sober and simple notions among the [Canadian] people."[5]

A few examples will help to illustrate the applicability of the doctrine in an environmental context. Nuisance doctrine has been successfully invoked against an operation whose fumes and emissions damaged the plaintiff's commercial gardens,[6] and by an orchard owner whose fruit trees experienced damage attributable to the use of salt for de-icing an adjacent highway.[7] Another successful plaintiff was a corporate landlord whose use of his property was materially interfered with and whose ability to earn rents was undermined by excessive noise and vibration following the introduction of new equipment by a long-established manufacturing plant in a mixed residential and industrial neighbourhood.[8] A homeowner in Quebec succeeded under a provision of the province's *Civil Code* roughly comparable to nuisance against the operators of a telecommunications tower that had the effect of attracting birds to the neighbourhood. The combined impact of the noise and the smell of excrement—on and off her property—interfered with the resident's ability to enjoy her yard, thereby lessening the value of her property.[9] Noise, smoke, litter, and offensive odours emanating from a rural landfill operation led to an injunction and a substantial award of damages.[10]

Notwithstanding such successful claims, the courts clearly recognize a number of defences, and plaintiffs in nuisance face a number of other significant obstacles. Defendants may seek to undermine the

---

5   Morden J in *Walker v Pioneer Construction Co* (1975), 8 OR (2d) 35 at 48 (HCJ), quoting with approval from *Clerk and Lindsell on Torts*, 11th ed (London: Sweet & Maxwell, 1954) at 564.

6   *Walker v McKinnon Industries Ltd*, [1949] OR 549 (HCJ), var'd [1950] OWN 309 (CA).

7   *Schenck v Ontario* (1981), 34 OR (2d) 595 (HCJ), aff'd (1984), 49 OR (2d) 556 (CA), aff'd (*sub nom Schenck v Ontario (Minister of Transportation & Communications)*), [1987] 2 SCR 289.

8   *340909 Ontario Ltd v Huron Steel Products* (1990), 73 OR (2d) 641 (HCJ).

9   *Bolduc v Bell Mobilité Cellulaire* (1994), 17 CELR (NS) 102 (CQ). For a convenient overview of Quebec's environmental law framework, see L. Giroux and P. Halley, "Environmental Law in Quebec" in E Hughes, AR Lucas, & WA Tilleman, eds, *Environmental Law and Policy*, 3d ed (Toronto: Emond Montgomery, 2003) c 4. Issues around fault and compliance with approvals in the nuisance context also arose in *St Lawrence Cement Inc v Barrette*, above note 1.

10   *Nippa v CH Lewis (Lucan) Ltd* (1991), 7 CELR (NS) 149 (Ont Gen Div), (1991), 7 CELR (NS) 163 (CA).

plaintiff's case with evidence indicating that plaintiffs are abnormally sensitive to interference[11] or perhaps that the plaintiff consented in some way to the nuisance.[12] Prescriptive rights may be acquired by defendants who are able to show that the activity complained of and otherwise amounting to a nuisance was carried out continuously for a period of twenty years or more to the knowledge of the plaintiffs or their predecessors who failed to take action against it.[13] It is also noteworthy, given that "[t]he primary *raison d'être* of nuisance is to equip a party who is suffering damage to his land or interference with his use of the land with a means of forcing the party causing that damage to stop doing so," that nuisance cannot be used on a retroactive basis to secure compensation for the subsequent effects of activity that did not amount to nuisance when the activity actually occurred.[14]

Defendants may also seek to immunize their operations against nuisance claims on the grounds that the activity complained of is the inevitable consequence of express statutory authorization and was accordingly given implicit legislative protection.

In *Tock v St. John's (City) Metropolitan Area Board*,[15] where a blocked sewer operated by the defendant municipality resulted in flood damage to the plaintiff homeowner, the Supreme Court of Canada considered the defence of statutory authority. The Court was divided in its analysis of the appropriate treatment of inevitable consequences, with three members proposing to restrict the defence to damage caused by actions specifically required by legislation. Another member of the Court suggested that the defence would be available if the defendant could establish that no other methods of carrying out the work would have avoided damage. In a third opinion, two justices indicated that consideration of statutory authority should be incorporated in the general calculus of reasonableness in a nuisance analysis. "[G]iven all the circumstances, [is it] reasonable to refuse to compensate the aggrieved party for the damages he has suffered?" In *Tock* the defendant municipality was unable to satisfy the Court's requirements and could not avail itself of the defence in the context of the following statutory provision:

> 154. (1) The council may . . . construct, acquire, establish, own and operate

11   *MacNeill v Devon Lumber Co* (1987), 82 NBR (2d) 319 (CA).
12   *Pattison v Prince Edward Region Conservation Authority* (1988), 3 CELR (NS) 212 (Ont CA).
13   *Russell Transport Ltd v Ontario Malleable Iron Co*, [1952] OR 621 (Co Ct).
14   *Smith v Inco*, above note 3 at para 64.
15   [1989] 2 SCR 1181 [*Tock*].

(a) a public water supply system . . .
(b) a public sewerage system . . . and
(c) a storm drainage system . . .

(2) For the purposes of subsection (1) the council may
(a) acquire any waters required for the purpose of providing a sufficient supply of water for the town, and
(b) acquire by purchase or expropriation any lands adjacent to such waters to prevent pollution of those waters.

(3) For the purpose of exercising its powers under subsection (1) the council may lay out, excavate, dig, make, build, maintain, repair and improve all such drains, sewers, and water supply pipes as the council deems necessary.[16]

This language was considered by the Court to be permissive and not mandatory.

The Supreme Court subsequently affirmed the traditional view of the defence of statutory authority when it endorsed the following description:

The defendant must negative that there are alternate methods of carrying out the work. The mere fact that one is considerably less expensive will not avail. If only one method is practically feasible, it must be established that it was practically impossible to avoid the nuisance. It is insufficient for the defendant to negative negligence. The standard is a higher one. While the defence gives rise to some factual difficulties, in view of the allocation of the burden of proof they will be resolved against the defendant.[17]

Defendants may, however, enjoy more explicit immunity from nuisance claims on the basis of express legislative exclusions. These are especially common in relation to agricultural operations. A typical example of such a "right to farm" provision is from Saskatchewan:

The owner or operator of an agricultural operation is not liable to any person in nuisance with respect to the carrying on of the agricultural operation, and may not be prevented by injunction or other order of any court from carrying on the agricultural operation on the

---

16   *The Municipalities Act*, SN 1979, c 33, s 154.
17   *Ryan v Victoria*, [1999] 1 SCR 201 at para 55, quoting Sopinka J from *Tock*, above note 15 at 1226. For recent examples, see *Willis v Halifax (Regional Municipality)*, 2010 NSCA 76; *Susan Heyes Inc v Vancouver (City)*, 2011 BCCA 77.

grounds of nuisance where the owner or operator uses normally accepted agricultural practices.[18]

Although "right to farm" legislation does not operate to exempt farm operations from environmental legislation, some provinces have extended agricultural immunity to restrictive local bylaws. Virtually all provinces adopted "right to farm" legislation in some form or other.[19]

Plaintiffs contemplating a claim in nuisance may also have to confront an awkward and uncertain distinction between private and public nuisance, the latter more difficult to pursue though arguably more relevant to environmental protection. Anchored in the proprietary interests of potential plaintiffs, the private nuisance claim as described above offers the prospect of redress against environmental harm almost in direct proportion to the self-interest of the individuals affected. In contrast, public nuisance doctrine provides a basis for legal action against the perceived causes of environmental harm when that harm involves injury to or interference with public rights, a situation in which individual litigants have no automatic entitlement or standing to pursue a claim.

In cases of public nuisance, the attorney general is presumed to be the most suitable party to initiate litigation on behalf of the general interests of the community. Individuals seeking to proceed with public nuisance claims on behalf of the wider community — in effect to represent the public interest for purposes of the litigation — have been required as a condition of standing to obtain the attorney general's permission to proceed or to demonstrate that they have suffered special damages as a result of the defendant's interference with public rights.

The potentially restrictive application of the special damages test is illustrated in *Hickey v Electric Reduction Co*,[20] where commercial fishermen in Placentia Bay, Newfoundland, were denied standing to proceed in public nuisance against an industrial polluter on the grounds that

---

18   *The Agricultural Operations Act*, SS 1995, c A-12.1, s 3(1). For consideration of this issue in Ontario, see *Pyke v TriGro Enterprises* (2001), 55 OR (3d) 257 (CA).

19   *Agricultural Operation Practices Act*, RSNB 2011, c 107; *Agricultural Operations Practices Act*, RSA 2000, c A-7; *Farm Practices Act*, SNS 2000, c 3; *The Farm Practices Protection Act*, CCSM c F45; *An Act Respecting the Preservation of Agricultural Land and Agricultural Activities*, RSQ c P-41.1; *Farm Practices Protection (Right to Farm) Act*, RSBC 1996, c 131; *The Agricultural Operations Act*, SS 1995, c A-12.1; *Farming and Food Production Protection Act, 1998*, SO 1998, c 1; *Farm Practices Act*, RSPEI 1988, c F-4.1; *Farm Practices Protection Act*, SNL 2001, c F-4.1.

20   (1971), 2 Nfld & PEIR 246 (Nfld TD).

despite commercial losses their right to fish in public waters was simply "a right in common with all Her Majesty's subjects."

In a more recent decision, the relationship between public and private nuisance was also considered. In *Sutherland v Vancouver International Airport Authority*, residents of a Richmond, British Columbia, subdivision launched nuisance proceedings in response to aircraft noise. The noise levels interfered with speech outside the plaintiffs' homes, affecting their use of patios, gardens, and other outdoor amenities. The trial judge found that the aircraft noise inside the house "interfered to a degree transcending annoyance." The British Columbia Court of Appeal, while upholding the finding that the noise of the airport constituted nuisance, ultimately accepted the government's argument that the nuisance was statutorily authorized and overturned the ruling. In so doing, however, the Court of Appeal directly addressed the argument that since the conduct to which the residents objected constituted public nuisance it could only be challenged with the consent of the attorney general:

> In my opinion, the plaintiffs succeeded in establishing the elements of private nuisance: unreasonable and substantial interference with the use and enjoyment of their lands. They are not to be denied a remedy because the defendants' conduct in the circumstances also amounts to a public nuisance.[21]

2) Negligence

To succeed in negligence, the plaintiff must establish that the defendant's failure to meet a standard of care to which the plaintiff was entitled has caused damage for which compensation is being sought. In the environmental context, claims of this nature might arise in connection with physical injury or property damage following on the defendant's use or handling of contaminants or other hazardous substances.

A plaintiff advancing a civil claim in negligence must first establish that the defendant owed that party a duty of care. In *Donoghue v Stevenson*, Lord Atkin explored the "general conception of relations giving rise to a duty of care" and remarked:

> The rule that you are to love your neighbour becomes in law, you must not injure your neighbour; and the lawyer's question, Who is my neighbour? receives a restricted reply. You must take reasonable

---

21   *Sutherland v Vancouver International Airport Authority*, 2002 BCCA 416 at para 34.

care to avoid acts or omissions which you can reasonably foresee would be likely to injure your neighbour. Who, then, in law is my neighbour? The answer seems to be—persons who are so closely and directly affected by my act that I ought reasonably to have them in contemplation as being so affected when I am directing my mind to the acts or omissions which are called in question.[22]

It must then be demonstrated that the defendant's conduct fell short of the standard of care reasonably expected in the circumstances. Such standards may be derived by the court from an examination of applicable statutory requirements, on the basis of normal practices, or in light of the conduct that would be expected from a reasonable person. Those holding themselves out as experts or professionals in a particular field will be charged with a higher standard of care, as will anyone undertaking an activity, however desirable, which poses risks to others. Plaintiffs in negligence will face the further requirement of demonstrating that the defendant's breach of a duty or standard of care was the cause of their injury, and that the damage complained of was not so remote as to have been unforeseeable.

In contrast with riparian claims and trespass actions, negligence requires the plaintiff to provide proof of damages. Physical injury and property damage, however difficult they may be to quantify, have long been considered compensable. In the absence of personal injury or property damage, however, purely economic losses have not ordinarily been recoverable.[23] This limitation may now be softened by a Supreme Court of Canada decision holding that expenditures taken to safeguard property interests or to preserve bodily integrity may constitute re-coverable economic loss even in the absence of actual physical damage or personal injury.[24]

Negligence principles have figured prominently in another stream of environmental cases where claims are not made directly against those originally responsible for environmental damage but against others whose acts or omissions subsequently exposed the plaintiffs to economic losses. The *Sevidal v Chopra* litigation arose in connection with the purchase of a residential property that had been contamin-ated several decades earlier with radioactive soil.[25] At the time of the agreement of purchase and sale, the vendors failed to disclose that radioactive soil dating from experimental research work in the 1940s

22   [1932] AC 562 at 580 (HL).
23   *Rivtow Marine Ltd v Washington Iron Works* (1973), [1974] SCR 1189.
24   *Winnipeg Condominium Corp No 36 v Bird Construction Co*, [1995] 1 SCR 85.
25   (1987), 64 OR (2d) 169 (HCJ).

had been found in the vicinity. Nor did they disclose additional information that came to their attention between the date of the agreement and the date of closing to the effect that the Atomic Energy Control Board had found radioactive contamination on their property. Prior to closing, the purchasers read newspaper reports concerning radioactive soil in the area, but not on the property they intended to buy. However, on the basis of assurances from an official of the AECB, they decided to proceed with the transaction. The AECB was found liable for negligently misrepresenting the condition of the property under the doctrine of *Hedley Byrne & Co Ltd v Heller & Partners Ltd*.[26] Liability of this kind has made governments extremely cautious about certifying the environmental condition of land. For their part, the vendors were found liable in deceit for failing to disclose a dangerous latent defect in the property.

In *Heighington v Ontario*, provincial officials were found liable in negligence for failing to remedy radioactive contamination of the soil although the condition of the soil was known to them, and the *Public Health Act* as then in existence imposed a duty on the Department of Health to abate conditions injurious or dangerous to public health. "In all the circumstances," stated the Ontario Court of Appeal, "the provincial officials were negligent in that, in breach of the *Public Health Act*, they failed to take reasonable steps to cause to be removed such radioactive material, including contaminated soil, as might endanger the health of future occupants of the land."[27]

Claims have also been made against legal professionals for failing to detect environmental liabilities in real estate transactions or for failing to protect their clients against such liabilities. In a recent BC case, legal advisors to a property development firm were found to have breached the duty of care owed in circumstances where they neither discovered a pollution abatement order relating to the land in question nor insisted on appropriate contractual safeguards in the agreement. As the court determined that these failings were not in fact the cause of the plaintiff's losses, the action was dismissed.[28]

Damages otherwise resulting from the defendant's negligence may be reduced where the plaintiff's own negligence was a contributing factor. Thus, a plaintiff property owner was contributorily negligent for its failure to seal the floor of a fuel tank storage room, thereby allowing

---

26   (1963), [1964] AC 465 (HL).
27   (1989), 69 O.R. (2d) 484 at 486 (CA).
28   *Fraser Park South Estates v Lang Michener Lawrence and Shaw* (2001), 84 BCLR (3d) 65 (CA).

further damage to occur following a spill initially caused by the negligent conduct of the fuel oil supplier.[29]

There are also indications of increasing resort to allegations of regulatory negligence against public officials whose conduct or decisions may appear to be causally connected to some form of environmental injury.[30] The general principles applicable to such claims, including an important distinction exempting policy decisions (as distinct from operational responsibilities), from the realm of liability were discussed in *Just v British Columbia*:

> As a general rule, the traditional tort law duty of care will apply to a government agency in the same way that it will apply to an individual. In determining whether a duty of care exists, the first question to be resolved is whether the parties are in a relationship of sufficient proximity to warrant the imposition of such a duty. In the case of a government agency, exemptions from this imposition of duty may occur as a result of the nature of the decision made by the government agency. That is, a government agency will be exempt from the imposition of a duty of care in situations which arise from purely policy decisions.
>
> In determining what constitutes a policy decision, it should be borne in mind that such decisions are generally made by persons of a high level of authority in the agency, but may also be made by persons of a lower level of authority. The characterization of such a decision rests on the nature of the decision and not on the identity of the actors. As a general rule, decisions concerning budgetary allotments for departments or government agencies will be classified as policy decisions. Further, it must be recalled that a policy decision is open to challenge on the basis that it is not made in the *bona fide* exercise of discretion. If after due consideration it is found that a duty of care is owed by the government agency and no exemption by way of statute or policy decision-making is found to exist, a traditional torts analysis ensues and the issue of standard of care required of the government agency must next be considered.[31]

29   *G & S Haulage Ltd v Park Place Centre Ltd*, 2011 NSCA 29.
30   *Tottrup v Alberta (Minister of Environmental Protection)*, [2000] AJ No. 435 (CA); *Quebec (AG) v Girard*, [2004] JQ no 13624 (CA); *Taylor v Canada (Attorney General)*, 2012 ONCA 479.
31   *Just v British Columbia* (1989), 64 DLR (4th) 689 at 708 (SCC). See also *Cooper v Hobart*, [2001] 3 SCR 537; *Edwards v Law Society of Upper Canada*, [2001] 3 SCR 562; *Holland v Saskatchewan*, 2008 SCC 42.

In the context of claims against government agencies and officials, notice requirements and limitation periods are important considerations.[32]

3) Strict Liability

Originating as an application of nuisance principles in the 1866 decision of Mr. Justice Blackburn in *Rylands v Fletcher*, the doctrine of strict liability for damages caused when dangerous substances escape from the defendant's lands to injure the lands of another now offers potential relief in circumstances involving environmental harm.[33] Injury to persons or property resulting from the escape of such substances as sewage, industrial chemicals, pesticides, fuels, and gases may be compensable notwithstanding the exercise of reasonable care by the defendant to prevent the escape.

Blackburn J's formulation of the principle of liability indicated that "the person who for his own purposes brings on his lands and collects and keeps there anything likely to do mischief if it escapes, must keep it in at his peril." Those failing to contain the cause of such mischief are "*prima facie* answerable for all the damage which is the natural consequence of its escape." In confirming this interpretation, the House of Lords qualified the application of the rule by confining it to situations involving the "non-natural" use of land. That consideration has been variously approached by succeeding generations of judicial interpreters who have endeavoured to comply with Lord Moulton's observation that "[i]t is not every use to which land is put that brings into play that principle. It must be some special use bringing with it increased danger to others, and must not merely be the ordinary use of the land or such a use as is proper for the general benefit of the community."[34] Thus, even dangerous uses, if common or generally accepted in a particular locale, might not give rise to liability under the doctrine in *Rylands v Fletcher*, while potentially harmful activities carried on for the general benefit of the community rather than for private advantage or profit might equally fall within the exceptions to the rule.[35]

The doctrine in *Rylands v Fletcher* was reconsidered by the House of Lords in a prominent controversy involving a tannery whose solvent-handling practices eventually resulted in the contamination of an underground aquifer used for municipal supply purposes by the Cam-

---

32 *Public Authorities Protection Act*, RSO 1990, c P-38; *Proceedings Against the Crown Act*, RSO 1990, c P-27; *Berendsen v The Queen*, 2001 SCC 55.
33 (1866), LR 1 Ex 265, confirmed by (1868), LR 3 HL 330.
34 *Rickards v Lothian*, [1913] AC 263 at 280 (PC).
35 For example, *Danku v Fort Frances (Town)* (1976), 14 OR (2d) 285 (Dist Ct).

bridge Water Company.[36] The House of Lords was emphatic in rejecting a lower court finding to the effect that the use and storage of substantial quantities of industrial chemicals was a natural or ordinary use of land in the context of the industrial community in which the tannery was located. Lord Goff remarked:

> Indeed I feel bound to say that the storage of substantial quantities of chemicals on industrial premises should be regarded as an almost classic case of non-natural use; and I find it very difficult to think that it should be thought objectionable to impose strict liability for damage caused in the event of their escape.[37]

More fundamentally, the House of Lords in *Cambridge Water* considered whether it was necessary for the plaintiff to establish foreseeability of harm of the relevant type in a claim under the *Rylands v Fletcher* principle and concluded that this was indeed an essential ingredient of the tort. On the basis that the contamination of water supplies resulting from spilled chemicals travelling a significant distance underground was not foreseeable during the period (pre-1976) when the defendants were using the solvents in question, the tannery escaped liability.

The requirements and implications of *Rylands v Fletcher* were extensively discussed in the Ontario Court of Appeal decision in *Smith v Inco*, a case arising from nickel oxide emissions from a refinery in Port Colborne between 1918 and 1984. With reference to the nature of industrial activity in this instance, the court stated:

> Any industrial activity, and perhaps even more so a refinery, certainly carries with it the potential to do significant damage to surrounding properties if something goes awry. The claimants did not, however, . . . demonstrate that Inco's operation of its refinery for over 60 years presented "an exceptionally dangerous or mischievous thing" or that the circumstances were "extraordinary or unusual." To the contrary, the evidence suggests that Inco operated a refinery in a heavily industrialized part of the city in a manner that was ordinary and usual and did not create risks beyond those incidental to virtually any industrial operation. In our view, the claimants failed to establish that Inco's operation of its refinery was a non-natural use of its property.[38]

---

36   *Cambridge Water Co Ltd v Eastern Counties Leather Plc*, [1994] 2 AC 264 (HL).
37   *Ibid* at 309.
38   *Smith v Inco*, above note 3 at para 103.

4) Breach of Statutory Duty

The Supreme Court of Canada in *Canada v Saskatchewan Wheat Pool* discussed the suggestion that breach of statute would in itself constitute the basis of tortious action for which damages might be recoverable. The decision indicated firmly that breach of statutory duty ought not to be regarded as an independent source of liability. Rather, proof of the breach and resulting damages may be evidence of negligence, with the statutory formulation of the duty serving to indicate "a specific, and useful, standard of reasonable conduct."[39] Consistent with this analysis, in *McGeek Enterprises v Shell Canada*, an Ontario court found that the defendant's breach of the provincial *Gasoline Handling Act* was insufficient to ground liability in negligence.[40]

5) Trespass

Intentional and direct entry onto another person's land, or placing or allowing some substance or material onto that land, may constitute a trespass in the absence of such lawful justification or excuse as consent or licence, necessity, or statutory authorization. Thus, in *Hole v Chard Union*,[41] defendants committed a trespass by discharging refuse and sewage into a stream passing directly through the plaintiff's property. The requirement of directness, however, has sometimes precluded trespass claims of an environmental nature when substances—sprayed insecticides, for example—have drifted onto plaintiffs' lands. Trespass, being actionable per se without proof of damage, entitles the plaintiff to recover nominal or general damages for the fact of the interference or to injunctive relief, which may be particularly appropriate in the case of a continuing trespass. Arguments concerning the rejuvenation or extension of this historic cause of action have recently emerged in connection with the use of genetically modified organisms, especially in western Canada.[42]

---

39 *Canada v Saskatchewan Wheat Pool*, [1983] 1 SCR 205 at 228. Now see *Ingles v Tutkaluk Construction Ltd*, [2000] 1 SCR 298. As underlined by the Supreme Court of Canada, "the proper remedy for breach of statutory duty by a public authority, traditionally viewed, is judicial review for invalidity": *Holland v Saskatchewan*, above note 31 at para 9.

40 *McGeek Enterprises v Shell Canada* (1991), 6 OR (3d) 216 (Gen Div).

41 [1894] 1 Ch 293 (CA).

42 *Monsanto Canada Inc v Schmeiser*, [2004] 1 SCR 902; *Hoffman v Monsanto Canada Inc*, 2005 SKQB 225, aff'd (2007), 28 CELR (3d) 165 (Sask CA).

6) Riparian Rights

Landowners whose property borders a natural watercourse are entitled under the doctrine of riparian rights to take action to preserve the natural quantity and quality of the adjacent water subject to the reasonable use of other riparians. The principle was articulated in *John Young v Bankier Distillery Co*, where Lord MacNaghten explained that a riparian owner is "entitled to the water of his stream, in its natural flow, without sensible diminution or increase and without sensible alteration in its character or quality."[43]

Defendants have sometimes asserted the importance, reasonableness, or utility of the activity which an aggrieved riparian seeks to enjoin. In *McKie v KVP Co*, where objection was taken to pollution from a pulp mill, arguments of this kind were advanced and emphatically rejected by the trial judge, who awarded damages and an injunction against the defendant company: "Some evidence was given on behalf of the defendant to show the importance of its business in the community, and that it carried it on in a proper manner. Neither of these elements is to be taken into consideration in a case of this character, nor are the economic necessities of the defendant relevant to be considered."[44] In the aftermath of the company's final appeal to the Supreme Court of Canada, however, the Ontario legislature dissolved the injunction, confining the riparian plaintiffs to damages alone.[45]

B. ASSESSING THE COMMON LAW

As forums for dealing with private claims concerning the environment, the courts offer all the attractions regularly associated with formal adversarial procedures. Litigation initiated by aggrieved individuals defending property-based interests has strong advocates.[46] One experienced observer has expressed some of the attractions this way:

> The injured person can initiate action on his own, without the need to rely on any government agency to protect his interest. He controls the choice of lawyers, medical and other scientific experts to assist him. The parties themselves or their legal advisors maintain control

---

43   [1893] AC 691 at 698 (HL).
44   *McKie v KVP Co*, [1948] OR 398 at 410 (HCJ).
45   *The KVP Company Limited Act, 1950*, SO 1950, c 33.
46   E Brubaker, *Property Rights in the Defence of Nature* (London: Earthscan Publications, 1995).

over the timing and choice of strategies through every stage of the negotiations. Except in the case of infants and certain persons deemed by law to be incapable of making informed judgments without assistance, the decision of the plaintiff whether to accept a settlement offer need not be approved by any bureaucracy. Moreover, if the matter goes to trial, it is decided by an independent judiciary designed, at least in theory, to be above political or partisan pressures, and whose decisions are subject to appeal to higher courts.[47]

Yet those who have experienced such litigation, and other commentators, including presiding judges, have identified important limitations in the ability of traditional courts to resolve modern environmental controversies in a fully satisfactory and conclusive manner.

The constraints take several forms. Some are procedural in nature. They concern such questions as who is eligible to proceed with this litigation; or, as it is ordinarily expressed, does the would-be plaintiff have standing? Other obstacles to private litigation include the expense associated with lengthy and often complex proceedings involving expert witnesses and potential liability for legal costs.[48] Certain difficulties also arise in connection with the burden of proof, notably in situations where scientific evidence is inconclusive or where expert opinion is divided. Cases of this kind are further complicated by the long latency periods sometimes required for actual damage to appear from exposure to toxic substances.[49] Additional reservations are expressed on occasion about remedial constraints: damages will often be difficult to calculate and are widely considered an inadequate form of compensation where serious environmental harm has taken place. Moreover, with the exception of injunctive relief, judicial remedies generally come into play after the damage has occurred, a situation that is immensely frustrating to those who are anxious to emphasize preventive approaches to environmental problems.

---

47   J Swaigen, "The Role of the Civil Courts in Resolving Risk and Uncertainty in Environmental Law" (1991) 1 J Envtl L & Prac 199 at 208.

48   *Canadian Environmental Law Assn v Canada (Minister of the Environment)* (1999), 34 CELR (NS) 159 (FCA). See also C Tollefson, "When the Public Interest Loses: The Liability of Public Interest Litigants for Adverse Costs Awards" (1995) 29 UBC L Rev 303; C McCool, "Costs in Public Interest Litigation: A Comment on Professor Tollefson's Article, 'When the Public Interest Loses'" (1996) 30 UBC L Rev 309; C Tollefson, D Gilliland, & J DeMarco, "Towards a Costs Jurisprudence in Public Interest Litigation" (2004) 83 Can Bar Rev 473.

49   To some degree difficulty of this nature may be alleviated by statute. See, for example, *Limitations Act*, SO 2002, c 24, Sched B, s 17: "There is no limitation period in respect of an environmental claim that has not been discovered."

As environmental law overall evolves to reflect such emerging principles as sustainability, pollution prevention, polluter pay, and precaution, the common law will come under close scrutiny for its congruence and ability to keep pace. That courts are aware of a series of new challenges on the common law horizon has recently been acknowledged by the Supreme Court of Canada where Binnie J remarked in *British Columbia v Canadian Forest Products Ltd*:

> It seems to me there is no legal barrier to the Crown suing for compensation as well as injunctive relief in a proper case on account of public nuisance, or negligence causing environmental damage to public lands, and perhaps other torts such as trespass, but there are clearly important and novel policy questions raised by such actions. These include the Crown's potential liability for inactivity in the face of threats to the environment, the existence or non-existence of enforceable fiduciary duties owed to the public by the Crown in that regard, the limits to the role and function and remedies available to governments taking action on account of activity harmful to public enjoyment of public resources, and the spectre of imposing on private interests an indeterminate liability for an indeterminate amount of money for ecological or environmental damage.[50]

There have been indications, however, of some legislative willingness to address some of the uncertainties and limitations of the common law framework in the environmental context.

C. STATUTORY CIVIL LIABILITIES

A number of recent legislative measures have established new statutory civil liabilities for environmental damage. For example, the Alberta *Environmental Protection and Enhancement Act* created a civil cause of action for the benefit of any person who suffered loss or damage as a result of conduct constituting an offence for which the defendant was convicted under the Act.[51] Although the plaintiff is still required to proceed with the action in a court of competent jurisdiction, the effect of the statute is to relieve plaintiffs of the obligation to show that the defendant owed them a duty of care, or of establishing the relevant standard of care which the defendant failed to meet. In cases of conduct contravening the *AEPEA*, the Act also offers injunctive relief to

---

50   *British Columbia v Canadian Forest Products Ltd*, 2004 SCC 38 at para 81.
51   RSA 2000, c E-12, s 219 [*AEPEA*].

"[a]ny person who has suffered, is suffering or is about to suffer loss or damage."[52]

In a somewhat similar manner, the Ontario *Environmental Bill of Rights, 1993* resolves the standing problem in public nuisance claims:

No person who has suffered or may suffer a direct economic loss or direct personal injury as a result of a public nuisance that caused harm to the environment shall be barred from bringing an action without the consent of the Attorney General in respect of the loss or injury only because the person has suffered or may suffer direct economic loss or direct personal injury of the same kind or to the same degree as other persons.[53]

Other statutory liabilities for losses and the costs of preventing or cleaning up damage arising in the context of spills are described in Chapter 10.

D. CLASS ACTION LEGISLATION

Since environmental damage frequently entails injury to numerous parties or potential plaintiffs, provisions to facilitate proceedings on behalf of multiple victims are of considerable importance. In addition to rules of procedure allowing for "representative" actions and the inherent jurisdiction of the courts relating to their proceedings, considerable attention has been directed to legislation establishing the framework for class actions.[54]

In *Comité d'environnement de la Baie v Société d'électrolyse et de chimie Alcan*, the Quebec Court of Appeal, with reference to the province's class action legislation, authorized a class action on behalf of 2,400 property owners seeking some $20 million compensation for damages attributed to particulate emissions from the defendant's operations.[55] The court recognized the existence of distinctions between various members of the applicant class in relation to exposure and the extent of damages, but it found sufficient common ground in relation to technical evidence and the standard of care to justify permitting an action

---

52   *Ibid*, s 225. See also *Canadian Environmental Protection Act, 1999*, SC 1999, c 33, ss 39–41.
53   *Environmental Bill of Rights, 1993*, SO 1993, c 28, s 103(1).
54   *Class Proceedings Act*, SO 1992, c 6; *Class Proceedings Act*, RSBC 1996, c 50; *Class Actions Act*, SS 2001, c C-12.01; *Class Proceedings Act*, SNS 2007, c 28; *Western Canadian Shopping Centres Inc v Dutton*, 2001 SCC 46.
55   [1990] RJQ 655.

which, given the comparatively small size of individual losses, would not otherwise have proceeded. As the court expressed its assessment of the relevant considerations:

> The class action recourse seems to me a particularly useful recourse in appropriate cases of environmental damage. Air and water pollution rarely affect just one individual or one piece of property. They often cause harm to many individuals over a large geographic area. The issues involved may be similar in each claim but they may be complex and expensive to litigate, while the amount involved in each case may be relatively modest. The class action, in these cases, seems an obvious means for dealing with claims for compensation for the harm done when compared to numerous individual law suits, each raising the same issues of fact and law.[56]

Despite this sympathetic account of the objectives of environmental class actions, certification has generally not been as readily available in other jurisdictions: applicants for certification under class proceedings legislation must satisfy all necessary preconditions in order to succeed in having the class of litigants recognized. In *Kwicksutaineuk/Ah-Kwa-Mish First Nation v BC (Minister of Agriculture and Lands)*, class certification was denied to a group described as "all aboriginal collectives who have or assert constitutionally protected aboriginal and/or treaty rights to fish wild salmon" in an area where aquaculture operations had been authorized.[57]

Section 5 of Ontario's statute of class proceedings indicates that a class action shall be certified where a class proceeding would be the *preferable* means to resolve *common issues* on behalf of an *identifiable class of persons* relating to a cause of action disclosed in the pleadings by a qualified plaintiff or defendant. Those experienced in environmental class action litigation suggest that certification is generally more easily obtained in the context of a discrete environmental incident rather than in relation to ongoing pollution. In *Cotter v Levy*, although the composition of the class of appropriate plaintiffs was contested, the Plastimet fire in Hamilton was an event well suited to certification.[58] On the other hand, in *Hollick v Metro Toronto*, the circumstances proved to be more problematic for the would-be plaintiffs. In *Hollick*, the certification application was made on behalf of roughly 30,000 persons who might have been affected over an extended period of years by exposure

---

56 *Ibid* at 660. For a recent Quebec certification decision, see *Carrier c Québec (Procureur général)*, 2011 QCCA 1231.

57 2012 BCCA 193 at para 1.

58 *Cotter v Levy*, [2000] OJ No 1086 (SCJ).

to noxious fumes and gases associated with the City of Toronto's Keele Valley landfill site. After initial success on the certification application, the plaintiffs suffered reversal in the divisional court which held that there was no identifiable class of persons and in the Court of Appeal where a majority of the court found "no common issue to justify the certification of a class action because the individuals' lives have been affected, or not affected, in a different manner and degree." On further appeal, the Supreme Court of Canada was satisfied as to the existence of an identifiable class and as to the existence of common issues. It concluded, however, that a class action was not the *preferable* procedure for the resolution of those issues.

The preferability analysis set out by the court had three aspects relating to the principal advantages of class actions: economical use of judicial resources, improved access to justice, and the potential to encourage modification of the tortfeasor's behaviour. Despite its conclusion that these goals would not be achieved by certification of the *Hollick* class action, the courts emphasized that environmental class actions are not necessarily precluded by the analysis. Each application for certification must be tested on its own facts.[59] Another major application immediately presented an opportunity for such further testing.

In *Pearson v Inco Ltd*, claims for physical, emotional, property, and business damages were brought against several defendants by a large group of residents of Port Colborne, Ontario where a nickel refinery operated for many years. In addressing the application for certification of the proceedings as a class action, Justice Nordheimer highlighted the complexities of the case. He anticipated that the matter would:

inevitably disintegrate into the need for thousands of individual trials with potentially tens, if not hundreds, of thousands of individual issues to be resolved. Consequent on that reality, will be the need for examinations for discovery of each and every one of the 20,000 members of the proposed class. In an action for damages arising from contamination, it is necessary to determine the exposure of each of the claimants to the contaminants. There is also a need to know the individual claimant's health history and their personal habits as they would relate to possible exposure to the contaminants. Further compounding the complexity of such a claim in this case is that there is considerable variation in contaminant levels across the area of concern.

---

59   *Hollick v Metro Toronto (Municipality)* (1999), 32 CELR (NS) 1 (Ont CA), aff'd [2001] SCJ No 67.

At the Ontario Court of Appeal, a more limited group of Port Colborne residents succeeded in obtaining certification to pursue the class action in relation to a more narrowly-circumscribed common issue associated with losses to property values.[60] The successful defendant was eventually awarded reduced payment of its substantial costs claim with payment assessed against the Class Proceedings Fund administered by the Law Foundation of Ontario.[61]

Initiatives intended to facilitate litigation on behalf of classes or groups of victims of environmental harm continue in provinces with and without class action legislation.[62]

FURTHER READINGS

BELANGER, M, *Développement jurisprudentiel au Québec en matière de recours collectifs environnementaux* (2010) Riseo 2010-3, online: www.riseo.fr/IMG/pdf/Riseo_2010-3_Observation_1.pdf.

BRANCH, W, *Class Actions in Canada*, loose-leaf (Aurora, ON: Canada Law Book, 2005–)

DeMARCO, J, D Gilliland, & C Tollefson, "Towards a Public Interest Costs Jurisprudence" (2004) 83 Can Bar Rev 473

FAIETA, MD, *et al*, *Environmental Harm: Civil Actions and Compensation* (Toronto: Butterworths, 1996)

FAIETA, MD, "Civil Liability for Environmental Torts" (2004) Ann Rev. Civil Lit 21-58

KALMAKOFF, JJ, "'The Right to Farm': A Survey of Farm Practices Protection Legislation in Canada" (1999) 62 Sask L Rev 225

---

60 *Pearson v Inco Ltd*, [2005] OJ No. 4918 (CA), leave to appeal to SCC refused, [2006] SCCA No 1. For discussion of the results of the litigation, reconstituted as *Smith v Inco*, see above notes 3 and 14.

61 *Smith v Inco Ltd*, 2012 ONSC 5094.

62 *Windsor v Canadian Pacific Railway*, 2006 ABQB 348; *Paron v Alberta (Environmental Protection)*, 2006 ABQB 375; *Ring v Canada (Attorney General)*, 2010 NLCA 20; *MacQueen v Ispat Sidbec Inc*, 2006 NSSC 208. For discussion of Saskatchewan's class action legislation, see M. Olszynski, "*Hoffman v Monsanto Canada Inc*: Looking for a Generous Approach to the Elephant in the Garden" (2005) 16 J Envtl L & Prac 53. See also H McLeod-Kilmurray, "*Hoffman v Monsanto*: Courts, Class Actions, and Perceptions of the Problem of GM Drift" (2007) 27(3) Bulletin of Science, Technology & Society 188 at 197–98.

MCLAREN, JPS, "The Common Law Nuisance Actions and the Environmental Battle: Well-Tempered Swords or Broken Reeds?" (1972) 10 Osgoode Hall LJ 513

MCLEOD-KILMURRAY, H, "*Hollick* and Environmental Class Actions: Putting the Substance into Class Action Procedure" (2002–3) 34 Ottawa L.R. 263

———, "Proceeding With (Pre)Caution: Environmental Principles as Interpretive Tools in Applications For Pre-trial Injunctions" (2009) 32 Dal LJ 295

NADON, O, "Civil Liability Underlying Environmental Risk-Related Activities in Quebec" (1998) 24 CELR (NS) 141

ONTARIO, LAW REFORM COMMISSION, *Report on the Law of Standing* (Toronto: Ontario Law Reform Commission, 1989)

TOLLEFSON, C, "Costs and the Public Interest Litigant: *Okanagan Indian Band* and Beyond" (2006) 19 Can J Admin L & Prac 39

WILDSMITH, BH, "Of Herbicides and Human Kind: Palmer's Common Law Lessons" (1986) 24 Osgoode Hall LJ 161

CHAPTER 6

ENVIRONMENTAL REGULATIONS AND APPROVALS

The prevalence of environmental regulations is consistent with a general tendency described by Justice Cory, formerly of the Supreme Court of Canada:

> Regulatory measures are the primary mechanisms employed by governments in Canada to implement public policy objectives . . . . It is difficult to think of an aspect of our lives that is not regulated for our benefit and for the protection of society as a whole. From cradle to grave, we are protected by regulations; they apply to the doctors attending our entry into this world and to the morticians present at our departure . . . . The more complex the activity, the greater the need for and the greater our reliance upon regulation and its enforcement.[1]

Although critics might dispute Justice Cory's concluding assertion, an explanation along the lines he sets out might well be offered to account for the extensive body of regulations that has been formulated to protect the environment from various forms of degradation.

The basic purposes of an environmental protection regime are typically embodied in statutory schemes and in statements of official policy. In Canada actual performance requirements are generally established by regulation or administrative guidelines. This chapter addresses some of the issues associated with designing such standards before turning to the relationship between standards and the permits

---

1   *R v Wholesale Travel Group Inc*, [1991] 3 SCR 154 at 220–22.

or approvals usually required by those whose operations entail impacts on or discharges into the natural environment of air, land, and water.

A. STANDARD-SETTING

1) Introduction

Standard-setting in the environmental context has been described as "the process of deciding how much pollution will be allowed to enter the environment each year."[2] Yet it is important to appreciate that pollution standards are associated—explicitly or implicitly—with underlying goals relating to environmental quality. Standards are technical instruments intended to promote or maintain certain objectives, whether those objectives are expressed in terms of environmental quality and human health, biological diversity, economic development and resource productivity, sustainability, or something else. Thus, an important relationship exists between environmental principles such as those described in Chapter 1, and legislative and regulatory practice. By way of example, if sustainability is an intended policy outcome, it will be appropriate to incorporate measures or indicators for assessing sustainability in regulatory standards; or, in situations involving certain health risks, it may be appropriate to incorporate the precautionary principle into the standard-setting process.

Standards may be formulated in various ways, some directed at allowable emission levels (emission standards), others based on actual measurements of environmental quality in the relevant media, whether air, water, or land (ambient-quality standards), or possibly in terms of operational practices or design and technology requirements (design standards).[3]

Each of these approaches has a contribution to make, although their comparative merits are subject to heated discussion. Advocates of emission standards or limits applicable to particular industrial operations and other dischargers of pollutants point to their obvious administrative and legal convenience. Monitoring is comparatively straightforward and violators are far more readily identifiable than in the case of environmental quality objectives where the relationship between observed environmental deterioration and any specific source

---

2   D Macdonald, *The Politics of Pollution* (Toronto: McClelland & Stewart, 1991) at 159.

3   For a valuable general commentary, see R Macrory, *Regulation, Enforcement and Governance in Environmental Law* (Oxford: Hart Publishing, 2010) c 9.

or sources among hundreds of discharges is rarely so clear. Yet ambient-quality standards have the virtue of maintaining the regulatory focus on overall results whereas emission limits (especially those formulated in terms of effluent concentrations or production ratios) have sometimes failed to address the fundamental issue of levels of overall pollution that are acceptable in light of broader goals such as sustainability or biodiversity.[4] In other words, environmental deterioration may continue to occur even though dischargers are meeting emission standards. Design standards may appear attractive from business and administrative perspectives in that, once the appropriate technology or process has been identified, one can readily determine whether it has been adopted or implemented. Critics of technology standards, however, lament the separation of the manner of environmental protection from results, especially in areas where the environmental risk is severe but technical performance standards are bounded by such concepts as "practicable" or "economically achievable." From the perspective of economic efficiency, other observers regard technology-based standards as excessively costly in comparison with the alternatives that might be developed if industry were given economic incentives to innovate.[5]

The Canadian tendency has been to control pollutant discharges on the basis of emission standards or limits for specified substances. Limits may ultimately be expressed in various ways; they may be stated, for example, in terms of effluent concentrations or in terms of linkages to production levels. Alternatively, absolute discharge levels may be established on daily, seasonal, or annual bases. A zero-discharge standard or even outright bans on the use of particular toxic substances are not unknown, and may become more common as further evidence accumulates to demonstrate that the assumption that pollutants are gradually rendered harmless through diffusion is unreliable.[6]

---

4   Macdonald, above note 2; S Boehmer-Christiansen, "Environmental Quality Objectives Versus Uniform Emission Standards" in D Freestone & T Ijlstra, eds, *The North Sea: Perspectives on Regional Environmental Co-operation* (London: Graham and Trotman, 1990) c 12. The differences between ambient quality standards and emission limits correspond in some respects to the debate between proponents of overall emission reductions and intensity targets in relation to greenhouse gases.

5   See Chapter 17.

6   For a detailed examination of standard-setting procedure in relation to pesticides, see "The Standard Setting Framework" in Kathleen Cooper, *et al*, *Environmental Standard Setting and Children's Health* (Canadian Environmental Law Association and the Ontario College of Family Physicians, Environmental Health Committee, May 2000) c 3, online: www.cela.ca/publications/cardfile. shtml?x=1114.

Canadian practice has been typical of many jurisdictions in that discharge standards often lack clear and explicit linkages to overall objectives for environmental quality or to the condition of the receiving medium. However, certain quality objectives do exist for air and water. These can serve as benchmarks or background signals for those responsible for the detailed operation of the regulatory and approvals regime, triggering responses or influencing decisions even if they are not directly enforceable.

As described by the Canadian Council of Ministers of the Environment (CCME), it is possible for Canada-wide standards (CWS) to include qualitative or quantitative standards, guidelines, objectives, and criteria relating to health and environmental protection. "CWSs will include a numeric limit (for example, ambient discharge, or product standard), a commitment and timetable for attainment, a list of preliminary actions to attain the standard, and a framework for reporting to the public."[7] The standards themselves lack legal force and may be implemented in each jurisdiction according to that jurisdiction's own preferences.

2) Air

In relation to air, the federal government has for some time produced a set of non-binding *Ambient Air Quality Objectives* for several key pollutants, including suspended particulate matter. For each of the designated pollutants, three concentration levels were established on an annual, daily, and hourly basis. The *tolerable* level suggested a threshold at which a response is required in the interests of public health. The *acceptable* level (roughly approximating WHO guidelines) indicated adequate protection against environmental and health effects. The *desirable* level represents a long-term goal for air-quality improvement.[8] As expressed by one group of observers, "a level of pollution may be considered unacceptable, but still tolerable, or it may be acceptable, but better air quality would be desirable."[9]

In addition to such objectives for ambient air quality at sites throughout Canada, and as discussed in connection with the international context, targets were established under various international

---

7   Canada-wide Standards, CCME, online: www.ccme.ca/ourwork/environment.
     html?category_id=108.

8   *Ambient Air Quality Objectives*, C Gaz 1989, I.3642 ; *National Ambient Air Objectives for Particulate Matter* (1998).

9   D Estrin & J Swaigen, *Environment on Trial*, 3d ed (Toronto: Emond Montgomery, 1993) at 481.

agreements for reductions in total emissions of sulphur, NOx, VOCs, and heavy metals. At the provincial level, regulations or guidelines concerning air quality[10] and regulations covering emissions elaborate the regime in considerable detail.[11]

In October 2012, federal, provincial, and territorial ministers of the environment agreed at meetings of the CCME to adopt a new Air Quality Management System (AQMS). The AQMS will build upon existing initiatives and will be established at the federal level as objectives pursuant to *CEPA 1999* sections 54 and 55. The AQMS incorporates additional tools to safeguard air quality in the interests of public health and environmental protection. Proposed new measures include: Canadian Ambient Air Quality Standards for particulate matter and ozone with others to follow in respect of sulphur dioxide and nitrogen dioxide; base-level industrial emission requirements for major industrial sectors; an air zone management framework; the designation of regional air sheds to facilitate responses to cross-border pollution; and an inter-governmental working group to address emissions from transportation.[12]

3) Water

In relation to surface water quality, objectives have been formulated through planning procedures undertaken by the federal and provincial governments. These are often regional in scope or oriented around a particular drainage area such as the Fraser River or the St. Lawrence.

In 1986 Ontario introduced a Municipal/Industrial Strategy for Abatement (MISA), an initiative that has been described as the "keystone" of that province's attempts to control the discharge of contaminants into surface waters.[13] MISA's ultimate objective was described as the "virtual elimination" of persistent toxic contaminants (includ-

---

10   For a province by province comparison of standards for selected contaminants, see Alberta Environmental Protection, *A Comparison of Alberta's Environmental Standards* (March 1999).

11   RRO 1990, Reg 346 (General—Air Pollution) was replaced by O Reg 419/05 "Air Pollution—Local Air Quality." The new air quality regulation whose sectoral implementation is to be phased in over a fifteen-year period brings Ontario practice closer to air quality assessment methodologies developed by the US Environmental Protection Agency. Further changes are intended to increase compatibility between provincial monitoring and reporting requirements under O Reg 127/01 and the federal National Pollutant Release Inventory. See Chapter 18.

12   Online: www.ccme.ca/ourwork/air.html?category_id=146.

13   Ontario, Ministry of the Environment, *Municipal/Industrial Strategy for Abatement (MISA): A Policy and Program Statement of the Government of Ontario on*

ing toxic metals and toxic organics) from all discharges into Ontario's waterways.

Significantly, MISA approached the problems of analysis and regulation by focusing on municipalities and several industrial sectors: electric power, inorganic chemicals, iron and steel manufacturing, metal casting, mines, petroleum refining, pulp and paper, and organic chemical manufacturing. Industrial operations in each of the designated sectors were first required to monitor their discharges of a specified list of contaminants. Detailed abatement regulations have been based on the monitoring results.[14] In view of the length of time since the introduction of the MISA program, observers have begun to call for review and revision.

Significant water initiatives have also been introduced elsewhere. Alberta, following comprehensive legislative reform of licensing arrangements, has continued to address water quality and allocation issues through the provincial Water for Life program.[15] Manitoba reorganized administrative arrangements concerning a wide range of water-related governmental responsibilities by establishing a ministry of Water Stewardship.[16] Quebec has pursued an extensive series of reforms relating to water basin management, water rights, and quality. Since 2008 British Columbia has been engaged in modernizing the *Water Act*[17] with a view to new legislation on water sustainability.[18] This process is ongoing.

Although this text offers no discussion of water allocation issues, it should be noted that issues of water distribution and supply are of great concern across the country.[19]

Controlling Municipal and Industrial Discharges into Surface Waters (Toronto: Ministry of the Environment, 1986).

14 Petroleum refining: O Reg 537/93; pulp and paper: O Reg 760/93; industrial minerals: O Reg 561/94; metal casting: O Reg 562/94; metal mining: O Reg 560/94; electric power generation: O Reg 215/95; organic chemical manufacturing: O Reg 63/95; inorganic chemicals: O Reg 64/95; iron and steel manufacturing: O Reg 214/95.

15 *Water Act*, RSA 2000, c W-3; www.waterforlife.gov.ab.ca; JO Saunders, "Institutional Relationships and Alberta's *Water for Life* Strategy" (Calgary: Canadian Institute of Resources Law, Occasional Paper 32, 2010).

16 *The Water Protection Act*, CCSM c W65.

17 RSBC 1996, c 483.

18 Online: www.livingwatersmart.ca/water-act.

19 M Valiante, "The Great Lakes Charter Annex, 2001" (2003) 13 J Envtl L & Prac. 47; A Kwasniak, "Quenching Instream Thirst: A Role for Water Trusts in the Prairie Provinces" (2006) 16 J Envtl L & Prac 211; N Bankes & A Kwasniak, "The St. Mary's Irrigation District Licence Amendment Decision" (2005) 16 J Envtl L & Prac 1; DW Schindler and WF Donahue, "An impending water crisis

4) Drinking Water

Drinking water supplies in Canada are drawn from both surface and groundwater sources, demonstrating vital connections between environmental protection and human health. Illnesses and tragic deaths as well as other indications of contamination have resulted in greater public attention to issues surrounding drinking water quality.[20]

Municipal waterworks provide local water treatment and distribution services within an overall framework established at the provincial level. In addition to matters relating to the administration and financing of waterworks and other operational considerations including technical and staffing requirements for different types and sizes of facilities, drinking water quality standards may also be prescribed. *Guidelines for Canadian Drinking Water Quality*, formulated and revised through the ongoing deliberations of federal and provincial specialists, set out relevant parameters. Several provinces have incorporated the essence of these guidelines into provincial regulations.[21]

In the aftermath of the Walkerton, Ontario, and North Battleford, Saskatchewan incidents, policy reviews were conducted across the country[22] often leading to legislative or regulatory reforms intended to

---

in Canada's western prairie provinces," online: www.pnas.org/cgi/doi/10.1073/pnas.0601568103.

20 Background or issue papers prepared for the Walkerton Inquiry provide a comprehensive overview of legal, constitutional, technical, and social aspects of the drinking water supply system, largely with reference to Ontario in a comparative context. See online: www.archives.gov.on.ca/en/e_records/walkerton/part2info/commissuepapers/index.html.

21 *Drinking Water Protection Regulation*, BC Reg 200/2003, as amended by BC Reg 300/2004, 352/2005; *Potable Water Regulation*, A Reg 277/2003; *Regulation respecting the quality of drinking water*, RRQ c Q-2, r 40; *Potable Water Regulation-Clean Water Act*, NB Reg 93-203; *Safe Drinking Water Act, 2002*, SO 2002, c 32 and *Ontario Drinking Water Quality Standards*, O Reg 169/03; *Water Regulations, 2002*, RRS, c.E-10.21, Reg 1; *Drinking Water Safety Regulation*, Man Reg 40/2007; *Drinking Water and Wastewater Facility Operating Regulations*, PEI Reg EC710/04; *Water and Wastewater Facilities and Public Drinking Water Supplies Regulations*, NS Reg 186/2005.

22 Alberta, *Water for Life: Alberta's Strategy for Sustainability* (Edmonton: Alberta Environment, 2003); British Columbia, *A Water Conservation Strategy for British Columbia* (Victoria: Ministry of the Environment, 1999); Newfoundland and Labrador, *Source to Tap: Water Supplies in Newfoundland and Labrador* (St John's: Newfoundland & Labrador Department of Environment, 2001); Nova Scotia, *A Drinking Water Strategy for Nova Scotia* (Halifax: Ministry of the Environment & Labour, 2002); Northwest Territories, *Managing Drinking Water Quality in the Northwest Territories* (Yellowknife: Policy, Planning and Evaluation, 2003).

safeguard sources of drinking water supply.[23] Such initiatives form part of a multi-barrier or source-to-tap approach to drinking water safety.

Particular concern has been expressed about the need for an enhanced legal framework applicable to drinking water safety in First Nations communities. This issue remains unresolved despite substantial financial investment, policy analysis, and legislative proposals.[24]

B. PERMITS, LICENSING, AND APPROVALS

Depending on the nature and scope of a proposed activity, environmental licences, permits, or approvals will be required as a precondition to development or operations. Such authorizations provide relief from the blanket prohibitions against harmful discharges that are frequently found in basic environmental legislation. In actual operational situations the permitting process therefore plays an important role in implementing or elaborating general standards set out in objectives or embodied in regulations.

In Ontario, several environmental statutes deal with permit requirements, but the *Environmental Protection Act* is illustrative:

> No person shall, except under and in accordance with a certificate of approval issued by the Director,
>
> (a) construct, alter, extend or replace any plant, structure, equipment, apparatus, mechanism or thing that may discharge or from which may be discharged a contaminant into any part of the natural environment other than water; or
>
> (b) alter a process or rate of production with the result that a contaminant may be discharged into any part of the natural environment other than water or the rate or manner of discharge of a contaminant into any part of the natural environment other than water may be altered.[25]

Through the approvals process, each of the relevant environmental ministries seeks to ensure compliance with applicable environmental legislation, regulation, policies, and guidelines. "At least in theory," one

23 *Drinking Water Protection Act*, SBC 2001, c 9; *Clean Water Act*, SO 2006, c 22; *Regulation respecting the quality of drinking water*, RRQ c Q-2, r 18.1.1.

24 Standing Senate Committee on Aboriginal Peoples, *Safe Drinking Water for First Nations* (May 2007), online: www.parl.gc.ca/Content/SEN/Committee/391/abor/rep/rep08jun07-e.htm; Bill S-8, *An Act respecting the safety of drinking water on First Nation lands*, 1st Sess, 41st Parl, 2012.

25 *Environmental Protection Act*, RSO 1990, c E.19, s 9 [*OEPA*].

experienced commentator has explained, "the system is intended to en-sure that activities which discharge potential contaminants into the air, water or onto the land, are subject to technical scrutiny to ensure that pollution controls are utilized and contamination of the environment minimized."[26] It must be emphasized, however, that to a considerable degree it is the terms and conditions attached to individual approvals which establish the detailed legal requirements for operations. The de-tails of the licensing processes vary depending upon the circumstances. But applications accompanied by supporting documentation will gen-erally proceed through stages of technical review leading to a draft ap-proval or certificate accompanied by a series of conditions, including, for example, qualifications for personnel, or provision of emergency response equipment. Conditions attached to approvals may deal with various aspects of the applicant's site and operations. Some will address administrative considerations such as entry and inspection, the disclo-sure of information, reporting, and monitoring. Operating standards detailing authorized emission levels will be set and may be accompan-ied by a description of actions to be taken in the event that they are exceeded.

The scope of matters to be addressed in conditions accompanying an approval is established initially by legislation or regulation. A per-mit under British Columbia's *Environmental Management Act* illustrates how the authorization process may be used to impose specific oper-ational requirements on applicants:

> A director may issue a permit authorizing the introduction of waste into the environment subject to requirements for the protection of the environment that the director considers advisable and, without limit-ing that power, may do one or more of the following in the permit:
>
> (a) require the permittee to repair, alter, remove, improve or add to works or to construct new works and to submit plans and speci-fications for works specified in the permit;
>
> (b) require the permittee to give security in the amount and form and subject to conditions the director specifies;
>
> (c) require the permittee to monitor, in the manner specified by the director, the waste, the method of handling, treating, trans-porting, discharging and storing the waste and the places and things that the director considers will be affected by the dis-

---

26   RM Fishlock, "Orders and Approvals of the Ontario Ministry of the Environ-ment" (Paper presented to Canadian Bar Association—Ontario, 1991 Institute of Continuing Legal Education, *Environmental Law: An Environmental Primer*, 19 January 1991).

charge of the waste or the handling, treatment, transportation or storage of the waste;

(d) require the permittee to conduct studies and to report information specified by the director in the manner specified by the director;

(e) specify procedures for monitoring and analysis, and procedures or requirements respecting the handling, treatment, transportation, discharge or storage of waste that the permittee must fulfill;

(f) require the permittee to recycle certain wastes, and to recover certain reusable resources, including energy potential from wastes.[27]

Statutory authority to require financial assurances in connection with approvals is also common.[28] The assurances may take a variety of forms including cash, letters of credit, or an approved bond. They are intended to relate to specified action in connection with works including "measures appropriate to prevent adverse effects upon and following the cessation or closing of the works."[29] Requirements for pollution-liability insurance coverage may sometimes be included,[30] together with other financial terms.[31]

As is commonly the case, Alberta's EPEA appears to rely heavily on regulations to establish the range of issues that may be expected in an approval.[32] However, extensive authority is regularly conferred on the senior official responsible for decisions about approvals. Thus, the Alberta legislation, in addition to providing for regulations respecting terms and conditions, indicates that the director "may issue an approval subject to any terms and conditions the director considers appropriate" while explicitly stating that such terms and conditions "may be more stringent, but may not be less stringent, than applicable terms and conditions provided for in the regulations."[33] The director or manager, as the case may be, clearly enjoys a substantial grant of discretionary power concerning the issuance of an environmental compliance

---

27 *Environmental Management Act*, SBC 2003, c 53, s 14(1) [*BCEMA*].

28 *OEPA*, above note 25, Part XII. Details on the administration of the financial assurances provisions may be found in *Guideline F-15 Financial Assurance Guideline* (Ontario Ministry of the Environment, June 2011).

29 *OEPA*, above note 25, s 132(1)(c).

30 Environmental liability coverage has rarely been required by the Ontario's Ministry of the Environment as a condition of an approval. MD Faieta, "Liability Insurance for Environmental Contamination in Ontario" (1991) 2 CILR 125 at 127.

31 See also *Environmental Protection and Enhancement Act*, RSA 2000, c E-12 [*AEPEA*].

32 *Ibid*, s 85(1)(a) and 86(1)(a).

33 *Ibid*, s 68(2) & (3).

approval and also in regard to the alteration, revocation, or suspension of such certificates.[34]

The existence of discretion in the environmental regulatory-approvals process is sometimes regarded critically. Some commentators identified the scope of discretion as potentially problematic for companies attempting to negotiate a suitable response where pollution has occurred, while others considered that the absence of legislative precision facilitates corporate evasion of desirable environmental norms.[35] Yet there are reasons for maintaining discretion and for the bargaining and negotiation that accompany its exercise. Such reasons derive from the uncertainties that pervade environmental issues:

> [T]he fisheries officials who drafted legislation that prohibited putting slash, stumps or other debris into water frequented by fish knew very well that this prohibition could not be automatically enforced. To do so would be scientifically and technically unreasonable and politically unacceptable. The difficulties are that it is unclear in what circumstances such debris is harmful to fish (though in some cases it is clearly harmful), it is unclear what alternate technologies are available for avoiding the putting of debris in water if logging and land clearing are to be permitted, and it is impossible to determine if the harm to fish will outweigh the social benefits derived from the logging or clearing land.[36]

Situations of this kind require individualized decision making within the overall legal framework.

Applicants have often experienced frustrating delays in the approvals process. Some of the delays may be attributed to deficiencies contained in applications, and thus might have been avoided by more careful advance preparation on the part of the applicant. However, when a substantial backlog developed in one province, environmental officials acknowledged the existence of inherent delays in the process which have "at times, compromised the competitiveness of businesses."[37] The desire to reduce administrative complexity and delays has prompted recent legislative measures to standardize or elimin-

---

34 *OEPA*, above note 25, s 20.3.

35 H Poch, *Corporate and Municipal Environmental Law* (Toronto: Carswell, 1989) at 161.

36 AR Thompson, *Environmental Regulation in Canada: An Assessment of the Regulatory Process* (Vancouver: Westwater Research Centre, University of British Columbia, 1980) at 35–36.

37 F Carnerie, *The Approval Process: A Regulatory Regime in Transition* (Toronto: Canadian Institute of Environmental Policy, 1992) at 15.

ate the need for certain forms of approvals. Thus, Ontario took steps some years ago to streamline certain approvals and to exempt other activities from ordinary approvals requirements. The activities eligible for one or other of these forms of treatment are activities whose environmental impact was considered to be "predictable and controllable" so long as they are conducted in a manner that is consistent with rules to be set out in regulations (the "permit by rule" model).[38] The attraction of such streamlining where impact is properly classified as "predictable and controllable" or exemptions for activities whose impacts are deemed insignificant should be set against the loss of flexibility in tailoring licence approvals to distinctive local circumstances, and against the risk of cumulative impacts.[39]

Ontario has continued its efforts to streamline applications for environmental compliance approvals through the use of online procedures and sectoral guidance involving an Environmental Activity and Sector Registry.[40] Environmental compliance approvals offer the opportunity of replacing multiple permits with one approval applicable to all activities on a given site. Alberta, also concerned with the potential for regulatory delay and complexity, has proposed a degree of consolidation in the approvals process whereby a new regulator would assume responsibility for approval functions currently distributed between the Energy Resources Conservation Board and the provincial Ministry of Environment and Sustainable Resource Development.[41]

C. APPEAL MECHANISMS AND PUBLIC PARTICIPATION

Decisions with respect to approvals and licences may ordinarily be appealed by the applicant to a senior environment official or to an administrative body with authority to review and amend the initial determination. The composition of appeal bodies will be set out in statutory provisions together with a statement of the powers and duties of

---

38   *Environmental Approvals Improvement Act*, SO 1997, c 7.

39   David McRobert indicates that to the extent some approval requirements are replaced by standardized approvals there will also be a reduction in opportunities for public participation pursuant to the *Environmental Bill of Rights, 1993*. D McRobert, "The Nuts, Bolts and Rest of the Machinery: An Update on Ontario's *Environmental Bill of Rights* and the Work of the Environmental Commissioner" (Insight Information, September 2001) 20–22.

40   O Reg 245/11; O Reg 255/11; O Reg 261/11.

41   Bill 2, *Responsible Energy Development Act*, 1st Sess, 28th Leg, Alberta, 2012–2013.

the appellate institution. Time limits on the filing of appeals will also be specified in legislation or regulations. Basic procedures and such related matters as costs awards will generally be addressed alongside the fundamental issue of the availability of an administrative appeal.[42] In the Quebec case, for example, an unsuccessful applicant for a certificate of authorization under the *Environment Quality Act*[43] is entitled under section 96 of the *EQA* to a process resembling appeal proceedings before the Territory and Environment Division of the Administrative Tribunal of Quebec.

Opportunities for wider public participation in the development of environmental regulations and in decisions concerning permit and licensing approvals have historically been limited.[44] The former case reflects a long-standing assumption about the nature of the legislative process, while the traditional exclusion of the public from deliberations relating to individual permit or licence applications has been premised on the assumption that members of the public are not ordinarily affected by a matter between the applicant and regulatory officials or that public interests, including environmental interests, are adequately represented by such officials.[45]

Developments such as environmental bills of rights and specific statutory requirements for public notice and comment have often, though not universally, increased the scope for public participation in both settings. In Saskatchewan, the *Environmental Management and Protection Act* provides that "[e]xcept in circumstances that are considered by the Lieutenant Governor in Council to be an emergency, the minister shall seek advice and provide a reasonable opportunity for the public to be heard respecting any prescribed regulation or any prescribed amendment to a regulation pursuant to this Act."[46]

---

42   *AEPEA*, above note 31, Part 4; Alta Reg 114/93; *BCEMA*, above note 27, Part 8; *Environment Act*, SNS 1994–95, c 1, Part XIV; *Clean Environment Act*, RSNB 1973, c C-6, s.14; *OEPA*, above note 25, Part XIII; *Canadian Environmental Protection Act, 1999*, SC 1999, c 33, ss 243–27 [*CEPA 1999*]. Not all tribunals are authorized to award costs. See *Ontario (Director, Environmental Protection Act) v Becker Milk Co* (2005), 78 OR (3d) 556 (SCJ).

43   *Environment Quality Act*, RSQ c Q-2 [*EQA*].

44   For background, see JF Castrilli & CC Lax, "Environmental Regulation-Making in Canada: Towards a More Open Process" in J Swaigen, ed, *Environmental Rights in Canada* (Toronto: Butterworths, 1981) 334. *Pim v Ontario (Minister of the Environment)* (1978), 23 OR (2d) 45 (Div Ct).

45   *Sierra Club of Western Canada v British Columbia* (1984), 11 Admin LR 276 (BCSC); *Sea Shepherd Conservation Society v British Columbia* (1984), 55 BCLR 260 (SC).

46   *Environmental Management and Protection Act, 2002*, SS 2002, c E-10.21, s 81(3). A similar provision appears in the *Manitoba Environment Act*, CCSM c E125, s 41(2).

Alberta's *EPEA* also provides opportunities in specified circumstances for persons other than the holder of an approval to participate in appeal proceedings involving decisions of the director, provided that the person is "directly affected by the Director's decision."[47] In *Kostuch v Alberta Environmental Appeal Board*, an environmental advocate sought standing before the board in connection with a decision of the director to extend a previously approved date of commencement for construction of a cement plant in the vicinity of an area she used for recreational pursuits.[48] The decision of the EAB to deny standing was upheld by the Alberta Court of Queen's Bench, following the reasoning of the Court of Appeal in relation to similar language in another statute. The Court of Appeal had stated: "When considered in the context of the regulatory scheme, it is apparent that the right of appeal is confined to persons having a personal rather than a community interest in the matter."[49]

The Alberta Court of Appeal elaborated its approach to the interpretation of "directly affected" in relation to environmental appeals by public interest representatives:

> The use of the modifier "directly" with the word "affected" indicates an intent on the part of the Legislature to distinguish between persons directly affected and indirectly affected. An interpretation that would include any person who has a genuine interest would render the word "directly" meaningless, thus violating fundamental principles of statutory interpretation.[50]

On an exceptional basis, the Ontario *Environmental Bill of Rights, 1993* (*OEBR*) provides an opportunity for public involvement in appeal proceedings where these are otherwise available in relation to certain designated instruments, including statutory permits and other authorizations. Any person resident in Ontario with an interest in the decision on such instruments may, on a timely basis, seek leave to appeal from the relevant appellate body. While the interest necessary to support a leave application under the *OEBR* is therefore broader than the "directly affected" test, the granting of leave to appeal is subject to a severe two-part test. Leave to appeal should be granted only where, in light of relevant law and policy, there is good reason to believe that

---

47   AEPEA, above note 31, s 91(1).
48   *Kostuch v Alberta (Environmental Appeal Board)* (1996), 182 AR 384 (QB).
49   *CUPE Local 30 v WMI Waste Management of Canada Inc* (1996), 34 Admin LR (2d) 172 at 178 (Alta CA).
50   *Friends of the Athabasca Environmental Assn v Alberta (Public Health Advisory & Appeal Board)* (1996), 181 AR 81 at 84 (CA).

the decision was unreasonable and where it appears that significant environmental harm could result from that decision.[51]

In *Re Residents Against Co Pollution Inc*, numerous applications were made under the OEBR for leave to appeal air-emissions and sewage-works approvals issued to Petro Canada in connection with the proposed expansion of the company's Mississauga refinery.[52] Applicants argued variously that the director's decision had not been based on a holistic, ecosystem approach; that guidelines respecting the separation of residential and industrial land had not been followed; that source and ambient air-quality testing were ignored in favour of modelling estimates, and so on, all of which factors were presented as evidence of unreasonableness. In the view of the appeal board, these considerations failed to satisfy the first element of the test for granting leave to appeal. However, the board did accept that procedural irregularities, lack of public notice, and a condition of the air approval concerning the retention of records were such that no director, acting reasonably, would have decided as the director did in this case. In turning to the second test of significant harm to the environment, the EAB (now the Environmental Review Tribunal) ruled that the possibility of such harm (in this case associated with SO_2 concentrations in an apartment building) was sufficient. The board accordingly granted leave to appeal in relation to the issues of record retention and the sulphur-dioxide risk.

In *Dawber*, another comparatively rare example of a successful application for leave to appeal under the OEBR, the Environment Review Tribunal agreed that principles such as ecosystem protection, precaution and public participation found in the ministry's policy Statement of Environmental Values could be relevant to the determination of unreasonableness even where regulatory standards had been met:

> The Tribunal does not agree that approval of a CofA based upon compliance with numerical standards in regulations is automatically or necessarily a reasonable decision if reliance upon those standards results in a failure to observe provisions in other laws and policies also applicable to the decision.[53]

51 *Environmental Bill of Rights, 1993*, SO 1993, c 28, ss 38 and 41.
52 (1996), 20 CELR (NS) 97 (OEAB). See also *Federation of Ontario Naturalists v Ontario (Director, Ministry of the Environment)* (1999), 32 CELR (NS) 92 (OEAB); *Friends of the Jock River v Ontario (Director, Ministry of the Environment)* (2002), 44 CELR (NS) 69 (OERT); *Simpson v Ontario (Director, Ministry of the Environment)* (2005), 18 CELR (3d) 123 (OERT).
53 *Dawber v Director (Ministry of the Environment)*, [2007] OERTD No 25 at para 31.

In reaching this conclusion, the tribunal carefully analysed the scope and limitations of its own authority:

> The . . . laws and policies that apply to the Directors' decisions are not themselves the subject of the test . . . and the Tribunal is not seized with the task of assessing the reasonableness or adequacy of their content, at least not directly. The Tribunal does not have the mandate to require changes to those laws and policies or to impose upon the Directors a duty to achieve a higher standard of environmental protection than those laws and policies require. Instead, the reasonableness of the Directors' decisions must be assessed in the context of the legal regime within which they occur . . . . However, it is appropriate to inquire whether and to what extent the Directors' decisions considered, incorporated and reflected relevant law and policies.[54]

Even in the absence of appeal mechanisms, interested individuals and public interest groups may be entitled to seek judicial review of the decision maker's exercise of its statutory powers in relation to licensing approvals and also in connection with administrative orders and environmental assessment. Judicial review proceedings permit courts to enquire into the manner in which administrative decisions have been taken with a view to ensuring that procedural requirements have been fulfilled, that the tribunal's conduct has been free of bias as that concept is understood in administrative law, and that no reviewable errors have been made in relation to questions of jurisdiction, law, fact, and discretion. Distinctive administrative law remedies may be available.[55]

Access to judicial review is dependent on the standing of the applicant, that is, on the recognition of the applicant's eligibility to present its concerns before the court. Liberalized rules of standing that developed initially in relation to constitutional claims and later extended to administrative action in the *Finlay* decision[56] have been influential in establishing the concept of public interest standing and thereby facilitating access to the courts. On a discretionary basis, the courts may grant public interest standing to an applicant who is either directly

---

54 *Ibid* at para 28. In a judicial review challenge to the decision, the Ontario Divisional Court concluded that the Tribunal's decision to grant leave to appeal where the Statement of Environmental Values had not been applied by the Director was a reasonable one. *Lafarge Canada Inc v Ontario (Environmental Review Tribunal)*, [2008] OJ No. 2460.

55 On the availability of the entitlement of third party complainants to interlocutory relief where the validity of an environmental approval was in question, see *Calvé v Gestion Serge Lafrenière inc*, [1999] JQ no 1334 (CA).

56 *Finlay v Canada (Minister of Finance)*, [1986] 2 SCR 607.

affected or genuinely interested as a citizen in a serious and justiciable issue that would not otherwise be brought to trial in a reasonable and effective manner.[57]

Public interest standing has figured prominently in several recent environmental controversies. In *MiningWatch Canada v Canada (Minister of Fisheries and Oceans)*, a coalition of twenty groups and organizations sought to challenge a decision involving significant issues in federal environmental assessment. In granting standing on a public interest basis, the court concluded that "there is no evidence to suggest that others might raise the important issue raised by the applicant."[58] In *Morton v British Columbia (Minister of Agriculture and Lands)*, wilderness groups, environmental organizations, and fishing interests wanted to challenge aquaculture permitting procedures. The court clearly acknowledged the environmental *bona fides* of the applicants and, in granting public interest standing, added that "[i]t is not inconceivable that the legislation might be challenged by an unsuccessful applicant for a fish farm licence, but such an individual would not necessarily be affected by the impugned legislation in the way or to the extent that the petitioners may be."[59]

Although the Supreme Court of Canada has confirmed that the principles applicable to public interest standing should be interpreted in a liberal and generous manner, there are clear indications that public interest standing cannot be open-ended.[60] In a number of cases, prospective environmental litigants have failed to obtain public interest standing on the grounds that the issues involved were neither constitutional nor truly administrative,[61] or because the applicant had failed to satisfy the tests of being directly affected by or genuinely interested in the alleged wrong.[62] Public interest standing on the *Finlay* principles has also been restricted formally to government action, with one court

---

57 For the application of this test to grant standing in environmental cases, see *Western Canada Wilderness Committee v British Columbia (Minister of Environment & Parks)* (1988), 2 CELR (NS) 245; *Reese v Alberta (Ministry of Forestry, Lands & Wildlife)* (1992), 123 AR 241 (QB); *Friends of the Island Inc v Canada (Minister of Public Works)*, [1993] 2 FC 229 (TD).

58 2007 FC 955 at para 184.

59 2009 BCSC 136 at para 92.

60 *Canadian Council of Churches v Canada (Minister of Employment & Immigration)*, [1992] 1 SCR 236.

61 *Hunter v Saskatchewan* (1994), 122 Sask R 161 (QB).

62 *Shiell v Atomic Energy Control Board* (1995), 17 CELR (NS) 286 (Fed TD); *Manitoba Naturalists Society Inc v Ducks Unlimited Canada* (1991), 79 Man R (2d) 15 (QB).

observing that "[p]ublic interest standing should not be conferred to enable a party to sue a private individual or corporation."[63]
CEPA 1999 provides for public participation in connection with a wide range of government decision making, including the development of regulations, and the issuance of approvals and orders under the act. Opportunities to file objections or to request the formation of boards of review are consistent with the statutory duty of the government of Canada to "encourage the participation of the people of Canada in the making of decisions that affect the environment."[64] Participation is facilitated in part by the creation in connection with *CEPA 1999* of an Environmental Registry.[65] Section 13(1) outlines information to be included:

> The Environmental Registry shall contain notices and other documents published or made publicly available by the Minister, and shall also include, subject to the *Access to Information Act* and the *Privacy Act*,
> (a) notices of objection and of any approval granted under the Act;
> (b) a copy of every policy and of every proposed regulation or order made under this Act; and
> (c) copies of documents submitted to a court by the Minister relating to any environmental protection action.

FURTHER READINGS

DeMarco, JV, & P Muldoon, *Environmental Boards and Tribunals in Canada: A Practical Guide* (Markham: LexisNexis, 2011)

Elgie, SAG, "Environmental Groups and the Courts: 1970–1992" in G Thompson, ML McConnell, & LB Huestis, eds, *Environmental Law and Business in Canada* (Aurora, ON: Canada Law Book, 1993) at 185

Franson, MAH, RT Franson, & AR Lucas, *Environmental Standards: A Comparative Study of Canadian Standards, Standard Setting Processes and Enforcement* (Edmonton: Environment Council of Alberta, 1982)

Laplante, B, "Environmental Regulation: Performance and Design Standards" in GB Doern, ed, *Getting It Green: Case Studies in Canadian Environmental Regulation* (Toronto: CD Howe Institute, 1990) at 59

---

63 *Shiell v Amok Ltd* (1987), 58 Sask R 141 (QB).
64 *CEPA 1999*, above note 42, s 2(1)(e).
65 *Ibid*, s 12; online: www.ec.gc.ca/ceparegistry.

LEVY, AD, "The Scope of Liability and Exercise of Discretion in Recent Decisions of the Ontario Environmental Appeal Board" (1996) 6 J Envtl L & Prac 223

ONTARIO, MINISTRY OF ENVIRONMENT, *Modernization of Approvals: Inter-jurisdictional Comparison of Alternative Approval Methods: Overview and Best Practices* (Program Planning and Implementation Branch, April 2010)

THOMPSON, AR, *Environmental Regulation in Canada: An Assessment of the Regulatory Process* (Vancouver: Westwater Research Centre, University of British Columbia, 1980)

CHAPTER 7

ADMINISTRATIVE COMPLIANCE MECHANISMS

A. COMPLIANCE AND ADMINISTRATIVE ENFORCEMENT

Beyond the underlying framework of environmental standards that an industrial, commercial, or other applicant may be expected to meet after the required approvals and authorizations have been obtained, lie questions relating to compliance and eventually to the implications of non-compliance; that is, what levels of compliance are being achieved and what are the consequences of failing to satisfy (or even disregarding) applicable environmental norms?

Alternative strategies for encouraging environmental performance have been actively debated: some commentators advocate a conciliatory approach, while others have promoted a sanctions-based or penal model of enforcement.[1] The discussion has been influenced not only by evidence of the potential effectiveness of these general alternatives in environmental terms, but also by external developments affecting the context in which enforcement efforts are undertaken. The introduction of the *Charter of Rights and Freedoms* with its evolving implications

---

1 K Hawkins, *Environment and Enforcement: Regulation and the Social Definition of Pollution* (Oxford: Clarendon Press, 1984) is a classic reference work on the general debate. Canadian developments are surveyed in D Chappell, *From Sawdust to Toxic Blobs: A Consideration of Sanctioning Strategies to Combat Pollution in Canada* (Ottawa: Supply & Services, 1989).

for administrative procedures, prosecutorial practices, and penalty regimes, and an appreciation of administrative enforcement costs in periods of fiscal restraint are notable examples of such influences.[2]

The compliance mechanisms considered in this chapter include a range of measures to monitor environmental performance, to issue warnings and administrative orders, and even to impose penalties through an administrative process. Other approaches to compliance such as the prosecution of offences or the use of voluntary agreements are discussed in Chapters 8 and 16 respectively.

B. REPORTING OBLIGATIONS

The terms and conditions applicable to operating licences and permits will frequently impose regular reporting obligations that provide officials with information on an ongoing basis concerning the normal operations of approved sites and facilities. Water treatment facilities will be expected to conduct regular testing and report results. The operators of waste disposal sites may be required to report the nature and volume of materials collected by or delivered to them. In addition, statutory reporting obligations are now common in connection with spills and other irregular discharges of contaminants. The *OEPA* requires every person who discharges or causes or permits the discharge of a contaminant "out of the normal course of events" that causes or is likely to cause an adverse effect to notify the ministry forthwith.[3] Specific notification requirements apply in Ontario when a pollutant is spilled, that is, discharged, into the natural environment from or out of a structure, vehicle, or other container in a manner that is abnormal in quality or quantity in light of all the circumstances of the discharge.[4] Reporting obligations may be found in other provincial legislation, especially relating to gasoline and other fuels, and in such federal statutes as the *Fisheries Act*[5] and *CEPA 1999*. Under the latter there is a statutory requirement to report imposed on some individuals, while the legislation permits others to report both releases and likely releases of toxic substances.[6]

2   Canada (Director of Investigation & Research, Combines Investigation Branch) v Southam Inc, [1984] 2 SCR 145; R v Wholesale Travel Group Inc, [1991] 3 SCR 154.
3   Environmental Protection Act, RSO 1990, c E.19, s 15 [OEPA].
4   Ibid, s 92.
5   RSC 1985, c F-14, s 38(4) [FA].
6   Canadian Environmental Protection Act, 1999, S.C. 1999, c 33, ss 95–96 [CEPA 1999].

A legal issue of considerable sensitivity is possible prosecutorial use of information provided by those subject to regulatory reporting requirements on the grounds that it may violate the principle against self-incrimination and therefore be inconsistent with fundamental justice under the *Charter*. As expressed by Chief Justice Lamer: "Any state action that coerces an individual to furnish evidence against him- or herself in a proceeding in which the individual and the state are adversaries violates the principle against self-incrimination. Coercion, it should be noted, means the denial of free and informed consent."[7]

In *R v Fitzpatrick*, the Supreme Court of Canada considered the principle in the context of charges of catching and retaining fish in excess of a fixed quota brought against a British Columbia fisherman where the only evidence presented by the prosecution was a "hail report" and a "daily fishing log." The accused had been required by section 61 of the *Fisheries Act* to provide these reports to authorities. Justice La Forest, writing for the Court, concluded that the principle against self-incrimination was not offended by the use of the reports for prosecutorial purposes. In the context of a regulated industry, the fisherman and the state were not in an adversarial relationship, nor were the reports obtained through coercion since the accused, having chosen to participate in a licensed industry, could be presumed to know of and to have accepted the conditions under which the information was made available to fisheries officers.[8]

Further insights into the relationship between the principle against self-incrimination and regulatory reporting requirements emerge from subsequent decisions. As Justice Iacobucci remarked in *White*:[9]

> The principle against self-incrimination demands different things at different times, with the task in every case being to determine exactly what the principle demands, if anything, within the particular context at issue.

In *Jarvis*,[10] the Court explained that the context may be determined by the "predominant purpose" of the reporting. In the absence of an "adversarial relationship" in the context of regulatory reporting, no violation of the principle against self-incrimination, and thus of section 7 of the *Charter*, would arise from subsequent prosecutorial use of the information.

---

7   *R v Jones*, [1994] 2 SCR 229 at 249.
8   *R v Fitzpatrick* (1996), 18 CELR (NS) 237 (SCC).
9   *R v White*, [1999] 2 SCR 417 at para 45.
10   *R v Jarvis*, [2002] 3 SCR 757.

C. INSPECTIONS

Inspections are an additional mechanism available to administrative officials seeking information on the compliance status of businesses that are operating within the framework of an environmental permit and regulatory system. The terms and conditions of licences will frequently contain provisions concerning ongoing inspections of operations. However, environmental legislation itself regularly provides for inspections by designated officials who are authorized to "enter and inspect" certain premises in connection with the administration of the environmental regime, or, as it is expressed in *CEPA 1999*, for the purpose of ensuring compliance with the Act and regulations.[11]

Routine administrative inspections may be conducted for a number of purposes other than investigation of possible statutory violations with a view to prosecution. Inspections may be undertaken

- to locate and identify pollution;
- to confirm compliance with statutes, regulations, certificates of approval, or administrative orders;
- to identify, contain, clean up, and prevent future repetitions of incidents such as emissions or spills;
- to examine opportunities to reduce pollution or for preventive and corrective action;
- to discuss and attempt to resolve neighbourhood complaints about pollution;
- to determine whether proposed construction or alterations should be approved; and
- to ensure that pollution control equipment has been constructed as applied for and approved.[12]

Statutory powers of inspection typically authorize inspectors or abatement officials at any reasonable time to enter non-residential premises to determine whether environmental contaminants have caused

---

11   *CEPA 1999*, above note 6, s 218(1). See also *OEPA*, above note 3, s 165, as am by SO 1998, c 35, s 25; *Ontario Water Resources Act*, RSO 1990, c O.40, s 24, as am by SO 1998, c 35, s 29; *Pesticides Act*, RSO 1990, c P11, as am by SO 1998, c 35, s 26, *Environmental Management Act*, SBC 2003, c 53; *Environmental Protection and Enhancement Act*, RSA 2000, c E-12, s 26 [*AEPEA*]; *Environment Act*, SNS 1994–95, c 1, s 119(1) [*NSEA*]; *Environment Act*, SM 1987–88, c 26, s 20; *Saskatchewan Environmental Management and Protection Act, 2002*, SS 2002, c E-10.21, s 2.3(2) [*EMPA*].

12   D Saxe, *Inspections and Searches in the Environmental Context* (Toronto: Environment Ontario, 1987).

or threaten to cause adverse effects, or to enter such premises in the reasonable belief that waste will be found there. Premises in or from which the official reasonably believes a contaminant is or may be released into the environment are also subject to inspection, as are places that are or should be subject to an environmental licence, permit, or approval. Other locations which, in the reasonable belief of the inspector, are likely to contain documentation relating to regulated or approved activities may also be entered without warrant pursuant to the inspection power.[13]

Having entered the premises, officials may undertake a range of activities in furtherance of the inspection. Depending on the legislative particulars in each jurisdiction, they may, for example, take photographs or audiovisual recordings, operate equipment or machinery; conduct tests and take samples, or make reasonable oral or written inquiries.[14]

In the context of constitutionally protected interests in privacy, extensive authority of this nature is controversial. It is justified, however, in relation to administrative objectives that can perhaps be achieved only through inspection. As expressed by La Forest J in *Thomson Newspapers*, the citizen's expectations of privacy vary depending on the activity in which he or she is engaged, and it is generally accepted that regulation serves, at least in part, to maintain compatibility between individual self-interest and the collective goals or aspirations of the community. Inspection provides one mechanism for ensuring that balance:

> The restaurateur's compliance with public health regulations, the employer's compliance with employment standards and safety legislation, and the developer's or homeowner's compliance with building codes or zoning regulations, can only be tested by inspection, and perhaps unannounced inspection, of their premises.[15]

---

13   *OEPA*, above note 3, s 156 (1)(d); *NSEA*, above note 11, ss 119(1)(a)–(e); *AEPEA*, above note 11; *EMPA*, above note 11, s 2.3(2)(c); *CEPA 1999*, above note 6, s 218; *FA*, above note 5, ss 38(3)–(3.5).

14   *OEPA*, above note 3, ss 156(1)(n)–(t); *AEPEA*, above note 11, s 188(5). The powers of provincial officers under the *OEPA*, the *Ontario Water Resources Act*, and the *Pesticides Act* were substantially enhanced by the *Environmental Statute Law Amendment Act*, SO 1998, c 35; *EMPA*, above note 11, s 2.3(9). In order to determine compliance, provincial officers in Ontario have recently been given authority to require a response to "reasonable inquiries," including telephone inquiries: *OEPA*, above note 3, s 157.0.1.

15   *Thomson Newspapers Ltd v Canada (Director of Investigation & Research)*, [1990] 1 SCR 425 at 507, La Forest J.

Even if the validity of inspection functions has been acknowledged in this way, the uncertain boundary between inspection for regulatory purposes and investigations associated with the anticipated use of prosecutorial powers remains extremely sensitive.[16]

Noting in a comprehensive introduction to the *CEPA 1999* that inspections and investigations are clearly distinguished within the legislation, Meinhard Doelle explains the purpose and use of the former:

> Inspections are carried out to verify compliance with the CEPA . . . .
> Under section 218, inspections may be carried out at any reasonable time as long as the enforcement officer has reasonable ground to believe that the place to be inspected contains a substance to which the CEPA applies. Dwelling places can only be entered with a search warrant or the consent of the occupant. The CEPA provides for search warrants for inspections in cases where access is refused. It is important to note that such refusal may lead to prosecution itself, turning an inspection into an investigation. According to the compliance policy, inspections will be carried out according to a program of inspections complemented by spot checks. In addition to general compliance, inspections may be carried out as follow-up to warnings, directions, Ministerial orders, environmental compliance orders, injunctions, environmental alternative measures, and court orders that require further action by an offender. Decisions about inspections may also be influenced by information provided by members of the public, whistle blowers, and by alterations made at facilities subject to control under the CEPA.[17]

Some jurisdictions resorted to publicity concerning the compliance status of licensed and approved operations on the assumption that the knowledge of shareholders, consumers, financial associates, or the public generally would spur business officials to remedy deficiencies. British Columbia's environment department historically released a *Noncompliance Report* which identified those operations found to be out of compliance with waste-management permits and provincial environmental regulations during the relevant period. It is now more common for environmental agencies to report upon their own record and actions taken to promote compliance.[18]

---

16   *R v Inco Ltd* (2001), 54 OR (3d) 495 (CA). This case is discussed in Chapter 8.

17   M Doelle, *Canadian Environmental Protection Act & Commentary: 2005/2006* (Markham, ON: LexisNexis Butterworths, 2005) 42–43.

18   Following the 2001 BC provincial election, the name of the ministry was changed to the Ministry of Water, Land, and Air Protection. Now see online: www.env.gov.bc.ca/main/compliance-reporting. Compliance reports for Ontario

D. ADMINISTRATIVE ORDERS

Authority to issue administrative orders promoting compliance with environmental legislation is common across Canada. Such orders may operate to control sources of existing pollution, to terminate specified activities, or to impose preventive or remedial obligations. Administrative compliance powers of this nature are customarily conferred upon senior officials, including the minister of an environment department, to be exercised in statutorily prescribed circumstances. The validity or legality of these instruments thus demands that they be used only in a manner that conforms to their legislative origins. As a matter of practice, apart from emergency situations, administrative orders are generally resorted to after discussion and consultation have failed to resolve an environmental situation.

The Supreme Court of Canada recently considered the use of an administrative order issued against a Quebec company whose property was contaminated.[19] The specific authority under which the order had been issued reads in part:

> Where the Minister believes on reasonable grounds that a contaminant is present in the environment in a greater quantity or concentration than that established by regulation . . . he may order whoever had emitted, deposited, released or discharged . . . all or some of the contaminant to furnish him with an environmental characterization study, a programme of decontamination or restoration of the environment describing the work proposed for the decontamination or restoration of the environment and a timetable for the execution of the work.[20]

When the company against whom an administrative order had been issued pursuant to this provision challenged it, the court noted frankly: "As discretionary and broad as the power to make orders appears to be, nonetheless important procedural requirements circumscribe it." Following a detailed review of the specific requirements applicable in the circumstances of the case, LeBel J provided valuable general insights into the nature of administrative authority in the environmental context:

---

may be found online: www.ene.gov.on.ca/environment/en/industry/compliance_ and_enforcement/index.htm; for Alberta, online: environment.alberta.ca/0941. html; and for Quebec, online: www.mddep.gouv.qc.ca/Infuseur/mois_ condamnations.asp.

19 *Imperial Oil v Quebec*, [2003] 2 SCR 624 [*Imperial Oil*].
20 *Environment Quality Act*, RSQ c Q-2, s 31.42.

When the Minister has to make a specific decision concerning someone subject to the law, he must comply with precise procedural obligations . . . . Generally speaking, those obligations require that he
give notice to the person concerned, receive and review the represen-
tations and information submitted by that person and give reasons to
that person for his decision. The effect of this procedural framework
is that the Minister must carefully and attentively examine the observations submitted to him. However, that obligation is not equivalent
to the impartiality that is required of a judge or an administrative de-
cision-maker whose primary function is adjudication. In performing
his functions, the Minister is involved in the management of an environmental protection system. He must make decisions in a context
in which the need for the long-term management of environmental
problems plays a prominent role, and in which he must ensure that
the fundamental legislative policy on which the interpretation and
application of environment quality legislation are based is implemented. The Minister has the responsibility of protecting the public
interest in the environment, and must make his decisions in consideration of that interest.[21]

Insofar as failure to comply with administrative orders constitutes
an offence, a party wishing to challenge such orders should generally
do so directly by means of judicial review as was done in *Imperial Oil*,
or on the basis of a statutory right of appeal where available. An alternative way to challenge an administrative order in the context of
enforcement proceedings is known as *collateral attack*, but such an approach is contentious and potentially problematic.[22] In *R v Consolidated
Maybrun Mines Ltd*, the accused ignored an environmental order concerning PCB containment measures at an abandoned mine site until
charged with failing to comply. Elements of the defence included an
attack on the original justification for the order and on its reasonableness, prompting the court to distinguish between a challenge that the
decision maker lacked jurisdiction to make the order from the outset
and a challenge to the effect that otherwise lawful jurisdiction had
been exercised without reasonable grounds. Only the former challenge
could be pursued on the basis of collateral attack. General observations by the SCC emphasize the status of administrative orders in the
environmental context in relation to the rights of those to whom such
orders are directed:

---

21   *Imperial Oil*, above note 19 at para 34.
22   *R v Consolidated Maybrun Mines Ltd*, [1998] 1 SCR 706.

It is clear from a review of the Environmental Protection Act that its purpose is not simply to repair damage to the environment resulting from human activity, even if we assume that repairs will always be possible, but primarily to prevent contamination of the province's environment. Such a purpose requires rapid and effective means in order to ensure that any necessary action is taken promptly. This purpose is reflected both in the scope of the powers conferred on the Director and in the establishment of an appeal procedure designed to counterbalance the broad powers conferred on the Director by affording affected individuals an opportunity to present their points of view and assert their rights as quickly as possible.[23]

With reference to several provincial regimes, the following discussion illustrates various circumstances in which different types of administrative orders may be employed.

1) Control Orders

Control orders, as they have generally been known in Ontario, permit statutorily appointed officials to require designated parties to implement measures to control the illegal discharge of a contaminant into the natural environment where that discharge has been established on the basis of a written report. It is a precondition of any control order that a prohibited contaminant has been discharged into the natural environment, or that a discharge contravening section 14 or the regulations is occurring.[24]

Monitoring obligations, equipment installation or replacement, and operational procedures are among the types of measures typically included in such orders.[25] Orders of this nature may be directed to the owner or previous owner of the source of the contaminant, to a person who was or is in occupation of the source of contaminant, or to a person who has or had "charge management or control" of the source of contaminant.[26] The designated recipient of a control order is entitled to fifteen days' notice, accompanied by the director's reasons for propos-

---

23   *Ibid* at para 59.

24   *OEPA*, above note 3, s 7. The power was originally conferred on directors, presumptively a small class of senior officials. In practice, the category was extended to facilitate the issuance of orders. The 1998 *Environmental Statute Law Amendment Act* provided some clarification of the statutory basis upon which abatement officers might issue field orders. Further amendments restricted the availability of control orders to situations involving "adverse effects." See SO 2005, c 12, s 1(4).

25   *OEPA*, above note 3, s 124.

26   *Ibid*, s 7.

ing the order and by the report on which it is based.[27] The person to whom the order is directed may thereupon make submissions to the director or may appeal to Ontario's Environmental Review Tribunal.[28]

The appeal will not automatically trigger a stay of the Ontario order. Instead, the appeal board has discretion on the application of a party to stay the order, but it may not do so in cases where a stay would produce danger to the health or safety of any person, impairment or serious risk of impairment of the quality of the natural environment, or injury or damage or serious risk of injury or damage to any property or to plant or animal life.[29]

In Alberta, comparable authority to issue what is known as an enforcement order is available to the provincial director, based on the director's opinion that a contravention of the *Environmental Protection and Enhancement Act* has occurred.[30]

2) Stop Orders

Although a control order may be used for the purpose of stopping the discharge of a contaminant into the natural environment,[31] an alternative exists in the form of a stop order. Such orders, also written and accompanied by reasons, require immediate compliance on the part of the person to whom they are served.[32] Yet the preconditions of a stop order are more restrictive than those of a control order, and for this reason, stop orders have been used comparatively infrequently. Before issuing a stop order the director must—on reasonable and probable grounds—be of the opinion that an existing discharge of contaminant is occurring in such a way that it constitutes an immediate danger to human life, health, or property.[33]

---

27   *Ibid*, s 127.
28   *Ibid*, ss 127, 140, and 143. In the exercise of this authority, the Environmental Review Tribunal is the successor to the Environmental Appeal Board.
29   *Ibid*, s 143.
30   *AEPEA*, above note 11, ss 210-215; see also *NSEA*, above note 11, s 125; *EMPA*, above note 11, s 4; *Environment Act*, CCSM c E125, s 24.
31   *OEPA*, above note 3, s 124 (1)(b); see also *NSEA*, above note 11, s 126.
32   *OEPA*, above note 3, ss 8 and 129.
33   *Canada Metal Co v MacFarlane* (1973), 1 OR (2d) 577 (HCJ). For consideration by the Ontario Environmental Review Tribunal of an order in the nature of a stop order, see *Echo Bay Milling Ltd v Ontario (Director, Ministry of the Environment)*, 2003 CarswellOnt 4335 (ERT).

3) Preventive Orders

In the absence of statutory contraventions, but in anticipation of pollution, administrative orders may also be used to prevent or minimize environmental damage.[34] Orders of a preventive nature require reasonable and probable grounds[35] and are typically subject to appeal.[36]

The pollution prevention order under British Columbia's *Environmental Management Act* illustrates this type of environmental protection authority.[37] Where a director is satisfied on reasonable grounds that an activity is being carried out in such a manner that the release of a substance would likely cause pollution of the environment, the director may order any of the following to be done at the expense of the person to whom the order was directed:

a) provide to the director information the director requests relating to the activity, operation, or substance;
b) undertake investigations, tests, surveys, or any other action the director considers necessary to prevent the pollution and to report the results to the director;
c) acquire, construct, or carry out any works or measures that are reasonably necessary to prevent the pollution;
d) adjust, repair, or alter any works to the extent reasonably necessary to prevent the pollution.

One or more of the following could be served with an order of this kind:

a) a person who previously had or or had at the time possession, charge, or control of the substance;
b) a person who previously did anything or who was at the time doing anything that could have caused the release of the substance;
c) a person who previously owned or occupied or at the time owned or occupied the land on which the substance was located.

The nature of these orders is such that courts will construe statutory powers to impose preventive measures strictly. As explained in relation to the *OEPA*, "it authorizes state intervention into the activity of a per-

---

34 *OEPA*, above note 3, s 18, as am by SO 2005, c 12, ss 1(8) & (9); *AEPEA*, above note 11, ss 102 & 103.
35 See *R v Consolidated Maybrun Mines Ltd* (1992), 9 CELR (NS) 34 (Ont Prov Div), rev'd in part (1993), 12 CELR (NS) 171 (Ont Gen Div) [*Maybrun*].
36 *OEPA*, above note 3, s 140; *AEPEA*, above note 11, s 84. Nova Scotia's authority in connection with an emergency situation appears to have comparable applicability: *NSEA*, above note 11, s 128.
37 *Environmental Management Act*, SBC 2003, c 53, s 81.

son on his own land before any offence has been committed, and without providing any offsetting protection or benefit by compliance." In other words, the director may "intrude with his own view of risk management while leaving the person with full responsibility for the risk."[38]

4) Remedial Orders

Remedial orders are now also commonly in place to require cleanup and restoration measures.[39] In light of the tendency to associate their use with emergency situations where delay entails the risk of continuing environmental damages, cleanup orders are not always subject to pre-compliance appeal or judicial review.[40] Where water supplies have suffered or are at risk remedial obligations may include the provision of alternative supplies.

5) Environmental Protection Orders under *CEPA 1999*

At the federal level, *CEPA 1999* provides for Environmental Protection Compliance Orders (EPCOs) that are roughly equivalent to the types of administrative order available under provincial legislation. These orders are confined in their application to circumstances in which enforcement officers reasonably believe that contraventions of the Act have occurred or will occur in relation to a range of designated activities largely related to substances governed by the Act.[41] Orders "reasonable in the circumstances and consistent with the protection of the environment and public safety" may require that measures be taken to:

- refrain from doing anything in contravention of *CEPA 1999* or the regulations, or do anything to comply with the Act or regulations;
- stop or shut down any activity, work, undertaking, or thing for a specified period;
- cease the operation of any activity or any part of a work, undertaking, or thing until the enforcement officer is satisfied that the compliance will be achieved.

EPCOs may be directed to any person who causes or contributes to the alleged contravention or who owns or has the charge, management, or control of the substance or any product containing the substance to

---

38   *Maybrun*, above note 35 at 41 (Ont Prov Div).
39   *AEPEA*, above note 11, s 113; *OEPA*, above note 3, s 17; *Contaminated Sites Remediation Act*, CCSM c C205, s 17.
40   *OEPA*, above note 3, s 122.
41   *CEPA 1999*, above note 6, ss 234–42.

which the alleged contravention relates or the property on which the substance or product is located.[42]

6) Fairness and the Allocation of Liability for Administrative Orders

Simply by way of introduction to a subject that is more fully discussed in Chapter 11 in connection with contaminated lands, it is useful to note the existence of debate over the allocation of liability for compliance amongst a range of potentially responsible parties. Pursuant to the various statutory schemes, it is possible that directions may be issued to people to remedy pollution that originated prior to the passage of the legislation authorizing the orders or directed at those who were not directly responsible for the environmental damage to which they may be required to respond.[43] Legislation may be used to clarify the manner in which departmental officials should exercise their discretion in addressing orders in these circumstances. Alberta, for example, enumerated factors that are to be given consideration by the director in deciding to issue an environmental protection order to a person responsible for a contaminated site:

(a) when the substance became present in, on, or under the site;

(b) in the case of an owner or previous owner of the site,

   (i)   whether the substance was present in, on, or under the site at the time that person became an owner;

   (ii) whether the person knew or ought reasonably to have known that the substance was present in, on, or under the site at the time that person became an owner;

   (iii) whether the presence of the substance in, on, or under the site ought to have been discovered by the owner had the owner exercised due diligence in ascertaining the presence of the substance before he became an owner, and whether the owner exercised such due diligence;

   (iv) whether the presence of the substance in, on, or under the site was caused solely by the act or omission of an independent third party;

   (v)   the price the owner paid for the site and the relationship between that price and the fair market value of the site had the substance not been present in, on, or under it;

---

42   *Canada v IPSCO Recycling Inc*, 2003 FC 1518.
43   *British Columbia Hydro and Power Authority v British Columbia (Environmental Appeal Board)*, [2005] SCJ No 2.

(c) in the case of a previous owner, whether that owner disposed of his interest in the site without disclosing the presence of the substance in, on, or under the site to the person who acquired the interest;

(d) whether the person took all reasonable care to prevent the presence of the substance in, on, or under the site;

(e) whether a person dealing with the substance followed accepted industry standards and practice in effect at the time or complied with the requirements of applicable enactments in effect at the time;

(f) whether the person contributed to further accumulation or the continued release of the substance on becoming aware of the presence of the substance in, on, or under the site;

(g) what steps the person took to deal with the site on becoming aware of the presence of the substance in, on, or under the site;

(h) any other criteria the Director considers to be relevant.[44]

A task force report prepared for the Canadian Council of Ministers of the Environment on factors relevant to the allocation of liability for contaminated sites proposed a very similar series of considerations for adoption in other jurisdictions.[45]

Even in the absence of legislative guidance, decision makers have addressed the problem of apportioning responsibility for environmental costs under administrative regimes. In *Re 724597 Ontario Ltd*, more familiarly known as *Appletex*, the Ontario Environmental Appeal Board examined the question of allocating cleanup, waste removal, and decommissioning costs under a director's order aimed at the environmental problems associated with anabandoned wool knitting and dyeing mill.[46] The order, issued in 1993, was directed at the company itself, its president, and two investors whose involvement dated from 1989 as part of an initiative to restore the bankrupt operation. Noting the possibility of "a high degree of unpredictability and potential unfairness"[47] in the manner in which director's orders under the *EPA* might be issued, the board sought guidance in the CCME principles. These, it concluded, require decision makers to examine the particular circumstances of each case rather than adopting a "deep pockets" solution. Ultimately, follow-

---

44   *AEPEA*, above note 11, s 129(2).
45   Canadian Council of Ministers of the Environment, Core Group on Contaminated Site Liability, *Contaminated Site Liability Report: Recommended Principles for a Consistent Approach across Canada* (23 March 1993).
46   *Re 724597 Ontario Ltd* (1994), 13 CELR (NS) 257 (OEAB).
47   *Ibid* at 284.

ing a review of the application of the CCME principles to the *Appletex* situation, the EAB amended the director's order in relation to several of the parties, largely revoking the liability of one of the individuals.[48]

The introduction of "fairness" and "equity" to decisions on the allocation of liability under administrative orders remains controversial from several perspectives. Observers question, for example, the evidentiary, procedural, and administrative cost implications of a shift towards fault-based determinations. Nevertheless, courts have acknowledged that it is legitimate for decision makers to take account of the fairness factors:

> First, the Tribunal determines the issue of jurisdiction, which is whether or not an order can be made against a party. If it determines that it has jurisdiction to make an order, the next stage is to determine whether it should make an order. In exercising its discretion, the Tribunal is entitled to consider issues of fairness.[49]

E. ADMINISTRATIVE MONETARY PENALTIES

Although breaches of regulatory provisions, including environmental legislation, have traditionally been viewed as matters for prosecutorial action, increasingly frequent statutory enactments have introduced an alternative process in the form of administrative penalty mechanisms, occasionally described as administrative monetary penalties (AMP). AMP provisions should be distinguished from ticketable offences where the manner of initiating the proceedings is modified but the matter remains within the jurisdiction of the courts.[50]

Sanctions resulting from administrative, rather than judicial, proceedings are generally expected to provide less costly and more expeditious enforcement. They will also possibly be found more convenient from the perspective of offenders who accept the administrative determination of the contravention, a process that does not result in a

---

48   An appeal by the director was dismissed. *Re 724597 Ontario Ltd* (1995), 18 CELR (NS) 137 (Ont Div Ct), leave to appeal refused (11 March 1996), (Ont CA) [unreported].

49   *Montague v Ontario (Ministry of Environment)*, [2005] OJ No. 868 (Div Ct). For more recent developments, including *Kawartha Lakes (City) v Ontario (Director, Ministry of the Environment)*, 2012 ONSC 2708, see Chapter 11.

50   See, for example, *CEPA 1999*, above note 6, s 310(1); *Wild Animal and Plant Protection and Regulation of International and Interprovincial Trade Act*, SC 1992, c 52, s 23; *Migratory Birds Convention Act, 1994*, SC 1994, c 22, s 19.

criminal record. For precisely this reason, however, some observers question whether AMPs will serve as an effective deterrent.

Administrative penalty schemes will ordinarily involve a notification procedure setting out the details of the violation and the financial penalty determined to be applicable. British Columbia legislation provides an illustration:

> Subject to the regulations, if a director is satisfied on a balance or probabilities that a person has
> (a) contravened a prescribed provision of this Act or the regulations,
> (b) failed to comply with an order under this Act, or
> (c) failed to comply with a requirement of a permit or approval issued or given under this Act,
>
> the director may serve the person with a determination requiring the person to pay an administrative penalty in the amount specified in the determination.[51]

An administrative hearing on the appropriateness of the penalty, or possibly an administrative appeal or review of the entire offence and penalty proceeding, will generally be set out in legislation governing administrative penalty schemes of this type.[52]

Alberta implemented an administrative penalty arrangement in the *AEPEA*, under which the director, if of the opinion that a contravention of designated sections of the Act or regulations has occurred, may impose a penalty as provided for by regulation.[53] With regard to the level of penalty to be assessed and the AMP scheme, the Alberta appeal board remarked:

> The Board believes the amount of the penalty must reflect the regulatory matrix and associated criteria. The Board believes that to achieve the goal of deterrence, the penalty must also be high enough so that those who violate the law without reasonable excuse will not be able to "write off" the penalty as an acceptable trade-off for the harm or potential harm done to Alberta's environment.[54]

---

51 *Environmental Management Act*, above note 37, s 115.

52 Environmental AMPs have been provided for in Alberta (*AEPEA*, above note 11, the *Public Lands Act*, the *Forests Act*), British Columbia (*Forest Practices Code, Administrative Remedies Regulation*, BC Reg 166/95), New Brunswick (*Clean Air Act, Administrative Penalties Regulation*, NB Reg 98-41), Nova Scotia (*NSEA*, above note 11), and Ontario (*Environmental Protection Act, Ontario Water Resources Act, Pesticides Act*).

53 *Administrative Penalty Regulation*, Alta Reg 143/95.

54 *Hayspur Aviation Ltd v Alberta (Department of Environmental Protection)*, [1997] AEABD No 9. For an explanation of the current formula for determining AMPs,

Between April 2000 and March 2006, 138 AMPs were imposed under the *AEPEA*, resulting in total assessed penalties of $668,000. Individual penalties ranged from a low of $500 to a high of $29,500.

Ontario's venture into the realm of administrative penalties has been in operation since August 2007. The *Environmental Penalties Regulation*[55] designates "regulated persons" who may be subject to the new penalty regime in relation to certain specified contraventions. It establishes applicable procedures including notice of intention to issue a penalty and a request for review. In determining the amount of the environmental penalty to be assessed, a formula combining the "monetary benefit" received by the regulated person and a "gravity component" for the contravention is utilized. The monetary benefit is calculated in relation to avoided and delayed costs, while the gravity component is determined in accordance with a classification system intended to distinguish less serious, serious, and very serious contraventions. In connection with a contravention of section 14 of the *Environmental Protection Act*, for example, a contravention is serious where it causes or may cause one or more of the following effects:

1. Localized injury or damage to any animal life.
2. Widespread or long-term interference with the normal conduct of business.
3. Widespread or long-term loss of enjoyment of the normal use of property.
4. Widespread damage to property, other than plant or animal life.
5. Damage to property, other than plant or animal life, such that the property cannot be restored, within a reasonable time, to the condition that existed immediately before the discharge occurred.[56]

On the other hand, a contravention of the same section is considered very serious where it causes or may cause the following:

1. Widespread injury or damage to plant or animal life.
2. Harm or material discomfort to any person.
3. An adverse effect on the health of any person.
4. The impairment of the safety of any person.[57]

Reductions to the basic administrative penalty are available in Ontario on the basis of such considerations as efforts to prevent or mitigate harm, or the existence of an environmental management system.

---

see online: environment.alberta.ca/documents/Administrative-Penalties.pdf.
55   *Environmental Penalties Regulation*, O Reg 222/07.
56   *Ibid*, s 10.
57   *Ibid*.

For its part, the federal government has also positioned itself to employ AMPs within the framework of the *Environmental Violations Administrative Monetary Penalties Act*.[58] Violations or contraventions subject to *EVAMPA* will be designated by regulation with reference to ten federal statutes: the *Antarctic Environmental Protection Act*, the *Canada National Marine Conservation Areas Act*, the *Canada National Parks Act*, the *Canada Water Act*, the *Canada Wildlife Act*, the *Canadian Environmental Protection Act, 1999*, the *International River Improvements Act*, the *Migratory Birds Convention Act, 1994*, the *Saguenay-St. Lawrence Marine Park Act* and the *Wild Animal and Plant Protection and Regulation of International and Interprovincial Trade Act*. Section 11 of the new legislation specifically addresses defences:

> 11. (1) A person, ship or vessel named in a notice of violation does not have a defence by reason that the person or, in the case of a ship or vessel, its owner, operator, master or chief engineer
> (a)   exercised due diligence to prevent the violation; or
> (b)   reasonably and honestly believed in the existence of facts that, if true, would exonerate the person, ship or vessel.
>
> (2) Every rule and principle of the common law that renders any circumstance a justification or excuse in relation to a charge for an offence under an Environmental Act applies in respect of a violation to the extent that it is not inconsistent with this Act.

Although it had been assumed that AMPs would, apart from administrative reviews, operate more or less without legal challenge, the explicit discussion in *EVAMPA* arises from the fact that questions were raised about the availability of a due diligence defence.[59] The controversy is in some respects a crossover from similar questions previously raised in other areas of the law. With regard to AMPs under the *Excise Tax Act*, the battle lines were sharply drawn by the unequivocal statement of Judge Bowman:

> That a person should be susceptible of being penalized administratively by a public servant without any possibility of exculpating himself by demonstrating due diligence is not only extraordinary. It is abhorrent. It is not less abhorrent because it is mechanically and routinely imposed by anonymous revenue officials and therefore quali-

---

58   SC 2009, c 14, s 126.
59   *MacMillan Bloedel Ltd v British Columbia* (1997), 23 CELR (NS) 47 at 51 (BC Forest Appeals Commission).

fies for the essentially meaningless rubric "administrative" rather than "criminal." A punishment is a punishment. Neither its nature nor its effect is tempered by the use of palliative modifiers.[60]

Courts of appeal in at least two provinces have also indicated their understanding that a due diligence defence ought to be available in the context of administrative penalties.[61] They have done so, however, with specific reference to the gravity or severity of the consequence of an administrative finding. There is thus some continuing basis for uncertainty about due diligence defences, at least where the actual burden of the penalty might be perceived as modest.

The range of measures described in this chapter, from devices oriented towards information gathering through administrative orders to administrative penalty regimes, are intended to ensure, by and large in a "business as usual" context, an acceptable level of compliance. Nevertheless, as noted in the following chapter, environmental law includes offences that have increasingly been the subject of formal enforcement proceedings.

FURTHER READINGS

COMMISSION FOR ENVIRONMENTAL COOPERATION, *Special Report on Enforcement Activities* (June 2001)

COOP, JD, "Beyond *Appletex*: The Status of 'Fairness' Litigation and the Challenges Posed by the Doctrine of 'Fairness'" (1996) 7 J Envtl L & Prac 115

COOP, JD, & J FAIRFAX, "Fairness Principle Overturned by Environmental Review Tribunal—The Pendulum Swings Yet Again" in SD Berger, ed, *Key Developments in Environmental Law, 2010* (Canada Law Book, 2010)

CROWLEY, R, & F THOMPSON, "Retroactive Liability, Superfund and the Regulation of Contaminated Sites in British Columbia" (1995) 29 UBC L Rev 87

---

60 *Pillar Oilfield Projects Ltd v R*, [1993] 2 GTC 1005 at 1009 (TCC). Now see *Canada (Attorney General) v Consolidated Canadian Contractors Inc* (1998), 231 NR 92 (FCA).

61 *504174 NB Ltée (fas Choo Choo's) c Nouveau-Brunswick (Ministre de la Sécurité Publique)* (2005), 279 NBR (2d) 307 (CA); *Whistler Mountain Ski Corp v British Columbia (General Manager Liquor Control and Licensing Branch)*, [2002] BCJ No 1604, 43 Admin LR (3d) 294 (CA).

Hughes, EL, AR Lucas, & WA Tilleman, eds, *Environmental Law and Policy*, 3d ed (Toronto: Emond Montgomery, 2003) c 10

CHAPTER 8

OFFENCES, PROSECUTION, AND PENALTIES

A. AN INTRODUCTION TO ENVIRONMENTAL OFFENCES

Not unexpectedly, prominent environmental offences are associated with environmental damage: prohibitions have been established against certain forms of conduct that cause or threaten to cause damage to the environment. The *Environment Quality Act* of Quebec provides an example in declaring that

> [n]o one may emit, deposit, issue or discharge or allow the emission, deposit, issuance or discharge into the environment . . . of any contaminant the presence of which in the environment . . . is likely to affect the life, health, safety, welfare or comfort of human beings, or to cause damage to or otherwise impair the quality of the soil, vegetation, wildlife or property.[1]

The *Ontario Water Resources Act* makes it an offence to discharge or cause or permit the discharge of any kind of material in or into any waters where the discharge may impair water quality.[2]

> Every person that discharges or causes or permits the discharge of any material of any kind into or in any waters or on any shore or

---

1   RSQ c Q-2, s 20.
2   *Ontario Water Resources Act*, RSO 1990, c O.40, s 30(1) [*OWRA*].

bank thereof or into or in any place that may impair the quality of the water or any waters is guilty of an offence.

Similarly, the federal *Fisheries Act* states that

no person shall deposit or permit the deposit of a deleterious substance of any type in water frequented by fish or in any place under any conditions where the deleterious substance or any other deleterious substance that results from the deposit of the deleterious substance may enter any such water.[3]

As broadly formulated as such prohibitions appear to be, the existence of exemptions must be noted. The *Fisheries Act*, in fact, contains its own express limitation in that the legislation itself indicates that no one contravenes the prohibition just cited "by depositing or permitting the deposit in any water or place of waste or pollutant of a type, in a quantity and under conditions authorized by regulations applicable to that water or place."[4]

In addition to their anti-pollution provisions, environmental statutes ordinarily establish a series of further offences. Failure to comply with regulatory requirements is an offence, as is the failure to obtain required licences, permits, or approvals, or failure to comply with any terms and conditions set out in these instruments. Non-compliance with valid administrative orders may be addressed through prosecution, and environmental legislation also typically makes it an offence to interfere with or disregard the regulatory process by failing to supply required information, or by providing false or misleading information, or by obstructing enforcement officials or failing to assist them as required.[5] Other environmental reporting obligations that may become the subject of prosecutorial redress relate to the occurrence of spills.

Offences in the environmental context are generally described as *regulatory* or *public welfare offences*. They differ in principle from what are commonly referred to in Canada as "true crimes." The theoretical distinctions were summarized by Mr Justice Cory in *R v Wholesale Travel Group Inc*:

---

3   *Fisheries Act*, RSC 1985, c F-14, s 36(3) [*FA*].
4   *Ibid*, s 36(4). The *Jobs, Growth and Long-term Prosperity Act*, SC 2012, c 19, further elaborates the scope of regulation-making authority in relation to deleterious substances.
5   *Canadian Environmental Protection Act, 1999*, SC 1999, c 33, ss 272–73 [*CEPA 1999*]; *FA*, above note 3, s 63, as am by SC 1991, c 1, s 18; *Migratory Birds Convention Act, 1994*, SC 1994, c 22, s 13, as am by SC 2005, c 23, s 9 [*MBCA*].

The objective of regulatory legislation is to protect the public or broad segments of the public . . . from the potentially adverse effects of otherwise lawful activity. Regulatory legislation involves a shift of emphasis from the protection of individual interests and the deterrence and punishment of acts involving moral fault to the protection of public and societal interests. While criminal offences are usually designed to condemn and punish past, inherently wrongful conduct, regulatory measures are generally directed to the prevention of future harm through the enforcement of minimum standards of conduct and care.[6]

Justice Cory then contrasted the nature of fault in the regulatory and criminal settings:

Since regulatory offences are directed primarily not to conduct itself but to the consequences of conduct, conviction of a regulatory offence may be thought to import a significantly lesser degree of culpability than conviction of a true crime. The concept of fault in regulatory offences is based upon a reasonable care standard and, as such, does not imply moral blameworthiness in the same manner as criminal fault. Conviction for breach of a regulatory offence suggests nothing more than that the defendant has failed to meet a prescribed standard of care.[7]

The social importance of harm prevention — that is, seeking to avoid potentially incalculable and often irreversible environmental damage by requiring a prescribed level of care or performance — thus explains the extension of offences to situations where actual harm may not have occurred.

Regulatory offences themselves may be further subdivided into three classifications—*mens rea*, strict liability, and absolute liability—which have particular significance for prosecutions. Regulatory offences, including environmental offences, fall overwhelmingly within the strict liability category. Commission of such offences, as explained by Dickson J in *R v Sault Ste Marie (City)*, will be established on a *prima facie* basis by the prosecution showing the doing of the prohibited act unaccompanied by evidence of the mental state of the accused. It is then "open to the accused to avoid liability by proving that he took all reasonable care. This involves consideration of what a reasonable man would have done in the circumstances." A second category of offences requires the prosecution to prove *mens rea*, "consisting of some positive

---

6   [1991] 3 SCR 154 at 219 [*Wholesale*].
7   *Ibid.*

state of mind such as intent, knowledge, or recklessness." This may be accomplished "either as an inference from the nature of the act committed, or by additional evidence." Absolute liability offences require proof of the *actus reus*, but it is not then "open to the accused to exculpate himself by showing that he was free of fault."[8]

In the absence of an express statutory classification of the regulatory offence as one of strict or absolute liability or involving *mens rea*, analysis of legislative intent begins with the presumption of strict liability that—depending on other factors present—might be displaced in favour of either *mens rea* or absolute liability. To classify an offence as one involving *mens rea* requires language signalling the importance of the accused's state of mind as a factor to be established by the prosecution. Words such as *wilfully, knowingly,* or *with intent,* are comparatively clear in this regard. It is less certain that words such as *participate* satisfy the standard, although it has been determined that wilful blindness may be equated with the *mens rea* standard of knowingly. "Deliberately choosing not to know something when given reason to believe further inquiry is necessary can satisfy the mental element of the offence."[9]

On the other hand, distinguishing between strict and absolute liability offences presents the challenge of determining whether the legislative body responsible for the enactment "had made it clear that guilt would follow proof merely of the proscribed act."[10] The primary, but not exclusive, considerations relevant to this determination include the subject matter of the legislation, the overall regulatory pattern, the importance of the penalty provided, and the precision of the language employed.[11]

Complications and a reorientation of incentives resulted from the *Charter of Rights and Freedoms.* Defence counsel traditionally argued that statutory provisions established strict liability rather than absolute liability offences. Due diligence defences rendered conviction less likely.[12] The strategic situation was somewhat altered by the *Charter*: "Counsel now perceive that any absolute liability offence accompanied by a possibility of imprisonment will contravene the *Charter* unless

---

8   *R v Sault Ste Marie (City)*, [1978] 2 SCR 1299 at 1325–26, 85 DLR (3d) 161 [*Sault Ste Marie*]. The framework for the classification of offences is reiterated in *Levis (City) v Tetreault*, [2006] SCJ No 12.

9   *R v Jorgensen*, [1995] 4 SCR 55 at 110, Sopinka J, with reference to s 163(2)(a) of the *Criminal Code*, RSC 1985, c C-46 [*Criminal Code*]

10   *Sault Ste Marie*, above note 8 at 1326.

11   J Swaigen, *Regulatory Offences in Canada: Liability and Defences* (Toronto: Carswell, 1992) at 32.

12   For discussion of due diligence, see Chapter 9.

saved by section 1; therefore, they argue that provisions create absolute liability offences, in the hope that they will be struck down."[13] Legislative revisions designed to ensure *Charter* conformity now make such opportunities less likely.[14]

B. INTERPRETING ENVIRONMENTAL OFFENCES IN THE COURTS

Notwithstanding the best efforts of those responsible for drafting legislation, disagreements will arise over the meaning and application of statutory provisions. Such disputes are most likely in the context of prosecutions where an accused business or individual faces potentially severe consequences upon conviction. In these circumstances, as can readily be illustrated with reference to offences mentioned in the previous section, judicial interpretation plays a significant role in elaborating the scope of liability.

The applicability of the strong general prohibition in section 20 of Quebec's *Environment Quality Act* was restricted on the basis of judicial analysis of its relationship to two other prohibitions, namely against discharging a contaminant prohibited by regulation and against discharging a contaminant in excess of the quantity authorized by regulation. In *Alex Couture Inc v Piette*, charges were brought under the general prohibition, section 20(3), against a company whose operations were subject to existing regulations. In the circumstances, the Quebec Court of Appeal concluded that the general anti-pollution clause had no application on the grounds that the government would hardly authorize and prohibit the same emission of a contaminant. Thus, the general prohibition against any discharge of a contaminant would not apply in the case of a contaminant whose discharge was governed by regulation.[15]

Prosecutions under section 36(3), the deleterious substance provision of the *Fisheries Act,* have raised numerous issues. Of particular importance, it has been asked whether the nature of the substance or the condition of the water after the introduction of the substance is the focus of attention. When a trial court in British Columbia concluded

---

13   Swaigen, above note 11 at 39.
14   But see *Whistler Mountain Ski Corp v British Columbia (General Manager Liquor Control and Licensing Branch)*, [2002] BCJ No 1604 (CA) for further discussion of the distinctions.
15   *Alex Couture Inc v Piette*, [1990] RJQ 1262 at 1268 (CA).

that the Crown's obligation was to establish that the water had been rendered deleterious by the addition of some substance, in this case Bunker C oil, the issue of interpretation proceeded to the Court of Appeal.[16]

Seaton JA decided that section 36(3) "prohibits the deposit of a deleterious substance, not the deposit of a substance that causes the water to become deleterious." As he explained: "once it is determined that Bunker C oil is a deleterious substance and that it has been deposited, the offence is complete without ascertaining whether the water itself was thereby rendered deleterious." Seaton JA was certain that Parliament could very well have expressed a prohibition against depositing a substance in water so as to render that water deleterious to fish, but that it had chosen a stricter prohibition.

The same provision was examined by the Ontario Court of Appeal in a high profile prosecution against a municipality. A unanimous panel determined that:

> The focus of s 36(3) is on the substance being added to the water frequented by fish. It prohibits the deposit of a deleterious substance in such water. It does not prohibit the deposit of a substance that causes the receiving water to become deleterious. It is the substance that is added to water frequented by fish that is defined, not the water after the addition of the substance. A deleterious substance does not have to render the water into which it is introduced poisonous or harmful to fish; it need only be likely to render the water deleterious to fish. The *actus reus* is the deposit of a deleterious substance into water frequented by fish. There is no requirement in s 36(3) . . . of proof that the receiving waters are deleterious to fish.[17]

These judicial explanations are consistent with the preventive orientation of environmental law.

A somewhat similar controversy regarding the scope of liability arose in connection with provincial legislation prohibiting the discharge into water of any material that "may impair" the quality of the water. Toronto Hydro was charged when mineral oil contaminated with PCBs escaped from underground vaults housing transformers and entered the drainage and sewage system leading to Lake Ontario. The company argued that the small quantity involved would not have impaired water quality in Lake Ontario. The proposition that the quantity

---

16   *R v MacMillan Bloedel (Alberni) Limited* (1979), 47 CCC (2d) 118.
17   *R v Kingston (City)*, 2004 CanLII 39042 at para 65 (Ont CA), leave to appeal to SCC refused, [2004] SCCA No 347.

or concentration rather than the nature of the material is determinative of impairment was rejected. Corbett J stated:

> the offence is constituted when the Crown proves that any material discharged . . . may impair the quality of the water course . . . The use of the words "may impair" shows the intention of the legislation is not to prohibit the results of certain acts but to prevent the discharge of any material which, by its nature, may impair the quality of the water course.[18]

A different formulation of the test was subsequently articulated in connection with charges of discharging activated sludge, a substance that is not always associated with adverse impacts on water quality. In *R v Imperial Oil* it was stated that:

> the offence is made out where the Crown proves beyond any reasonable doubt that the discharge of the material may impair the quality of the water, based upon not only the nature of the material, but also the nature and circumstances of the discharge of that material, including its quantity and concentration, as well as the time frame over which the discharge took place.[19]

The Court of Appeal subsequently endorsed the test as formulated in *Imperial Oil*, observing that:

> Inherently toxic substances will always fail that test, reflecting zero tolerance for discharging materials that, by their nature, may impair water quality. If the material in the discharge is not inherently toxic, then it will be necessary to consider the quantity and concentration of the discharge as well as the time frame over which the discharge took place.[20]

Another common source of interpretive uncertainty—the relationship between discharging, causing, and permitting—was addressed by the Supreme Court of Canada. As explained by Dickson J in *R v Sault Ste-Marie*, the discharging aspect of the offence relates to direct acts of pollution, while the causing dimension is associated with activity by the defendant that it is capable of controlling and that results in pollution. Permitting involves a passive lack of interference by the defendant, that is, a failure to prevent an incident which it should have foreseen.[21]

---

18   *R v Toronto Electric Commissioners* (1991), 6 CELR (NS) 301 at 316 (Ont Gen Div).
19   *R v Imperial Oil* (1995), 17 CELR (NS) 12 at 18 (Ont Prov Div).
20   *R v Inco Ltd* (2001), 54 OR (3d) 495 at 513 (CA).
21   *Sault Ste Marie*, above note 8 at 184–85 (DLR).

Issues of interpretation continue to arise and are currently antici-pated in connection with the new *Canadian Environmental Assessment Act, 2012*[22] and ongoing amendments to the *Fisheries Act*. With regard to the latter, for example, amendments to the habitat protection provi-sions have attracted considerable attention. The former section 35(1) declared that in the absence of ministerial authorization or regulation, "No person shall carry on any work or undertaking that results in the harmful alteration, disruption or destruction of fish habitat." In an initial round of revision, the prohibition against a work or undertak-ing has been elaborated by the addition of the word "activity," thereby inviting consideration about a possible expansion in the scope of the provision. A further set of amendments, not yet in force, would replace section 35(1) with the following:

> No person shall carry on any work, undertaking or activity that re-sults in serious harm to fish that are part of a commercial, recrea-tional or Aboriginal fishery, or to fish that support such a fishery.

This further set of amendments would define "serious harm to fish" as "the death of fish or any permanent alteration to, or destruction of, fish habitat," while also adding definitions for Aboriginal and com-mercial fisheries and for fish habitat.[23] Again, alongside the results of policy review and additional regulation, questions of interpretation are likely to arise concerning the relationship of permanent alteration to the former alteration, disruption, or destruction provisions, and so on.

C. THE *CRIMINAL CODE* AND THE ENVIRONMENT

The severity of potential sanctions available and the presumption of moral wrongdoing on the part of those convicted under criminal law makes criminalization attractive to those who regard environmental degradation as a serious affront to contemporary social values. However, Justice Cory acknowledged difficulties in the theoretical distinction be-tween degrees of moral fault in criminal and regulatory offences: "For example, is the single mother who steals a loaf of bread to sustain her family more blameworthy than . . . the manufacturer who, as a result of

---

22   See Chapter 12.
23   The *Fisheries Act* amendments were introduced through Bill C-38, *An Act to implement certain provisions of the budget tabled in Parliament on March 29, 2012 and other measures*, 1st Sess, 41st Parl, 2012 (Royal Assent, 29 June 2012).

negligence, sells dangerous products or pollutes the air and waters by its plant?"[24] As he further observed, the degree of moral blameworthiness attaching to certain types of conduct may change with changing social values.

The *Criminal Code* makes no express reference to environment. Nonetheless, certain existing provisions offer some scope to prosecute those responsible for environmentally harmful conduct, presuming that substantially similar charges have not been brought for alleged violations of the environmental regime itself.[25] For example, the *Code* indicates that everyone is criminally negligent who, in doing anything or in omitting to do anything that it is his or her duty to do, shows wanton or reckless disregard for the lives or safety of other persons.[26] The common nuisance provision makes it an offence to commit a common nuisance and thereby to endanger the lives, safety, or health of the public.[27] Other sections of the *Criminal Code* with environmental dimensions address mischief;[28] dangerous, offensive, volatile,[29] and explosive substances;[30] and certain offences against animals.[31]

Historically, some use was made of these provisions in relation to environmental damage, particularly in situations involving threats to public health. However, the *Criminal Code* provisions contain a number of important limitations that render them poorly suited and unreliable for use in the cause of environmental protection. A study for the Law Reform Commission of Canada (LRCC) found that some of the *Code's* existing provisions were too vaguely worded to facilitate successful environmental prosecutions, while the focus of others on threats and injury to the lives and safety of persons, or on damage to property rather than on environmental interests per se, undermined their utility. Having concluded that "existing *Code* offences do not effectively encompass serious pollution, and could not be revised to do so in a manner which would highlight the importance of a safe environment;

---

24   *Wholesale*, above note 6.

25   R v *Crowe* (1996), 20 CELR (NS) 235 (Ont Gen Div).

26   *Criminal Code*, above note 9, s 219. Amendments in this area following the Westray mining tragedy are discussed in Chapter 9.

27   *Criminal Code*, ibid, s 180; R v *Goodyear Tire & Rubber Co of Canada* (1996), 21 (CELR) (NS) 176 (Ont Prov Div).

28   *Criminal Code*, ibid, s 430.

29   *Ibid*, s 178.

30   *Ibid*, ss 79–82.

31   *Ibid*, ss 444–47. In 2008, the traditional summary offences of "injuring or endangering animals" and "causing unnecessary suffering" were re-designated as hybrid offences now involving the possibility of imprisonment: An Act to amend the Criminal Code (cruelty to animals), SC 2008, c 12.

nor could they be revised without diffusing the present goals and purposes of those offences,"[32] the LRCC recommended a new and distinct category of offences against the environment.[33]

The specific recommendations of the LRCC were not adopted, but the publication of the report coincided more or less with a serious strengthening of the enforcement capacity of many provincial environment ministries and with increasingly severe penalty regimes in a number of jurisdictions. In addition, section 274(1) of *CEPA 1999* creates something in the nature of a crime against the environment provision triggered by violations of *CEPA 1999* itself:

> Every person is guilty of an offence and liable on conviction on indictment to a fine or to imprisonment for a term of not more than five years, or to both, who, in committing an offence
>
> (a) intentionally or recklessly causes a disaster that results in a loss of the use of the environment, or
>
> (b) shows wanton or reckless disregard for the lives or safety of other persons and thereby causes a risk of death or harm to another person,

Subsection 274(2) specifically provides that sections 220 or 221 of the *Criminal Code* apply in the case of anyone contravening *CEPA 1999* whose wanton or reckless disregard for the lives or safety of others in fact causes death or bodily harm.

D. ENFORCEMENT POLICY AND PROSECUTORIAL DISCRETION

As public concern mounted over the inadequacies of environmental protection, the question of appropriate strategies for ensuring that established environmental standards would be respected attracted increasing attention. As discussed in Chapter 7, two general approaches—conciliatory and enforcement-based—were identified. The former generally consists of non-coercive measures and negotiations intended to encourage or promote environmental performance consistent with

---

32   Law Reform Commission of Canada, *Crimes against the Environment* (Ottawa: LRCC, 1985).

33   *Ibid* at 68. For a remarkable attempt to craft a comprehensive rule around "ecological sustainability" rather than pollution, see B Pardy, "In Search of the Holy Grail of Environmental Law: A Rule to Solve the Problem" (2005) 1 Journal of Sustainable Development Law and Policy 29.

established environmental standards. Canada's approach has been characterized as conciliatory in nature, or, in the words of one observer, as a "relatively closed, consensual and consultative approach with a small number of prosecutions."[34] An enforcement strategy, on the other hand, relies more heavily on the use of prosecution and formal penalties or sanctions.[35]

There is an important ongoing debate about the effectiveness of the alternative strategies. A number of studies appear to confirm the utility of a sanctions-based approach to regulatory legislation.[36] However, there are indications that in certain circumstances significant reductions in the discharge of environmental contaminants may be brought about without resort to substantial sanctions or penalties.[37] Defenders of a conciliatory strategy also note its contribution to the dissemination of knowledge. There is an informal benefit, it is argued, from the work of inspectors who are sometimes in a position to facilitate the transfer of experience and learning between different companies which have encountered similar environmental compliance challenges.

Although each general strategy has advocates and detractors, the debate about their comparative merits is seriously complicated by the inevitable relationships between the two approaches. Advocates of a conciliatory process have often been willing to acknowledge that the existence of sanctions resulting from the possibility of prosecution provides some reinforcement for their efforts. On the other hand, it has been argued that effective enforcement action depends upon moral as well as legislative "legitimacy" and that this is likely to be absent where the institutions and processes of compliance are ignored. "What is sanctionable," in the opinion of Keith Hawkins, "is not rule-breaking as such, but rule-breaking which is deliberately or negligently done, or rule-break-

---

34   PN Nemetz, "Federal Environmental Regulation in Canada" (1986) 26 Natural Resources J 551.

35   For a comprehensive discussion of differences between the two general approaches, see K Hawkins, *Environment and Enforcement: Regulation and the Social Definition of Pollution* (Oxford: Clarendon Press, 1984); in the Canadian context see D Chappell, *From Sawdust to Toxic Blobs: A Consideration of Sanctioning Strategies to Combat Pollution in Canada* (Ottawa: Supply & Services, 1989).

36   D Saxe, "The Impact of Prosecution of Corporations and Their Officers and Directors upon Regulatory Compliance by Corporations" (1991) 1 J Envtl L & Prac 91; R Brown & M Rankin, "Persuasion, Penalties, and Prosecution: Administrative v Criminal Sanctions" in ML Friedland, ed, *Securing Compliance: Seven Case Studies* (Toronto: University of Toronto Press, 1990) 325–53.

37   DN Dewees, "The Effect of Environmental Regulation: Mercury and Sulphur Dioxide" in Friedland, above note 36 at 354–91.

ing accompanied by unco-operativeness which amounts to a symbolic assault upon the enforcer's . . . authority and legitimacy."[38]

In relation to the issue of active implementation, a number of observers have argued that, although legislative and regulatory measures may be satisfactory in principle, enforcement efforts have been inconsistent and inadequate in practice. For example, studies and reports by the Canadian Environmental Advisory Council and by staff at the Law Reform Commission of Canada criticized Environment Canada during the 1980s for deficiencies in the enforcement of environmental legislation, or for what was described as an "implementation gap."[39] Various causes may be advanced to account for the "implementation gap" in environmental law, notably the fact that competition exists for the allocation of public prosecutorial resources. Justice officials carrying responsibility for the enforcement of a wide range of statutes applicable throughout the community must, in effect, allocate and ration personnel and available finances. In Saskatchewan, for example, before embarking upon a prosecution provincial justice decision makers systematically address the following questions:

i)   Is there a reasonable likelihood of conviction?

ii) Is it in the public interest to prosecute?

Consider the following in answering ii:

- The seriousness of the offence;
- Any mitigating or aggravating circumstances;
- The personal circumstances of the accused;
- The staleness of the alleged offence;
- The prosecution's effect on public order, morale, or public confidence in the administration of justice;
- The availability of alternatives to prosecution;
- The frequency of the offence in the community;
- The concern in the community over the offence;
- The likely sentence; and
- The attitudes and interests of the victim.[40]

---

38   Hawkins, above note 35 at xiv.

39   L Giroux, "A Statement by the Canadian Environmental Advisory Council on Enforcement Practices of Environment Canada" (June 1985); Law Reform Commission of Canada, *Pollution Control in Canada: The Regulatory Approach in the 1980s* (Study Paper) by K Webb (Ottawa: The Commission, 1988).

40   Saskatchewan Department of Justice, "The Role of Public Prosecution in the Justice System," quoted in M Bailey & A Ikwueme, *Report on Saskatchewan Environmental Law Review* (Saskatoon, SK: Centre for Studies in Agriculture, Law and the Environment, 2001) at 28.

An Alberta review panel on environmental law enforcement set out some of the considerations governing the operation of a sanctioning strategy. Prosecution, the panel explained, supplements the administrative process by signalling to polluters that prohibited conduct will not be tolerated. The imposition of a penalty deters not only the convicted accused but other potential offenders from future wrongdoing. The Alberta panel recommended that prosecution be used for clearly defined offences, with enforcement policy identifying certain crucial violations that constitute an automatic prosecutable offence:

> Since the current approach of Alberta Environment involving negotiation and abatement relies heavily on accurate monitoring and timely reporting, any breaches in this regard should be treated extremely seriously. Offences such as failure to report to authorities any uncontrolled releases, providing false information and failure to obtain a permit or license should also result in automatic prosecution.[41]

CEPA 1999 came into effect during a period of intense interest in stricter enforcement, a situation that encouraged the federal minister to emphasize the severity of the sanctions to be embodied in the legislation:

> Sanctions will include million-dollar-a-day fines. But more than fines are needed because they affect the balance sheet but not necessarily the polluters themselves. The new law will also place responsibility squarely where it belongs—on the shoulders of the chief executive officers and company presidents who commit violations or who permit them. They will be subject to jail sentences of one to five years. And the government intends to enforce the law with vigor.[42]

These widely quoted remarks contributed in an important way to the nature of the expectations attendant upon the introduction of *CEPA 1999*. There was thus considerable interest when officials responsible for *CEPA 1999*'s administration addressed the issues of enforcement and compliance in a policy statement:

> Compliance with the Act and its regulations is mandatory. Enforcement officials throughout Canada will apply the Act in a manner that is fair, predictable and consistent. They will use rules, sanctions and

---

41 Quoted in LB Huestis, "Enforcement of Environmental Law in Canada" in G Thompson, ML McConnell, & LB Huestis, eds, *Environmental Law and Business in Canada* (Aurora, ON: Canada Law Book, 1993) 243 at 255. Now see "Enforcement Program for the Environmental Protection and Enhancement Act" (Alberta Environmental Protection, 2 September 1994).

42 Hon Tom McMillan, Speech.

processes securely founded in law. Enforcement officials will administer the Act with an emphasis on prevention of damage to the environment. Enforcement officials will examine every suspected violation of which they have knowledge, and will take action consistent with this Enforcement and Compliance Policy. Enforcement officials will encourage the reporting to them of suspected violations of the Act.[43]

These remain the guiding principles of compliance and enforcement in connection with the administration of CEPA 1999.[44]

The specific measures envisaged to promote compliance include education and exchange of technical information, the elaboration of codes of practice and guidelines, inspections, oral and written warnings, increased monitoring, and the use of administrative orders, recalls, ticketing, and directions, as well as court-based proceedings, injunctions, civil claims for cost recovery, and prosecutorial action.

Environment Canada has reported annually on its enforcement efforts under CEPA 1999 using two broad categories and somewhat variable classification procedures. Enforcement *activities* include administrative verification, field, or site inspections and investigations. Enforcement *actions* include verbal and written warnings, directives, prosecutions, and some referrals to other agencies. The department has recently begun to make significantly greater use of Environmental Protection Compliance Orders under section 235 to prevent or stop designated violations of CEPA 1999.

As reported by the Commissioner of the Environment and Sustainable Development, Environment Canada's enforcement initiatives under CEPA 1999 for the 2010–2011 period included: 606 written warnings, three written directives, two prosecutions and forty-two environmental protection compliance orders. No use was made of tickets, injunctions, ministerial orders, or negotiated alternative measures. There were no convictions. The CESD report was sharply critical of Environment Canada's performance under CEPA 1999. The departmental response suggested that a number of recommendations to clarify priorities around human health and environmental risk, and to monitor performance more systematically, were being pursued.[45]

---

43 Environment Canada, *Canadian Environmental Protection Act Enforcement and Compliance Policy* (Ottawa: Supply & Services, 1988) at 9.

44 Online: www.ec.gc.ca/lcpe-cepa/default.asp?lang=En&n=5082BFBE-1&offset=2&toc=show. See also Environment Canada, *Compliance and Enforcement Policy for the Habitat Protection and Pollution Prevention Provisions of the Fisheries Act*, online: www.ec.gc.ca/alef-ewe/default.asp?lang=en&n=D6B74D58-1.

45 *2011 December Report of the Commissioner of the Environment and Sustainable Development*, (Ottawa: Office of the Auditor General, 2011) c 3 "Enforcing

Some observers of the enforcement record suggest that more frequent prosecutions, combined with higher fines resulting from legislative amendments, has a discernible impact on corporate behaviour. In particular, more vigorous enforcement measures are thought to encourage more conscientious attention to the necessity for environmental compliance. Dianne Saxe surveyed senior corporate officials in major Canadian firms with respect to the impact that prosecution for environmental non-compliance might have on their decisions. She concluded that prosecution "has a strong, statistically significant impact upon the environmental behaviour of corporations, both in actual, past behaviour and in predictions of future behaviour." In terms of specific conduct, Saxe reported that corporations that had experienced prosecution had higher levels of environmentally related spending than firms that had not been prosecuted. She also found indications that corporate executives would be more likely to take action to have their companies avoid environmental offences if they could be prosecuted personally for such offences.[46]

E. INVESTIGATIONS

A search or investigation for the purpose of obtaining evidence relevant to the prosecution of possible statutory violations differs in important respects from routine administrative inspections, even if, as in some jurisdictions, these activities may be conducted by the same officials.[47] The Supreme Court of Canada adopted the following distinction between searches and inspections in *Comité Paritaire de l'Industrie de la Chemise v Potash*:

> An inspection is characterized by a visit to determine whether there is compliance with a given statute. The basic intent is not to uncover a breach of the Act; the purpose is rather to protect the public. On the other hand, if the inspector enters the establishment because he has reasonable grounds to believe that there has been a breach of the Act, this is no longer an inspection but a search, as the intent is then es-

---

the *Canadian Environmental Protection Act, 1999*," online: www.oag-bvg.gc.ca/internet/English/parl_cesd_201112_e_36027.html.

46   D Saxe, above note 36.

47   For discussion in the environmental context, see Environment Canada, *Compliance and Enforcement Policy for CEPA, 1999*, online: www.ec.gc.ca/alef-ewe/default.asp?lang=En&n=AF0C5063-1&offset=6&toc=show.

sentially to see if those reasonable grounds are justified and to seize anything which may serve as proof of the offence.[48]

As one operational consequence of this distinction, officials involved in investigations must pay particular attention to fact-finding techniques, including the taking of witness statements and the identification and safeguarding of evidence such as samples that could eventually be required in court.

Although courts have acknowledged the basic legitimacy of the inspection process where abatement officials gather information for administrative compliance purposes, the potential use of information in prosecutions raises immediate concerns. In *Thomson Newspapers Ltd v Canada (Director of Investigation & Research)*, Justice La Forest referred to the suspicion and stigma attached to persons who are under investigation for a criminal offence when he asserted that "[f]or reasons that go to the very core of our legal tradition, it is generally accepted that the citizen has a very high expectation of privacy in respect of such investigations."[49] Certain *Charter* provisions are directly relevant to privacy interests in the course of investigative procedures. In particular, section 8 specifies that "everyone has the right to be secure against unreasonable search and seizure." This provision, according to the Supreme Court in *Canada (Director of Investigation & Research, Combines Investigation Branch) v Southam Inc*,[50] guarantees a reasonable expectation of privacy and makes warrantless searches presumptively unreasonable. A party seeking to justify a warrantless search faces the challenge of rebutting that presumption. Ordinarily, therefore, prior authorization obtained from an impartial arbitrator deciding on reasonable and probable grounds (established on the oath of the applicant) that an offence has taken place and that evidence can be found at the designated location will be necessary to establish the validity of the search or seizure.[51]

The interplay between the inspection/investigation distinction from *Comité Paritaire de l'Industrie de la Chemise* and the importance of protection against unreasonable investigative searches noted in *Thom-*

---

48   Translation from L Angers, "La recherche d'une protection efficace contre les inspections abusives de l'état: la Charte québécoise, la Charte canadienne et le Bill of Rights américain" (1986) 27 C de D 723 at 727–28, quoted in *Comité Paritaire de l'Industrie de la Chemise v Potash*, [1994] 2 SCR 406 at 417.

49   [1990] 1 SCR 425 at 507–8. The fact-specific nature of the expectation of privacy as assessed in "the totality of the circumstances" is discussed in *R v Mission Western Developments Ltd*, 2012 BCCA 167.

50   [1984] 2 SCR 145.

51   *Ibid* at 160–68.

son Newspapers and *Hunter v Southam* came to the fore in a prosecution against Inco for violations of the *Ontario Water Resources Act (OWRA)*.[52] After an officer of the Ministry of the Environment's Investigation and Enforcement Branch had been informed by abatement officials that a discharge had taken place from a mine waste treatment facility, the Investigation and Enforcement Branch (IEB) officer interviewed employees and requested documents relevant to the discharge. The company was subsequently charged.

It was the ministry's position that authority for the IEB officer's conduct was found in the warrantless inspection provisions of the *OWRA* section 15 which are reinforced by the possibility that charges of obstruction may be laid against those who fail to cooperate. In the Crown's submission, the statutory provisions involved no unreasonable incursion into the company's expectations of privacy as the information obtained corresponded to information to which the ministry was entitled within the general regulatory framework.

In the submission of Inco, on the other hand, the statutory provisions for inspections became inoperable at such point as the investigating officer had reasonable and probable grounds to lay charges. The Ontario Court of Appeal agreed that if reasonable and probable grounds existed before the interviews were conducted, the warrantless investigation was presumptively unreasonable as an interference with the company's expectation of privacy pursuant to *Hunter v Southam*. In such circumstances, the investigating officer would be required to obtain a warrant to proceed.

The SCC decision in *CanadianOxy Chemicals Limited* examined the scope of search warrants issued pursuant to section 487(1) of the *Criminal Code* in the context of strict liability or regulatory offences.[53] In particular, it was necessary to determine whether such warrants could authorize the collection of evidence relating to potential defences such as due diligence, or would they be confined to evidence related to the Crown's obligation to prove the offence. In *CanadianOxy*, following a reported discharge of chlorine into Burrard Inlet, a fisheries officer acting pursuant to a section 487(1) warrant had seized records relating to employee training, plant maintenance, and other matters that might permit a due diligence defence to be defeated by a demonstration of negligence.

---

52 *R v Inco Ltd*, above note 20, leave to appeal to SCC refused, [2001] SCCA No 436. See also *R v Jarvis*, [2002] 3 SCR 757.
53 *CanadianOxy Chemicals Ltd v Canada (AG)* (1999), 29 CELR (NS) 1.

Noting that the statutory phrase "evidence with respect to the commission of an offence" is a "broad statement," Major J judged the ordinary meaning of the phrase to encompass "all materials which might
shed light on the circumstances of an event which appears to constitute
an offence." He further concluded that the gathering of evidence under
warrant should not be restricted to the elements of the offence itself.

F. PRIVATE PROSECUTIONS AND OTHER CITIZEN INITIATIVES

Individuals and public interest groups who are dissatisfied with official
efforts to ensure environmental compliance or to pursue violations have
several enforcement options and environmental protection strategies.[54]

Citizens may encourage public authorities to take enforcement action, or they may initiate private prosecutions. Individuals contemplating a private prosecution of an offence may be advised to complain
formally and in writing to the appropriate enforcement agency in the
hope that it may yet undertake the case. If this does not occur, the
prosecution can be launched by laying an information concerning
the alleged offence and preparing for trial.[55] Indeed, there have been
some successful private prosecutions in the environmental context.[56]
One important example is provided by the successful *Fisheries Act*
prosecution of the City of Kingston which was initiated as a private
prosecution.[57] More recently, following the widely-publicized death of
hundreds of migratory birds in waste management facilities associated
with oil sands operations in northern Alberta, charges were initiated
by means of a private prosecution.[58] If the entitlement of private prosecutors to share in the proceeds from fines becomes more commonly
available, the incentive may encourage further use of this enforcement

---

54 J Brunnée, "Individual and Group Enforcement of Environmental Law in Que-
    bec" (1992) 41 UNBLJ 107; OE Delogu, "Citizen Suits to Protect the Environ-
    ment: The US Experience May Suggest a Canadian Model" (1992) 41 UNBLJ
    124; R Cotton & N Johnson, "Avenues for Citizen Participation in the Environ-
    mental Arena: Some Thoughts on the Road Ahead" (1992) 41 UNBLJ 131.
55 JS Mallet, *Enforcing Environmental Law: A Guide to Private Prosecution*, 2d ed
    (Edmonton: Environmental Law Centre, 2004).
56 *R v Sheridan* (1972), [1973] 2 OR 192 (Dist Ct).
57 *R v Kingston (City)*, above note 17. For the origins of the case, see *Fletcher v
    Kingston (City)* (1998), 28 CELR (NS) 229 (Ont Prov Div).
58 *R v Syncrude Canada Ltd*, 2010 ABPC 229.

mechanism.[59] Such actions have served on occasion to draw attention to gaps in official enforcement action.[60]

Canadian commentators have expressed the view that private prosecutions are costly, difficult, and fraught with hazards; in the words of one observer, "[t]he weak-spirited need not even try."[61] In addition to the likelihood that the private prosecutor's investigative resources and access to legal services are limited, the attorney general retains authority under section 579(1) of the *Criminal Code* to stay proceedings at any time before judgment. In the absence of flagrant impropriety, the attorney general's decision to intervene and order a stay is unreviewable.[62] Elizabeth Swanson and Elaine Hughes also conclude that the courts have not proven effective as a means to compel government officials to undertake environmental enforcement actions. In support of their argument they cite *Canadians for the Abolition of the Seal Hunt v Canada (Minister of Fisheries & Environment)*,[63] an unsuccessful attempt to obtain an order of *mandamus* to require the federal minister of fisheries to enforce existing regulations as a means of minimizing cruelty in the hunt. Yet Swanson and Hughes acknowledge the value of judicial commentary in highlighting the controversy and the nature of public expectations.[64] The intense interest of concerned citizens in appropriate environmental enforcement activity in the face of limited public resources has underlined the need for governments to address regulatory negligence claims. Such actions might be brought by persons injured as a result of alleged deficiencies in enforcement practices.[65]

In addition to private prosecution, certain provisions in recent environmental legislation permit individuals to call for or initiate public investigation of alleged offences on the basis of documented applications to designated officials.[66] Thus, under *CEPA 1999* any Canadian

---

59 *Penalties and Forfeitures Proceeds Regulations*, CRC, c 827; *Environment Act*, SY 1991, c 5, s 19(2) [*YEA*]; *Environmental Rights Act*, RSNWT 1988 (Supp), c 83, s 5 [*NWTERA*].

60 SAG Elgie, "Environmental Groups and the Courts: 1970–1992" in Thompson, McConnell, & Huestis, above note 41, 185 at 206–7.

61 RW Proctor, "Individual Enforcement of Canada's Environmental Protection Laws: The Weak-spirited Need Not Try" (1991) 14 Dal LJ 112 at 132.

62 *Kostuch v Alberta (AG)* (1995), 174 AR 109 (CA), leave to appeal to SCC refused, [1995] SCCA No 512.

63 (1980), [1981] 1 FC 733 (TD).

64 EJ Swanson & EL Hughes, *The Price of Pollution: Environmental Litigation in Canada* (Edmonton: Environmental Law Centre, 1990) at 110–12.

65 M Mittelstaedt, "Ontario Prepares Negligence Defence" *The [Toronto] Globe and Mail* (18 February 1997) A1; *Quebec (AG) v Girard*, [2004] JQ no 13624 (CA).

66 *CEPA 1999*, above note 5, s 17.

resident eighteen years of age or older who alleges an offence has been committed under the Act may apply to the minister to have the matter investigated.[67] Should the minister fail to investigate and report within a reasonable time or respond unreasonably to the investigation, the individual applicant is entitled to launch an environmental protection action under the Act.[68] Under the Ontario *Environmental Bill of Rights, 1993 (OEBR)*, any two residents of the province may apply for an investigation by the responsible minister of an alleged contravention of any Act, regulation, or instrument prescribed under the *OEBR*. Such applications are made in the first instance to the environmental commissioner, who forwards the request to the appropriate minister and thereafter monitors the response process.[69]

Somewhere between a dozen and fifteen applications for review or requests for investigations are generally received by the Environmental Commissioner of Ontario (ECO) each year and forwarded to the relevant ministry for response. One example will serve to indicate how such initiatives might proceed. In August 2002, the ECO forwarded to the Ministry of the Environment an application for investigation submitted by the Sierra Club. It was generally alleged that Ontario Power Generation's (OPG) five coal-fired plants were responsible for the deposition of mercury into bodies of water in Ontario. More specifically, the application alleged contravention of section 30(1) of the *OWRA* which prohibits the discharge into Ontario's waters of any material that "may impair" water quality.[70] The application also alleged that OPG contravenes section 36(3) of the federal *Fisheries Act*, which prohibits the deposit of a "deleterious" substance into Canadian waters frequented by fish.[71] MOE did not conduct an investigation under the *Fisheries Act* on the grounds that in Ontario "the investigation and enforcement of the *FA* is the responsibility of Environment Canada." The ministry carried out an investigation under the *OWRA* amounting to a paper review of the evidence. The ministry concluded that "there is not, at this time, a reasonable prospect of a successful prosecution of OPG or any of its officers or directors with respect to the mercury emissions from the coal-fired plants, nor would it now be in the public interest

---

67   *CEPA 1999, ibid.* See also *NWTERA*, above note 59, s 4; Alberta *Environmental Protection and Enhancement Act*, RSA 2000, c E-12, s 196 [*AEPEA*]; *Environment Act*, SNS 1994–95, c 1, s 115; *YEA*, above note 59, s 14.

68   *CEPA 1999*, above note 5, s 22.

69   *Environmental Bill of Rights, 1993*, SO 1993, c 28, Part V.

70   *OWRA*, above note 2, s 30(1).

71   Environmental Commissioner of Ontario, *Annual Report 2003–2004*, online: www.eco.on.ca/english/publicat/ar2003.pdf at 122.

to commence such a prosecution under the *OWRA*."[72] The ECO reports annually on the outcome of applications and provides a general assessment of ministry responses.[73]

The *North American Agreement on Environmental Cooperation* (*NAAEC*) provides another mechanism to pursue grievances concerning environmental enforcement. Individuals and non-governmental organizations may make submissions to the secretariat of the Commission for Environmental Co-operation asserting that a "[p]arty [to the agreement] is failing to effectively enforce its environmental law." If the submissions satisfy criteria specified in *NAAEC*, the secretariat may request a response from the party named in the submission. Consideration of the response may lead to the preparation of a factual record for presentation to the council, the commission's governing body comprised of the environmental ministers of Canada, Mexico, and the United States, and on the basis of a two-thirds vote by council the factual record may be made publicly available.[74]

Certain interpretive issues arise in connection with the citizen submission process under the *NAAEC*. In particular, consideration must be given to the scope of "environmental law" within the context of the submission provision. Furthermore, there has been scope for disagreement and uncertainty around what is meant by failure to enforce effectively. Chris Tollefson usefully describes what is and what is not contemplated by the arrangements:

> [T]he NAAEC does not require parties to protect the environment from harm. Parties are allowed to freely choose their own preferred level of environmetal protection. The NAAEC does, however, require that parties 'effectively enforce' environmental laws they enact, which are presumably designed to achieve their chosen level of environmental protection. In short, the citizen submission process is not about preventing environmental harm *per se*, but rather about holding governments responsible for enforcing environmental laws.[75]

---

72   *Ibid* at 123.

73   Environmental Commissioner of Ontario, *Losing Touch: Annual Report 2011/2012*, Part 1, online: www.eco.on.ca/uploads/Reports-Annual/2011_12/ Losing%20Touch%20I%20EN.pdf; Environmental Commissioner of Ontario, *Losing Our Touch: Annual Report 2011/2012*, Part 2, online: www.eco.on.ca/ blog/2012/10/02/2011-12-annual-report.

74   *North American Agreement on Environmental Cooperation*, 12 and 14 September 1993, 32 ILM 1480. For discussion of procedures applicable to citizen submissions, see online: www.cec.org/citizen.

75   C Tollefson, "Stormy Weather: The Recent History of the Citizen Submission Process of the North American Agreement on Environmental Cooperation" in

Despite the obstacles and limitations of the citizen submission process, a number of Canadian applications have been successful in compelling the preparation of a factual record.[76]

G. PENALTIES, REMEDIAL ORDERS, AND SENTENCING PRINCIPLES

The sentencing of those convicted of environmental offences has generally been intended to serve the same ends as penalties imposed on other wrongdoers. Punishment along with deterrence of further violations either by the convicted offender or by others are basic objectives, although considerable emphasis is placed on the goal of environmental protection in the public interest that underpins the overall regulatory regime.[77]

To promote compliance, Canadian jurisdictions have intermittently revised their penalty provisions by increasing the severity of the potential consequences of ignoring environmental protection requirements. Individuals convicted under Manitoba's *Environment Act*, for example, are subject in the case of a first offence to a fine of not more than $50,000 or a term of imprisonment of up to six months, or to both. In the case of subsequent offences, the fine and potential prison term are increased to $100,000 and one year respectively. Corporate accused face a fine of up to $500,000 for a first offence and up to $1,000,000 for subsequent convictions.[78] In some jurisdictions, corporate offenders may also be subject to profit stripping.[79] As discussed more fully in the following chapter, increases in the personal exposure of corporate officers and directors to prosecution have appeared.[80]

J Kirton & V MacLaren, eds, *Linking Trade, Environment and Social Cohesion: NAFTA Experiences, Global Challenges* (Aldershot, UK: Ashgate, 2002) at 161.

76 For information on Canadian submissions resulting in factual records, see online: www.cec.org/Page.asp?PageID=1226&SiteNodeID=543, with particular reference to files on BC Hydro, BC Logging, BC Mining, Oldman River II, Ontario Logging, Ontario Logging II, Montreal Technoparc, Pulp and Paper, and Quebec Automobiles.

77 For discussion, see Swanson & Hughes, above note 64 at 180–82.

78 The *Environment Act*, CCSM c E125, s 33. Roughly equivalent fines are now also available in Ontario in connection with convictions under the *Environmental Protection Act*, and under the *OWRA*, above note 2, as a result of the *Environmental Enforcement Statute Law Amendment Act*, SO 2005, c 12.

79 *AEPEA*, above note 67, s 216; *MBCA*, above note 5, s 13(5).

80 *Environmental Protection Act*, RSO 1990, c E.19, s 194; *CEPA 1999*, above note 5, s 280.1.

At the federal level, the *Environmental Enforcement Act* introduced enforcement and penalty provisions to nine statutes and designated regulations.[81] The environmental statutes affected by the changes are:

- the *Antarctic Environmental Protection Act*;
- the *Canada National Marine Conservation Areas Act*;
- the *Canada National Parks Act*;
- the *Canada Wildlife Act*;
- the *Canadian Environmental Protection Act, 1999*;
- the *International River Improvements Act*;
- the *Migratory Birds Convention Act, 1994*;
- the *Saguenay-St. Lawrence Marine Park Act*;
- the *Wild Animal and Plant Protection and Regulation of International and Interprovincial Trade Act*.

The overall scheme of the new fine structure and its basic rationale are indicated in the following table:

Table 8.1   *Environmental Enforcement Act* — Fines

Offender	Type of Offence	Summary		Indictment	
		Min.	Max.	Min.	Max.
Individuals	Most serious offences	$5,000	$300,000	$15,000	$1 M
	Other offences	N/A	$25,000	N/A	$100 000
Small Corporations and Ships under 7,500 tonnes	Most serious offences	$25,000	$2 M	$75,000	$4 M
	Other offences	N/A	$50,000	N/A	$250 000
Corporations and Ships over 7,500 tonnes	Most serious offences	$100,000	$4 M	$500,000	$6 M
	Other offences	N/A	$250,000	N/A	$500,000

Source: Environment Canada: www.ec.gc.ca/alef-ewe/default.asp?lang=En&n=7CB7E78A-1

Courts have considered and ordered prison sentences in a variety of circumstances involving environmental offences. These have included contempt as well as substantive offences under environmental legislation. In *R v Jetco Manufacturing Ltd*,[82] a sentence of one year's imprisonment for contempt plus a further month up to a total of fifteen months for every day of delay in undertaking remedial work was ordered. The convictions of both the corporate defendant and the president were set aside on appeal on the grounds that it had not been satisfactorily

81   SC 2009, c 14.
82   (1986), 1 CELR (NS) 79 (Ont HCJ).

established in evidence that the defendants had notice of the prohibition order, violation of which was the basis of the contempt.[83] In *R v BEST Plating Shoppe Ltd*,[84] Siapas, the president of BEST, was sentenced to a term of imprisonment not exceeding six months in an application for a contempt order arising from repeated violations of a prohibition order made pursuant to the former Ontario *Municipal Act* concerning discharges in contravention of Metropolitan Toronto's sewer-use by-law. On *Charter* grounds, the contempt finding against the individual defendant was set aside on appeal.[85] Following a trial of the contempt charges, BEST's president was convicted and sentenced to six months' imprisonment.[86] In *R v Blackbird Holdings Ltd*, a convicted director was jailed for violation of an environmental statute rather than on the basis of contempt.[87] In *R v Cardinal*, a thirty-day jail term to be served intermittently was imposed on an accused convicted of multiple counts of fish and wildlife offences.[88] Overall however, the use of imprisonment in Canadian environmental cases has been rare.[89]

In the context of public welfare offences such as environmental offences, consideration of imprisonment or significant financial penalties is closely associated with deterrence. The following discussion outlines the judicial basis of concern for this objective:

> In our complex interdependent modern society . . . regulatory statutes [such as ecological conservation statutes] are accepted as essential in the public interest. . . .
>
> With reference to these offences, deterrence is not to be taken only in its usual negative connotation of achieving compliance by threat of punishment. Recently [this court] . . . referred to deterrence in a more positive aspect:
>
>> But in a crime of this type the deterrent quality of the sentence must be given paramount consideration, and here I am using the term deterrent in its widest sense. A sentence by emphasizing community disapproval of an act, and branding it as reprehensible has a more educative effect, and there-

---

83   *R v Jetco Manufacturing Ltd* (1987), 57 OR (2d) 776 (CA).
84   (1986), 1 CELR (NS) 85 (Ont HCJ).
85   *R v BEST Plating Shoppe Ltd* (1987), 59 OR (2d) 145 (CA).
86   *Metropolitan Toronto (Municipality) v Siapas* (1988), 3 CELR (NS) 122 (Ont HCJ).
87   (1990), 6 CELR (NS) 119 (Ont Prov Offences Ct), var'd (1991), 6 CELR (NS) 138 (Ont Prov Div), leave to appeal refused (1991), 6 CELR (NS) 116 (Ont CA).
88   2010 ABQB 673.
89   *R v Varnicolor Chemical Ltd* (1992), 9 CELR (NS) 176, [1992] OJ No 1978 (Prov Div); *R v Demacedo*, [1992] BCJ No 2254 (Prov Ct); *R v Fontaine*, [1992] BCJ No 2640 (Prov Ct); *R v Underwood* (29 March 1996) (Alta QB).

by affects the attitude of the public. One then hopes that a person with an attitude thus conditioned to regard such conduct as reprehensible will not commit such an act.

This aspect of deterrence is particularly applicable to public welfare offences where it is essential for the proper functioning of our society for citizens at large to expect that the basic rules are established and enforced to protect the physical, economic and social welfare of the public.[90]

The remedial powers of courts have been extended beyond fines and imprisonment to include authority to order restoration work, to prevent or reduce the likelihood of recurrence of environmental harm, or to impose other potentially costly obligations in connection with a conviction.[91] In addition to any other punishment under *CEPA 1999*, the court—subject to the nature and circumstances of the offence—may make a variety of other enumerated orders:

(*a*) prohibiting the offender from doing any act or engaging in any activity that may result in the continuation or repetition of the offence;

(*b*) directing the offender to take any action that the court considers appropriate to remedy or avoid any harm to the environment that results or may result from the act or omission that constituted the offence;

(*c*) directing the offender to prepare and implement a pollution prevention plan or environmental emergency plan;

(*d*) directing the offender to carry out environmental effects monitoring in the manner established by the Minister or directing the offender to pay, in the manner prescribed by the court, an amount for the purposes of environmental effects monitoring;

(*e*) directing the offender to implement an environmental management system that meets a recognized Canadian or international standard;

(*f*) directing the offender to have an environmental audit conducted by a person of a class and at the times specified by the court and directing the offender to remedy any deficiencies revealed during the audit;

(*g*) directing the offender to publish, in the manner directed by the court, the facts relating to the conviction;

---

90   *R v Cotton Felts Ltd* (1982), 2 CCC (3d) 287 (Ont CA).
91   For a well-documented early review of environmental enforcement see Huestis, above note 41.

(h) directing the offender to notify, at the offender's own cost and in the manner directed by the court, any person aggrieved or affected by the offender's conduct of the facts relating to the conviction;

(i) directing the offender to post any bond or pay any amount of money into court that will ensure compliance with any order made under this section;

(j) directing the offender to submit to the Minister, on application by the Minister made within three years after the date of conviction, any information with respect to the offender's activities that the court considers appropriate and just in the circumstances;

(k) directing the offender to compensate the Minister in whole or in part, for the cost of any remedial or preventative action taken by or caused to be taken on behalf of the Minister as a result of the act or omission that constituted the offence;

(l) directing the offender to perform community service, subject to any reasonable conditions that may be imposed in the order;

(m) . . .

(n) directing the offender to pay, in the manner prescribed by the court, an amount for the purposes of conducting research into the ecological use and disposal of the substance in respect of which the offence was committed or research relating to the manner of carrying out environmental effects monitoring;

(o) directing the offender to pay, in the manner prescribed by the court, an amount to environmental, health or other groups to assist in their work in the community where the offence was committed;

(p) directing the offender to pay, in the manner prescribed by the court an amount to an educational institution for scholarships for students enrolled in environmental studies; and

(q) requiring the offender to comply with any other reasonable conditions that the court considers appropriate and just in the circumstances for securing the offender's good conduct and for preventing the offender from repeating the same offence or committing other offences.[92]

Some legislation, including the Manitoba statute whose penalty provisions were noted above, confers on judges a licence-revocation power that may be exercised "where in the opinion of the judge the in-

---

92   *CEPA 1999*, above note 5, s 291; see also *Wild Animal and Plant Protection and Regulation of International and Interprovincial Trade Act*, SC 1992, c 52, s 22(6); *FA*, above note 3, s 79.2.

dividual [or corporation] is unwilling or unable to remedy the situation or condition giving rise to the offence."[93]

The task of determining the most appropriate sentencing option in the circumstances of a successful environmental prosecution rests with the court. The judiciary therefore constitute a vital element of the compliance and enforcement structure, and so the principles applicable to their sentencing decisions are of considerable importance.

Principles on sentencing in environmental cases as articulated by Stewart J in *R v United Keno Hill Mines Ltd*[94] set out a framework for evaluating the available options. Relevant considerations include the nature of the environment affected by the offence; the degree of damage and the deliberateness of the offence, together with the accused's attitude and any indication of remorse; evidence of efforts made to comply; the nature and size of the corporation and any realization of profits from the offence; previous criminal record; and other evidence of the character of the convicted corporation or individual.

It is also possible for the legislature to address the matter of considerations relevant to sentencing, as was done in the case of pollution offences under the *Canada Shipping Act, 2001* which stipulates that a maximum fine of $1,000,000 may be ordered on conviction. The statute itself identifies factors to which the court may have regard in determining punishment:

(a) the harm or risk of harm caused by the offence;

(b) an estimate of the total costs of clean-up, of harm caused, and of the best available mitigation measures;

(c) the remedial action taken, or proposed to be taken, by the offender to mitigate the harm;

(d) whether the discharge or anticipated discharge was reported in accordance with the regulations . . .

(e) any economic benefits accruing to the offender that, but for the offence, the offender would not have received; and

(f) any evidence from which the court may reasonably conclude that the offender has a history of non-compliance with legislation designed to prevent or to minimize pollution.[95]

---

93 Manitoba *Environment Act*, above note 78, s 33.
94 (1980), 10 CELR 43 (Y Terr Ct). For an extensive recent discussion of sentencing factors, see *R v Northwest Territories Power Corp*, 2011 NWTTC 3.
95 *Canada Shipping Act, 2001*, SC 2001, c 26, s 191(4). See also *CEPA 1999*, above note 5, s 287. Whether the absence of explicit reference to general deterrence as an enumerated consideration will affect sentencing remains to be determined. See *R v BWP*, 2006 SCC 27.

The new range of fines introduced to a suite of federal environmental statutes through the *Environmental Enforcement Act* is intended to be administered with reference to a common set of statutorily-prescribed considerations. As now set out in *CEPA 1999*, the amount of the fine should be increased to account for relevant aggravating factors including the following:

(a) the offence caused damage or risk of damage to the environment or environmental quality;

(b) the offence caused damage or risk of damage to any unique, rare, particularly important or vulnerable component of the environment;

(c) the offence caused harm or risk of harm to human health;

(d) the damage or harm caused by the offence is extensive, persistent or irreparable;

(e) the offender committed the offence intentionally or recklessly;

(f) the offender failed to take reasonable steps to prevent the commission of the offence despite having the financial means to do so;

(g) by committing the offence or failing to take action to prevent its commission, the offender increased revenue or decreased costs or intended to increase revenue or decrease costs;

(h) the offender committed the offence despite having been warned by an enforcement officer of the circumstances that subsequently became the subject of the offence;

(i) the offender has a history of non-compliance with federal or provincial legislation that relates to environmental or wildlife conservation or protection; and

(j) after the commission of the offence, the offender
    (i) attempted to conceal its commission,
    (ii) failed to take prompt action to prevent, mitigate or remediate its effects, or
    (iii) failed to take prompt action to reduce the risk of committing similar offences in the future.[96]

The legislation confirms that the absence of an aggravating factor is not to be considered as a mitigating factor, and requires judges to give reasons where they are satisfied of the existence of an aggravating factor or factors that will not be used to increase the amount of the fine.

Notable even in the context of sentencing principles is the need to assess and balance direct environmental protection and restoration measures alongside more traditional punitive and deterrence con-

---

96   *CEPA 1999*, above note 5, s 287.1(2).

siderations. Thus counsel, even at the time of argument on sentencing, must reflect carefully on the suitability of possible penalties to various underlying objectives of the environmental law regime, including prevention, restoration, and environmental protection.

Creative sentencing decisions are beginning to emerge. When, during refuelling of the motor vessel "Lil Buddy LS 855," gasoline was discharged into the waters of British Columbia's Pitt River, contrary to oil pollution prevention regulations under the *Canada Shipping Act*, the court, upon conviction of the accused company, ordered a comparatively modest fine. In addition, however, the company was required to pay a further sum, ultimately to be made available to a community environmental organization to support its work on conservation and protection of fish and fish habitat.[97]

Several hundred birds were trapped and most died in bitumen (a mat "several inches thick, viscous and cohesive with the consistency of a frothy roofing tar") on the surface of a large settling basin where "tailings" from oil sands production are deposited.[98] When Syncrude Canada was convicted under the Alberta *EPEA and the Migratory Birds Convention Act, 1994* in connection with this extensive damage to wildlife, Crown and defence counsel prepared a joint submission on sentencing projects. By court order, Syncrude was required to contribute financially to three initiatives:

1. Research through the Avian Protection Project at the University of Alberta ($1,300,000);
2. The Waterfowl Habitat Fund of the Alberta Conservation Association ($900,000); and
3. The Wildlife Management Technician Diploma Program at Keyano College ($250,000).

In addition, Syncrude was required to review and enhance measures within its own Waterfowl Protection Plan to safeguard water birds.

FURTHER READINGS

BERGER, SD, *The Prosecution and Defence of Environmental Offences* (Toronto: Emond Montgomery, 1993)

CAMPBELL, GS, "Fostering a compliance culture through creative sentencing for environmental offences" (2004) 9 Can Crim L Rev 1-33

---

97   *R v Forrest Marine Ltd* (29 April 2005) (BC Prov Ct).
98   *R v Syncrude Canada Ltd*, 2010 ABPC 299 at paras 1–3.

COMMISSION FOR ENVIRONMENTAL COOPERATION, *Special Report on Enforcement Activities* (June 2001)

DUNCAN, LF, *Enforcing Environmental Law: A Guide to Private Prosecutions* (Edmonton: Environmental Law Centre, 1990)

HALLEY, P, *Le droit penal de l'environnement: l'interdiction de polluter* (Montreal: Yvon Blais, 2001)

HALLEY, P, & A GAGNON-ROCQUE, "La sanction en droit pénal canadien de l'environnement: la loi et son application" (2009) 50 Cahiers de droit 919

HUGHES, EL, & LA REYNOLDS, "Creative Sentencing and Environmental Protection" (2009) 19 J Envtl L & Prac 105

LAW REFORM COMMISSION OF CANADA, *Sentencing in Environmental Cases* (Study Paper) by J Swaigen & G Bunt (Ottawa: the Commission, 1985)

LIBMAN, R, *Libman on Regulatory Offences in Canada* (Salt Spring Island: Earlscourt Legal Press, 2002)

SWAIGEN, J, *Regulatory Offences in Canada: Liability & Defences* (Toronto: Carswell, 1992)

VALIANTE, M, "'Welcomed Participants' or 'Environmental Vigilantes'? The *CEPA* Environmental Protection Action and the Role of Citizen Suits" (2002) 25 Dal LJ 81

WEBB, K, "Taking Matters into Their Own Hands: The Role of Citizens in Canadian Pollution Control Enforcement" (1991) 36 McGill LJ 770

CHAPTER 9

CORPORATE ENVIRONMENTAL OBLIGATIONS AND DIRECTORS' AND OFFICERS' LIABILITY

A. THE LIABILITY OF CORPORATIONS

Among the principal forms of business organizations—sole proprietorships, partnerships, and corporations—the last, corporations, has attracted particular attention from an environmental perspective. Despite many variations in corporate form, from small, not-for-profit entities to major multinational firms, in the environmental context corporations are regarded as serious sources of potential harm whose operations require careful supervision and control.

While the nature and magnitude of the risks create an obvious public interest in channelling corporate behaviour in ways that reduce the likelihood of environmental damage, the practical problems of influencing corporate behaviour through the legal regime must be faced. Those who rely on legal mechanisms, criminal sanctions in particular, have had to consider how a regime of prohibitions and penalties will affect corporate operations. In the context of corporate accused, some aspects of criminal law pose especially intriguing problems. The need, in relation to the prosecution of certain offences, to establish a guilty mind or some form of intent on the part of accused corporations is one obvious example.

Although it may be argued that corporate action ultimately depends on human agency, or that the corporation can never act alone, the tendency is to subordinate philosophical dilemmas in the context of holding corporations responsible for wrongdoing. One analysis sets out the normative and practical arguments. First, justice requires that everyone in breach of penal law be equally subject to prosecution. "It is hardly fair," the analysis continues, "that individuals committing rather petty crimes, almost always entailing only one or a few victims, are subject to prosecution and imprisonment while a corporation might cause harm on a far grander scale, yet escape punishment." Second, although individual actions within a corporate environment may not constitute a crime when considered separately, the cumulative impact can be criminal and blameworthy; to exempt the corporation from liability would be to permit such conduct to go unchecked. Moreover, corporations, because of the collectivity of individuals involved, can and do behave as the persons that they, in strict point of law, are. Corporations are therefore susceptible to stigmatization (harm to status or reputation), and deterrence in the same way individuals are. Finally, access to resources, information, and expertise makes corporations better able to take measures to avoid the commission of criminal offences than individuals ordinarily are.[1]

Another approach to the conceptual challenges of holding corporations accountable for criminal offences attributed to them is to minimize the criminal dimensions of the situation. Such an approach is hinted at by Chief Justice Lamer, who expressed the opinion that "when the criminal law is applied to a corporation, it loses much of its 'criminal' nature and becomes, in essence, a 'vigorous' form of administrative law." Since the stigma attached to conviction is effectively reduced to a financial penalty, the corporation—which cannot be imprisoned—is in a completely different situation than is an individual.[2] As discussed below, recent changes to the *Criminal Code* in the aftermath of the Westray Mine disaster appear to have increased the direct exposure of corporations to criminal liability.

Corporate liability for environmental violations has rested on a variety of grounds. One means of linking the responsibility of the corporation directly with the conduct of individuals in its employ takes the form of vicarious liability. Such an approach appears in some regulatory legislation, Alberta's *Environmental Protection and Enhancement Act*, for example, where it is provided that

> for the purposes of this Act, an act or thing done or omitted to be done by a director, officer, official, employee or agent of a corpora-

---

1   MA Bowden & T Quigley, "Pinstripes or Prison Stripes? The Liability of Corporations and Directors for Environmental Offences" (1995) 5 J Envtl L & Prac 209 at 222.
2   *R v Wholesale Travel Group Inc*, [1991] 3 SCR 154 at 182.

tion in the course of his employment or in the exercise of his powers or the performance of his duties shall be deemed also to be an act or thing done or omitted to be done by the corporation.[3]

Corporations may also be held liable directly if their actions are identified with the conduct of some individual, typically a senior official, who is seen for the purpose as being the "directing mind" of the corporation. Depending on the circumstances, there may be several directing minds, as the Supreme Court of Canada explained in *Canadian Dredge & Dock*,

> a corporation may . . . have more than one directing mind. This must be particularly so in a country such as Canada where corporate operations are frequently geographically widespread. The transportation companies, for example, must of necessity operate by the delegation and sub-delegation of authority from the corporate centre; by the division and subdivision of the corporate brain; and by decentralizing by delegation the guiding forces in the corporate undertaking.[4]

The inquiry required by this theoretical identification of the corporation with a directing mind was more fully explained by the SCC in a subsequent decision:

> the focus of [the] inquiry must be whether the impugned individual has been delegated the "governing executive authority" of the company within the scope of his or her authority. I interpret this to mean that one must determine whether the discretion conferred on an employee amounts to an express or implied delegation of executive authority to design and supervise the implementation of corporate policy rather than simply to carry out such policy. In other words, the Courts must consider who has been left with the decision-making power in a relevant sphere of corporate activity.[5]

For purposes of the *Criminal Code*, amendments were introduced following the Westray Mine experience where, in May 1992, twenty-six miners died in a coal mine explosion. A public inquiry found that management had either disregarded or even encouraged a number of

---

3   *Environmental Protection and Enhancement Act*, RSA 2000, c E-12, s 253 [*AEPEA*]. Clauses of this type address the attribution of conduct to the corporation, but are insufficient to attribute an employee's mental state to the corporation insofar as the mental element of an offence is concerned. See *R v Safety-Kleen Canada Inc* (1997), 32 OR (3d) 493 (CA).

4   *R v Canadian Dredge & Dock Co*, [1985] 1 SCR 662 at 693.

5   *The Rhone v The Peter B Widener*, [1993] 1 SCR 497 at 520–21.

hazardous or illegal practices which contributed to the explosion.[6] Legislative changes now set out principles for attributing criminal liability to "organizations" in relation to the conduct of individuals determined to be their "representative." As a result of the new provisions, corporations may now more readily face prosecution for both intentional offences and offences grounded on proof of negligence.[7]

Although a degree of uncertainty still surrounds the actual mechanisms of accountability for environmental offences, corporations are clearly expected to comply with the entire range of environmental requirements including anti-pollution provisions, licensing conditions, spills reporting, and cleanup obligations, the duty to implement administrative orders, and so on. They may accordingly face prescribed penalties.

B. DIRECTORS' AND OFFICERS' LIABILITY

Despite the imposition of liability on corporations, the practical impact remains uncertain, notably in relation to the potential of conviction to alter environmentally harmful behaviour. How, it is asked, can a monetary penalty—generally modest in relation to corporate assets, and possibly even paid for by consumers in the form of marginally higher prices—effectively promote environmental compliance? The assumption has been made that to ensure that corporations will devote adequate resources to compliance it is necessary to engage the attention of their most senior policy makers through personal liability. In the words of Chief Justice Stewart of the Yukon Territorial Court: "Fining corporations leaves the upper echelon policy makers relatively unscathed. Fining corporate policy makers reduces somewhat the impotency of levying fines against corporate assets." Personal liability, he argued, "is the most effective method of ensuring that persons with the power to shape corporate policy are deterred from either active or passive acquiescence in the development of corporate policies precipitating violations."[8]

In *R v Northwest Territories Power Corp*, another northern judge insisted on the need to penalize individuals directly for corporate wrong-

---

6   Westray Mine Public Inquiry, *The Westray Story: A Predictable Path to Disaster, Report of the Westray Mine Public Inquiry* by Justice K Peter Richard, Commissioner, online: www.gov.ns.ca/lwd/pubs/westray.

7   *Criminal Code*, RSC 1985, c C-46, ss 22.1 & 22.2.

8   *R v United Keno Hill Mines Ltd* (1980), 10 CELR 43 at 52 and 55 (Y Terr Ct).

doing. Where it appeared that a regulated public corporation—having pleaded guilty to a violation of subsection 36(3) of the *Fisheries Act*—would simply recover the cost of a fine through its rate base, Justice Bourassa concluded that the defendant regarded the matter as "but an annoying, irritating obligation, rather than an important continuing responsibility."[9] To encourage a more responsible approach and to prevent future offences, Bourassa J chose to involve directors in sentencing and concluded that he would require the directors and chief executive officer "to apologize to the public for the corporation's negligence."[10] In explaining the sentence, he formulated a rationale based on the fact that directors accept "the responsibility of overseeing and directing corporate management. They reflect the corporate character, and must be accountable for it."[11] The responsibilities of directors, he further observed, extend to "the policies, priorities and values inherent in the corporation's operations."[12] In making the link between individual conduct and corporate environmental performance, Bourassa J stated:

> To impact upon the directors of a corporate defendant is likely . . . to prevent further offences, in that the directors will realize that they are and will be accountable for their acts (or omissions)—that they cannot shelter behind a corporate veil.[13]

Although Bourassa J's order for an apology was struck down on appeal,[14] the objective of promoting corporate compliance by means of imposing accountability on directors and other senior officers has gained acceptance.

Even in the absence of express statutory provision, corporate officials have long been liable to prosecution as parties to a corporate offence on the grounds that they aided or abetted the corporation in the commission of the wrongful act. But express liability provisions for directors and other corporate officials are now frequently found in environmental legislation. *CEPA 1999*, for example, explicitly imposes personal liability on individuals, including officers and directors:

> If a corporation commits an offence under this Act, any director, officer, agent or mandatory of the corporation who directed, authorized, assented to, acquiesced in or participated in the commission

---

9   *R v Northwest Territories Power Corp* (1989), [1990] NWTR 115 at 119 (Terr Ct).
10 *Ibid* at 123.
11 *Ibid* at 122.
12 *Ibid.*
13 *Ibid* at 122–23.
14 *R v Northwest Territories Power Corp*, [1990] NWTR 125 (SC).

of the offence is a party to and guilty of the offence, and is liable on conviction to the penalty provided for by this Act for an individual in respect of the offence committed by the corporation, whether or not the corporation has been prosecuted and convicted.[15]

In addition to their customary responsibilities for corporate operations, officers and directors have also been more clearly singled out in provincial and territorial legislation for personal liability in relation to corporate environmental practices.[16]

A range of uncertainties relating to the necessary elements of directors' and officers' liability somewhat limited the prosecutorial appeal of such provisions. In particular, the nature of conduct (passive or active) that would amount to assent or acquiescence was not entirely clear.[17] Moreover, given the underlying assumption that directors' and officers' liability serves to improve corporate performance in the environmental field, prosecutors may be required to demonstrate actual influence and perhaps control of relevant aspects of corporate activity.

Partially as a consequence of the ambiguities, Ontario reformulated the environmental responsibility of directors and officers in 1986, imposing on them a "duty to take all reasonable care to prevent the corporation from causing or permitting . . . unlawful deposit, addition, emission or discharge,"[18] and making failure to carry out that duty an offence. A roughly comparable duty is now found in section 280(2) of CEPA 1999:

> Every director and officer of a corporation shall take all reasonable care to ensure that the corporation complies with
> (a) this Act and the regulations; and
> (b) orders and directions of, and prohibitions and requirements imposed by, the Minister and enforcement officers and review officers.

The intention of the Ontario initiative, according to one well-placed observer, was that the amendments would "serve a normative and edu-

---

15 Canadian Environmental Protection Act, 1999, SC 1999, c 33, s 280 [CEPA 1999]. Similar federal provisions are found in the Transportation of Dangerous Goods Act, 1992, SC 1992, c 34, s 39 [TDGA]; and the Fisheries Act, RSC 1985, c F-14, s 78.2, as am by SC 1991, c 1, s 24.

16 AEPEA, above note 3, s 232; Environment Act, CCSM c E125, s 35; Environment Act, SNS 1994–95, c 1, s 164 [NSEA]; Environmental Protection Act, RSPEI 1988, c E-9, s 32(3).

17 See CEPA 1999, above note 15, s 280.1; and for similarly worded provisions, see D Saxe, Environmental Offences: Corporate Responsibility and Executive Liability (Aurora, ON: Canada Law Book, 1990) at 131–36.

18 Environment Enforcement Statute Law Amendment Act, 1986, SO 1986, c 68, s 17.

cational function by bringing home to corporate officials their personal obligation to the public to govern the corporation in a manner that gives priority to the establishment and proper operation of pollution prevention systems."[19]

In the context of applying the new Ontario provision, an important procedural issue arose, one engaging underlying considerations associated with evidentiary responsibilities in the prosecution of regulatory offences, and directly affecting the utility and effectiveness of the provision. It was understood by some that the Crown would have the procedural burden of establishing not only that a corporation had engaged in a prohibited activity but also that the officer or director charged under section 194 had failed to take reasonable care in attempting to prevent the offence. On the other hand, it was argued that evidentiary responsibility regarding due diligence rested with the accused. In *R v Bata Industries Ltd*,[20] the court concluded that, notwithstanding the statutory language, the failure to take all reasonable care was not an element of the *actus reus* that the prosecution must prove beyond a reasonable doubt. Rather, the defendants would continue to bear the burden of establishing due diligence on a balance of probabilities. This interpretation was subsequently rejected in another provincial court decision, *R v Commander Business Furniture Inc*, where Hackett J concluded that:

> the . . . wording . . . is such that the Crown must prove not only that the director is engaged in an activity that may result in the discharge of a contaminant, but it must also prove that he or she failed to take all reasonable care to prevent it. In my view, this goes beyond proof of an actus reus or a discharge which caused an adverse effect.

Hackett J further explained his understanding of the content of the Crown's obligations as calling for actual evidence concerning the conduct or non-performance of the accused:

> To prove a failure to take all reasonable care, in my view, means that the Crown must prove an act or failure to act which amounts to negligent conduct or an objective intention beyond a reasonable doubt. The words . . . indicate to me that the legislature intended that the

---

19 J Swaigen, "Ontario's *Environment Enforcement Statute Law Amendment Act, 1986*" (1987) 2 CELR (NS) 14 at 19. For further discussion see J Swaigen, *Regulatory Offences in Canada: Liability & Defences* (Toronto: Carswell, 1992) at 152–57.

20 (1992), 9 OR (3d) 329 (Prov Ct). Charges were laid under both the Ontario *Environmental Protection Act*, RSO 1990, c E.19 [*OEPA*] and the *Ontario Water Resources Act*, RSO 1990, c O.40 [*OWRA*]. Convictions were registered under the *OWRA*, while the *OEPA* charges were stayed.

fault for this offence must be proved by the Crown rather than, as it is the case in most strict liability offences, disproved by the defence on a balance of probabilities.[21]

Further legislative amendment to the *OEPA* in 2005 more clearly asserts the conclusion reached in *Bata*. The amended section 194(1) extended the range of environmental offences which "every director or officer or a corporation has a duty to take all reasonable care to prevent the corporation" from committing. Failure to carry out that duty is made an offence pursuant to section 194(2), and the evidentiary burden relating to fulfilment of the duty is assigned to the accused as follows:

> If a director or officer of a corporation is charged with an offence under subsection (2) in connection with a specific contravention of the corporation, the director or officer has the onus, in the trial of the offence, of proving that he or she carried out the duty under subsection (1) in connection with that contravention.[22]

This provision has attracted considerable interest and attention on the part of corporate advisors seeking to ensure that appropriate means to demonstrate due diligence are in place, should an officer or director be called upon to establish the all reasonable care defence. Indeed, the early *Bata* proceedings were extremely successful from the perspective of "consciousness raising" for directors and officers. Publicity surrounding the Ministry of the Environment's decision to charge the chairman and chief executive officer of Bata, along with two other senior officials who were eventually convicted, contributed significantly to the level of awareness of directors' and officers' responsibilities with respect to the environment.

Recent changes to Quebec's *Environment Quality Act* (*EQA*) elaborate circumstances affecting the liability of directors and officers in that province:

> 115.40. If a legal person or an agent, mandatary or employee of a legal person, partnership or association without legal personality commits an offence under this Act or the regulations, its director or officer is presumed to have committed the offence unless it is established that the director or officer exercised due diligence and took all necessary precautions to prevent the offence.[23]

---

21   (1992), 9 CELR (NS) 185 at 250–51 (Ont Prov Ct).
22   *OEPA*, above note 20, s 194 (2.1).
23   SQ 2011, c 20, s 26.

Decisions to expand and make explicit the liability of directors and officers have been premised on some combination of perceived wrongdoing and the assumption that personal exposure to penalties would induce the individuals whose decisions govern corporate behaviour to address environmental considerations more forthrightly and systematically.[24] Although the evidence is inconclusive, there is some support for the premise. For example, one survey found that "corporate executives reported that attention to environmental matters at the highest levels of the firm, and corporate efforts to avoid pollution, would be greater if corporate executives faced the possibility of personal prosecution for pollution."[25] Another observer remarked anecdotally that, in the aftermath of written warnings to individual officers and directors of companies with three or more convictions under Metro Toronto's sewage-control bylaws, at least eight of the nineteen companies involved initiated measures to prevent future contraventions.[26]

In *Bata* the trial judge had endeavoured to ensure that the personal liability of the officials convicted would not be diffused. He therefore issued an order prohibiting the corporation from indemnifying the individual officers for the financial penalties imposed by the judgment. That order was subsequently determined by the Court of Appeal to have been improperly made against Bata in light of the purpose of the probation orders under the *Provincial Offences Act* and in light of detailed provisions governing indemnification set out in Ontario's *Business Corporations Act*.[27]

1) Strict Liability and Environmental Due Diligence

The defence of due diligence, which is available to an accused facing prosecution for a strict liability offence,[28] is often specifically incorporated in environmental legislation. Whether expressed as "all due diligence"[29] or as "all reasonable measures to comply"[30] or in the form

---

24 For a review of the arguments, see Saxe, above note 17 at 31–45.
25 Saxe, *ibid* at 53–54; see also D Saxe, "The Impact of Prosecution of Corporations and Their Officers and Directors upon Regulatory Compliance by Corporations" (1991) 1 J Envtl L & Prac 91.
26 H Poch, *Corporate and Municipal Environmental Law* (Toronto: Carswell, 1989) at 60–62.
27 RSO 1990, c B.16, s 136; *R v Bata Industries Ltd* (1995), 25 OR (3d) 321 (CA) [*Bata*].
28 On the availability of a due diligence defence in the context of administrative penalties, see Chapter 7.
29 *CEPA 1999* above note 15, s 283; *Fisheries Act*, above note 15, s 78.6.
30 *TDGA*, above 15, s 40.

of "a duty to take all reasonable care,"[31] the concept entails a demonstration that the accused's conduct prior to the offence satisfies the expected standard.

In the context of a prosecution, the due diligence standard has been subject to judicial consideration. It has been remarked, for example, that "[r]easonable care and due diligence do not mean superhuman efforts. They mean a high standard of awareness and decisive, prompt and continuing action."[32] What constitutes adequate due diligence for any particular defendant in the context of a given environmental offence will be a matter for determination by the court.

In the *Bata* decision, Ormston Prov J outlined certain general principles of a director's due diligence:

(a) Did the board of directors establish a pollution prevention "system" . . . *i.e.*, was there supervision or inspection? Was there improvement in business methods? did he exhort those he controlled or influenced?

(b) Did each director ensure that the corporate officers have been instructed to set up a system sufficient within the terms and practices of its industry of ensuring compliance with environmental laws, to ensure that the officers report back periodically to the board on the operation of the system, and to ensure that the officers are instructed to report any substantial non-compliance to the board in a timely manner?

Directors, Ormston J further observed,

(c) . . . are responsible for reviewing the environmental compliance reports provided by the officers of the corporation, but are justified in placing *reasonable* reliance on reports provided to them by corporate officers, consultants, counsel or other informed parties.

(d) The directors should substantiate that the officers are promptly addressing environmental concerns brought to their attention by government agencies or other concerned parties including shareholders.

(e) The directors should be aware of the standards of their industry, and other industries which deal with similar environmental pollutants or risks.

(f) The directors should immediately and personally react when they have noticed the system has failed.

---

31   *OEPA*, above note 20, s 194.
32   *R v Courtaulds Fibres Canada* (1992), 9 CELR (NS) 304 at 313 (Ont Prov Ct), Fitzpatrick Prov J.

Within this general profile and dependent upon the nature and structure of the corporate activity, one would hope to find remedial and contingency plans for spills, a system of ongoing environmental audit, training programs, sufficient authority to act and other indices of a pro-active environmental policy.[33]

In determining whether the due diligence standard has been met, the courts have identified a number of factors that must be weighed and balanced. These include: nature and gravity of the adverse effect; foreseeability of the effect, including abnormal sensitivities; alternative solutions available; legislative or regulatory compliance; industry standards; character of the neighbourhood; efforts (if any) made to address the problem; period of time over which such efforts were made, and promptness of response; matters beyond the control of the accused, including technological limitations; skill level expected of the accused; complexities involved; preventive systems; economic considerations; and actions of officials. This set of considerations was thoroughly analyzed and applied by Tjosvold J of the Alberta Provincial Court in the Syncrude prosecution.[34]

That general systems of due diligence may have been encouraged by recent jurisprudential pronouncements is welcome. But in a noteworthy decision, the British Columbia Court of Appeal made clear that while the structural framework of a system of due diligence may be a necessary component of a defence to strict liability offences, this will not always be sufficient. In R v Imperial Oil that court emphasized an important distinction between general systems of due diligence and due diligence in relation to the specific event giving rise to charges. While the defendant corporation, charged when plant effluent killed fish in Burrard Inlet, argued that it was entitled to rely on the advice of a chemical supplier that its product was not toxic to fish, and that its general program of identifying and remedying potential sources of environmental risk would shortly have addressed the situation, a majority of the court took a different view. The company had not specifically contemplated in a timely manner the implications of a release by means of its effluent discharge of what was in fact a toxic substance into neighbouring water.[35] Some further insight into what a corporation may be expected to contemplate for the purpose of safeguarding itself against the success of such charges is provided by the courts' observation in R v MacMillan Bloedel that the "foresight required will vary

---

33   R v Bata Industries (1992), 7 CELR (NS) 245 at paras 134–35 (Ont Prov Div).
34   R v Syncrude Canada Ltd, 2010 ABPC 229 at paras 125–28.
35   R v Imperial Oil (2000), 36 CELR (NS) 109 (BCCA).

with the level of expertise generally acceptable in a given industry, and a link can be made to the factor of industry standards."[36]

The challenges of demonstrating due diligence will vary with particular circumstances—a fact which was highlighted in *R v Petro Canada*. Here, the company had been charged with causing a gasoline spill from an undetermined location in an extensive network of pipes. Given its inability to identify the specific source of the leak, and thus to point to directly-related due diligence measures, the company's due diligence defence emphasized the safety systems it had established to detect spills and leakage. The trial court rejected this attempt to show diligence on the grounds that the cause of the leak was not established. In setting this determination aside and ordering a retrial of the matter, the court of appeal indicated that it is unnecessary for a defendant to identify the exact source or cause of harm in order to invoke the defence. As Goudge, JA explained, however, there would be a clear advantage in being able to point more precisely to the source of harm:

> where the accused can do this, it may be able to narrow the range of preventative steps that it must show to establish that it took all reasonable care. However, where . . . the accused cannot prove the precise cause of the pipe failure that due diligence defence is not rendered unavailable as a result. That being said, it must be emphasized that to invoke the defence successfully in such circumstances, the accused must show that it took all reasonable care to avoid any foreseeable cause.[37]

2) The Environmental Audit

An environmental audit process offers some measure of independent review, assessment, or evaluation of performance in relation to expected and required standards. Although sometimes described as "self-inspection," the audit is most likely to be conducted by consultants or specialized professionals provided with authority to examine a company's operations, to make inquiries concerning practices and procedures, to compare these with corporate policy and existing regulatory requirements and to report their findings back to the senior administration. The audit serves increasingly as a vital element in systems of due diligence and in programs of prevention. That is, in the event of prosecution for a strict liability offence, the existence of an audit program may

---

36   (2002), 220 DLR (4th) 173 (BCCA).
37   *R v Petro-Canada* (2003), 63 OR (3d) 219 at 224 (CA).

be of assistance in support of the reasonable care defence.[38] Audits and other forms of self-inspection also play a preventive role in that they allow conscientious management to identify sources of operational risk and to implement further measures to reduce the potential for environmental harm.

The precise nature of an adequate and effective environmental audit has not been standardized in Canada. However, one definition set out the essential criteria and basic objectives this way:

> [E]nvironmental audit is a systematic, documented, objective evaluation of a facility's management, operations, and equipment that may have either a direct or indirect effect on the environment with a view to assessing (1) compliance with corporate policies, which should include meeting regulatory requirements; (2) risks of exposure to liability for environmental damage; and (3) opportunities for reducing, reusing or recycling wastes.[39]

In the context of *CEPA 1999*'s enforcement and compliance policy, audits are described as

> [i]nternal evaluations by companies and government agencies to verify their compliance with legal requirements as well as their own internal policies and standards. They are conducted by companies, government agencies, and others on a voluntary basis, and are carried out by either outside consultants or employees of the company or facility from outside the work unit being audited. Audits can identify compliance problems, weaknesses in management systems, or areas of risk. The findings are documented in a written report.[40]

Audits may be initiated in a variety of circumstances and for a range of purposes. Certain business transactions such as mergers, acquisitions, and financings may trigger an audit requirement. Alternatively, self-evaluation may be undertaken in the aftermath of new knowledge concerning previously unanticipated sources of risk. Some operations will conduct environmental audits on a more or less routine basis as a matter of general due diligence, in connection with planning annual

---

38 See *Bata*, above note 27; *R v Rio Algom Ltd* (1988), 66 OR (2d) 674 (CA); *R v J Clark & Son Ltd* (1979), 25 NBR (2d) 488 (Prov Ct). See ME Deturbide, "Corporate Protector or Environmental Safeguard? The Emerging Role of the Environmental Audit" (1995) 5 J Envtl L & Prac 1 at 10, n 30.

39 DR Cameron, *Environmental Concerns in Business Transactions: Avoiding the Risks* (Toronto: Butterworths, 1993) at 81.

40 Environment Canada, *Canadian Environmental Protection Act Enforcement and Compliance Policy* (Ottawa: March 2001) at 17 [*CEPA 1999 Policy*].

programs of financial expenditure or risk-assessment and insurance reporting.

The specific objectives selected will influence the scope of the audit and the manner in which it is carried out. When employed as an ongoing management tool, for example, greater emphasis will be placed on systems, processes, and practices in possible need of attention if future environmental accidents and liability are to be avoided. On the other hand, in the context of real estate transactions, preventive objectives may be much less significant; the parties may be primarily concerned with legal compliance and indications of potentially costly environmental liability existing at a specific time. Such knowledge may allow the parties to a transaction to appreciate the risks involved more fully and encourage them to structure their relationship or transactional risks accordingly.

Although precise objectives dictate the manner in which self-evaluation processes are carried out, in general they will involve an intensive site inspection including careful observation of facilities in operation, a review of records and documentation, personnel interviews, and an analysis and examination of adjacent properties. The findings at this stage may suggest the need for follow-up work such as sampling and testing to help in resolving uncertainties and in formulating appropriate recommendations for remedial action.

Those participating in the audit will have been selected on the basis of the particular expertise each contributes to the investigation and analysis. Other operational decisions in the conduct of an audit or self-evaluation are often influenced by concern about the potential for adverse consequences of the findings. Documented non-compliance and identified deficiencies may expose the subject of the audit to legal liability and negative publicity as well as to the expense of remedial measures. For these reasons the environmental-audit process is frequently treated as a confidential matter. Indeed, counsel may recommend measures intended to secure a form of solicitor-client privilege for the audit report. It may be suggested, for example, that the audit team should report directly to counsel, that confidentiality agreements should be entered into with all consultants, and that copies should be marked "confidential" and access to them restricted.

Courts are diligent in scrutinizing claims of privilege, and it is not every report prepared for or under the direction of counsel that will satisfy the requirements of the privilege doctrine. In *R v McCarthy Tetrault*[41] certain documents seized by the Crown from counsel for

---

41   (1992), 9 CELR (NS) 12 (Ont Prov Div).

a corporate accused pursuant to a search warrant were subject to a privilege claim. The documents had been prepared by counsel in the course of a meeting with the client in which discussion of a potential environmental prosecution took place. Although counsel insisted that the meeting was for the purpose of communicating confidential information and to prepare legal advice, notice circulated prior to the meeting had referred to it as an environmental audit. The Crown sought to characterize the meeting in this latter way to suggest that it occurred for internal corporate purposes rather than in relation to legal advice and was therefore not privileged. In assessing the competing characterizations, MacDonnell Prov J insisted that "[a] claim of privilege will not be established by merely asserting it." A sworn statement by the solicitor affirming his or her belief that a substantial and *bona fide* purpose of the communication was to obtain legal advice will generally be required. A solicitor who is aware of any other purpose for the communication which is subject to a claim of privilege is under a high duty to make disclosure so that the court can assess the claim fairly.[42]

As the origins of the *McCarthy* case indicated, enforcement officials may seek access to audit reports in connection with prosecutorial investigations.[43] Some reconciliation must therefore be established between the desire to promote self-assessments for their beneficial potential and the deterrent effect of using audits against those who voluntarily initiated them. As a matter of official practice, and more recently in legislation in some jurisdictions, attempts have been made to offer assurances against the abuse of audit reports in prosecution. These initiatives recognize the desirability of encouraging self-examination as a means of stimulating corrective action.[44]

CEPA 1999 enforcement and compliance policy confirms that inspectors will not request environmental audit reports during routine inspections to verify compliance with the Act.[45] However, audit reports may be required in the course of investigations; if so, they may be obtained on the basis of a search warrant or without warrant in exigent circumstances "when the delay necessary to obtain a warrant would likely result in danger to the environment or human life, or the loss or destruction of evidence."[46]

---

42   *Ibid* at 23.
43   Should questions arise concerning searches and seizure of law office records for which solicitor-client privilege is claimed, see *Lavallee, Rackel & Heintz v Canada (AG)* (2002), 167 CCC (3d) 1 (SCC).
44   *NSEA*, above note 16, s 75.
45   *CEPA 1999 Policy*, above note 40 at 17.
46   *Ibid*.

Aspects of the matter are addressed by statute in Nova Scotia, where compliance with a negotiated agreement or with an administrative order will ensure that any person "who voluntarily provides the Department with detailed information obtained through an environmental audit or environmental-site assessment about non-compliance with the requirements of this Act by that person, shall not be prosecuted for the non-compliance."[47] There is no immunity, however, in cases where the department's knowledge of non-compliance was obtained independently prior to receiving information from the person.

Apart from judicial insistence on an audit or equivalent as a condition of avoiding conviction for strict liability offences, the environmental audit has not become a general legal requirement. Waste and packaging audits, however, may come to be seen as an exception.[48] It is also noteworthy that the disclosure of audit information may arise outside the context of inspections, investigations, or prosecution. Such a situation arose recently when the Canada–Newfoundland and Labrador Offshore Petroleum Board received an Access to Information (AIA) Request asking for the disclosure of "all documents pertaining to integrated safety and environmental protection audits and inspections of offshore drilling operations conducted by the Board since Jan. 1 2008." As the subject of some of those audits or inspections, Hibernia Management and Development objected to release by the Board of certain documents on the grounds of privilege, personal information, and the presence of commercial or technical information of a confidential nature. The company's challenge to disclosure was unsuccessful.[49]

C. FINANCIAL-DISCLOSURE OBLIGATIONS, SHAREHOLDER ACCOUNTABILITY, AND SUSTAINABILITY REPORTING

Public availability of relevant information, especially in combination with economic incentives, has considerable potential to influence be-

---

47   *NSEA*, above note 16, s 70(1). Under the Nova Scotia legislation, environmental audit means "a process of independently obtaining and evaluating evidence about an environmental matter to determine the relationship between the environmental matter and the established standards and criteria," and environmental-site assessment means "the process by which an assessor seeks to determine whether a particular property is or may be subject to contamination."
48   See *OEPA*, above note 20, s 176(4)(1).
49   *Hibernia Management and Development Co v Canada–Newfoundland and Labrador Offshore Petroleum Board*, 2012 FC 417.

haviour. Not surprisingly, therefore, those anxious to enhance the foundations of environmental protection encourage corporate disclosure relating to environmental issues. In a summary that is perhaps equally applicable to the role of individual shareholders and ethical investment groups, one valuable commentary explains the importance of environmental information to financial institutions:

> Mandating disclosure of environmental liabilities and costs under securities laws and other company legislation can facilitate financiers' appraisal of the environmental behaviour of businesses. In theory, if accurate information is publicly available, market forces can respond by feeding environmental costs and performance into the cost and terms of finance.[50]

Financial reports prepared in accordance with generally accepted accounting principles (GAAP) can reveal certain environmental liabilities directly in financial statements where satisfactory estimates can be made, or in the form of accompanying notes where the nature of a potential liability is known but its magnitude or monetary significance remains too uncertain to quantify reliably. In this way the fact that assets have been devalued as a consequence of environmental contamination, that costs will be incurred to remediate property or to compensate injured parties, or that pending litigation may affect operations and earnings, may be brought to the attention of investors.[51] In addition, securities laws contribute to the dissemination of information about environmental matters affecting the financial position of businesses whose shares are offered to the public.

Securities legislation, supplemented by policy guidance, seeks to protect investors from unfair, improper, or fraudulent practices and to foster efficient capital markets supported by public confidence.[52] The connection between environmental law and securities regulation derives from the potential cost of corporate liability for environmental claims or cleanup and restoration obligations as well as the negative effects of adverse publicity associated with environmental damage. Thus, rules that require companies whose securities are offered to the public to disclose relevant information in a prospectus or other investor-oriented documentation and on a continuing basis during the course of

---

50   BJ Richardson, "Financing Environmental Change: A New Role for Canadian Environmental Law" (2004) 49 McGill LJ 145 at 195.
51   The introduction to Canada of International Financial Reporting Standards to replace GAAP beginning in 2011 is expected to increase the level of financial disclosure around environmental matters.
52   *Securities Act*, RSO 1990, c S.5, s 1.1.

operations are gradually being extended to include disclosure obligations concerning environmentally related liabilities.

Although not directly applicable in Canada (except as they apply to Canadian companies required to comply in the United States), developments in US securities law—with the *Sarbanes-Oxley Act*[53] serving as a striking example—are influential and have been considered relevant in the interpretation of securities legislation in Canada.[54] The significance of the US experience for Canadian companies and investors makes it worthwhile to note the results of a recent attempt by the US Government Accountability Office to assess the performance of the SEC in the environmental area:

> Little is known about the extent to which companies are disclosing environmental information in their filings with SEC. Determining what companies should be disclosing is extremely challenging without access to company records, considering the flexibility in the disclosure requirements. Despite strong methodological limitations, some studies provide tentative insights about the amount of environmental information companies are disclosing and the variation in disclosure among companies. However, the problem in evaluating the adequacy of disclosure is that one cannot determine whether a low level of disclosure means that a company does not have existing or potential environmental liabilities, has determined that such liabilities are not material, or is not adequately complying with disclosure requirements.[55]

The situation in Canada appears to be equally uncertain, although important disclosure initiatives are now underway.

In Canada, securities regulation has evolved as a provincial responsibility. Numerous recommendations and proposals to establish a national regulatory framework have foundered.[56] However, initiatives such as national policy statements and a multijurisdictional disclosure system have been taken to reduce inconsistencies and to alleviate inconvenience.

---

53   *Sarbanes-Oxley Act of 2002*, Pub L 107-204, 116 Stat 745 (2002) [*Sarbanes-Oxley Act*].

54   *Pacific Coast Coin Exchange of Canada v Ontario (Securities Commission)*, [1978] 2 SCR 112.

55   US Government Accountability Office, *Environmental Disclosure: SEC Should Explore Ways to Improve Tracking and Transparency of Information* (GAO-04-808, July 2004), online: www.gao.gov/cgi-bin/getrpt?GAO-04-808.

56   *Reference re Securities Act*, 2011 SCC 66.

Initially through policy statements[57] accompanying legislation, and more recently through formally enforceable rules, regulatory bodies in all provinces have elaborated disclosure requirements. Disclosure principles concerning environmental liabilities flow from a basic obligation to provide full, true, and plain disclosure of matters that would reasonably be expected to affect the value of the issuer's securities. General obligations to disclose risk factors in a prospectus, while not specifically imposing environmental disclosure, encourage due diligence investigations that may indicate the need to disclose and discuss environmental matters to potential investors. Complex legislation, diverse environmental circumstances, and real problems with quantification make it difficult to determine with precision whether there are matters requiring disclosure on the basis that some fact "significantly affects or would reasonably be expected to have a significant effect on the market price or value of the securities." To evaluate an environmental concern appropriately from the perspective of securities regulations not only "necessitates . . . an understanding of the laws that are in place but also requires an appreciation of the interplay between local sensitivity, local enforcement, the current state of the art of remediation, and the size and nature of the company."[58]

Companies recognized as reporting issuers of securities face continuous-disclosure obligations that require them to disclose on an ongoing basis, through press releases, all "material changes"; the latter have been defined as any "change in the business, operations or capital of the issuer that would reasonably be expected to have a significant effect on the market price or value of any of the securities." In 1993, the Ontario Securities Commission observed that an injunction application by environmental enforcement officials to restrain a securities issuer from pursuing a principal aspect of its operations on the basis of environmental non-compliance would appear *prima facie* to constitute a material change. Indeed, the commission added that

> given the current high public sensitivity to environmental issues, proceedings instituted . . . for non-compliance with environmental legislation [raise] something of a spectre and may be more likely to be a material change for an issuer than some other lawsuits, given

---

57 On the enforcement limitations of policy statements, see *Ainsley Financial Corp v Ontario (Securities Commission)* (1994), 21 OR (3d) 104 (CA).

58 SHT Denstedt & SR Miller, "Due Diligence in Disclosing Environmental Information for Securities Transactions" (1995) 33 Alta L Rev 231 at 250.

the impact it may have on the public image and consequently on the business affairs of the company.[59]

Ten years later, in a document addressing continuous disclosure obligations, the Canadian securities regulators set out environmental disclosure requirements and explained their applicability to information forms and reports. National Instrument 51-102 identified five key environmental matters: environmental risks; trends and uncertainties; environmental liabilities; asset retirement obligations; and financial and operational effects of environmental protection requirements. A guidance statement provided in connection with what is referred to as Management's Discussion and Analysis Report offered the following advice to decision makers trying to determine whether an environmental matter relating to their company would be material and therefore subject to disclosure: "Would a reasonable investor's decision whether or not to buy, sell or hold securities in your company likely be influenced or changed if the information in question was omitted or misstated? If so, the information is likely material."[60]

In 2010, the Canadian Securities Administrators, representing provincial and territorial regulators, published a more elaborate guidance statement on environmental reporting.[61] The guidance is intended to provide assistance to reporting securities issuers with respect to requirements for continuous disclosure previously set out in National Instrument 51-102. Before discussing four categories of disclosure obligations, the guidance document articulates the background considerations that increasingly call attention to environmental matters in business: interrupting operations (including supply and distribution chains, personnel, and physical assets) resulting in material unplanned costs, such as costs to address an environmental accident; affecting the issuer's licence to operate; affecting capital expenditure decisions and the viability of projects; changing consumer preferences; affecting the issuer's reputation; altering access to and the cost of capital; affecting the affordability and availability of insurance; and providing new business opportunities.

Evolving Canadian securities law requirements for environmental disclosure, as introduced here, are supplemented by a further array of

---

59   *Re Sheridan* (1993), 16 OSC Bull 6345 at 6349.

60   Canadian Securities Regulatory Authorities, National Instrument 51-102, *Continuous Disclosure Obligations* (NI-51-102); and Form 51-102F1, "Management's Discussion and Analysis" at 2.

61   Canadian Securities Administrators, *Environmental Reporting Guidance*, (CSA Staff Notice 51-333, 27 October 2010).

measures and initiatives that have enhanced the availability of corporate environmental information. In this regard, each of the following is of some interest: the influence of shareholder activism on corporate accountability and disclosure; voluntary corporate reporting associated with corporate social responsibility or indicators of sustainability; the interest of financial institutions in environmental information; and, a potential acceleration in demands for specific environmental information linked to greenhouse gas emissions and climate change.

Legislation establishing the rights of shareholders in the context of corporate governance has established principles applicable to investors' participation in decision making, including opportunities to call for the circulation of proposed resolutions, the solicitation of proxies and so on. With regard to proxy circulation, an earlier version of the CBCA provided that

> a corporation is not required to comply with a shareholder's request if it clearly appears that the proposal is submitted by the shareholder primarily for the purpose of enforcing a personal claim or redressing a personal grievance against the corporation or its directors, officers or security holders, or primarily for the purpose of promoting general economic, political, racial, religious, social or similar causes.[62]

Under this rule, several Canadian shareholder proposals associated with social or environmental causes were never circulated, and, accordingly, lost whatever opportunity advance circulation might have afforded to solicit additional support.[63]

Less restrictive legislation now appears to offer more potential for shareholder requests to receive the benefits of advance circulation in that the current rule states that a shareholder resolution need not be circulated when "it clearly appears that the proposal does not relate in a significant way to the business or affairs of the corporation."[64] Arguably, expanding requirements for environmental disclosure bring environmental considerations more closely within the well-recognized parameters of the business or affairs of the corporation.

In addition, on a voluntary basis, a number of firms have begun to produce environmental reports on their operations for the information of investors and the public generally. The environmental research and consulting group Stratos undertook a survey of "sustainability re-

---

62 *Canada Business Corporations Act*, SC 1974–75, c 33, s 131(5)(b).
63 *Greenpeace Foundation of Canada v Inco Ltd*, [1984] OJ No 274 (HCJ); *Varity Corp v Jesuit Fathers of Upper Canada et al* (1987), 59 OR (2d) 459 (HCJ), aff'd (1987), 60 OR (2d) 640 (CA).
64 *Canada Business Corporations Act*, RSC 1985, c C-44, s 137(5)(b.1).

porting" in Canada.[65] For the purposes of this survey, a "sustainability report" was defined

> to include reports that provide substantial information on a company's management and performance related to one or more aspects of sustainability beyond financial performance. This broad term encompasses environmental, social, community, corporate responsibility, and corporate social responsibility reports, along with annual reports that include five or more pages of environmental and /or social information, including performance data.

The Stratos survey documented substantial recent growth in the number of reporting companies, with significant sectoral variations. Financial institutions, utilities, and companies in the resources sector were most common within the ranks of reporting businesses. Although much of the report is devoted to an assessment of the types of information provided (sustainabilility indicators) and to areas of potential improvement, a basic explanation was offered of the underlying business rationale for reporting. Three factors were of primary importance:

- Enhance corporate reputation by differentiating yourself from competitors and gaining a competitive advantage in capital, labour and customer markets;
- Improve internal operations through cost savings and more effective use of internal resources and building internal alignment and capacities of employees;
- Build stronger external relationships by publicly sharing information on your economic, environmental and social performance with key stakeholder groups.[66]

Sustainability reporting is a comparatively new undertaking, by no means yet subject to the formal requirements associated with financial reporting and securities regulation. Activity is nevertheless underway to establish standards, identify best practices, and otherwise enhance the comprehensiveness and reliability of information provided. The *Global Reporting Initiative* (GRI), for example, is the outcome of collaboration between the United Nations Environment Program and the Coalition for Environmentally Responsible Economies. The GRI has formulated indicators and guidelines for sustainability reporting to address the following environmental dimensions of sustainability: materials use;

---

65   Stratos Inc, "Building Confidence: Corporate Sustainability Reporting in Canada" (November 2003), online: www.stratos-sts.com/wp-content/uploads/2013/04/2003_11_CSR-Building-Confidence.pdf.
66   *Ibid* at 6.

energy use; water use; biodiversity; emissions, effluents, and waste; performance of suppliers; environmental impacts of products and services; and compliance.[67]

Other factors are contributing to increasing interest in and requirements for corporate reporting on environmental performance. In particular, the emergence of markets for green house gas emissions brings with it a need for transparent and verifiable reporting of a corporation's assets and liabilities from an energy use and emissions perspective that is likely to encourage further integration of financial and environmental disclosure.[68] The Carbon Disclosure Project (CDP) provides a further example of encouragement for voluntary data reporting. The CDP is an international not-for-profit that provides a global collection of self-reported climate change data. The CDP enables companies, governments, and cities around the world to measure, disclose, manage, and exchange information on greenhouse gas emissions and water standards in order to mitigate environmental risks.[69]

FURTHER READINGS

ARCHIBALD, T, KE JULL, & KW ROACH, *Regulatory and Corporate Liability: From Due Diligence to Risk Management*, loose-leaf (Aurora, ON: Canada Law Book, 2004–)

DETURBIDE, ME, "Accessibility of Environmental Audit Reports: A New Business Privilege?" (1999) 8 J Envtl L & Prac 279

GIROUX, E, "L'entreprise de l'audit environnemental: perspectives de developpement national et international dans les secteurs de l'environnement et du commerce" (1997) 38 C de D 71

MOFFET, J, "Ontario's Policy on Access to Environmental Evaluations: The Creation of an Audit Privilege" (1997) 7 J Envtl L & Prac 311

RICHARDSON, BJ, Socially Responsible Investment Law: Regulating the Unseen Polluters, (Oxford UP, 2008)

SAXE, D, *Environmental Offences: Corporate Responsibility and Executive Liability* (Aurora, ON: Canada Law Book, 1990) cc 5, 6, & 7

---

67 Global Reporting Initiative, *Sustainability Reporting Guidelines* (2002), online: www.aeca.es/comisiones/rsc/documentos_fundamentales_rsc/gri/guidelines/gri_guidelines_2002.pdf.
68 For discussion of greenhouse gas trading and market instruments generally, see Chapters 17 and 19.
69 Online: www.cdproject.net.

STRANZ, NJ, "Beyond *R v Sault Ste Marie*: The Creation and Expansion of Strict Liability and the 'Due Diligence' Defence" (1992) 30 Alta L Rev 1233

SWAIGEN, J, Regulatory Offences in Canada: Liability & Defences (Toronto: Carswell, 1992) cc 5 & 6

CHAPTER 10

ENVIRONMENTAL VALUATION AND COMPENSATION

A. THE NATURE OF ENVIRONMENTAL DAMAGE

Environmental damage and other losses suffered as a result of ongoing pollution, accidents or spills, general degradation, or the over-exploitation and mismanagement of resources may take many forms. Physical contamination of a short- or long-term nature is an obvious example, with or without destruction of plant and animal life, or biodiversity loss. In severe situations it is also possible to imagine that contamination will have permanently or irreversibly undermined the regenerative capacity or resilience of the affected ecosystem. Losses here may also entail the reduction or elimination of what we are coming to appreciate as ecological services such as water supply, climate stabilization, nutrient cycling, or pollination. Insofar as human populations are concerned, individuals may suffer adverse health effects, physical damage to property, or economic losses, singly or in combination. On occasion it is possible to speak of entire communities as the victims of environmental harm, arising, for example, from the contamination of food and water supplies. Financial compensation might then focus on payments to those—including the public—who have suffered losses or incurred expenses associated with remedying environmental damage or taking measures to prevent the spread of such damage.[1]

---

1   For discussion of restoration, see Chapter 11.

Many aspects of environmental damage as just discussed fall outside the scope of compensation as generally understood in the context of tort claims. For purposes of comparison it is worthwhile to review that approach prior to examining alternative approaches to environmental losses:

> Traditionally, the courts considered the only measure of compensation for damage to property to be the diminution in value caused by the tortfeasor's wrong, that is, the difference between the property value before and after the occurrence of damage. The cost of restoring or repairing the property, if considered at all, was simply regarded as a means of determining the diminution of value. However, in many cases, the distinction is irrelevant. Where the cost of restoration is equal to or less than the diminution of capital value, the repair is always recoverable, even if the plaintiff does not actually incur the cost. Moreover, where the repairs fail to restore the property to its original value, the plaintiff is entitled to the cost of repair and to an additional sum to compensate for the residual deficiency. However, where the cost of restoring the property is greater than the diminution of value the cases are divided as to which measure of damages should be applied. Most cases follow the traditional approach so that the plaintiff is only entitled to damages sufficient to compensate for a diminution of property value. However, damages will be measured according to the cost of repair if restoration alone will make good the plaintiff's loss .... The latter approach will only be adopted if the plaintiff actually intends to effect repairs and if the cost of such repairs is reasonable.[2]

As environmental losses are more fully appreciated in a context that encompasses recognition of such principles as polluter pay, intergenerational equity, and the values of biodiversity and ecological integrity, attention has shifted from individualized claims to a more broadly conceived framework for evaluating compensation. As seen in *British Columbia v Canadian Forest Products Ltd*[3] (discussed later in this chapter), the willingness of courts to explore new issues around the valuation of environmental losses introduces methodological and evidentiary challenges.

---

2   LN Klar *et al*, *Remedies in Tort*, vol 4, loose-leaf (Toronto: Carswell, 1999–) at 27.
3   *British Columbia v Canadian Forest Products Ltd*, 2004 SCC 38 [Canfor].

B. EVALUATING ENVIRONMENTAL LOSSES

The issue of the value of environmental losses and of nature more generally has considerable significance for official attitudes towards resource development, sustainability, and the level of compensation. But it should be noted that "values toward nature have not been static in western society."[4] One stream of thinking promotes wise management of natural resources, recognizing both the limited extent of forests and waterways, for example, and their potential to contribute to economic development. Properly conserved and efficiently managed, natural resources represent an ongoing source of wealth for society. This attitude to the valuation of nature is essentially utilitarian: we value nature to the extent that we can use it for our purposes. "We" are human beings, and the purposes are very much our own.

Human purposes need not be confined exclusively to the consumption of resources for sale in the marketplace. As expressed by one commentator, important elements of human freedom may be associated with environmental quality: "Sustaining living standards is not the same thing as sustaining people's freedom to have—or safeguard—what they value and to which they have reason to attach importance. Our reason for valuing particular opportunities need not always lie in their contribution to our living standards."[5] Indeed, a good deal of thought has been devoted to the task of extending our understanding of the values and uses of the natural environment. Today, more decision makers will acknowledge recreational, scientific, aesthetic, and historical values in addition to other utilitarian measures of nature, even including the contribution of ecological services. There is less agreement, however, on the calculus to be applied if a dispute arises about preserving wilderness for public use and enjoyment or extracting its component parts. We have a fair idea of the market value of standing timber: some minor variation on "volume × unit price" will provide an approximation. It has proven much more difficult to place a value on pleasure and enjoyment, or the planetary advantages we are less able to take for granted now that they are being undermined.

---

4   RB Payne, "The Forest and the Trees: Non-Timber Values and Forest Management in Ontario" (Witness Statement Number 4, Filed on Behalf of Forests for Tomorrow); *Re Proposed Class Environmental Assessment by the Ministry of Natural Resources for Timber Management on Crown Lands in Ontario* (1990), 4 CELR (NS) 50 (OEAB).

5   A Sen, "Why We Should Preserve the Spotted Owl," *London Review of Books* 26:3 (5 February 2004) 10.

How much is a wild river winding through an old-growth forest worth to lovers of the outdoors? Or, what is the value of a wetland region as habitat or for its role in filtering and restoring water? The formulae are of considerable interest, even if their practical utility is often unclear.[6] One might approach the challenge of valuing natural resources by posing the question as one of compensation for loss. That is, supposing that the environment suffered damage — or even destruction — as a consequence of some wrongful act, what amount of compensation should be paid by those responsible?

If everyone agrees that compensation should be based on the value or worth of the loss, there are great differences of opinion concerning the relevant factors. For some, the value of natural resources or the environment is equated with *utility* alone: we have lost value to the extent that we have lost use. Others are more willing to acknowledge additional bases of valuation associated with inherent or *intrinsic* qualities of nature or non-utilitarian considerations. Those who propose the inclusion of intrinsic values in the calculus might elaborate their position in several ways. Even if we do not use resources, we value them because of the *option* or potential for use that they represent. In addition, we value them on the basis of a desire to pass them on to future generations in the form of a *bequest*. Intrinsic valuation would also recognize the importance of the mere *existence* of environmental assets without regard to their actual use by present or future generations. Advocates of intrinsic value would defend their views with the further argument that in each case — option value, bequest value, and existence value — individuals would be willing to pay to protect environmental resources.

The analysis becomes even more complicated as the debate moves on from the kinds of values that might be recognized for purposes of compensation to the task of assigning numbers to those values. Methodology is a highly controversial matter. On the one hand are those who advocate a market-based approach to valuation. They suggest that compensation for loss or damage to a resource is simply the difference between its original market value and the commercial value or price after the damage has been done. The market-based approach is

---

6   For purposes of the following summary, I have relied heavily on an early condensation of some legal/economic literature prepared for the Ontario Law Reform Commission and published in Ontario Law Reform Commission, *Report on Damages for Environmental Harm* (Toronto: Queen's Printer, 1990). For a more recent and more comprehensive examination of the value debate, see M Bowman, P Davies, & C Redgwell, eds, *Lyster's International Wildlife Law*, 2d ed (Cambridge UP, 2010), c 3.

defended by its adherents with the claim that markets alone reflect real willingness to pay. In other words, only the actual behaviour of consumers establishes values. They might have some sympathy with the use of surrogate markets to establish environmental values, but that is the extent of their flexibility. For example, the costs of travel and expenses associated with getting to wilderness might represent the value of the wilderness experience. However, even this methodology restricts the value of wilderness to the value of its use.

Critics, on the other hand, reject the market model, in part because it is just that, a model. Markets for most natural resources do not really exist, they say, and so even if you know what someone might pay for a quantity of lumber, the price is not indicative of the value of the forest. What gets left out includes the intrinsic value of the resource, its service as habitat, and values that attach to resources by virtue of public enjoyment of them. For people with this view, the challenge is to move from assertions about unpriced values to actual quantification. One approximation of the value of a damaged natural resource centres on the cost of replacing it or of restoring it to its original condition.[7] Another suggested methodology known as the contingent-valuation approach involves the use of questionnaires and survey techniques in an attempt to determine the monetary value people would place on non-marketable items such as threatened species, free-running streams, and clear skies. Among the reservations expressed about an approach based on hypothetical transactions, serious controversy has arisen about whether sellers' hypothetical prices are more reliable measures than buyers' willingness to pay, for respondents differ in their valuations depending on whether they are gaining something or giving it up.

Yet alongside theoretical debates, practical attempts are underway to apply our current level of knowledge and understanding to environmental evaluation at regional and ecosystem levels.[8] A valuable example of this type of work is *Counting Canada's Natural Capital: Assessing the Real Value of Canada's Boreal Ecosystems*, a study intended by its authors "to begin to identify, inventory and measure the full economic value of the many ecological goods and services provided by Canada's boreal

7   For a class action claim by a group of cottage owners seeking the entitlement to be reimbursed for the cost of measures necessary to rehabilitate a lake injured by a fish-farming operation, see *Assoc pour la protection du Lac Heney c Gestion Serge Lafreniere inc*, [2001] JQ no 1730 (SC).

8   N Olewiler, *The Value of Natural Capital in Settled Areas of Canada* (Stonewall, MN: Ducks Unlimited Canada and Nature Conservancy Canada, 2004), online: www.cmnbc.ca/sites/default/files/natural%2520capital_0.pdf.

region."[9] The study, for which a distinctive accounting procedure was formulated, initially identified ecosystem services provided within the boreal region:

> atmospheric stabilization; climate stabilization; disturbance avoidance; water stabilization; water supply; erosion control and sediment retention; soil formation; nutrient cycling; waste treatment; pollination; biological control; habitat; raw materials; genetic resources; and recreational and cultural use.[10]

By way of results, the authors provided estimates of annual market values for natural capital extraction (timber, minerals, water) and non-market value estimates for the year 2002. The market value for natural capital extraction was adjusted to take account of environmental and social costs with the result that the *net* market value of natural capital extraction in the boreal region for the baseline year was $37.8 billion. For the same year, the total non-market value of boreal ecosystem services was estimated at $93.2 billion.[11] The principal components of the ecosystem services category with their estimated values were as follows:

- Flood control and water filtering by peatlands—$77 billion
- Pest control services by birds in the boreal forest—$5.4 billion
- Nature-related activities—$4.5 billion
- Flood control, water filtering, and biodiversity value by non-peatland wetlands—$3.4 billion
- Net carbon sequestration by the boreal forests—$1.85 billion

In observing that non-market values of boreal ecosystem services amounted roughly to 2.5 times the net market value of natural capital extractions from the region, authors of *Counting Canada's Natural Capital* remark that the study "affirms the relative importance of ecosystem functions that have no markets in which their services are traded, and the potential cost of replacement if human-made infrastructure can replace their services."[12]

---

9   M Anielski & S Wilson, *Counting Canada's Natural Capital: Assessing the Real Value of Canada's Boreal Ecosystems* (Ottawa: Canadian Boreal Initiative and Pembina Institute, 2005), online: www.borealcanada.ca/documents/Boreal_Wealth_Report_Nov_2005.pdf at 15. In light of limitations in publicly available data, the authors caution that their work is a first step towards an accounting of the ecological wealth of the boreal region.

10   *Ibid* at 2.

11   *Ibid* at 31.

12   *Ibid* at 62. See also *Canadian biodiversity: ecosystem status and trends 2010* (Canadian Councils of Resource Ministers: Ottawa, 2010), online: www.biodivcanada.ca/ecosystems.

An international research initiative on *The Economics of Ecosystems and Biodiversity* (TEEB) has also embarked on a program of environmental valuation that is intended ultimately to assist decision makers at the national and international levels. In a 2010 synthesis report, TEEB participants clearly set out the objective underlying ongoing research:

> Applying economic thinking to the use of biodiversity and ecosystem services can help clarify two critical points: why prosperity and poverty reduction depend on maintaining the flow of benefits from ecosystems; and why successful environmental protection needs to be grounded in sound economics, including explicit recognition, efficient allocation, and fair distribution of the costs and benefits of conservation and sustainable use of natural resources. . . . Valuation is seen not as a panacea, but rather as a tool to help recalibrate the faulty economic compass that has led us to decisions that are prejudicial to both current well-being and that of future generations. The invisibility of biodiversity values has often encouraged inefficient use or even destruction of the natural capital that is the foundation of our economies.[13]

Even as foundational research is underway into the valuation of environmental services, specific controversies come before the courts.

C. VALUING ENVIRONMENTAL LOSSES IN COURT

In *British Columbia v Canadian Forest Products Ltd (Canfor)*,[14] the Supreme Court of Canada had an opportunity to consider several aspects of environmental valuation. While many matters remain unresolved, the Court's discussion of the issues provides important guidance. To begin, an extended review and commentary on the use, existence and inherent values of ecosystems and natural resources was set out. This was accompanied by reference to measurement methodologies and US cases where these have been adopted. Binnie J's majority opinion demonstrates acceptance of the conceptual framework for valuing environmental losses and also the judicial willingness to address the evidentiary and other implications when such cases come before the courts.

---

13   TEEB, *The Economics of Ecosystems and Biodiversity: Mainstreaming the Economics of Nature: A synthesis of the approach, conclusions and recommendations of TEEB* (2010), online: www.teebweb.org.
14   Above note 3.

"A claim for environmental loss, as in the case of any loss, must be put forward based on a coherent theory of damages, a methodology suitable for their assessment, and supporting evidence."[15]

In *Canfor*, the Crown, in seeking damages for harm to public forest resources resulting from fire for which the defendant was largely responsible, failed to meet the applicable standard. Binnie J stated:

> I do not . . . agree that the Crown can succeed in an unpleaded claim for "ecological" or "environmental" damage simply because the Crown on this issue occupies the moral high ground. The Court and the alleged wrongdoer are entitled to require the Crown to adduce a proper evidentiary basis. Such evidence would be subject to cross-examination. Citation of articles in scholarly journals . . . is no substitute for evidence.[16]

The type of evidence a court would expect to see was illustrated elsewhere in the judgment. It would relate, for example, to:

- The nature of the wildlife, plants and other organisms protected by the environmental resource in question, and in particular whether rare or commercially valuable species are put at risk by damage or destruction of the ecosystem.
- The uniqueness of the ecosystem from a biological perspective.
- The environmental services provided by the resource, such as water quality and erosion control.
- The recreational opportunities afforded by the resource.
- The subjective or emotional attachment of the public to the damaged or destroyed area.[17]

Where an appropriate plaintiff is available to present relevant evidence for testing and scrutiny by the defendant, the court remains committed to fairness between the parties: "Quantification of the loss must be 'fair to both the plaintiff and the defendant. . . fairness is best achieved by avoiding both undercompensation and overcompensation'."[18] Some observers suggest that overcompensation for environmental losses is unlikely.[19]

---

15   *Ibid* at para 12.
16   *Ibid* at para 145.
17   *Ibid* at para 141.
18   *Ibid* at para 59.
19   For discussion of *Canfor's* implications for environmental valuation, see MZP Olszynski, "The Assessment of Damages Following the Supreme Court's Decision in *Canfor*" (2005) 15 J Envtl L & Prac 257.

Considerations somewhat related to environmental valuation may arise in injunction applications where the concept of irreparable harm must be addressed. Several British Columbia cases relating to old-growth forests and timber management provide some indication of judicial attitudes and approaches to the notion of irreparable harm. In *MacMillan Bloedel Ltd v Mullin*, an Aboriginal community with un-determined land rights sought an injunction against forest operations.[20] Seaton JA stated in awarding the injunction that: "[i]f logging proceeds and it turns out that the Indians have a right to the area with the trees standing, it will no longer be possible to give them that right . . . . The courts will not be able to do justice in the circumstances."[21] In *Westar Timber Ltd v Gitskan Wet'suwet'en Tribal Council*, Esson JA, in determining whether to grant an injunction against road construction designed to permit timber access, took into account the uniqueness of the area whose preservation was at stake.[22] On the other hand, in *Wiigyet v Kispiox Forest District*, Thackrey J indicated a concern for the impact on industry if an injunction were to be granted: "It is simply not possible to measure the damages of failed businesses, closed mills and people migrating from the area."[23] And, having heard of the impact on the for-est, he remarked: "[b]ut I cannot find that what is described makes the area in question any different than other pristine forest areas of British Columbia. It is sad that we cannot preserve every tract in a state that would be in total harmony with all calls of nature and of all claims of identifiable groups."[24]

Even where there are indications that matters of fundamental im-portance are at stake, as, for example, in the cause of action created under the Ontario *Environmental Bill of Rights, 1993* in the case of ac-tual or imminent contravention of prescribed instruments causing or threatening "significant harm to a public resource of Ontario," it is specifically stated that "[n]o award of damages shall be made" even if the plaintiff is entitled to judgment.[25] Compensation, accordingly, has been more commonly associated with various forms of governmental losses and the damages or injuries of individuals.

---

20   (1985), 61 BCLR 145 (CA).
21   *Ibid* at 159.
22   (1989), 37 BCLR (2d) 352 (CA).
23   (1990), 51 BCLR (2d) 73 at 81 (SC).
24   *Ibid* at 80.
25   SO 1993, c 28, ss 84 and 93(2).

D. STATUTORY APPROACHES TO COMPENSATION FOR ENVIRONMENTAL DAMAGE

Statutory compensation schemes are directed at a number of issues, including the scope and nature of compensable damages, the manner in which payments are to be distributed to eligible claimants, and possible limitations on the liability of those responsible for the environmental harm. There is a marked tendency to promote remedial action by facilitating the recovery of cleanup and prevention costs. The underlying assumption, especially evident in relation to spills legislation, is that quick responses can greatly lessen overall costs and losses in the area of environmental damage. British Columbia's *Environmental Management Act* section 47 provides an example of remediation costs:

> (3) For the purpose of this section, "costs of remediation" means all costs of remediation and includes, without limitation,
> (a) costs of preparing a site profile,
> (b) costs of carrying out a site investigation and preparing a report
> . . . ,
> (c) legal and consultant costs associated with seeking contributions from other responsible persons, and
> (d) fees imposed by a director, a municipality, an approving officer or the commission under this Part.
>
> (4) . . .
> (5) Subject to section 50 (3) [minor contributors], any person, including, but not limited to, a responsible person and a director, who incurs costs in carrying out remediation of a contaminated site may commence an action or a proceeding to recover the reasonably incurred costs of remediation from one or more responsible persons in accordance with the principles of liability set out in this Part.
> . . .
> (9) The court may determine in accordance with the regulations, unless otherwise determined or established under this Part, any of the following:
> (a) . . .
> (b) whether the costs of remediation of a contaminated site have been reasonably incurred and the amount of the reasonably incurred costs of remediation[26]

---

26 *Environmental Management Act*, SBC 2003, c 53.

British Columbia courts have now begun to outline their approach to determining the scope of recoverable costs of remediation.[27] The civil cause of action provided for in *CEPA 1999* allows any person who has suffered loss or damage resulting from contravention of the Act or regulations to recover damages.[28] In addition to establishing a civil cause of action for damages *CEPA 1999* authorizes court orders to be made at the time sentence is imposed to require the convicted offender to compensate an aggrieved person (on application) for loss or damage to property that resulted from commission of the offence.[29] Such orders, if not respected forthwith, may be made enforceable against the offender as a civil judgment by filing the order in the superior court of the province in which the conviction was obtained.[30] New to *CEPA 1999* are Environmental Protection Alternative Measures (EPAMs). These are described as measures, other than judicial proceedings that are used to deal with a person who is alleged to have committed an offence under the Act. The outcome of the EPAM process, which has been likened to a criminal diversion program, will be embodied in an agreement. Satisfactory evidence of compliance with the agreement by the alleged offender will result in dismissal of the charge. From the perspective of the present discussion of compensation for environmental loss or damage, it should be noted that agreements reached through the EPAM process may contain terms similar to authorized terms for sentencing convicted offenders, including the taking of any action appropriate to remedy or avoid harm to the environment from the offence.[31]

Following a conviction under the *Transportation of Dangerous Goods Act, 1992,* the court is authorized to order monetary or other compensation "for any remedial action taken or damage suffered by another person arising out of the commission of the offence."[32] In contrast to this broadly crafted eligibility provision, other statutory compensation opportunities are more closely circumscribed. Thus, only licensed commercial fishermen are eligible under the *Fisheries Act* to recover for "all loss of income" shown to have been incurred as a result of an unauthorized deposit of a deleterious substance.[33] Another special com-

---

27 *Workshop Holdings Ltd v CAE Machinery,* 2006 BCSC 389; *Canadian National Railway v ABC Recycling,* 2006 BCCA 429.
28 *Canadian Environmental Protection Act, 1999,* SC 1999, c 33, s 40.
29 *Ibid,* s 292(1).
30 *Ibid,* s 292(2).
31 *Ibid,* ss 295–309.
32 SC 1992, c 34, s 34(1)(b).
33 *Fisheries Act,* RSC 1985, c F–14, s 42(3).

pensation regime operates for the benefit of farmers whose crops have been rendered unmarketable as a consequence of pesticide residues.[34]

The Maritime Pollution Claims Fund, established in 1973 under the *Canada Shipping Act* was subsequently replaced by the Ship-source Oil Pollution Fund (SOPF)[35] now authorized by the *Marine Liability Act*. Liability and compensation arrangements for oil pollution damage are integrated with the international framework on civil liability for oil pollution damage.[36] In the first instance, shipowners are liable for the cost of oil damage, cleanup, and preventive measures caused by their ships.[37] Where damages cannot be recovered from shipowners or other relevant sources, compensation claims may be directed to the SOPF Fund.[38]

In the event of a nuclear incident at a Canadian nuclear facility (as defined in the *Nuclear Liability Act*, section 2), compensation for property damage and personal injury may be obtained through a nuclear power claims commission established under the federal *Nuclear Liability Act*.[39] Once created, such a commission would assume responsibility—subject to regulations—for determining eligibility for compensation. The establishment of a commission has the effect of staying all judicial proceedings relative to the particular incident in question. In *Energy Probe v Canada (AG)*,[40] compensation provisions established under the *Nuclear Liability Act* were challenged on several grounds, including inconsistency with sections 7 and 15 of the *Canadian Charter of Rights and Freedoms*.[41] As summarized by the Ontario Court of Appeal in preliminary proceedings, the applicants argued that the compensation ceiling actually promotes the use of nuclear energy:

> The thrust of the evidence is that the development of nuclear energy is encouraged by the Act, and may even be dependent upon the lim-

34   *Pesticide Residue Compensation Act*, RSC 1985, c P-10.
35   For a discussion of the initial operation of the SOPF, see MD Faieta *et al*, *Environmental Harm: Civil Actions and Compensation* (Toronto: Butterworths, 1996) at 396–403.
36   *Protocol to Amend the International Convention on Civil Liability for Oil Pollution Damage*, 27 November 1992, 1956 UNTS 255, as amended.
37   *Marine Liability Act*, SC 2001, c 6, s 51.
38   *Ibid*, ss 84 & 85. For further commentary and information, see the office of the administrator online: www.ssopfund.gc.ca/english/index.asp.
39   RSC 1985, c N-28.
40   (1989), 68 OR (2d) 449 (CA), leave to appeal to SCC refused (1989), 37 OAC 160n (SCC) [*Energy Probe*].
41   D Poch, "The Nuclear Liability Act: Nuclear Power Versus Legal Rights" in *Report of the Canadian Bar Association Committee on Sustainable Development in Canada: Options for Law Reform* (Ottawa: Canadian Bar Association, 1990) 98.

itations of liability contained within it. Insurance or other forms of security against potential claims would be needed throughout the industry without the protection of the Act and this would add measurably to the costs of nuclear energy development, encouraging implementation of alternative energy sources. Thus a link is put between the Act and the creation and proliferation of nuclear reactors.[42]

The action was eventually dismissed.[43] However, failure to adjust the ceiling on liability upwards to take account of inflation and to keep pace with other jurisdictions has attracted renewed criticism that the liability cap serves as a subsidy for nuclear power.[44]

Another specific compensation regime, in this case designed in the aftermath of regional environmental contamination, illustrates the precision with which compensation arrangements can be tailored. Following more than a decade and a half of intermittent and difficult negotiations involving the federal and provincial governments, the forest industry companies, and Indian communities, a settlement of claims regarding mercury pollution of the English and Wabigoon Rivers was reached in November 1985.[45] The settlement, whose implementation ultimately required legislative confirmation, provided for the creation of a special decision-making tribunal charged with the administration of applications for mercury-poisoning compensation by members of the Islington and Grassy Narrows Indian bands. The problematic issues of causation and entitlement to damages were resolved in the settlement by an agreement about the "known condition[s]" of mercury poisoning and by permitting the tribunal to determine eligibility on the basis of symptoms, signs, or conditions that were "reasonably consistent with mercury poisoning and capable of significantly impairing the quality of life or limiting the activities of an applicant."[46] The settlement limited the financial obligations of the forest industry companies, placed the Ontario government in the position of underwriting costs exceeding the initial capacity of the fund to satisfy them, and eliminated any existing and future rights of action of the bands or their individual members "in respect of any claims and causes of action that are the subject of the settlement."

42　*Energy Probe*, above note 40 at 452 (CA).

43　*Energy Probe v Canada (AG)* (1994), 17 OR (3d) 717 (Gen Div). See also Chapter 4.

44　J Wood, "Canada's Nuclear Liability" *Fraser Forum* (May/June 2011) 35.

45　*Energy Probe v Canada (AG)*, above note 43. The background is described in AM Shkilnyk, *A Poison Stronger than Love: The Destruction of an Ojibwa Community* (New Haven, CT: Yale University Press, 1985).

46　*English and Wabigoon River Systems Mercury Contamination Settlement Agreement Act*, 1986, SO 1986, c 23, s 1, definition of "condition."

Compensation arrangements are frequently incorporated into the terms and conditions attached to land-use approvals where environmental losses may be anticipated or are expected to occur. Thus, landowners in the immediate vicinity of waste-disposal or management sites are often eligible for compensatory payments linked to market-value losses on their properties. Not all decision makers, however, have the authority to impose compensation funds in connection with approvals, and it has been held in an Ontario decision that "if the legislature intended that the Board should have the power to require compensation of those whose properties have or may lose value because of the operation of the site, it would have specifically so provided."[47]

E. LIABILITY AND COMPENSATION FOR SPILLS

Incidents involving adverse environmental consequences will occur despite reasonable efforts to avoid them. As one provincial public information guide painted the scene: "Equipment failure, accidents on highways, railways or waterways, human error, third party involvement—any number of factors may combine to create a spill incident."[48] Moreover, in the absence of prompt and appropriate responses, environmental damage may extend beyond the immediate location of the spill, increasing both the difficulty and cost of restoration. For a variety of substantive and procedural reasons, however, common law liability has provided an inadequate stimulus to immediate post-incident response.[49] Accordingly, several jurisdictions recognized the importance of remedial spills legislation.

Saskatchewan, in 1983, was first to implement legislation governing reporting and cleanup responsibilities for spills.[50] That province's former *Environmental Management and Protection Act* also authorized those who had suffered loss or damage from a pollutant discharge to take civil action against the owner or person having control of the pollutant, although recovery has, on occasion, proven to be problem-

---

47 *Re Guelph (City)* (1995), 15 CELR (NS) 241 at 245 (Ont Div Ct).
48 Environment Ontario, *Spills Response Program* (Toronto: Queen's Printer, 1988) at 4.
49 JW Harbell, "Common Law Liability for Spills" in SM Makuch, ed, *The Spills Bill: Duties, Rights and Compensation* (Toronto: Butterworths, 1986) 1.
50 *Environmental Management and Protection Act*, SS 1983–84, c E–10.2; *Environmental Management and Protection Act, 2002*, SS 2002, c E-10.21; *Environmental Spill Control Regulations*, RRS, c D-14, Reg 1.

atic.[51] In November 1985 Ontario proclaimed its so-called "Spills Bill," which took the form of amendments to the province's *Environmental Protection Act* of 1978.[52] As explained by early commentators, the spills legislation "should superimpose liability over the common law, where intent, fault, reasonable use, escape, extent of damage, duty of care and foreseeability are not an issue. Rather, the ownership and control of the spilled pollutant is the primary question."[53]

To promote timely and effective measures in response to spills, the Ontario legislation proceeded on several fronts. Thus, a pollutant "spill" was broadly defined and the duties now arising in such an eventuality under the "Spills Bill" are such that "virtually any person could be affected by its provisions."[54] The legislation imposes a duty to give notice to the ministry and others of the circumstances of the spill and of remedial action taken or proposed. Where an "adverse effect" is associated with the spill, owners and persons having control of the pollutant prior to the spill have cleanup responsibilities requiring them to do "everything practicable to prevent, eliminate or ameliorate the adverse effects or to restore the natural environment."[55] But where appropriate actions are not forthcoming, the minister has extensive authority to direct that suitable actions be taken by agents or employees of the ministry or by others.

In terms of compensation for losses associated with spills, the central provision of the Ontario legislation indicates that the Crown, in right of the province or of Canada, and any person are entitled to compensation for loss or damage incurred as a direct result of the spill and for all reasonable cost and expense incurred in carrying out preventive and remedial orders issued in connection with the spill.[56] Loss or damage for purposes of this section includes personal injury, loss of life, loss of use or enjoyment of property, and pecuniary loss, includ-

---

51 *Busse Farms Ltd* v *Federal Business Development Bank* (1998), 168 DLR (4th) 27 (Sask CA).

52 See now RSO 1990, c E.19, Part X [*OPEA*]. Similar schemes are found in other jurisdictions. See *Environmental Management Act*, SBC 2003, c 53, ss 79–80 [*EMA*]; *Spills Reporting Regulation*, BC Reg 263/90; and *Spill Cost Recovery Regulation*, BC Reg 250/98.

53 Harbell, above note 49 at 25.

54 D Estrin, *Handle with Caution: Liability in the Production, Transportation and Disposal of Dangerous Substances* (Toronto: Carswell, 1986) at 5.

55 A claim under these provisions of the *OEPA*, above note 52, against a parent corporation which was not actually involved in activity on the site of its subsidiary at the time contamination occurred was rejected in *United Canada Malt Ltd* v *Outboard Marine Corp of Canada* (2000), 48 OR (3d) 352.

56 *OEPA*, above note 52, s 99(2).

ing loss of income.[57] As formulated, the legislation therefore addresses potential problems of standing and foreseeability for purposes of spills. Although strict liability applies to loss or damage from spills, the liability of owners and controllers of spilled pollutants is absolute in relation to the costs of cleanup.[58]

FURTHER READINGS

BOWMAN, M, "Biodiversity, Intrinsic Value, and the Definition of Environmental Harm" in Michael Bowman & Alan Boyle, eds, *Environmental Damages in International and Comparative Law: Problems of Definition and Valuation* (New York: Oxford University Press, 2002)

DAILY, G, *Nature's Services: Societal Dependence on Natural Ecosystems* (Washington, DC: Island Press, 1997)

ELGIE, S, & A LINTNER, "The Supreme Court's *Canfor* Decision: Losing the Battle but Winning the War for Environmental Damages" (2005) 38 UBC L Rev. 223

FAIETA, MD, *et al*, *Environmental Harm: Civil Actions and Compensation* (Toronto: Butterworths, 1996)

OLSZYNSKI, MZP, "The Assessment of Environmental Damages following the Supreme Court's Decision in *Canfor*" (2005) 15 J Envtl L & Prac 257

———, "Environmental Damages after the Federal *Environmental Enforcement Act*: Bringing Ecosystem Services to Canadian Environmental Law?" (2012) 50 Osgoode Hall LJ 129

ONTARIO LAW REFORM COMMISSION, *Report on Damages for Environmental Harm* (Toronto: Queen's Printer, 1990)

SWAIGEN, JZ, *Compensation of Pollution Victims in Canada* (Study prepared for the Economic Council of Canada) (Ottawa: Supply & Services Canada, 1981)

WORLD BANK, *How Much is an Ecosystem Worth: Assessing the Economic Value of Conservation* (Washington DC: World Bank, 2004)

WRUCK, J, "The Federal Environmental Damages Fund" (2004) 5 CELR (3d) 120

---

57   *Ibid.*
58   See also *EMA*, above note 52, s 47.

CHAPTER 11

REMEDIATION AND RESTORATION OF CONTAMINATED LANDS

A. INTRODUCTION

Persistent contamination is now recognized as a widespread and challenging problem. Canada faces a costly remedial agenda, with environmental law helping importantly to establish standards and to allocate costs.

In 1990, an inquiry conducted for the Law Reform Commission of Canada identified 8,784 waste disposal sites, many of which were considered to be sources of contamination. Only Quebec at that time had prepared a more comprehensive list in which the province identified some 11,000 properties known to be contaminated from waste or otherwise. A subsequent assessment undertaken on behalf of the National Round Table on the Environment and the Economy (NRTEE), resulted in an inventory of 30,000 locations under the general description of "brownfield sites," and originating in a variety of ways. In addition to known waste-disposal sites and scrapyards, hundreds of which may present continuing environmental and human-health risks, numerous other locations suffer toxic contamination. These include industrial sites associated with mining operations, with coal gasification plants, or metal and petroleum refineries. As well, there are old coking plants, chemical company facilities, electroplating establishments, and businesses whose operations once involved various forms of solvents, paints, and sealants or wood-preserving compounds.

The Sydney Tar Ponds in Nova Scotia, identified as problematic in 1982, represent one of the more intractable examples of widespread industrial contamination. The overall site contained 700,000 tonnes of toxic sludge accumulated over a century from the operations of a coking plant and steel mill. The condition of the site defied a series of federal-provincial cleanup efforts and continued to alarm nearby residents over health concerns.[1] Pursuant to a Memorandum of Agreement signed by the governments of Canada and Nova Scotia in May 2004, significant additional funding was committed and the province established a new organization, the Sydney Tar Ponds Agency (STPA), to pursue remediation. Some contaminants are to be removed for destruction elsewhere, while other materials will be treated on-site prior to the implementation of containment measures, restoration and landscaping. Detailed plans developed by the STPA have now been subject to joint environmental assessment review under federal and Nova Scotia legislation. In December 2012, Canada and Nova Scotia announced completion of the process to contain contaminants at the site.[2]

Even rural lands, traditionally regarded as essentially pastoral and subsequently absorbed into suburban residential housing projects, have been found to contain toxic hazards. In some cases leaking underground fuel-storage tanks pose the risk, yet there have been examples of radioactive contamination in unexpected locations. The *Sevidal v Chopra* and *Heighington* cases involved liability for radioactive contamination found in residential settings nearly half a century after wartime experimental use of agricultural property.[3] The impact on surface and groundwater quality of asphalt waste, which was disposed of in accordance with accepted practices in the 1960s, recently raised important questions of liability in Ontario.[4]

Over and above historic sources of contamination, which are at least researchable and discoverable in principle, are spill and accident sites. These are virtually impossible to locate reliably because of their largely random occurrence and the absence — until quite recently — of systematic reporting procedures and obligations.

There is a tendency to distinguish several dimensions of the cleanup task. Remediation is often understood to centre on the initial challenges of identifying and eliminating or neutralizing contaminants through a variety of mechanical, physical, chemical, and biological

---

1   For information from the Sydney Tar Ponds Agency on ongoing developments see online: www.tarpondscleanup.ca.

2   Online: www.tpsgc-pwgsc.gc.ca/biens-property/sydney/rspns-federal-eng.html.

3   *Sevidal v Chopra* (1987), 64 OR (2d) 169 (HCJ); *Heighington v Ontario* (1989), 69 OR (2d) 484 (CA).

4   *Berendsen v Ontario* (2008), 34 CELR (3d) 223 (Ont Sup Ct J), rev'd 2009 ONCA 845, leave to appeal to SCC granted, [2010] SCCA No 24 (QL) [*Berendsen*].

techniques.[5] A subsequent step, environmental restoration, may be described as "measures taken to return a site to previolation conditions"[6] or, somewhat more elaborately, as *"bringing a part of the natural environment from a state of decay, injury or loss back to its original self-sustaining condition, so that it will support all the forms of life which formerly inhabited it."*[7] When used with reference to the spill of a contaminant under the *OEPA*, restoring the natural environment means to "restore all forms of life, physical conditions, the natural environment and things existing immediately before the spill of the pollutant that are affected or that may reasonably be expected to be affected by the pollutant."[8] Before discussing a number of issues associated with the legal framework for remediation, it is helpful to underline some of the distinctive challenges presented by contaminated lands:

> Contamination is rarely static; its presence in the surface and subsurface of land, including groundwater, changes over time. Contamination does not respect property boundaries, so that site contamination can contribute toward liability for off-site migration, and a site contaminated by an off-site source may, after remediation, become recontaminated. . . . The regulatory environment dealing with contamination and people's perceptions of contamination can evolve, resulting in changes to the risk and liability occasioned by contamination over time, even without any change in the contamination itself. Remedial technologies can develop and improve, but so can detection methods, finding contamination tomorrow where none was identified today.[9]

One of the listed factors, the regulatory environment, has indeed been significantly transformed. We have recognized the extent of contamination across the country. We have formulated remedial programs, including programs influenced by a growing appreciation of the "polluter-pays" principle. We have increasingly recognized the interests of third parties.

In regard to broader interests, the National Round Table on the Environment and the Economy demonstrated important leadership in

5   Insight Educational Services, *Clean-up of Contaminated Sites: Regulations and State of the Art Technologies* (Mississauga: Insight Press, 1991).
6   WA Tilleman, ed, *The Dictionary of Environmental Law and Science* (Toronto: Emond Montgomery, 1994) at 244.
7   D Saxe, "Reflections on Environmental Restoration" (1992) 2 J Envtl L & Prac 77 at 78 (emphasis in original).
8   *Environmental Protection Act*, RSO 1990, c E.19, s 91(1) [*OEPA*].
9   KM van Rensburg, "Deconstructing *Tridan*: A Litigator's Perspective" (2004) 15 J Envtl L & Prac 85 at 92.

the course of its work on the redevelopment of brownfields. The initiative culminated in a call by the NRTEE for a national brownfields redevelopment strategy with an emphasis on sites where both cleanup costs and redevelopment potential are judged to be high. Typically, it is suggested, such properties will be found in urban centres and along transportation corridors where municipal services are already in place.

In releasing its strategy, the NRTEE articulated the objective as being to provide all participants in brownfield redevelopment with a clear, fair, and consistent public policy regime to bring greater certainty and efficiency to questions of liability and risk management and to promote a co-ordinated effort on liability and risk management among all levels of government. In connection with liability for contaminated lands in the context of brownfield redevelopment, a task force reported to the NRTEE with six recommendations:

2.1 Allow binding contractual allocation of liability.
2.2 Provide for termination of regulatory liability.
2.3 Provide for termination of civil liability after a limitation period.
2.4 Create an insurance fund [to deal with subsequent claims].
2.5 Apply site-specific assessment and approvals regimes.
2.6 Provide regulatory approvals for remediation.[10]

Coincident with debate encouraged by the NRTEE, several Canadian jurisdictions examined reforms to the legislative framework applicable to remediation and liability for contaminated lands. While the detailed arrangements operating in each province still differ in important ways, they address a comparable range of questions: What process determines the designation of a site as contaminated? What instruments should be available to require or promote remediation of contaminated lands? What is the range of parties who may be considered responsible for the remediation effort or its costs; what principles ground their liability, and what is the extent of that liability? What standard of remediation is to be achieved; by whom should it be determined that the standard has been met? What form, if any, of official certification or approval of the remediation process or its results will be provided? In what circumstances, if any, might exposure to further liability be reopened following completion of the required remediation? What measures will be available to safeguard the interests of third parties in remediation initiatives? What exemptions may be applicable?

---

10 *Cleaning up the Past, Building the Future: A National Brownfield Redevelopment Strategy for Canada* (Ottawa: NRTEE, 2003) 25–30.

B. SITE REMEDIATION REQUIREMENTS

Requirements to remediate former industrial sites or to restore them after use to an environmentally acceptable standard will sometimes provide an illustration of the polluter-pays principle.[11] Such obligations may be imposed by general legislation, or they may appear as terms and conditions of operating approvals or administrative orders.[12] In some circumstances, remediation actions may be court ordered.[13] Moreover, in dealings with original owners, purchasers or leaseholders have become increasingly inclined to insist upon, or at least to bargain for, some level of cleanup, assurance about the condition of the property, or commitment to participate in remedial work that may be found necessary.[14] Owners, of course, are equally concerned that a property be returned to them in satisfactory condition after occupation by some other operation. Thus, private arrangements and obligations also figure in the delineation of cleanup requirements, both as to their existence and with respect to the standard of remediation that must be provided or financed. Before examining statutory schemes, aspects of possible private arrangements may be briefly noted.

In *Westfair v Domo*, a gas bar operator, after occupying a leased site in Winnipeg for nearly twenty-five years, decommissioned the property and returned it to the landlord.[15] The remedial work cost about $400,000 and included excavation and removal of underground tanks and lines, the removal and treatment of contaminated soil, installation of a plastic liner or barrier, and backfill using clean material. Following this work, the property was considered to be in reasonable condition, generally in compliance with provincial guidelines and suitable for the site's highest and best use—commercial development. The property was not, however, in a condition equivalent to its original state at the time the leasing arrangement began. The landlord therefore sued to enforce a higher standard of remediation. Its claim, based on an implied contractual obligation for the lessee to return property in an uncontaminated condition, failed. Morse J expressed the view that

---

11   *Imperial Oil v Quebec*, [2003] 2 SCR 624.

12   See Chapter 7.

13   *OEPA*, above note 8, s 190(1); *Environmental Protection and Enhancement Act*, RSA 2000, c E-12, ss 213(1) and 234(1) [*AEPEA*].

14   DR Cameron, *Environmental Concerns in Business Transactions: Avoiding the Risks* (Toronto: Butterworths, 1993) cc 12 & 13.

15   *Westfair Foods Ltd v Domo Gasoline Corp*, [1999] MJ No 1 (QB), aff'd (1999), 33 CELR (NS) 93 (Man CA).

in the case of a commercial retail gasoline operation where a land-lord must know of the likelihood of contamination of the soil arising merely from the day-to-day operation of the facility and where the landlord benefits financially from the sale of increased quantities of gasoline, a tenant, upon termination of the lease, should not, in the absence of a specific provision in the lease to the contrary, be re-quired to restore the land to its original condition.[16]

Other courts have been more inclined to insist that leased prop-erty is to be returned in an uncontaminated condition on the basis of an implied term. In an Alberta decision, *Darmac Credit*, the view was expressed that

> in today's commercial world, unless a lease provides otherwise, it is implied within a lease that lands are to be returned uncontaminated. Contaminated lands are not saleable lands.[17]

In numerous cases, persistent contamination is in fact the consequence of industrial operations that were carried out in compliance with previous permit standards. Accordingly, the situation has often presented governments seeking to promote the remediation of contaminated sites with a complex challenge from the perspective of allocating cleanup and restoration costs on a principled basis.[18]

Where government agencies have incurred expenses in connection with environmental remediation or restoration measures, they are frequently authorized to recover the costs from persons responsible for the damage or from funds specifically created for the purpose. The *Arctic Waters Pollution Prevention Act*, for example, establishes the absolute liability of those engaged in resource exploration and development, shipping, or mainland or island-based undertakings in the Arctic and Arctic waters for costs and expenses incurred to repair or remedy any condition arising from unauthorized deposits of waste, or for the purpose of reducing or mitigating any damage to or

---

16 In an Ontario case involving contamination of property by a significant leak from a neighbouring gas station, the court determined that the plaintiff was entitled to have its site restored to the "pristine" condition it had been in prior to the leak. See *Tridan Developments Ltd v Shell Canada Products* (2002), 57 OR (3d) 503 (CA), leave to appeal to SCC refused, [2002] SCCA No 98.

17 *Darmac Credit Corp v Great Western Containers Inc* (1994), 163 AR 10 (QB). For other decisions along similar lines, see *Progressive Enterprises Ltd v Cascade Lead Products Ltd*, [1996] BCJ No 2473 (SC); and *O'Connor v Fleck* (2000), 35 CELR (NS) 16 (BCSC).

18 Situations of this kind are also extremely problematic for private litigants. See, for example, *Berendsen*, above note 4.

destruction of life or property, so long as the expenditures "can be established to have been reasonably incurred in the circumstances."[19] Cleanup costs are also recoverable under the *Fisheries Act* and from the Maritime Pollution Claims Fund in connection with oil-spill damage.[20] Other remediation requirements have been imposed on a sectoral basis. Specific requirements apply, for example, to those whose activity involves the use of underground storage tanks, oil and gas wells, mineral properties, and forest resources.[21]

Saskatchewan's *Environmental Management and Protection Act, 2002* now explicitly provides for measures to deal with contaminated sites.[22] The process unfolds pursuant to designation of a contaminated site by the minister where he or she is of the opinion that a substance that is causing, may cause or has caused an adverse effect is present in the area. Designations are based upon any standards, guidelines, or criteria adopted by the minister and may apply to adverse effects of discharges that occurred before or after the coming into force of the legislation in October 2002. The broad potential for designation is highlighted by its clear application even to activities that were, at the time of the discharge, giving rise to adverse effects, lawful or unregulated. In the words of section 11(8) of the Act, a contaminated site designation may be made notwithstanding that:

(b) the substance was discharged in accordance with this Act or any other Act, Act of the Parliament of Canada or regulations made pursuant to any of those Acts; or

(c) the discharge of the substance was not prohibited by this Act or any other Act, Act of the Parliament of Canada or regulations may pursuant to any of those Acts . . .

Public notice of the contaminated site designation, including a description of the site, will then be published in the *Gazette* while written notice must be given to parties specified in section 12 as follows:

(a) any person who, in the opinion of the minister, is a person responsible for the discharge that resulted in the contaminated site;

---

19 *Arctic Waters Pollution Protection Act*, RSC 1985, c A-12, ss 6–7.
20 *Fisheries Act*, RSC 1985, c F-14, s 42.
21 See, for example, *Crown Forest Sustainability Act*, SO 1994, c 25, ss 55–64; and *AEPEA*, above note 13, s 220.
22 *Environmental Management and Protection Act, 2002*, SS 2002, c E-10.21, s 10 *et seq* [*EMPA*]. For a detailed examination of remediation arrangements under the old and new *EMPAs* in Saskatchewan, see J Kelly Brown, "Contaminated Site Liability in Saskatchewan: On the 'Right Track' to Remediation?" (2003) 12 J Envtl L & Prac 55.

(b) any owner and occupier of land directly affected by the designation;

(c) the municipality in which the contaminated site is located . . .

In addition, written notice will also be provided to persons whose interests in land affected by the designation are on record under the land titles act or registry.

Each "person directly responsible for a discharge" related to the designated contaminated site is then required to undertake a series of actions set out in detail according to section 14, together with the minister's authority to respond:

(2) (a) prepare a remedial action plan for the contaminated site; and

(b) if there are any other persons directly responsible for the discharge, enter into a written agreement with those other persons . . . that provides for:

(i) the remedial action that must be taken; and

(ii) the apportionment of costs of taking that action.

(3) The person or persons directly responsible for a discharge shall submit the remedial action plan and any agreements for remedial action to the minister for approval.

(4) On receipt of a remedial action plan and an agreement . . . the minister may:

(a) approve the remedial action plan and any agreement;

(b) refuse to approve the remedial action plan and any agreement; or

(c) direct that changes be made to the remedial action plan and any agreement.

(5) On approval by the minister . . . every person who submitted a remedial action plan and agreement . . . shall comply with the terms of the approved remedial action plan and any approved agreement.

Those who comply with the terms of an approved remedial action plan are immunized from further orders, known in the legislation as environmental protection orders (EPOs). Those failing to meet their obligations are subject to a broad range of administrative orders intended to bring about remediation of the contaminated site.

The general Ontario approach developed from a series of guidelines intended to elaborate on the Ministry of the Environment and Energy's use of its legislative authority in relation to remediation of contaminated lands. The Ontario guidelines described elements of three possible approaches for responding to contamination in the context of cleanup or redevelopment. The "background" approach referred to naturally occurring, ambient, or background soil-quality criteria existing in the relevant area, while the "generic" approach associated specified land uses with soil and groundwater-quality criteria expected to safeguard against adverse environmental and human health effects. A third permitted approach was derived from site-specific risk assessment. Brownfields legislation has now provided a more detailed and comprehensive framework to address remediation and associated liability issues in the province.[23]

In addition to the new remediation requirements, in connection with a successful action under section 84 of the *OEBR* relating to significant harm to a public resource, the court has authority to order parties to the proceedings to negotiate a restoration plan. Such plans are expected to address, "to the extent that to do so is reasonable, practical and ecologically sound," such issues as

(a) the prevention, diminution or elimination of the harm;
(b) the restoration of all forms of life, physical conditions, the natural environment and other things associated with the public resource . . . ; and
(c) the restoration of all uses, including enjoyment, of the public resource.[24]

It is possible that *OEBR* restoration plans could also address harm to a public resource indirectly in that research on preventive technologies and community education or health programs might be incorporated.

In Alberta, specified lands, that is, lands identified by regulations and on or in respect of which an activity is carried out, are subject to the conservation and reclamation provisions of the *AEPEA* and must be restored to "an equivalent land capability." Operators on specified lands must conserve and reclaim such lands in accordance with any applicable approval, the terms and conditions of an environmental protection order dealing with conservation and reclamation, and official directions. An inspector, when satisfied that conservation and reclamation have been completed as required, may issue a reclamation certificate to the operator.[25]

Where some form of certification or approval follows the completion of a remedial program, governments remain cautious about the implica-

---

23 Ontario, Ministry of the Environment, *Guideline for Use at Contaminated Sites in Ontario* (Toronto: Ministry of the Environment, 1996). Site-condition standards, similar to the current guidelines, are now prescribed by regulation pursuant to *An Act to Encourage the Revitalization of Contaminated Land (Brownfields Statute Law Amendment Act)*, RSO 2001, c 17. See also O Reg 153/04.
24 *Environmental Bill of Rights, 1993*, SO 1993, c 28, s 95(2)
25 *AEPEA*, above note 13, Parts 5 & 6; *Conservation and Reclamation Regulation*, Alta Reg 242/99.

tions of providing such documentation. British Columbia addressed this issue in connection with compliance certificates following satisfactory remediation of contaminated lands under the province's former *Waste Management Act* by providing that, other than in cases where bad faith can be established, "no action lies and no proceeding may be brought against the Crown, the minister or an employee of the ministry because of anything arising out of the issue of a certificate of compliance."[26]

C. LIABILITY ALLOCATION ISSUES

Among the most sensitive and controversial matters in the field of remediation is the issue of allocating cleanup costs among past and present property owners, business operators, financial participants, and other potential contributors.

To identify potential contributors requires important judgments about the principles to be applied to the allocation of cleanup costs. Are cleanup costs viewed as a matter of individual or social responsibility? Does it matter that waste discharges or the other practices that may have resulted in contamination were not unlawful, perhaps even permitted, at the time damages occurred? Is it significant that the community as well as individuals may have benefited from the environmentally harmful activity in the sense that an employment base was created, taxes paid, and so on? Where contributors have been identified—whatever the criteria—are there grounds for limiting the extent of that liability, or for apportioning it among a group of contributors? These are the kinds of issues that have to be faced in designing liability regimes.[27] Saskatchewan's answers to some of these questions have been noted in the previous section.

Principles on contaminated sites liability formulated by CCME in 1993[28] were adopted by a number of administrative bodies[29] and variations can be found in some provincial legislation.[30]

---

26   *Waste Management Act*, RSBC 1996, c 482, ss 26 & 27. Now see BC's *Environmental Management Act*, SBC 2003, c 53, Part 4; and the *Contaminated Sites Regulation*, BC Reg 375/96.

27   N Vlavianos, "Creating Liability Regimes for the Clean-up of Environmental Damage: The Literature" (2000) 9 J Envtl L & Prac 145.

28   Canadian Council of Ministers of the Environment, *Recommended Principles* (May 1993). In 2003 the CCME reassessed the continuing applicability of the original principles. Now see *Recommended Principles on Contaminated Sites Liability, 2006*, online: www.ccme.ca/assets/pdf/csl_14_principles_e.pdf.

29   *Re 724597 Ontario Ltd* (1994), 13 CELR (NS) 257 (OEAB).

30   *AEPEA*, above note 13, s 129(2).

A British Columbia legislative initiative on contaminated sites formalized principles of liability, including exemptions and cost-allocation mechanisms as well as possibilities for public consultation in a remediation program.[31] In the first instance, it defined current or former owners (including tenants) and operators. An "owner" means a person who is in possession of, has the right of control of, occupies, or controls the use of real property, including, without limitation, a person who has any estate, legal or equitable, in the real property. An "operator" is described as a person who is or was in control of or responsible for any operation located at a contaminated site.

Under specified conditions, secured creditors and other persons designated by regulations also face responsibility for remediation. Certain exemptions are then established, including exemptions for owners or operators who are able to establish that

(i)   at the time the person became an owner or operator of the site,
    (a)   the site was a contaminated site,
    (b)   the person had no knowledge or reason to know or suspect that the site was a contaminated site, and
    (c)   the person undertook all appropriate inquiries into the previous ownership and uses of the site and undertook other investigations, consistent with good commercial or customary practice at that time, in an effort to minimize potential liability,
(ii) if the person was an owner of the site, the person did not transfer any interest in the site without first disclosing any known contamination to the transferee, and
(iii) the owner or operator did not, by any act or omission, cause or contribute to the contamination of the site.[32]

The BC Supreme Court had occasion to consider the scheme of the Act and particularly the scope of the definitions of owner and operator as these concepts relate to the concepts of control and responsibility in the case of *Beazer East Inc v British Columbia (Environmental Appeal Board)*.[33] The case centred on the potential liability of a parent corporation for contamination on the site of its subsidiary, though it is only necessary here to present Tysoe J's general remarks on the control and responsibility issues:

---

31   BC *Environmental Management Act*, above note 26, Part 4.
32   *Ibid*, s 46(d).
33   *Beazer East Inc v British Columbia (Environmental Appeal Board)* (2000), 36 CELR (NS) 195 (BCSC).

In general terms, it is my view that the intention of the Legislature was to include persons who made decisions or had the authority to make decisions with respect to any operation on the site. These are the persons who are potentially culpable because they were the ones who made or could have made decisions in relation to operations on the site, which may have included operations that caused or contributed to the contamination. A person who makes the decisions with respect to an operation is "in control" of the operation and a person who has the authority to make the decisions with respect to an operation is "responsible" for the operation. In my opinion, a person who is responsible for an operation is one who is accountable for the operation but the accountability is not necessarily legally enforceable.

I also believe in using the word "responsible," the Legislature intended to include persons who brought about an operation in the sense of causing the operation to be carried on or carried out. Such a person would be responsible for the operation because, but for the actions or decision of that person, the operation would not have been carried on or carried out.[34]

Manitoba legislation on contaminated sites approaches the question of allocating costs by providing, among other mechanisms, for "apportionment agreements." Those charged with deciding whether to approve such agreements are required to take all other relevant factors into account but must specifically "apply the principle that the primary responsibility for the remediation of a contaminated site lies with the person or persons who contaminated it and that they should bear the responsibility for the remediation in proportion to their contributions to the contamination."[35] Appeal mechanisms under the *Contaminated Sites Remediation Act* involve Manitoba's Clean Environment Commission (CEC) and the minister of the environment. Decisions of the CEC may, with leave, be appealed to the Manitoba Court of Appeal on questions of law or jurisdiction.

Notwithstanding indications, as canvassed above, that fairness factors associated with degrees of responsibility, knowledge, and reasonable behaviour in relation to the experience of contamination may be taken into account in allocating liability for cleanup costs, courts have upheld remediation orders directed at innocent parties. Thus, when

34   *Ibid* at 227. For discussion of the scope of remediation costs recoverable under the BC legislation, see *Canadian National Railway Co v ABC Recycling*, [2005] BCJ No. 982 (SC). See also *No 158 Seabright Holdings Ltd v Imperial Oil Ltd*, 2001 BCSC 1330 at para 47; and *Workshop Holdings Ltd v CAE Machinery Ltd*, 2003 BCCA 56.

35   *Contaminated Sites Remediation Act*, CCSM c 205, Part 5.

residential furnace oil entered city property and, if unchecked, would have threatened a nearby lake, environmental officials issued a cleanup order against the Kawartha Lakes municipality. The city protested that it was an innocent victim of the inaction of other parties and that it was unfair that it should have to pay the costs of remediation. The Ontario Superior Court determined that the order was not unreasonable in the circumstances of uncontrolled and continuing damage and was indeed consistent with the purpose of the legislation, that is, the protection of the environment.[36]

D. THE ENVIRONMENTAL LIABILITY OF LENDERS, RECEIVERS, AND TRUSTEES

The importance of environmental considerations for financial and real estate transactions has grown markedly since the 1980s, particularly as a consequence of statutory extensions of environmental liability to persons other than those who caused or were in some way directly responsible for environmental harm. In Ontario, for example, owners or former owners and a person who has or had the charge, management, or control of the source of a contaminant are liable to receive control orders or stop orders.[37] An order to take preventive measures may be issued to a person who owns or owned or who has or had management or control of an undertaking or property if the discharge of a contaminant from the property or undertaking will or is likely to result in an adverse effect and the required measures are necessary or desirable to prevent the discharge or lessen its adverse effects.[38]

Expansive approaches to such concepts as "person responsible," "owner," or "care, management, and control" had the potential to extend environmental liability to institutions and individuals whose original connection with contaminated properties was financial in nature rather than operational. Thus, lenders in general, mortgagees in particular, and others such as trustees and receivers acting on their behalf found their interests intertwined to a sometimes alarming degree with environmental legislation governing environmental protection and cleanup and restoration obligations on contaminated lands.

---

36   *Kawartha Lakes (City) v Ontario (Director, Ministry of the Environment)*, 2012 ONSC 2708.

37   OEPA, above note 8, ss 7 & 8. Comparable powers respecting waste removal are established under *ibid*, s 43.

38   *Ibid*, s 18.

In *Re Canadian National Railway*, the Ontario Divisional Court considered a mortgagee's liability under an administrative order calling for study of contaminated industrial lands and an assessment of remedial alternatives.[39] Among the issues raised was the possibility that mortgagees might exercise "control" so as to become "persons responsible" under the applicable legislation. In the circumstances of the case, and notwithstanding its knowledge of contamination amounting to breach of the covenant of good repair, the mortgagee who was not in possession was not liable. The Ontario Divisional Court explained that the mortgagee might have exercised a power of re-entry and taken control of the property:

> Once in control of the property it could be a person responsible under the Act if, at that time, it was found that the plant was the source of contaminant . . . . The fact that the technical, legal ownership of the plant is in the mortgagee does not make it an owner within the definition of a person responsible . . . . If a mortgagee has taken no active steps with respect to gaining or obtaining control of the property, it is not responsible.[40]

The Divisional Court's decision, besides contributing to a fuller understanding of "care, management, and control" in Ontario legislation was also notable for the sensitivity of the surrounding policy implications. While some observers characterized the analysis as an obstacle to attempts by the Ministry of Environment to impose clean-up costs on private parties rather than the public at large, others welcomed the result, arguing that "[i]t is too often assumed that current landowners should be made responsible for the condition of their land. However, where those conditions were created by others at a time when our current environmental sensitivity did not exist, is it unreasonable to suggest that society at large should pay for the cost of returning the environment to its natural state?"[41] But as *Re Canadian National Railway* was proceeding through the courts, the Ontario legislature expanded liability for cleanup costs to previous owners and other parties who may not themselves have caused pollution.[42]

39　*Canadian National Railway v Ontario (Director appointed under the Environmental Protection Act) (sub nom Re Canadian National Railway)* (1991), 3 OR (3d) 609 (Div Ct), aff'd (1992), 7 OR (3d) 97 (CA).

40　*Ibid* at 623–24 (Div Ct).

41　H Dahme, "Northern Wood Preservers: A Case of Contaminated Land" (1991) 2:5 Environmental Law Alert 1 at 2.

42　*OEPA*, above note 8, s 7.

Concern about the extension of liability prompted the Canadian Bankers Association to lament "that environmental protection law in Canada punishes the innocent as well as the guilty; that lenders and investors who are not polluters are being asked to pay the penalty for environmental damage caused by others." The association warned policy makers about the economic effects of environmental initiatives directed at "deep pockets" rather than actual polluters.[43] However, the policy issues were by no means one-sided. Aside from financing clean-up costs after damage has occurred, an important virtue of expanded liability lies in its potential to recruit financial institutions to the cause of systematic, preventive environmental monitoring. As one commentator concluded, "lenders must increasingly look to self-protection through careful investigation and the establishment and maintenance of on-going monitoring programs before a lending decision is made."[44]

When borrowers default, lenders may resort to receiverships to recover funds advanced, or bankruptcy proceedings may be initiated with the appointment of a trustee. In such circumstances of limited and uncertain financial resources, conflicts over environmental liabilities are particularly acute. In *Panamericana de Bienes y Servicios SA v Northern Badger Oil & Gas Ltd*, the Alberta Court of Appeal held that an order of the Alberta Energy Resources Conservation Board concerning well-abandonment procedures represented a general obligation for environmental work in the public interest, which the receiver/manager must pay out of the proceeds of disposition of a bankrupt company's assets prior to a distribution to secured creditors according to the scheme of the federal *Bankruptcy Act*.[45]

In the absence of statutory limitations on liability for costs of environmental cleanup and restoration, the possibility exists that receivers may face personal liability where such costs exceed the value of the assets under administration. To protect themselves from such risks, receivers and trustees, at the time of their appointment, have occasionally sought court assurances to limit the potential extent of environmental liabilities to the value of the debtor's assets, and to ensure that they will be paid for their services. Courts have shown some sympathy for these applications:

---

43   Canadian Bankers Association, Sustainable Capital: The Effect of Environmental Liability in Canada on Borrowers, Lenders and Investors (November 1991).
44   P Lalonde, "Lenders and Their Agents Beware: The *Northern Badger* Case" (1991) 2:6 Environmental Law Alert 1 at 3. For further consideration of the importance of financial arrangements in environmental protection, see Chapter 17.
45   (1991), 81 DLR (4th) 280 (Alta CA) [*Panamericana*].

> The balancing of values in this case falls in favour of protecting the health and safety of society over the rights of creditors . . . but there is also a need in modern society for trustees to take on the duty of winding up insolvent estates. The evidence before me indicates that no trustee can be found who will take on the bankruptcy . . . without a guarantee that he or she will be entitled to trustee's fees to be deducted from the amount paid out under the Order, and will have no personal liability for the costs of cleanup of the contaminated site . . . . In keeping with the findings I have made . . . I direct that in the event there are insufficient funds to meet the requirements of the Order, the payment of funds pursuant to the Order must be subject to a reduction equal to the amount of the trustee's fees.[46]

Such willingness to accommodate the concerns of persons acting on behalf of creditors has certainly not been universal, and exemption from environmental liabilities has been denied where courts have felt this would amount to rewriting legislation.[47]

A series of amendments to section 14.06 of the federal *Bankruptcy Act* alleviated some of the uncertainties by providing that

> Notwithstanding anything in any federal or provincial law, a trustee is not personally liable in that position for any environmental condition that arose or environmental damage that occurred,
>
> (a) before the trustee's appointment; or
>
> (b) after the trustee's appointment unless it is established that the condition arose or the damage occurred as a result of the trustee's gross negligence or wilful misconduct . . . .[48]

Accompanying provisions addressed options available to trustees in the context of remedial orders. The status of environmental remediation orders in the context of insolvency has figured prominently in recent litigation.

A widely awaited decision of the Supreme Court of Canada in 2012 involved aspects of the relationship between environmental remediation orders and the interests of creditors' in insolvency proceedings under the *Companies' Creditors Arrangement Act* (CCAA).[49] The legislation establishes a distinctive process for resolving financial claims against an insolvent corporate debtor, including arrangements to apportion or compromise those debts. The precise question ultimately

---

46   *Re Lamford Forest Products Ltd* (1991), 63 BCLR (2d) 388 at 396 (SC).
47   *Standard Trust Co v Lindsay Holdings Ltd* (1994), 15 CELR (NS) 165 (BCSC).
48   *An Act to Amend the Bankruptcy Act*, SC 1992, c 27, SC 1997, c 12.
49   *Newfoundland and Labrador v AbitibiBowater Inc*, 2012 SCC 67.

addressed by the majority was simply "whether orders issued by a regulatory body with respect to environmental remediation work can be treated as monetary claims under the *Companies' Creditors Arrangement Act*."[50] By way of conclusion, the court determined that where the circumstances of a regulatory order are such that it can be considered "monetary" in nature and thus a "provable claim" within the CCAA process, the order will not enjoy priority relative to other claimants against the limited assets of the insolvent company. The specific challenge on which the court advised in considerable detail was for the CCAA court to determine "[i]n the environmental context . . . whether there are sufficient facts indicating the existence of an environmental duty that will ripen into a financial liability owed to the regulatory body that issued the order."[51]

This decision emerged from a prolonged dispute between AbitibiBowater and the government of Newfoundland and Labrador. When Abitibi entered a period of financial distress, the company sought protection under the *CCAA*. Subsequently, the province issued environmental protection orders calling on AbitibiBowater to prepare remediation action plans for five former industrial sites and to complete the remediation program. Other factors, notably provincial expropriation of several of these sites and other ongoing controversies between government and the company, produced a "unique set of facts."[52]

The province argued that the environmental remediation orders were not claims within the framework of the *CCAA* and therefore could not be stayed by a *CCAA* court and made subject to a claims procedure order. The SCC majority agreed with the determination of the *CCAA* court, however, that in the circumstances, the regulatory obligations were "truly financial and monetary in nature."

To the extent that broader considerations of environmental policy were involved, the SCC majority took note of constitutional dimensions of the provincial argument:

> If the Province's actions indicate that, in substance, it is asserting a provable claim within the meaning of federal legislation, then that claim can be subjected to the insolvency process. Environmental claims do not have a higher priority than is provided for in the *CCAA*. Considering substance over form prevents a regulatory body from artificially creating a priority higher than the one conferred on the claim by federal legislation. . . . [A] province cannot disturb the pri-

---

50   *Ibid* at para 1.
51   *Ibid* at para 3.
52   *Ibid* at para 50.

ority scheme established by the federal insolvency legislation. Environmental claims are given a specific, and limited, priority under the *CCAA*. To exempt orders which are in fact monetary claims from the *CCAA* proceedings would amount to conferring upon provinces a priority higher than the one provided for in the *CCAA*.[53]

In addition, the majority observed that Parliament was aware of the need for regulatory agencies to perform remediation work on occasion, and in such situations, remediation costs are subject to the insolvency process with the claim secured by a charge on the contaminated real property and certain other related property and benefits from a priority under the *CCAA*, section 11.8(8). "Thus, Parliament struck a balance between the public's interest in enforcing environmental regulations and the interest of third-party creditors in being treated equitably."[54] The majority analysis continued with the observation that:

> If Parliament had intended that the debtor always satisfy all remediation costs, it would have granted the Crown a priority with respect to the totality of the debtor's assets. In light of the legislative history and the purpose of the reorganization process, the fact that the Crown's priority under s. 11.8(8) *CCAA* is limited to the contaminated property and certain related property leads me to conclude that to exempt environmental orders would be inconsistent with the insolvency legislation. As deferential as courts may be to regulatory bodies' actions, they must apply the general rules.[55]

It is also noteworthy that the majority responded to broader questions of principle, including the status of the polluter-pay principle that some interveners had raised:

> These parties argue that treating a regulatory order as a claim in an insolvency proceeding extinguishes the debtor's environmental obligations, thereby undermining the polluter-pay principle. . . . This objection demonstrates a misunderstanding of the nature of insolvency proceedings. Subjecting an order to the claims process does not extinguish the debtor's environmental obligations any more than subjecting any creditor's claim to that process extinguishes the debtor's obligation to pay its debts. It merely ensures that the creditor's claim will be paid in accordance with insolvency legislation. Moreover, full compliance with orders that are found to be monetary in

---

53   *Ibid* at para 19.
54   *Ibid* at para 32.
55   *Ibid* at para 33.

nature would shift the costs of remediation to third-party creditors, including involuntary creditors, such as those whose claims lie in tort or in the law of extra-contractual liability. In the insolvency context, the Province's position would result not only in a super-priority, but in the acceptance of a "third party-pay" principle in place of the polluter-pay principle.[56]

In a forceful dissent, the Chief Justice sought to distinguish regulatory obligations from monetized claims and explained her understanding of the differing consequences:

> If [the EPA orders] are not claims that can be compromised in restructuring, the Abitibi respondents ("Abitibi") will still have a legal obligation to clean up the sites following their emergence from restructuring. If they are such claims, Abitibi will have emerged from restructuring free of the obligation, able to recommence business without remediating the properties it polluted, the cost of which will fall on the Newfoundland and Labrador public.[57]

As the Chief Justice explained, corporations seeking to restructure under the *CCAA* will frequently be subject to ongoing regulatory orders relating, for example, to matters like employment, energy conservation, and the environment. "The corporation remains subject to these obligations as it continues to carry on business during the restructuring period, and remains subject to them when it emerges from restructuring unless they have been compromised or liquidated."[58] She quoted approvingly from the Alberta Court of Appeal decision in *Panamericana* regarding the *Bankruptcy Act*:

> The duty is owed as a public duty by all the citizens of the community to their fellow citizens. When the citizen subject to the order complies, the result is not the recovery of money by the peace officer or public authority, or of a judgement for money, nor is that the object of the whole process. Rather, it is simply the enforcement of the general law. The enforcing authority does not become a "creditor" of the citizen on whom the duty is imposed.[59]

In her assessment of the relevant circumstances: "The distinction between regulatory obligations under the general law aimed at the protection of the public and monetary claims that can be compromised in

---

56   *Ibid* at para 40.
57   *Ibid* at para 64.
58   *Ibid* at para 71.
59   *Ibid* at para 73.

CCAA restructuring or bankruptcy is a fundamental plank of Canadian corporate law."[60]

The "unique set of facts" presented in Abitibi, together with continued debate over the nature of regulatory orders and over the circumstances in which they might be characterized as monetary claims provide indications that further consideration of priorities is warranted. Regulatory bodies, lenders, and other potential creditors may also be expected to reassess future actions in light of their understanding of the incentives arising from the decision.[61]

E. CONTAMINATED-SITES INVENTORY AND PUBLIC-REMEDIATION PROGRAMS

Practitioners have become more alert to potential environmental problems whether the indications are provided by historic use, topography, and the character of the neighbourhood or district, or based on specific information. Thus armed, legal advisers in real estate transactions may initiate on-site examinations or otherwise more actively pursue searches, investigations, and negotiations to protect their clients' interests in relation to environmental risk.

Notwithstanding much effort to focus on preventive measures, the toxic legacy demands a costly and substantial response that is currently ongoing. That challenge, however, is a formidable one.

Following the announcement of federal funding in 1989, the CCME initiated a National Contaminated Sites Remediation Program (NCSRP). The jointly funded $250-million program was designed to pursue three objectives over a five-year period: to promote the remediation of contaminated lands on the basis of the polluter-pays principle; to encourage the development of innovative remediation technologies; and to fund the cleanup of abandoned or orphan sites that pose high risks.[62] The orphan category originally included about fifty of the estimated thousand contaminated sites that had been identified when the program was established. As of 1995 when the NCSRP was concluded,

---

60 *Ibid* at para 74.
61 See *Re Nortel Networks Corp*, 2012 ONSC 1213 for a very informative analysis of how decision makers might hope to respond to challenges presented by the fact that "insolvency statutes such as the CCAA and the BIA do not mesh very well with environmental legislation," *ibid* at para 101.
62 G Letourneau & BA Chomyn, "Contaminated Lands: A Canadian Perspective" (1991) 32 C de D 1073 at 1076.

remediation was either completed or under way at forty-five of the orphan sites.[63]

Although the NCSRP included some preliminary attempt to inventory and address contamination of federal government properties such as airports, government laboratories, ports and harbours, lighthouse stations and military facilities, the slow pace of progress in dealing with approximately 780 such contaminated sites attracted criticism.[64] As of March 2011, one-third of federal contaminated site files were considered closed and no longer requiring action. However, half the sites in the federal inventory of contaminated sites were still awaiting assessment.[65]

In the context of the IJC's concern for Great Lakes water quality, a restoration program was put in place in the form of so-called remedial action plans (RAPs). These are applicable to forty-three areas of concern (AOCs) where a previous lack of action and the failure of preventive or cleanup initiatives had resulted in the persistence of toxic and other contaminants. As outlined in an annex to the 1987 *Great Lakes Water Quality Agreement* (*GLWQA*), the RAP process begins with the identification of impaired water uses and an analysis of the causes of that impairment. Remedial measures to restore impaired uses are then formulated and implemented with the involvement of all interested agencies and the local community. Systematic monitoring of progress identifies continuing problems and was intended to facilitate a transition towards ongoing ecosystem protection.

The IJC has a responsibility to review each RAP for compliance with the objectives of the *GLWQA* and to determine whether the remedial effort in place represents a systematic and comprehensive ecosystem approach. Despite persistent frustrations, the IJC judged the RAP program to be "one of the success stories" of the *GLWQA*.[66] The RAP process itself is considered to be a decentralized, "bottom-up" initiative whose operations should promote cooperation and coordination on the part of all levels of government and interested stakeholders. Neverthe-

---

63 Canadian Council of Ministers of the Environment, *National Contaminated Sites Remediation Program: Annual Report 1994–95* (Winnipeg: Canadian Council of Ministers of the Environment, 1995).

64 *2002 October Report of the Commissioner of the Environment and Sustainable Development* (Ottawa: Office of the Auditor General, 2002) c 2 "The Legacy of Federal Contaminated Sites."

65 *Report of the Commissioner of the Environment and Sustainable Development to the House of Commons: The Commissioner's Perspective* (Ottawa: Office of the Auditor General of Canada, Spring, 2012) c 3, "Federal Contaminated Sites and Their Impacts."

66 International Joint Commission, *Seventh Biennial Report on Great Lakes Water Quality* (Ottawa: International Joint Commission, 1994) at 36.

less, the IJC lamented the minor involvement of the two federal governments in relation to many of the shared AOCs, in connecting channels between and below the Great Lakes: "The level of joint activity varies greatly and is generally too limited. The limited coordination and "cultural" differences in how RAPs are seen as part of governmental processes have led to considerable frustration for the individual jurisdictions and the public in these areas."[67]

On behalf of the IJC, the Great Lakes Water Quality Board undertook a review of government resources and changing program thrusts relating to operations under the GLWQA at the national and provincial/ state levels.[68] Selected findings included:

- governments are making changes in what they do and how they deliver programs;
- a one-to-one relationship does not exist between resource expenditures and program delivery;
- a number of creative partnerships have been developed and are being developed that share responsibility for program delivery, create efficiencies, and build the institutional capacity to achieve ecosystem results;
- some agencies reported substantial reductions in resource expenditures for certain indicators;
- continued emphasis must be placed on evaluating program effectiveness based on measuring ecosystem results.

Progress towards the elimination of Areas of Concern has fallen well short of expectations, despite extensive remedial efforts. In the quarter-century of operations, only three of the original Canadian Areas of Concern have been formally de-listed—Severn Sound, Collingwood Harbour, and Wheatley Harbour. Contaminated sediments and inadequate waste-water treatment facilities have yet to be comprehensively and effectively addressed while natural processes of recovery following interventions and expenditures will require a great deal of time. A series of Canada–Ontario Agreements Respecting the Great Lakes Basin Ecosystem, including provisions directed towards Areas of Concern in Canada have been concluded and a further renewal is under negotiation in the context of recent amendments to the Great Lakes Water

---

67   Ibid at 35.
68   Great Lakes Water Quality Board, International Joint Commission, Review of Government Resources and Changing Program Thrusts as They Relate to Delivery of Programs under the Great Lakes Water Quality Agreement (Detroit, MI: Great Lakes Water Quality Board, 1998).

Quality Agreement.[69] The renewed Canada–US commitment to Areas of Concern is now addressed in Annex 1 to the Great Lakes Water Quality Agreement, 2012 which came into effect in February 2013.

FURTHER READINGS

ABDEL-AZIZ, A, & N CHALIFOUR, *The Canadian Brownfields Manual,* (Toronto: LexisNexis/Butterworths, 2004)

BERETI, RE, *British Columbia Environmental Management Legislation and Commentary* (Toronto: LexisNexis Canada, 2006–)

COBURN, F, & G MANNING, *Toxic Real Estate Manual* (Toronto: Canada Law Book, 1999–)

COLLINS, L, & H MCLEOD-KILMURRAY, "Toxic battery: A tort for our time?" (2008) 16 Tort Law Review 131

NADON, O, *La gestion et la responsabilité des terrains contaminés au Québec* (LexisNexis, 2009)

NRTEE, *Greening Canada's Brownfield Sites* (Ottawa: National Round Table on the Environment and the Economy, 1998)

SWAIGEN, J, *Toxic Time Bombs: The Regulation of Canada's Leaking Underground Storage Tanks* (Toronto: Emond Montgomery, 1995)

WINFIELD, M, & G JENISH, *Troubled Waters? A Review of the Performance of the Governments of Canada and Ontario under the 1994 Canada–Ontario Agreement Respecting the Great Lakes Basin Ecosystem* (Toronto: Canadian Institute for Environmental Law and Policy, 1999)

---

69 Letter from the Honourable Peter Kent, MP, Minister of the Environment, Government of Canada to the Honourable Jim Bradley, MPP, Minister of the Environment, Government of Ontario (15 June 2012), online: www.ec.gc.ca/lcpe-cepa/default.asp?lang=En&n=CD691860-1. See also *2008 March Status Report of the Commissioner of the Environment and Sustainable Development* (Ottawa: Office of the Auditor General of Canada, 2008) c 7 "Ecosystems—Areas of Concern in the Great Lakes Basin."

CHAPTER 12

ENVIRONMENTAL ASSESSMENT

A. OVERVIEW OF ENVIRONMENTAL ASSESSMENT

Environmental assessment, in the opinion of the Supreme Court of Canada, is "a planning tool that is now generally regarded as an integral component of sound decision-making."[1] It is important, again in the words of the court, because, "the growth of modern societies has shown the serious problems that can result from anarchic development and use of land, in particular those problems concerning public health and the environment."[2]

The basic idea is that certain proposed activities should be scrutinized in advance from the perspective of their possible environmental consequences. However, challenging design and operational questions may arise in the process of implementing this idea, and there has been considerable divergence of opinion about the legal status and weight to be given to assessment processes. At one extreme of the spectrum of opinion are those who think that assessment—not a bad idea in principle—is something that should be dispensed with in the interests of getting on with the real job of economic development. At the other end are those who view the satisfactory completion of a rigorous and

---

1   *Friends of the Oldman River Society v Canada (Minister of Transport)*, [1992] 1 SCR 3 at 71 [*Oldman River*].
2   *R v Al Klippert Ltd*, [1998] 1 SCR 737 at para 16.

comprehensive environmental assessment as an essential precondition of proceeding with any proposal. Yet, even among those who accept the importance of environmental assessment, there are significant divergences of opinion concerning the scope and implications of such proceedings.

The components of a generic environmental assessment regime raise questions such as the following:

1) To what activities does the environmental assessment process apply? To large or small operations; public or private operations; projects only, or also plans, programs, and even policies that are less directly associated with immediate physical impacts?[3]
2) By whom should the assessment be carried out? By the initiator of the proposal, professional consultants or an independent body?[4]
3) What is the standard and scope of assessment, including the meaning of environment?[5] Does environment include social, cultural, and economic factors? Will the assessment deal only with "direct" and "significant" impact, or will "indirect" and "cumulative" impact also be addressed?[6]
4) Is environmental assessment primarily concerned with the technical dimensions of specific proposed activity, or should it extend to consideration of the very purpose and utility of the proposal, or to other means of accomplishing the same goals?
5) Will the assessment documents be subject to some further process of review and scrutiny? By departments of government; by the pub-

---

3   *2004 October Report of the Commissioner of the Environment and Sustainable Development* (Ottawa: Office of the Auditor General, 2004) c 4, "Assessing the Environmental Impact of Policies, Plans, and Programs."

4   H Benevides, "Real Reform Deferred: Analysis of Recent Amendments to the *Canadian Environmental Assessment Act*" (2004) 13 J Envtl L & Prac 195.

5   Projects under assessment contribute, through greenhouse gas emissions, to climate change at the global level with extraordinary environmental impacts outside the vicinity or locale of the project itself, and well beyond the jurisdiction in which the proposed activity would be undertaken. How to incorporate these environmental impacts into the assessment process has been challenging. See, for example, *2003 October Report of the Commissioner of the Environment and Sustainable Development* (Ottawa: Office of the Auditor General, 2003) c 2, "Road Transportation in Urban Areas: Accountability for Reducing Greenhouse Gases"; and T Kruger, "The *Canadian Environmental Assessment Act* and Global Climate Change: Rethinking Significance" (2009-2010) 47 Alta L Rev 161.

6   C Tollefson & K Wipond, "Cumulative Environmental Impacts and Aboriginal Rights" (1998) 18 Environmental Impact Assessment Review 371; *2011 October Report of the Commissioner of the Environment and* Sustainable *Development,* (Ottawa: Office of the Auditor General, 2011) c 2, "Assessing Cumulative Environmental Effects of Oil Sands Projects."

lic; or through an administrative tribunal process? And are such reviews mandatory or discretionary?

6) What should a review body be authorized to decide or recommend?
7) What are the consequences of not completing, or not "passing," an environmental assessment? Can the proposed initiative be delayed or terminated?
8) Are follow-up measures available to provide for monitoring and to ensure compliance with an assessment decision?

Following their introduction in the 1970s, the first generation of environmental assessment procedures was under almost continuous scrutiny by those who wished to strengthen the process and by those who believed that existing requirements or approaches were already too burdensome. Environmental groups actively promoted improvements through policy reform and used the courts to test environmental assessment standards.[7]

Some proponents experienced uncertainty in relation to such factors as "the time frame, the information requirements, the procedure for hearings, the outcome, and the policy that would be applied." The *Al-Pac* proponents faced most of these uncertainties and even the more fundamental "question of whether its project would be subject to hearings at all."[8] Over and above the actual requirements of environmental assessment if it is applicable, industry often raised questions about inconsistencies and overlaps between Canadian jurisdictions. The concerns of industry and investors should be placed in context. Saskatchewan's Environmental Assessment Review Commission (SEARC) re-examined the files on 636 proposals that had been considered by the Department of Environment and Public Safety during an eleven-year period. A full environmental impact assessment (EIA) was requested for eighty of these (13 percent), although only thirty-five EIAs were completed. Only one board of inquiry was established (Rafferty/ Alameda) and only two proposals were denied approval to proceed. SEARC concluded that "the existing EA process has not been a major roadblock for those proposals it has affected."[9]

In terms of costs, some early estimates suggested that hearing costs for projects considered under the federal environmental assessment

---

7   RB Gibson & B Savan, *Environmental Assessment in Ontario* (Toronto: Canadian Environmental Law Research Foundation, 1986).
8   P Edwards, *The Al-Pac Review Hearings: A Case Study* (Edmonton: Environmental Law Centre, 1990) at 126.
9   *Report of the Saskatchewan Environmental Review Commission: Environmental Challenges* (Regina: The Commission, 1991) at 83.

and review process ranged between 0.026 and 0.5 percent of total project costs.[10] A subsequent survey carried out by the Economic Council of Canada suggested that the average cost of environmental assessments on major projects approximates 1 percent of the overall capital cost, with major projects understood to be those involving more than $3 million.[11]

On the other hand, certain benefits have been claimed for environmental assessment. For example, it has been asserted that by providing timely opportunities for reflection and public input, environmental assessments often serve to eliminate potential problems. Along with the avoidance or reduction of environmental damage, benefits include opportunities for public input into design and operational features, as well as cost savings resulting from the downscaling or cancellation of ill-conceived and unnecessary projects.[12] Negotiations over conditions of approval have often been central elements of environmental assessment. In the sense that these produce consensus or agreement on the means of resolving difficulties, they, too, have a positive impact.[13]

B. EVOLUTION OF FEDERAL ENVIRONMENTAL ASSESSMENT

Procedures first adopted as cabinet policy in 1973 and then reissued in 1984 as the *Environmental Assessment and Review Process Guidelines Order (EARPGO)* set out the original basis for federal environmental assessment.[14] Though treated by government officials as discretionary, the Federal Court of Canada eventually determined in litigation concerning Saskatchewan's Rafferty-Alameda dam proposals that the *EARPGO* was

---

10 Gibson & Savan, above note 7 at 411.

11 GE Neufeld, *A Preliminary Survey of the Impact of Environmental Assessments on Competitiveness* (Ottawa: Economic Council of Canada, 1992). Roughly comparable findings have been reported in other jurisdictions. See J Glasson, R Therivel, & A Chadwick, *Introduction to Environmental Impact Assessment*, 3d ed (London: Routledge, 2005) at 233–35.

12 Gibson & Savan, above note 7 at 409.

13 MI Jeffery, "Accommodating Negotiations in EIA and Project Approval Processes" (1987) 4 EPLJ 244; MI Jeffery, "Consideration and Analysis of Conditions of Approval Likely to be Imposed by the Environmental Assessment Board in Granting Project Approval" (1988) 1 Can J Admin L & Prac 21 [Jeffery, "Consideration"].

14 SOR/84-467.

legally binding and that compliance with its procedures was required.[15] By this time, preliminary legislative efforts were well under way to provide formal statutory authority for the federal environmental assessment process and to address uncertainties that had arisen in connection with the *Environmental Assessment and Review Process (EARP)*. Enacted in 1992 and proclaimed in 1995 on the completion of supporting regulations, the *Canadian Environmental Assessment Act (CEAA 1995)* reformulated the federal environmental assessment regime.[16] Although *CEAA 1995* was replaced in 2012, experience under the former regime illustrates several considerations of continuing relevance.

By way of introduction, the scope of application of federal environmental assessments under *CEAA 1995* proved to be remarkably problematic. Some insights may be gained from the Supreme Court of Canada's discussion of a similar issue in the context of the *Oldman River* decision under the *EARPGO*. After emphasizing the importance of first linking the exercise of legislative power in relation to the environment to the appropriate head of constitutional power, La Forest J remarked that "the extent to which environmental concerns may be taken into account in the exercise of a power may vary from one power to another."[17] Accordingly, he observed that the exercise of Parliament's jurisdiction over fisheries, a resource, and over navigation, an activity, will each involve "a somewhat different environmental role."[18] He also offered a hypothetical example suggesting that, once the constitutional basis for federal action had been established, the scope of an associated environmental assessment might indeed be quite extensive:

> [o]ne might postulate the location and construction of a new line which would require approval under the relevant provisions of the *Railway Act* . . . . That line may cut through ecologically sensitive habitats such as wetlands and forests. The possibility of derailment may pose a serious hazard to the health and safety of nearby communities if dangerous commodities are to be carried on the line. On the other hand, it may bring considerable economic benefit to those communities through job creation and the multiplier effect that it will have in the local economy. The regulatory authority might require that the line circumvent residential districts in the interests of

---

15 *Canadian Wildlife Federation Inc v Canada (Minister of the Environment)*, [1989] 3 FC 309 (TD), aff'd (1989), 4 CELR (NS) 1 (FCA).

16 Controversies surrounding the transition between EARPGO and CEAA 1995 persisted for some time. *See Inter-Church Uranium Committee Educational Cooperative v Canada (Atomic Energy Control Board)*, 2004 FCA 218.

17 *Oldman River*, above note 1 at 67.

18 *Ibid.*

noise abatement and safety. In my view, all of these considerations may validly be taken into account in arriving at a final decision on whether or not to grant the necessary approval.[19]

Those who anticipated a less complex and controversial operation for the legislated federal environmental assessment regime have been disappointed.

As expressed in the preamble and a purposes clause, CEAA 1995 was intended both to ensure that the environmental effects of projects are carefully considered before the federal government takes action in connection with them and to promote sustainable development. In addition, the legislation sought to ensure that projects within Canada or on federal lands do not cause significant adverse environmental effects on other jurisdictions and that opportunities are provided for public participation in the federal environmental assessment process.

For CEAA 1995 to apply to a particular initiative, it had first to be established that the initiative was a project within the terms of the legislation and not otherwise excluded. Projects, for the purposes of CEAA 1995, were of two types—first, undertakings in relation to physical works, that is, "any proposed construction, operation, modification, decommissioning, abandonment or other undertaking in relation to that physical work," and, second, activities unrelated to a physical work if those activities are designated by regulation in what is known as the Inclusion List.[20] The Inclusion List identified various physical activities associated with specified subject areas: national parks and protected areas; oil and gas projects; nuclear facilities; defence; transportation; waste management; fisheries;[21] wildlife; projects on Aboriginal lands; the north, and forests.

The applicability of CEAA 1995 further depended on the involvement of a federal authority in the exercise of one of a series of four statutorily defined powers, duties, or functions (commonly described as "triggers") in relation to the project. Ministers of the Crown, designated departments, and other statutory agencies, along with additional bodies prescribed by regulation, are federal authorities under CEAA 1995.[22]

---

19   Ibid at 66.
20   Canadian Environmental Assessment Act, SC 1992, c 37, s 2(1) [CEAA 1995] and the Inclusion List Regulations, SOR/94-637, as am by SOR/99-436, SOR/2000-309, SOR/2003-280, SOR/2003-349, SOR/2005-261, and SOR/2005-314.
21   AJ Kwasniak, "Slow on the Trigger: the Department of Fisheries and Oceans, the Fisheries Act and the Canadian Environmental Assessment Act" (2004) 27 Dal LJ 347.
22   Federal Authorities Regulations, SOR/96-280, as am by SOR/2000-44 and SOR/2001-44.

Despite the fact that an undertaking constituted a project within the meaning of *CEAA 1995* and involved a triggering action by a federal authority, it might still be exempt from environmental assessment when carried out in response to certain emergencies or on the basis of an *Exclusion List*.[23] On the other hand, even where *CEAA 1995* was not triggered by a federal authority, environmental assessment might have been undertaken in relation to projects with an interprovincial or international impact or an impact on federal lands where the minister was of the opinion that significant adverse environmental effects might have resulted.[24] *CEAA 1995* provided for four possible procedures or "tracks" ranging from screenings, through comprehensive study assessments, to panel reviews or mediation. Screening and the comprehensive study approach were carried out in the form of "self-assessments."

In practice, the application of federal environmental assessment on a legislative basis under *CEAA 1995* proved to be controversial. Particular concern arose about the scope, extent, or coverage of the environmental assessment process required by the Act. This concern had three aspects. Although they are closely interrelated, if not mutual substitutes, separate treatment helps to clarify the conceptual nature of each of the scoping issues.

1) The Scope of the Project

The first of the scoping issues related to the project itself. Section 2 defined a project as being "in relation to a physical work, any proposed construction, operation, modification, decommissioning, abandonment or other undertaking in relation to that physical work," whereas section 15(1) indicated that the responsible authority will determine the scope of the project in relation to which an environmental assessment had to be conducted. A liberal, generous determination of a project's scope would lead to a broader, more encompassing environmental assessment, whereas a narrower, more restricted approach to the scope of a project would confine the ambit of the associated environmental assessment. For example, a federal authority might have been asked to approve bridge construction across a navigable waterway when a company engaged in forest operations wished to establish a roadway between its cutting site and a mill. The project could be described as

---

23 *Exclusion List Regulations, 2007*, SOR/2007-108. See also *CEAA 1995*, above note 20, s 59(c.1).

24 *CEAA 1995*, *ibid*, ss 46–48.

the construction of a bridge, or as the construction of a bridge in a roadway, or as the construction of a bridge in a roadway linking forest operations and milling facilities.

2) The Scope of the Environmental Assessment

The second scoping issue arises under section 15(3) of *CEAA 1995* and involved the scope of the environmental assessment:

> Where a project is in relation to a physical work, an environmental assessment shall be conducted in respect of every construction, operation, modification, decommissioning, abandonment or other undertaking in relation to that physical work that is proposed by the proponent or that is, in the opinion of the responsible authority . . . likely to be carried out in relation to that physical work.

Debate centred on whether (and the degree to which) this provision might require environmental assessment to extend outside the scope of the project. In other words, what activity or other undertakings are "in relation to" the physical work the proponent proposes or are, in the opinion of the responsible authority, likely to be carried out "in relation to" that physical work. To return to the previous example, and assuming the physical work constituting the scope of the project was construction of a bridge, could it now be argued that the roadway or the forest operations made possible by the roadway were undertakings "in relation to" the bridge?

3) The Scope of Factors to Be Considered in the Environmental Assessment

CEAA 1995, having listed factors to be considered in either a screening or comprehensive study, provided further that the scope of the factors to be taken into consideration were to be determined by the responsible authority.

Divergent approaches to these three issues were apparent in an extensive record of litigation.[25] Several important points of contention were addressed by the Supreme Court of Canada in 2010 when the Court determined that:

---

25   *Friends of the West Country Association v Canada (Ministry of Fisheries and Oceans)* (1999), 31 CELR (NS) 239 (FCA); *Prairie Acid Rain Coalition v Canada (Minister of Fisheries and Oceans)*, 2006 FCA 31.

when the term "project" . . . is considered in context, the correct interpretation is "project as proposed" and not "project as scoped". This means that the determination of whether a project requires a comprehensive study is not within the discretion of the RA. If the project as proposed is listed in the CSL, a comprehensive study is mandatory.[26]

As the Court further explained in connection with the question of scoping:

> Regardless of the assessment track, the RA or Minister's discretion to scope a project and to scope the environmental assessment is outlined in s 15. Section 15(1) grants the discretion to scope to either the Minister, in the case of mediation or a review panel, or the RA. However, the exercise of this discretion is limited by s 15(3). Section 15(3) provides that an environmental assessment of a physical work shall be conducted in respect of every "construction, operation, modification, decommissioning, abandonment or other undertaking" in relation to the project. Consistent with the view that the "project as proposed by the proponent" is to apply in the absence of text or context to the contrary, the scoping of the project performed by the RA or Minister under s 15(1) is subject to s 15(3). In other words, the minimum scope is the project as proposed by the proponent, and the RA or Minister has the discretion to enlarge the scope when required by the facts and circumstances of the project. The RA or Minister is also granted further discretion by s 15(2) to combine related proposed projects into a single project for the purposes of assessment. In sum, while the presumed scope of the project to be assessed is the project as proposed by the proponent, under s 15(2) or (3), the RA or Minister may enlarge the scope in the appropriate circumstances.[27]

4) CEAA 2012

CEAA 1995 has been replaced with a significantly altered federal environmental assessment regime in the form of CEAA 2012.[28] The new legislation differs from its predecessor in several important respects.

Triggers associated with prescribed exercises of federal decision-making authority have been eliminated. Projects now subject to federal environmental assessment will ordinarily be identified through an initial regulatory listing[29] followed by a discretionary determination by

---

26   *Mining Watch Canada v Canada (Fisheries and Oceans)*, 2010 SCC 2 at para 34.
27   *Ibid* at para 39.
28   *Canadian Environmental Assessment Act*, 2012, SC 2012, c 19, s 52 [*CEAA 2012*].
29   *Regulations Designating Physical Activities*, SOR/2012-147.

the Canadian Environmental Assessment Agency (the CEA Agency) to require an EA upon completion of an initial review of the project as described by the proponent,[30] public comment, and the possibility of adverse environmental effects.[31] The minister of environment is also authorized to require an EA where he or she is of the opinion that "the carrying out of that physical activity may cause adverse environmental effects" or on the basis of public concerns.[32]

Environmental effects to be taken into account include changes to listed components of the environment including fish, migratory birds, or aquatic species as well as environmental changes on federal lands, of an inter-provincial nature, or occurring outside Canada. Socio-economic, health, and cultural impacts for Aboriginal peoples as well as effects on traditional land use are also included amongst environmental effects to be considered under *CEAA 2012*.[33]

The previous four tracks or modes of assessment — screening, comprehensive study, panel review, and mediation — have been reduced to an environmental assessment under section 22 or panel review under section 38. Moreover, the self-assessment approach (previously applicable in the case of screenings and comprehensive studies), has been eliminated such that all environmental assessments under *CEAA 2012* will be conducted by the CEAA Agency or by the National Energy Board or the Canadian Nuclear Safety Commission in the case of projects falling within their designated authority. These bodies have been designated as "responsible authorities" for purposes of *CEAA 2012*.[34]

Section 19 of *CEAA 2012* specifies the factors that must be considered in the context of a federal environmental assessment leading to a report.[35] These include:

(a) the environmental effects of the designated project, including the environmental effects of malfunctions or accidents that may occur in connection with the designated project and any cumulative environmental effects that are likely to result from the designated project in combination with other physical activities that have been or will be carried out;

(b) the significance of the effects referred to in paragraph (a);

(c) comments from the public . . .

---

30   *Prescribed Information for the Description of a Designated Project Regulations*, SOR/2012-148.

31   *CEAA 2012*, above note 28, s 10(b).

32   *Ibid*, s 14(2).

33   *Ibid*, s 5(1).

34   *Ibid*, s 15.

35   *Ibid*, s 22(b).

(d) mitigation measures that are technically and economically feasible and that would mitigate any significant adverse environmental effects of the designated project;

(e) the requirements of the follow-up program in respect of the designated project;

(f) the purpose of the designated project;

(g) alternative means of carrying out the designated project that are technically and economically feasible and the environmental effects of any such alternative means;

(h) any change to the designated project that may be caused by the environment;

(i) . . .

(j) any other matter relevant to the environmental assessment that the responsible authority, or—if the environmental assessment is referred to a review panel—the Minister, requires to be taken into account.

Authority for scoping the majority of these factors is specifically conferred upon the responsible authority, or, in the case of a review panel, upon the minister.[36]

Opportunities for public participation in an environmental assessment must be provided[37] with arrangements for participant funding available in the case of panel reviews.[38] In the case of decisions involving a certificate from the National Energy Board, participation is provided for "interested parties," defined in section 2(2) as a person who is directly affected or who has relevant information and expertise.[39]

Decision makers under *CEAA 2012* must ultimately decide whether, taking account of appropriate mitigation measures, the designated project is "likely to cause significant adverse environmental effects." Where significant adverse environmental effects are likely, the matter will be referred to cabinet to determine whether those effects are justified in the circumstances.[40] In cases where significant adverse effects are not likely, or where they are justified in the circumstances, decision makers must set out conditions applicable to the designated project,

---

36   *Ibid*, s 19(2).

37   *Ibid*, s 24.

38   *Ibid*, s 57.

39   *Ibid*, s 28. For consideration of issues related to interested parties in the context of a Joint Review Panel hearing into the Jackpine Mine Expansion, see the Panel's decision of 17 October 2012, online at: www.ceaa.gc.ca/050/documents/p59540/82626E.pdf.

40   *CEAA 2012*, above note 28, s 52.

including mitigation measures and a follow-up program.[41] The latter serve to verify the accuracy of the environmental assessment of a designated project and to determine the effectiveness of mitigation. Findings and conditions will finally be embodied in a decision statement.[42]

Other new features of *CEAA 2012* include the introduction of fixed timelines to streamline the overall environmental assessment process subject to potential extension in designated circumstances. *CEAA 2012* also provides for possible penalties where activities by the proponent may cause one of the specified environmental effects unless it has been determined that no environmental assessment is required or if the proponent has complied with conditions set out in the decision statement.[43]

Further features of *CEAA 2012* include provisions to recognize provincial environmental assessment processes as substitutes for[44] or even equivalent to[45] the federal regime. These arrangements replace the framework established in *CEAA 1995* to encourage harmonization through inter-jurisdictional cooperation in cases where both federal and provincial environmental assessments were otherwise applicable.[46]

C. PROVINCIAL ENVIRONMENTAL ASSESSMENT REGIMES

Provincial environmental assessment regimes have been established in all Canadian provinces (see table 12.1), although they differ, sometimes significantly, in detail.[47]

Table 12.1 Provincial Environmental Assessment Legislation

Alberta	*Environmental Protection and Enhancement Act*, RSA 2000, c E-12
	Activities Designation Regulation, Alta Reg 276/2003

---

41   *Ibid*, s 53.
42   *Ibid*, s 54.
43   *Ibid*, ss 6 and 99(1).
44   *Ibid*, s 34.
45   *Ibid*, s 37.
46   M Doelle, "*CEAA 2012*: The End of Federal EA As We Know It?" (2012) 24 J Envtl L & Prac 1 at 13–15.
47   For suggestions about reducing variations and inconsistencies, see the Canadian Council of Ministers of the Environment, "Sub-Agreement on Environmental Assessment," online: www.ccme.ca/assets/pdf/envtlassesssubagr_e.pdf.

British Columbia	*Environmental Assessment Act*, SBC 2002, c 43 *Reviewable Projects Regulation*, BC Reg 276/95, repealed by BC Reg 290/2003
Manitoba	*The Environment Act*, CCSM, c E125 *Licensing Procedures Regulation*, Man Reg 163/88 *Classes of Development Regulation*, Man Reg 164/88
New Brunswick	*Clean Environment Act*, RSNB 1973, c C-6 *Environmental Impact Assessment Regulation*, NB Reg 87/83
Newfoundland and Labrador	*Environmental Protection Act*, SNL 2002, c E-14.2 *Environmental Assessment Regulations, 2003*, NLR 54/03
Nova Scotia	*Environment Act*, SNS 1994–95, c 1 *Environmental Assessment Regulations*, NS Reg 26/95
Ontario	*Environmental Assessment Act*, RSO 1990, c E-18
Prince Edward Island	*Environmental Protection Act*, RSPEI 1988, c E-9
Quebec	*Environment Quality Act*, RSQ 1977, c Q-2 *Regulation respecting environmental assessment and review*, RRQ, c Q-2, r 23
Saskatchewan	*The Environmental Assessment Act*, SS 1979–80, c E-10.1

The application section of the Ontario *Environmental Assessment Act* states that the legislation applies to

(a) enterprises or activities or proposals, plans or programs in re-spect of enterprises or activities by or on behalf of Her Majesty in right of Ontario or by a public body or public bodies or by a municipality or municipalities;

(b) major commerical or business enterprises or activities or propos-als, plans or programs in respect of major commercial or busi-ness enterprises or activities of a person or persons, other than a person referred to in clause (a), designated by the regulations.[48]

That is, in the absence of designation by regulation, private-sector in-itiatives in Ontario are not covered by provincial environmental assess-ment requirements. Most of the designations, until recently, involved waste management, although as a consequence of deregulation energy sector projects are subject to environmental assessment on the basis of their environmental significance rather than their public or private nature.[49]

---

48   *Environmental Assessment Act*, RSO 1990, c E.18, s 3 [*OEAA*].

49   *Electricity Projects Regulation*, O Reg 116/01; *Waste Management Project*, O Reg 101/07; and "Guide to Environmental Assessment Requirements for Waste Man-agement Projects" (15 March 2007) online: www.ene.gov.on.ca/stdprodconsume/groups/lr/@ene/@resources/documents/resource/std01_079506.pdf. Along with

Once the applicability of the Act to a given undertaking has been confirmed, the Ontario requirements for environmental assessment are comprehensive. According to the statute, an environmental assessment ordinarily consists of the following:

(a) a description of the purpose of the undertaking;
(b) a description of and a statement of the rationale for,
     (i)   the undertaking,
     (ii)   the alternative methods of carrying out the undertaking, and
     (iii) the alternatives to the undertaking;
(c) a description of,
     (i)   the environment that will be affected . . .
     (ii)   the effects that will be caused . . .
     (iii) the actions necessary . . . to prevent, change, mitigate or remedy . . .
(d) an evaluation of the advantages and disadvantages to the environment . . .[50]

Moreover, the province's Environmental Review Tribunal articulated high standards for the process that must be followed by a proponent in preparing an environmental assessment. The process should be systematic and replicable for, in the view of the tribunal, the Ontario Act calls for "a wide-ranging investigation that involves a reasonable and logical application of criteria, so that the final result is consistent with the steps taken along the way."[51] Subsequent amendments in Ontario, while preserving the existing description of the requirements for an environmental assessment, call for the proponent to submit terms of reference following consultations with interested persons and to obtain approval from the minister for those terms of reference. While this allows a proponent to seek approval for terms of reference tailored to a particular project, the generic elements identified in the statute remain presumptive requirements.[52] Provision was also made for time limits applicable to various stages in the environmental assessment process.[53]

energy and waste management projects, the transit and transportation sector attracts reform attention.

50   *OEAA*, above note 48, s 5(3).
51   *Re North Simcoe Waste Management Assn* (1989), 5 CELR (NS) 98 at 117 (OMB & OEAB) [*North Simcoe*].
52   *Sutcliffe v Ontario (Minister of the Environment)*, [2004] OJ No 3473 (CA). See M Valiante, "Case Comment" (2003) 3 CELR (3d) 219.
53   See M Valiante, "Evaluating Ontario's Environmental Assessment Reforms" (1999) 8 J Envtl L & Prac 215; and AD Levy, "A Review of Environmental Assessment in Ontario" (2002) 11 J. Envtl. L. & Prac. 173. Continuing refinements are underway, see "Codes of Practice for Ontario's Environmental Assessment

Other provinces have more systematically provided for review of major resource and industrial projects and other private-sector initiatives, although the assessments required are not always as comprehensive as those provided for by Ontario. British Columbia's *Environmental Assessment Reviewable Projects Regulation*,[54] for example, specifically addressed a wide range of types of facilities and described the circumstances in which construction or modification projects would be considered reviewable. In particular, the regulation included reference to industrial projects in the organic and inorganic chemical industry; primary metals; non-metallic mineral product industries such as cement, glass, lime, and asbestos; forest products industries including pulp, paper, paperboard, de-inking, wood preservative, building-board manufacturers, and sawmills; pharmaceutical plants; fibre and textile facilities; tanneries; tire and tube plants; and lead-acid battery manufacturers. Additional types of activities that, depending on their size and other characteristics, will be reviewable include mining projects, energy facilities, water-management and diversion projects, waste-disposal operations, food-processing and transportation projects, and tourism and recreational projects.[55] In Alberta, environmental assessment is applicable to activities in the nature of "construction, operation or reclamation" if scheduled under the *Environmental Protection and Enhancement Act* or designated by regulation. For some initiatives environmental assessment is mandatory, but Alberta Environment's director may designate others on the basis of specified statutory criteria such as the location and size of the activity or the level of public concern.[56] The issues to be addressed in the provincial environmental assessment process itself will typically become the focus of discussion and negotiation between the proponent and the regulatory authority with overall supervisory responsibility. Legislative guidance on these matters again varies in detail. Alberta identified the following as issues for discussion in an environmental-impact assessment report (if re-

---

Process: Preparing and Reviewing Environmental Assessments and Class Environmental Assessments" (Draft published for Comments, 17 April 2007).

54 BC Reg 276/95, as amended. Now see *Environmental Assessment Act*, SBC 2002, c 43 [*BCEAA*]; and *Reviewable Projects Regulation*, BC Reg 14/2006. The *Environmental Management Act*, SBC 2003, c 53, s 78, also provides for ministerial designation of projects subject to environmental assessment.

55 For judicial review of environmental assessment reviewability decisions by the BC Environmental Assessment Office, see *Friends of Davie Bay v BC*, 2012 BCCA 293.

56 *Environmental Protection and Enhancement Act*, SA 1992, c E-13.3, s 42 [*AEPEA*]. Now see *Environmental Protection and Enhancement Act*, RSA 2000, c E-12.

quired), whose final form is determined in terms of reference set by a provincially designated environment director:

(a) a description of the proposed activity and an analysis of the need for the activity;

(b) an analysis of the site selection procedure for the proposed activity, including a statement of the reasons why the proposed site was chosen and a consideration of alternative sites;

(c) an identification of existing baseline environmental conditions and areas of major concern that should be considered;

(d) a description of potential positive and negative environmental, social, economic, and cultural impacts of the proposed activity, including cumulative, regional, temporal, and spatial considerations;

(e) an analysis of the significance of the potential impacts identified under clause (d);

(f) the plans that have been or will be developed to mitigate the potential negative impacts identified under clause (d);

(g) an identification of issues related to human health that should be considered;

(h) a consideration of the alternatives to the proposed activity, including the alternative of not proceeding with the proposed activity;

(i) the plans that have been or will be developed to monitor environmental impacts that are predicted to occur and the plans that have been or will be developed to monitor proposed mitigation measures;

(j) the contingency plans that have been or will be developed in order to respond to unpredicted negative impacts;

(k) the plans that have been or will be developed for waste minimization and recycling;

(l) the manner in which the proponent intends to implement a program of public consultation in respect of the undertaking of the proposed activity and to present the results of that program;

(m) the plans that have been or will be developed to minimize the production or the release into the environment of substances that may have an adverse effect.[57]

The agencies with responsibility to conduct environmental assessments typically have authority in the context of their ultimate decision making to attach terms and conditions to approvals. They may, for

---

57   *AEPEA*, above note 56, s 49. See also *BCEAA*, above note 54.

example, impose certain safeguards on the manner in which projects are implemented, or they may require forms of compensation and assistance for the benefit of those whose interests will be adversely affected when developments proceed. Post-development monitoring and follow-up obligations are frequently considered to be vital elements in ensuring that environmental damages are controlled or that sustainability remains achievable.[58]

D. PUBLIC PARTICIPATION AND FUNDING

Whether or not public participation is formally required, some level of public involvement has ordinarily been encouraged in the interests of a better process. If nothing more, public involvement in the planning and assessment process can contribute to "minimization of confrontation and delays."[59] Potential contributions have also been recognized in terms of legitimacy, accountability, and the importance of different perspectives, as well as, quite possibly, in terms of new information or more rigorous scrutiny of the proponent's case.

Statutory provision for some form of supplementary review and scrutiny of the assessment, including administrative proceedings and a hearings process, often permits public participation in decision making over and above opportunities for consultation that are ordinarily included in the initial preparation of the assessment document itself. Insofar as such hearings have generally been discretionary, however, several jurisdictions have experienced litigation directed at the status of these procedures. In particular, attempts have been made to require such procedures, rather than to leave decisions about their use to the discretion of officials.

Critics of the Nova Scotia Power Corporation's Point Aconi project were unsuccessful in their efforts to compel a public review of the proposal.[60] With reference to section 13 of the *EARPGO*, applicants asserted that the level and nature of public concern about the Point Aconi project was such that public review was desirable and that the minister of fisheries and oceans (representing the initiating department in the proceedings) had rejected panel review on the basis of irrelevant considerations. Efforts to compel reconsideration of the assessment

---

58 See, generally, Jeffery, "Consideration," above note 13.
59 *North Simcoe*, above note 51 at 110.
60 *Cantwell v Canada (Minister of the Environment)* (1991), 6 CELR (NS) 16 (TD), aff'd (6 June 1991), (Fed CA) [unreported].

process for road development to provide access to old-growth timber in Ontario's Temagami district or to "bump up" the assessment to a public-hearing process similarly failed,[61] as did claims for public participation requirements under Manitoba's *Environment Act*.[62] Despite insisting that basic environmental assessments must be undertaken where required, courts have demonstrated reluctance to scrutinize official judgments of those assessments with a high degree of intensity. In the words of Mr Justice Strayer: "It is not the role of the Court . . . to become an academy of science to arbitrate conflicting scientific predictions, or to act as a kind of legislative upper chamber to weigh expressions of public concern and determine which ones should be respected."[63]

The contribution of public participation to the environmental assessment process depends not only on the nature of the decision to be made but on the actual involvement of the public and the quality of that involvement. The costs of effective participation are frequently substantial. This is particularly so in the context of resource-management hearings where decisions often depend heavily on complex evidence and expert witnesses. Litigation concerning the availability of financial support for public-interest intervenors in administrative proceedings[64] and related commentary[65] produced a number of *ad hoc* responses.

Ontario's *Intervenor Funding Project Act*[66] represented an attempt to deal more systematically with intervenor finances in relation to the proceedings of a small group of designated tribunals. The statute set out conditions and criteria for pre-hearing funding applications. Funding might be awarded in relation to issues that "affect a significant segment of the public" and "affect the public interest and not just private interests." In assessing eligibility for funding, panel members were directed to consider a series of criteria:

(a) the intervenor represents a clearly ascertainable interest that should be represented at the hearing;

---

61   *Temagami Wilderness Society v Ontario (Minister of the Environment)*, [1989] OJ Nos 460 & 1522 (HCJ).

62   *Swampy Cree Tribal Council v Manitoba (Clean Environment Commission)* (1994), 94 Man R (2d) 188 (QB).

63   *Vancouver Island Peace Society v Canada*, [1992] 3 FC 42 at 51 (TD).

64   *Hamilton-Wentworth (Regional Municipality) v Hamilton-Wentworth Save the Valley Committee Inc* (1985), 51 OR (2d) 23 (Div Ct); *Reference Re Ontario Energy Board Act* (1985), 51 OR (2d) 333 (Div Ct).

65   R Anand & IG Scott, "Financing Public Participation in Environmental Decision Making" (1982) 60 Can Bar Rev 81.

66   RSO 1990, c I.13.

(b) separate and adequate representation of the interest would assist the board and contribute substantially to the hearing;

(c) the intervenor does not have sufficient financial resources to enable it to adequately represent the interest;

(d) the intervenor has made reasonable efforts to raise funding from other sources;

(e) the intervenor has an established record of concern for and commitment to the interest;

(f) the intervenor has attempted to bring related interests of which it was aware into an umbrella group to represent the related interests at the hearing;

(g) the intervenor has a clear proposal for its use of any funds which might be awarded; and

(h) the intervenor has appropriate financial controls to ensure that the funds, if awarded, are spent for the purposes of the award.

However, the *Intervenor Funding Project Act* was dissolved in 1996. Costs awards, as distinct from advance funding for participants, are still available where applicable criteria are satisfied.[67]

E. INTERJURISDICTIONAL COORDINATION

Current environmental regimes evidence a greater willingness than their predecessors to acknowledge and take into account extrajurisdictional implications, including the international consequences of development. This latter characteristic may be evidence of efforts to fulfil Canadian obligations anticipated in connection with the 1991 international *Convention on Environmental Impact Assessment in a Transboundary Context (Espoo)*.

Some recent developments—notably, the incorporation of cumulative impact, and the environmental assessment of policy and sustainability—may represent new sources of uncertainty. However, the revised regimes may also provide mechanisms to promote convergence among neighbouring provinces.

Another possible source of convergence is federal-provincial agreements concerning the coordination of environmental assessments when both levels of government have responsibilities.[68] The CCME act-

---

67 *OEAA*, above note 48, ss 18–22; *Environment Act*, CCSM c E125, s 13.2.

68 *BCEAA*, above note 54, s 14; Ontario, *Bill 76, An Act to Improve Environmental Protection, Increase Accountability and Enshrine Public Consultation in the En-*

ively promoted interjurisdictional harmonization of environmental assessment. Several agreements were reached embodying the principles of the 1998 Canada-wide Accord on Environmental Harmonization and the sub-agreement on environmental assessment.[69]

Coordination efforts are also being taken in relation to situations involving native self-government. *CEAA 2012*, for example, requires the responsible authority for a designated project to consult and cooperate with other "jurisdictions" defined in the act to include legislatively-established self-government bodies with environmental assessment authority, or such bodies created pursuant to a land claims agreement.[70]

Innovative institutions with responsibility for environmental assessment have already emerged in the context of comprehensive Aboriginal-claims agreements and other similar negotiations. In general, these are joint-management structures involving native and non-native participants in stages of decision making ranging from initial screening and recommendations through to final authority. Several of the recently created institutions are intended to operate in the northern territories. Of these, the arrangements provided in the *Inuvialuit Final Agreement* for an environmental impact screening committee and an environmental impact review board were not long in experiencing jurisdictional controversy vis-à-vis other approval bodies.[71]

In anticipation of further implementation of native self-government, several provinces have proposed or contemplated arrangements to coordinate decision making in relation to environmental assessment and planning.[72]

---

vironmental Assessment Act, 1st Sess, 36th Leg, 1996, cl 3.1; *AEPEA*, above note 56, s 55.

69   Beginning with environmental assessment agreements with several Western provinces in 1999 and 2000, agreements were reached between the federal government and British Columbia, Alberta, Saskatchewan, Manitoba, Ontario, Quebec and Yukon. As discussed above, *CEAA 2012*, above note 28, offers a different approach to harmonization.

70   *Ibid*, ss 2 and 18.

71   M Robinson & L Binder, "The Inuvialuit Final Agreement and Resource-Use Conflicts: Co-Management in the Western Arctic and Final Decisions in Ottawa" in M Passelac-Ross & JO Saunders, eds, *Growing Demands on a Shrinking Heritage: Managing Resource-Use Conflicts* (Calgary: Canadian Institute of Resources Law, 1992) 155.

72   See, for example, *BCEAA*, above note 54; *Crown Forest Sustainability Act, 1994*, SO 1994, c 25.

FURTHER READINGS

BOWDEN, M-A, & M OLSZYNSKI, "Old Puzzles, New Pieces: *Red Chris* and *Vanadium* and the Future of Federal Environmental Assessment" (2011) 89 Can Bar Rev 445

DEMARCO, JV, "Developments in Environmental Law: the 2009–2010 term — Two Decisions on Environmental Assessment" (2010) 52 Sup Ct L Rev (2d) 247

GREEN, A, "Discretion, Judicial Review and the *Canadian Environmental Assessment Act*" (2002) 27 Queen's LJ 785

HANEBURY, J, "Environmental Impact Assessment and the Constitution: The Never-Ending Story" (2000) 9 J Envtl L & Prac 169

HANNA, KS, ed, *Environmental Impact Assessment: Practice and Participation* (Don Mills, ON: Oxford University Press, 2005)

HAZELL, S, *Canada v The Environment: Federal Environmental Assessment 1984–1998* (Toronto: Canadian Environmental Defence Fund, 1999)

HOBBY, B, D RICARD, M BOURRY, & J DE PENCIER, *Canadian Environmental Assessment Act: An Annotated Guide* (Aurora, ON: Canada Law Book, 1997–)

KWASNIAK, A, "Slow on the Trigger: the Department of Fisheries and Oceans, the *Fisheries Act* and the *Canadian Environmental Assessment Act*" (2004) 27 Dalhousie LJ 347

———, "Environmental Assessment, Overlap, Duplication, Harmonization, Equivalency, and Substitution: Interpretation, Misinterpretation, and a Path Forward" (2009) 20 J Envtl L & Prac 1

LEVY, ALAN D, "A Review of Environmental Assessment in Ontario" (2002) 11 J Envtl L & Prac 173

PHILLIPSON, M, & M-A Bowden, "Environmental Assessment and Agriculture: An Ounce of Prevention Is Worth a Pound of Manure" (1999) 62 Sask LR 415

RUTHERFORD, S, & K CAMPBELL, "Time Well Spent? A survey of public participation in federal environmental assessment panels" (2004) 15 J Envtl L & Prac 71

CHAPTER 13

TOXIC SUBSTANCES

A. THE TOXICS CHALLENGE IN CANADA

The phrase *from sawdust to toxic blobs* has been used to describe a long-term transformation in the Canadian pollution-control agenda.[1] Public concern with a generalized and traditional understanding of pollution (visible emissions and discharges presumed to decompose without harm if released at "safe" levels) has given way to heightened anxiety over long-term threats to human and environmental health from certain types of contaminants. The concept of toxic substances offers the prospect of establishing some priorities for new regulatory and remedial efforts. Numerous American initiatives and references to "virtual elimination," to "zero discharge of toxic chemicals," and to the precautionary principle are increasingly part of these developments. For its part, Europe has proceeded further with the formulation of an initiative known as REACH for Registration, Evaluation, and Authorization of Chemicals, a program that will increasingly influence chemicals management around the world.[2]

---

1   D Chappell, *From Sawdust to Toxic Blobs: A Consideration of Sanctioning Strategies to Combat Pollution in Canada* (Ottawa: Supply & Services, 1989).

2   MA Orellana, "Europe's REACH: A New Chapter in International Chemicals Law" (2006) 6 Sustainable Development Law and Policy 21; Regulation (EC) No 1907/2006 of the European Parliament and of the Council of 18 December 2006, online: http://eur-lex.europa.eu/LexUriServ/LexUriServ.do?uri=oj:l:2006: 396:0001:0849:en:pdf.

Designation of persistent toxics for special attention was an important step in the process of acknowledging that, if the environment is contaminated, so, in time, will be the species, including humans, who occupy the planet. But labelling the category of persistent toxics does not lessen the challenge of identifying the characteristics and ultimately determining the contents of that category. In general, concern with toxics focuses on substances that are highly resistant to natural processes of degradation even as they disperse through air, water, and soil. They bioaccumulate within food chains, but even in trace amounts they may be capable of bringing about biological changes.[3]

Toxic chemicals, although they are understood to pose significant risks to ecosystems and to human health, have often resisted precise definition and assessment. It has sometimes been difficult to determine exactly what human and environmental harm is caused by particular toxic substances. Substances differ in degree of toxicity and in terms of the nature of their impact, as well as in the timing in which those consequences appear. Moreover, toxicity varies in relation to concentration, length, and conditions of exposure; some segments of the population, children and the elderly, for example, may be more vulnerable than others. To complicate understanding still further, toxicity may be influenced by the presence of other substances in the environment, with such combinations and their synergistic consequences remaining largely unknown. Yet, during the 1970s and 1980s, toxic contamination was recognized as a significantly more widespread and intractable problem than previously suspected or acknowledged.[4] Reference to a few much-discussed toxics serves as a reminder of recent developments and provides a partial setting for consideration of legal initiatives.

The displacement in 1988 of some 3,500 people as a consequence of PCB storage problems at Saint-Basile-le-Grand, Quebec, demonstrated the vulnerability of urban populations to toxic concentrations, just as the 1985 PCB spill on the Trans-Canada Highway near Kenora, Ontario, and revelations concerning the contamination of numerous Arctic sites and mammal populations demonstrated that remoteness was no guarantee of immunity. Although PCBs were already the subject of

---

3   Environment Canada, "Management of Toxic Substances," online: www.ec.gc.ca/toxiques-toxics/default.asp?lang=En&n=97324D33-1.

4   With advances in science and in measurement techniques, linkages between exposure and health impacts have often become more apparent. See T McClenaghan *et al*, "Environmental Standard Setting and Children's Health in Canada" (2003) 12 J Envtl L & Prac 245; D Davis, *When Smoke Ran Like Water: Tales of Environmental Deception and the Battle Against Pollution* (New York: Basic Books, 2002).

regulatory controls dating from the 1970s,[5] attention focused on PCBs again in the late 1980s amidst considerable controversy over storage, exports, appropriate disposal technology and costs, and the tainted fuel scam (in which gasoline was being laced with PCBs as a means of disposing of these wastes).[6]

Another symbolic episode in a decade of seemingly unexpected encounters with chemical hazards involved the mid-1980s "toxic blob" in the St. Clair River, a part of the Great Lakes system on the border with the United States. The origins of the "blob" were attributed at the time to the accidental spill of dry-cleaning fluid that combined on the river bottom with a number of more hazardous chemicals already present in sediment. Yet the precipitating incident was by no means an isolated occurrence; governmental research and journalistic investigation confirmed that, between 1972 and 1984, 275 toxic spills had taken place in the vicinity and that approximately half of these entered the river itself.[7]

Dioxins, the name referring to a family of chemical compounds including "the most toxic synthetic chemical ever tested in the laboratory," also secured a prominent place in the regulatory agenda of both the United States and Canada. Highly publicized incidents involving pulp mill effluents produced alarm and attracted federal and provincial reaction.[8] In *Gagnier v Canadian Forest Products Ltd*, a commercial crab fisherman sought damages from a pulp mill whose alleged discharge of dioxins and other toxic substances into BC's Howe Sound resulted in closure of the crab harvest by government officials. The claim was dismissed without resolution of the scientific matters in conflict on the grounds that the plaintiff had, in any event, failed to establish damage.[9]

Our overall approach to the challenges presented by the proliferation of new potentially dangerous substances falls within the general framework of decision making for risk management. William Leiss provides a condensed account of the evolving backdrop of contemporary risk management:

> In Western industrial societies, with respect to the intrinsic difficulties of carrying out credible risk management decision making

5   JF Castrilli & CC Lax, "Environmental Regulation-Making in Canada: Towards a More Open Process" in J Swaigen, ed, *Environmental Rights in Canada* (Toronto: Butterworths, 1981) at 349–59.
6   J Ferguson, "Fuel Laced with Toxic Wastes Sold in Lucrative Scam" *The Globe and Mail* (8 May 1989) A1.
7   Chappell, above note 1 at 13.
8   K Harrison & G Hoberg, "Setting the Environmental Agenda in Canada and the United States: The Cases of Dioxin and Radon" (1991) 24 Can J Pol Sci 3.
9   (1990), 51 BCLR (2d) 218 (SC).

itself, all of the low-hanging fruit has been picked. . . . These easier victories amounted to drawing firm conclusions from toxicology and epidemiology that unacceptable levels of risk exist, that exposures should be reduced, and that either governments or industry should pay the costs for risk reduction without further ado . . . . Now our risk management battles are almost entirely different, sometimes because the risk reduction gains are purchased at much higher prices, but even more importantly because the reasons for carrying on the battles themselves are so much murkier . . . .[10]

As Leiss explains, the significant advances in risk reduction achieved in the first half of the twentieth century were generally associated with quite distinct challenges in the fields of occupational health and safety, public health, and air pollution. This was attributable in part to the comparatively undeveloped state of such forms of risk-related inquiry as toxicology and epidemiology. Moreover, government acknowledgement of a degree of responsibility in relation to environmental risks came much later. Leiss describes the contemporary situation as follows:

Now with far broader sets of responsibilities for risk management, with ever-increasing public expectations for risk control, and faced with the iron law of exponentially mounting costs for incremental risk reduction, in principle governments should look at risk factors synthetically, i.e., from the standpoint of comparative efficiencies in resource allocations for risk reduction opportunities . . . .

With every advance our society makes in collective risk reduction, there are distinctive benefits to be reaped, both in terms of enhanced quality of life and longevity. But in most cases the marginal costs for risk reduction inexorably keep rising, so that with each passing day it becomes increasingly more important to allocate risk reduction resources wisely. This must mean, quite simply, that some public alarms would be addressed with dollars, while other concerns, however loudly expressed, would be answered only with explanations as to why the expenditures would not be made.[11]

In addition to the Canadian regulatory initiatives described below, it should be noted that a number of toxic substances have been subject to international controls such as the Stockholm Convention on persistent organic pollutants, or the Rotterdam Convention on prior informed consent. Negotiations respecting international controls on mercury

---

10   W Leiss, *In the Chamber of Risks: Understanding Risk Controversies* (Montreal: McGill-Queen's Press, 2001) at 183–84.

11   *Ibid* at 183–87.

emissions and releases were recently concluded with the expectation that an agreement to be known as the Minimata Convention will be signed in 2013.

B. THE *CANADIAN ENVIRONMENTAL PROTECTION ACT, 1999 (CEPA 1999)* AND TOXICS

An overview of the federal government's operations in relation to toxics concluded, early in 1982, that "no overall strategy or policy respecting toxic chemicals is in place to give guidance in priority setting and major resource allocation."[12] This report identified interdepartmental problems within the federal government and limitations in the availability of information from manufacturers and importers as among the challenges to be addressed. Although it regarded the federal government's involvement in the toxics field as essentially residual to the provincial role, a 1986 report also noted "a lack of coherence among programs and . . . a lack of overall priorities."[13] Not long afterwards, the Brundtland Report noted toxics specifically as a subject to be addressed in terms of "manufacture, marketing, use, transport, and disposal." The report added that the regulation "should normally be done at the national level, with local governments being empowered to exceed, but not to lower, national norms."[14] The challenges of coherence and priority-setting have persisted.

As enacted in 1988, the original *Canadian Environmental Protection Act (CEPA)*, in addition to consolidating several existing federal environmental initiatives, was intended to address many of the limitations of the *ECA* in relation to toxic substances. The continuing emphasis given to toxics is evident in the preamble to *CEPA 1999* that includes several specific references to this issue and to the manner in which it is to be handled:

---

12 Environment Canada, *Toxic Chemical Related Activities within the Federal Government (FY 81/82): An Overview* by JAS Walker & RD Hamilton (Ottawa: Supply & Services, 1982) at 19.

13 *Regulatory Programs: A Study Team Report to the Task Force on Program Review* (Ottawa: Supply & Services, 1986) at 211 [Neilson Task Force]; *Environmental Contaminants Act*, SC 1974–75, c 72.

14 World Commission on Environment and Development, *Our Common Future* (Oxford UP, 1987) at 219–20.

Whereas the Government of Canada acknowledges the need to virtually eliminate the most persistent and bioaccumulative toxic substances and the need to control and manage pollutants and wastes if their release into the environment cannot be prevented;

Whereas the Government of Canada is committed to implementing the precautionary principle that, where there are threats of serious or irreversible damage, lack of full scientific certainty shall not be used as a reason for postponing cost-effective measures to prevent environmental degradation;

Whereas the Government of Canada recognizes that the risk of toxic substances in the environment is a matter of national concern and that toxic substances, once introduced into the environment, cannot always be contained within geographic boundaries.

Building on the framework created by its predecessor, *CEPA 1999* elaborated procedures for assessing the toxicity of designated substances and provided options for managing those substances ultimately determined to be toxic according to statutory criteria. Apart from substances understood to be "inherently toxic," a substance is toxic according to section 64 of *CEPA 1999*

if it is entering or may enter the environment in a quantity or concentration or under conditions that

(a) have or may have an immediate or long-term harmful effect on the environment or its biological diversity;

(b) constitute or may constitute a danger to the environment on which life depends; or

(c) constitute or may constitute a danger in Canada to human life or health.

For the purpose of assessing toxicity, several categories of substances have been established and various forms of evaluation have been provided. Approximately 23,000 existing substances, currently in use in Canada, were recorded on the Domestic Substances List.[15] Certain of these were designated as Priority Substances and made subject to accelerated assessment.[16] By September 2006, all substances on the Domestic Substances List were further classified to identify those requir-

---

15   *Canadian Environmental Protection Act, 1999*, SC 1999, c 33, s 66 [*CEPA 1999*]. Substances and activities new to Canada are subject to a distinctive set of procedures in ss 80–89.

16   *Ibid*, ss 76(1) and 78.

ing further screening or assessment as Priority Substances because of exposure, inherent toxicity, persistence, or bioaccumulation.[17]

In 2009, within the framework of the Chemicals Management Plan, the government of Canada initiated a process to update the Domestic Substances List. Basic data gathering was undertaken with respect to approximately 500 substances for the 2008 calendar year. A second phase of chemicals review was launched in December 2012 encompassing a further 2700 substances.[18]

Assessment procedures, following what is described as a risk-based approach, are conducted on the basis of information obtained from a range of sources[19] or may involve reference to decisions made by other jurisdictions.[20] It is intended that assessments of substances be conducted through the application of a weight of evidence approach and with reference to the precautionary principle as defined in CEPA 1999.[21]

In section 77 the legislation contemplates several measures to be proposed by the responsible ministers following the assessments:

- no further action;
- add the substance to the Priority Substances List;
- add the substance to the Toxic Substances List;
- recommend virtual elimination in the case of persistent and bioaccumulative substances.[22]

CEPA 1999 provides opportunities for the review of various decisions or orders taken pursuant to the legislation.[23] Thus, Board of Review proceedings were initiated on behalf of Silicones Environmental Health and Safety Council of North America in connection with the

---

17 Ibid, ss 73–74. Of the 23,000 existing substances reviewed, some 4,000 were determined to be in need of detailed scrutiny, with roughly 500 of these singled out for priority attention. For links to related documentation and details on the status of assessment processes, see online: www.chemicalsubstanceschimiques. gc.ca. A new Chemicals Management Plan was announced in December 2006. See also, 2008 March Status Report of the Commissioner of the Environment and Sustainable Development (Ottawa: Office of the Auditor General, 2008) c 1 "Chemicals Management — Substances Assessed under the Canadian Environmental Protection Act, 1999."

18 Online: www.chemicalsubstanceschimiques.gc.ca/plan/approach-approche/ dsl-lis-eng.php#a2.

19 CEPA 1999, above note 15, ss 68, 70, & 71.

20 Ibid, s 75.

21 Ibid, s 76.1.

22 Persistence and Bioaccumulation Regulations, SOR/2000-107.

23 CEPA 1999, above note 15, ss 333–340.

proposed listing of Siloxane D5 as a toxic substance on *CEPA 1999*'s Schedule 1.[24]

In the case of substances determined to be toxic, their addition to the Toxic Substances List by order of the Governor in Council establishes the basis for a series of management alternatives. These include regulation, the implementation of pollution prevention planning, and the development of a program for virtual elimination.

On the recommendation of the ministers, listed toxic substances are subject to regulation by the Governor in Council respecting a wide range of issues:

(a) the quantity or concentration of the substance that may be released into the environment either alone or in combination with any other substance;

(b) the places or areas where the substance may be released;

(c) the commercial, manufacturing, or processing activity in the course of which the substance may be released;

(d) the manner in which and conditions under which the substance may be released into the environment;

(e) the quantity of the substance that may be manufactured, processed, used, offered for sale, or sold in Canada;

(f) the purposes for which the substance or a product containing it may be imported, manufactured, processed, used, offered for sale, or sold;

(g) the manner in which and conditions under which the substance or a product containing it may be imported, manufactured, processed, or used;

(h) the quantities or concentrations in which the substance may be used;

(i) the quantities or concentrations of the substance that may be imported;

(j) the countries from which or to which the substance may be imported or exported;

(k) the conditions under which, the manner in which, and the purposes for which the substance may be imported or exported;

(l) the total, partial or conditional prohibition of the manufacture, use, processing, sale, offering for sale, import or export of the substance or a product containing it;

---

24 For background discussion and the Board of Review interpretation of its mandate in connection with the assessment and scheduling of the substance in question, see online: http://cdr-siloxaned5-bor.ca/default.asp?lang=En&n= 9320DEF6-1&offset=15&toc=show.

(m) the total, partial, or conditional prohibition of the import or export of a product that is intended to contain the substance;

(n) the quantity or concentration of the substance that may be contained in any product manufactured, imported, exported, offered for sale, or sold in Canada;

(o) the manner in which, conditions under which, and the purposes for which the substance or a product containing the substance may be advertised or offered for sale;

(p) the manner in which and conditions under which the substance or a product containing it may be stored, displayed, handled, transported, or offered for transport;

(q) the packaging and labelling of the substance or a product containing it;

(r) the manner, conditions, places, and method of disposal of the substance or a product containing it, including standards for the construction, maintenance, and inspection of disposal sites;

(s) the submission to the Minister, on request or at any prescribed times, of information relating to the substance;

(t) the maintenance of books and records for the administration of any regulation made under this section;

(u) the conduct of sampling, analyses, tests, measurements or monitoring of the substance;

(v) the submission of samples of the substance to the Minister;

(w) the conditions, test procedures and laboratory practices to be followed for conducting sampling, analyses, tests, measurements, or monitoring of the substance;

(x) circumstances or conditions under which the Minister may . . . modify
   (i) any requirement for sampling, analyses, tests, measurements or monitoring, or
   (ii) the conditions, test procedures, and laboratory practices for conducting any required sampling, analyses, tests, measurements, or monitoring; and

(y) any other matter . . . necessary to carry out the purposes of this Part.[25]

For a selected list of existing regulations, see table 13.1.

Pollution prevention has been designated as a priority objective in the selection of options to manage risks associated with toxic substances.[26]

---

25 *CEPA 1999*, above note 15, s 93(1).

26 *Ibid*, s 90(1.1). In specified circumstances non-toxic substances affecting international air and water pollution may also be subject to pollution prevention initiatives.

To this end, *CEPA 1999* authorizes the minister of the environment to call for the preparation and implementation of pollution prevention plans. Such a requirement may be applicable to single substances or groups of substances and may be directed to a person or to a class of persons by means of a notice under section 56. More particularly, notices under section 56 may specify:

(a) the substance or group of substances in relation to which the plan is to be prepared;
(b) the commercial, manufacturing, processing, or other activity in relation to which the plan is to be prepared;
(c) the factors to be considered in preparing the plan;
(d) the period within which the plan is to be prepared;
(e) the period within which the plan is to be implemented; and
(f) any administrative matter necessary.

Those required to draw up a pollution-prevention plan must provide written declarations confirming that such a plan has been prepared and that it has been implemented.[27] Plans should be available at the relevant location for examination by enforcement officials, but plans themselves will not ordinarily be submitted unless specifically required by the minister for the purpose of determining and assessing preventive or control actions in respect of a substance or group of substances.[28]

The management option applicable to substances that are persistent, bioaccumulative, and released to the environment primarily as a result of human activity is virtual elimination. In this context, virtual elimination means "the ultimate reduction of the quantity or concentration of the substance in the release below the level of quantification specified by the ministers" where the level of quantification (LoQ) for a substance is "the lowest concentration that can be accurately measured using sensitive but routine sampling and analytical methods."[29] With the LoQ established for a given substance, the ministers will prescribe the permissible quantity or concentration of the substance that may be released. Their decision in this respect may be based on "environmental or health risks and any other relevant social, economic or technical matters."

As commentators have noted, the virtual elimination option does not, in fact, provide for elimination but only for controlled releases; and it does so, not with exclusive reference to environmental and health

---

27   *Ibid*, s 58.
28   *Ibid*, ss 59, 60(1), and 227(b). See also Environment Canada, *Guidelines for the Implementation of the Pollution Prevention Planning Provisions of Part 4 of the Canadian Environmental Protection Act, 1999 (CEPA, 1999)* (February 2001).
29   *CEPA 1999*, above note 15, s 65.

risks, but with respect to such risks set against or counterbalanced by social, economic, and technical matters.[30]

A notable provincial initiative on toxics management is now underway. In Ontario, the *Toxics Reduction Act, 2009* introduces requirements applicable to toxic substances as prescribed by regulation.[31] The legislation calls for toxic substance reduction plans that address opportunities—including targets and timetables—to reduce the use or creation of toxic substances at designated facilities.[32] Reduction options include materials or feedstock substitution; product design or re-formulation; equipment or process modification; spill and leak prevention; on-site re-use or re-cycling; improved inventory management or purchasing techniques; training or improved operating practices.[33] In addition, the Act establishes accounting procedures:

> The owner and the operator of a facility who are required under section 3 to ensure that a toxic substance reduction plan is prepared for a toxic substance shall ensure that, for each process at the facility that uses or creates the substance, the substance is tracked and quantified, in accordance with the regulations, to show how the substance enters the process, whether it is created, destroyed or transformed during the process, how it leaves the process and what happens to it after it leaves the process.[34]

Table 13.1 Regulations for Toxic Substances (Selected)

Federal Regulations
Asbestos Mines and Mills Release Regulations, SOR/90-3414
Chlor-Alkali Mercury Release Regulations, SOR/90-130
Chlorobiphenyls Regulations, SOR/91-152
Polybrominated Diphenyl Ethers Regulations, (SOR/2008-218)
Contaminated Fuel Regulations, SOR/91-486

---

30 M Valiante, "Legal Foundations of Canadian Environmental Policy: Underlining Our Values in a Shifting Landscape" in DL VanNijnatten & R Boardman, eds, *Canadian Environmental Policy: Context and Cases,* 2d ed (Don Mills, ON: Oxford University Press, 2002) at 15.

31 SO 2009, c 19. For background, see Ministry of the Environment, Policy Proposal Notice, "Creating Ontario's Toxics Reduction Strategy—a discussion paper" (27 August 2008), online: www.ebr.gov.on.ca/ERS-WEB-External/displaynoticecontent.do?noticeId=MTA0MzAy&statusId=MTU1ODkz#.

32 The designation of toxic substances and facilities closely tracks established lists under other statutory schemes. See O Reg 455/09, ss 3 & 4.

33 *Ibid,* s 17.

34 *Toxic Reduction Act, 2009,* s 9; see also O Reg 455/09, ss 12 & 13.

Federal Regulations
Export and Import of Hazardous Wastes Regulations, SOR/2005-149
Gasoline Regulations, SOR/90-247
New Substance Notification Regulations (Chemicals and Polymers), SOR/2005-247
New Substance Notification Regulations (Organisms), SOR/2005-248
PCB Waste Export Regulations, SOR/97-109
Prohibition of Certain Toxic Substances Regulations, 2003, SOR/2003-99
Prohibition of Certain Toxic Substances Regulation, 2005, SOR/2005-41
Pulp and Paper Mill Defoamer and Wood Chip Regulations, SOR/96-313
Pulp and Paper Mill Effluent Chlorinated Dioxins and Furans Regulations, SOR/92-267

C. TRANSPORTATION OF DANGEROUS GOODS

The 1979 derailment of chlorine tank cars and the evacuation of some 200,000 Mississauga, Ontario residents revealed significant deficiencies in provisions governing the transportation of dangerous substances.[35] Existing legal controls were considered to be too particularized and sectoral either to provide an effective response capability or to reduce the likelihood of such occurrences in the first place.[36] The volume and diversity of hazardous substances being shipped throughout Canada clearly indicated the need for a more systematic and comprehensive framework for prevention and response.[37]

In order "to promote public safety in the transportation of dangerous goods," the federal government legislated in the immediate aftermath of the Mississauga disaster to establish such a framework,

---

35 SCM Grange, Commissioner, *Report of the Mississauga Railway Accident Inquiry* (Ottawa: Supply & Services Canada, 1980).

36 M Rankin, "Dangerous Moves: The Law Responds to the Transportation of Dangerous Goods" (1990) 24 UBC L Rev 213.

37 Approximately 132 million tonnes of dangerous goods were transported in Canada in 2006 (the most recent year for which statistics are available). Road, rail, and marine transport modes accounted for 65 percent, 24 percent and 11 percent respectively. For the period 2004 to 2008, with roughly 30 million dangerous goods shipments estimated to have taken place annually in Canada, there were, on average, 400 reportable releases involving the transportation of dangerous goods. The large majority (90 percent) of these releases occurred in connection with road shipments. See Transport Canada, Audit, Evaluation and Advisory Services, *Evaluation of the Transportation of Dangerous Goods Program Activity* (Ottawa: Government of Canada, July 2011), online: www.tc.gc.ca/media/documents/corporate-services/tdg2011-eng.pdf.

although the legislation anticipated provincial collaboration as well as detailed regulations.[38] Under the *Transportation of Dangerous Goods Act (TDGA)*, such goods included any product, substance, or organism contained either "by its nature" or by regulation in a scheduled classification list. Nine general classifications derived from the *International Convention for the Safety of Life at Sea* are used: explosives, compressed gases, flammable liquids, flammable solids, oxidizers and organic peroxides, poisonous and infectious substances, radioactives, corrosives, and a miscellaneous category including dangerous wastes and environmentally hazardous substances. Following revisions in 1992, the Act applied in relation to all matters within the legislative authority of Parliament, including dangerous goods outside Canada that are carried on a ship or aircraft registered in Canada.[39]

Statutory requirements include duties concerning registration and classification, labelling, packaging, and documentation as well as staff training. Section 5 of the *TDGA* specifically prohibits anyone from: handling, offering for transport, or importing "dangerous goods unless . . . the person complies with all safety requirements that apply under the regulations; . . . [and] the goods are accompanied by all documents that are required under the regulations."[40] Moreover, the means of containment and transport must comply with all applicable prescribed safety standards and must display all applicable prescribed safety marks. "Handling" is also broadly defined to mean

> loading, unloading, packing, or unpacking dangerous goods in a means of containment for the purposes of, in the course of or following transportation and includes storing them in the course of transportation.

In anticipation that dangerous substances, despite precautions, might be released accidentally, the *TDGA* also imposes reporting requirements and an obligation to "take all reasonable emergency measures to reduce or eliminate any danger to public safety that results or may reasonably be expected to result from the release."[41]

---

38 *Transportation of Dangerous Goods Act*, RSC 1985, c T-19. By 1985, with the development of regulations completed, the new system was implemented (SOR/85-77, 1 July 1985).

39 *Transportation of Dangerous Goods Act, 1992*, SC 1992, c 34, s 3(1) [*TDGA*].

40 For examples of *TDGA* prosecutions, often combined with charges under *CEPA 1999*, above note 15, see *R v Snap-On Tools of Canada Ltd* (2001), 44 CELR (NS) 301, [2001] OJ No 5221 (Ct J); *R v Alberta Public Works* (2001), 292 AR 157, 40 CELR (NS) 99 (Prov Ct); *R v Leon-Ram Enterprises* (2001), 41 CELR (NS) 179 (Sask Prov Ct). See also *Canada (AG) v Cariboo Pulp and Paper Co*, [2007] BCJ No 2418 (SC).

41 *TDGA*, above note 39, s 18(2).

The *Transportation of Dangerous Goods Act, 1992* provides for controls on design and construction standards for containers and requires the preparation and prior approval by the minister of transport of emergency-response plans. The powers of inspectors, notably in relation to preventive orders, were increased. Arrangements have also been made for electronic computerized monitoring to allow firefighters and other front-line response-team members to identify the precise nature of goods in transit more promptly than has previously been possible. The scope of penalties and remedial orders incorporates power to prohibit a convicted offender from engaging in activities regulated by the Act, and a duty to compensate those who undertook remedial work on the environment as a consequence of the offence. There are additional requirements to assist in repairing the environment and to conduct or to finance research to improve safety arrangements.[42]

The *TDGA* appears to have provided an effective framework for inter-jurisdictional cooperation in a field where coordination among jurisdictions and among agencies is a central element of an effective regulatory regime.[43] Consistent treatment of intraprovincial transportation is promoted through provisions to encourage negotiated agreements with the provinces concerning the implementation and administration of the Act.[44] The provinces acknowledged the virtues of consistency in relation to the transportation of dangerous goods and legislated accordingly in relation to their own constitutional responsibilities.[45]

TDGA regulations were produced in "clear language" for the first time in 2001.[46]

D. PCBS

Polychlorinated Biphenyls (PCBs) have been used for several decades in industrial and commercial applications. In electrical transformers, for example, their lubricating and insulating capability was particularly attractive. However, in the 1960s and 1970s, health concerns led to prohibitions and controls on their use and manufacture. Although such

---

42   *Ibid*, s 34.
43   Rankin, above note 36 at 198.
44   *TDGA*, above note 39, s 4.
45   Measures to address coordination between *CEPA 1999*, above note 15, and the *TDGA*, above note 39, include *CEPA 1999*, Schedule 1 "List of Toxic Substances," s 13.
46   SOR/2001-286.

concerns later somewhat diminished, a complex regulatory regime addressing transportation, storage, and disposal issues remains in place.[47]

PCBs were banned in the United States in 1976 under the authority of section 6 of the *Toxic Substances Control Act*. In Canada, PCB production has been banned since 1980 and their continuing use has been restricted. Federal PCB storage controls were established on an interim basis under *CEPA* in the aftermath of the 1988 fire and evacuation at Saint-Basile-le-Grand, Quebec, and were subsequently implemented on a permanent basis.[48] The regulations establish storage requirements designed to prevent release of PCBs into the environment. Labelling and reporting duties, maintenance and inspection obligations, and emergency procedures are also addressed. Comparable and compatible requirements have been instituted at the provincial level.

Interprovincial PCB transportation within Canada is also governed by regulations, in this case pursuant to the *TDGA*. These call for equipment containing PCBs to be drained and sealed in suitable containers prior to shipment. Again, some provincial regimes are in place in connection with intraprovincial PCB transportation.[49]

The disposal of existing PCB stockpiles has remained extremely troublesome. PCBs have entered landfills, but the slow rate at which they break down has meant that destruction programs, primarily involving incineration, have been preferred. In Canada, disposal facilities were established at Swan Hills in Alberta, the first province to have eliminated its own stockpiled PCBs by means of a mandatory destruction program. To reduce risks associated with the transportation of PCBs, portable incineration units have been used elsewhere in the country. These facilities are costly and have not been available in sufficient numbers to address the overall problem. From 1988 to 1995 the federal government administered a PCB destruction program.[50]

PCBs have also been subject to the *Basel Convention on the Control of Transboundary Movements of Hazardous Wastes and Their Disposal*, whose effect was to encourage parties to the convention to dispose of

---

47   In *R v Consolidated Maybrun Mines*, (*sub nom R v Maybrun Mines Consolidated*) (1992), 9 CELR (NS) 42 (Ont Prov Div, Fraser Prov J found "no evidence presently available that would justify a finding that PCBs have an adverse effect on humans based on realistic exposure levels that could be obtained from environmental exposure."

48   *Storage of PCB Material Regulations*, SOR/92-507, as am by SOR/2000-102. Now see *PCB Regulations* (SOR/2008-273).

49   *R v TNT Canada Inc* (1986), 58 OR (2d) 410 (CA).

50   *Federal Mobile PCB Treatment and Destruction Regulations*, SOR/90-5, as am by SOR/93-231 and SOR/2000-105.

their hazardous waste domestically, "as far as is compatible with environmentally sound and efficient management," thereby minimizing transboundary shipments. Canada and the United States addressed transboundary hazardous waste on a bilateral basis.[51]

The Canadian government introduced export-control regulations to eliminate the risk of Canadian PCB spillage in foreign countries.[52] An exception was permitted in order to facilitate the return to the United States of PCBs associated with American military installations. In 1995 an amendment to the *PCB Waste Export Regulations*[53] banned all PCB exports to the United States very shortly after that country had relaxed its own import restrictions in the case of PCBs originating in Canada. The Canadian initiative was criticized as a measure to ensure PCB supplies for the Swan Hills facility and became the subject of a legal challenge on the part of many industrial operations that consider it invalid and unnecessarily costly.[54] As of February 1997, Canadian PCBs destined for destruction in the United States by incineration or other means were permitted under a detailed control regime requiring approvals, documentation, and insurance.[55]

In view of new federal authority relating to the export and import of hazardous waste and hazardous recyclable materials in sections 185 to 192 of *CEPA 1999*, consideration was redirected to regulatory revisions that would strengthen controls on imports of PCB wastes to Canada, harmonizing export and import requirements.

E. PESTICIDES

Although the Saint-Basile-le-Grand experience with PCBs and some other high-profile incidents might suggest that the primary focus of concern regarding toxics should be on accidental and comparatively isolated releases, other evidence points towards endemic practices creating systemic risks from toxics. Studies relating to pesticides demonstrate important concerns about the authorization and generalized

---

51 (1986) 22 ILM 1025.
52 PCB Waste Export Regulations, SOR/90-453.
53 *Ibid*, as am by *PCB Waste Export Interim Order*, PC 1995-2013, C Gaz 1995.I.4228.
54 T Weiler, "Application of the Federal Regulatory Policy to Regulatory Decision-Making: The Curious Case of the 1995 PCB Waste Export Interim Order" (1999) 8 J Envtl L & Prac 181.
55 *PCB Waste Export Regulations, 1996*, SOR/97-109, as am by SOR/2000-103.

application of chemical substances and continue to stimulate inquiry into the approvals process.[56]

As explained by Health Canada, the development and use of synthetic organic chemicals predates the Second World War and has subsequently grown steadily. Both insecticides and herbicides are extensively employed in a wide range of commercial as well as domestic applications. In addition to human exposure associated with direct contact, the general public is exposed to pesticides through residues on food and to a lesser extent in drinking water. The *Food and Drugs Act* provides mechanisms for constant monitoring of pesticide residues in foods, while the *Guidelines for Canadian Drinking Water* outline acceptable residue levels for pesticides that have entered the water system either directly through spills, off-target aerial spraying, run-off, or after filtering through the soil to groundwater.[57]

The Canadian regulatory regime combines a federal system of controls on the registration of chemical ingredients for use in pesticides with provincial regimes addressing licensing issues and the supervision of pesticide handling and application procedures. Municipal governments are increasingly involved in regulating the use of pesticides within their boundaries.[58]

1) The Federal Level

The federal *Pest Control Products Act*[59] established a registration requirement for any product, organism, or substance used to control, destroy, attract, or repel any pest. These so-called control products now also include control products derived from biotechnology. The pests targeted include any injurious, noxious, or troublesome animal, plant or other organism. The pesticide registration process, emphasizing health and risk assessments for control products, is carried out under the supervision of the Pest Management Regulatory Agency.[60]

---

56   G Hoberg, "Risk, Science and Politics: Alachlor Regulation in Canada and the United States" (1990) 23 Can J Pol Sci 257; Pesticide Registration Review Team, *Final Report: Recommendations for a Revised Federal Management Regulatory System* (Ottawa: Supply & Services, 1990).
57   Health Canada, *A Vital Link: Health and the Environment in Canada* (Ottawa: Supply & Services, 1992) at 54–58 [*A Vital Link*].
58   See, for example, City of Toronto, "Pesticides, Use of," By-law No 456-2003.
59   RSC 1985, c P-9.
60   For a description of the assessment process under the previous regime, see the report of the House Standing Committee on Environment and Sustainable Development, *Pesticides: Making the Right Choice for the Protection of Health and the Environment* (2000), online: http://cmte.parl.gc.ca/cmte/CommitteePublication.

Current federal legislation prohibits the sale, use or importation of any control product other than ones that have been registered, packaged, and labelled in the prescribed manner and that conform to prescribed standards, and requires that registered products be used in a manner consistent with the terms of registration. Additional offences relate to false, misleading, or deceptive advertising of control products or to manufacturing and distributing them contrary to regulations.[61] The previous Act, as described by Cullen J of the Federal Court, was "clearly designed to protect the health of the general public from the impact of products that may be dangerous, and imposes significant control mechanisms before a product is permitted to be registered."[62] The revised legislation now explicitly states in section 6(8) that "no person shall manufacture, possess, handle, store, transport, distribute, use or dispose of a pest control product in a way that endangers human health or safety or the environment."

Several hundred active chemical ingredients for pesticides have been registered in Canada, of which approximately 100 entered into regular use.[63] In the context of an application for registration, the applicant is required to furnish sufficient information to permit an assessment of the relevant control product and bears the burden of persuasion.[64] The decision to register is based ultimately upon a determination by the minister that the health and environmental risks and the value of the pest product are "acceptable." For purposes of that assessment, the legislation provides the following guidance:

> the health or environmental risks of a pest control product are acceptable if there is reasonable certainty that no harm to human health, future generations or the environment will result from exposure to or use of the product, taking into account its conditions or proposed conditions of registration.[65]

Considerable controversy has surrounded the manner in which determinations of acceptability are made, including the extent of public participation in the decision-making process.[66] Legal challenges under

---

aspx?COM=173&Lang=1&SourceId=36396 at c 8. For information on the responsibilities and operations of PMRA, see online: www.hc-sc.gc.ca/pmra-arla/english/aboutpmra/about-e.html.

61 *Pest Control Products Act*, SC 2002, c 28, s 6 [*PCPA, 2002*].

62 *Monsanto Canada Inc v Canada (Minister of Agriculture)* (1986), 1 FTR 63 at 64 (TD).

63 *A Vital Link*, above note 57 at 57.

64 *PCPA, 2002*, above note 61, s 7(6).

65 *Ibid*, s 2(2).

66 *2003 October Report of the Commissioner of the Environment and Sustainable Development* (Ottawa: Office of the Auditor General, 2003) c 1, "Managing the Safety

the previous legislation raised a number of issues which will be of continuing relevance. In *Pulp, Paper & Woodworkers of Canada, Local 8 v Canada (Minister of Agriculture)*, the registration of Busan 30WB, a chemical used to prevent discolouration from fungal growth in non-kiln-dried lumber, was challenged on several grounds in judicial review proceedings.[67] The Federal Court, Trial Division, held that the question of the sufficiency of the information provided in the application to enable the chemical to be properly evaluated was a condition precedent to the minister's discretion to register or not to register the control product. In the absence of sufficient information, the registration was therefore quashed. In another case, a claim for damages originating in the plaintiff's assertion that she suffered from "delayed neurotoxicity" as a consequence of the negligent registration of a pesticide, the Federal Court of Appeal indicated that the decision to register a control product was a policy decision. In the absence of ministerial bad faith, that action could not succeed.[68]

In addition to amendments to the pest control products registration process, the new *PCPA* is also noteworthy for the introduction of post-registration controls, including requirements for the reporting of adverse effects and timely re-evaluations of older pesticides to ensure that new information is taken into account.[69] The legislation also provides for a special review of a registered pest control product on the basis of a request by any person. Where the minister has reasonable grounds to believe that the health or environmental risks of the product are, or its value is, unacceptable, a special review is mandatory, notwithstanding the general program of re-evaluation.[70]

2) The Provincial Level

At the provincial level, pesticide-management legislation has generally provided for a licensing and permit scheme governing the sale and use of pesticides in a range of applications including forest management operations, agricultural settings, and commercial-extermination servi-

---

and Accessibility of Pesticides." For follow-up assessment, see *2008 March Report of the Commissioner of the Environment and Sustainable Development* (Ottawa: Office of the Auditor General, 2008) c 2, "Chemicals Management—Pesticide Safety and Accessibility."

67 (1991), [1992] 1 FC 372 (TD).

68 *Kuczerpa v Canada* (1993), 14 CRR (2d) 307 (FCA).

69 Under the Chemicals Management Plan, accelerated re-evaluation of older pesticides is underway, online: www.chemicalsubstanceschimiques.gc.ca/plan/index-eng.php.

70 *Wier v Canada (Minister of Health)*, 2011 FC 1322 at para 92.

ces.[71] Provincial pesticide regimes may include their own categorization of pesticide risks with corresponding requirements and conditions for the licensing, training, and supervision of users in various settings, accompanied by enforcement provisions and penalties for non-compliance. Notwithstanding prior federal registration of the relevant control product, issues relating to pesticide risk and safety continue to arise in the specific context of licensing and on-site applications.

As approved by the British Columbia Court of Appeal,[72] the approach to toxicity and risk to be taken by the Environmental Appeal Board in considering licence applications for pesticide use under the province's former *Pesticide Control Act* merits repetition in light of recent criticisms of limitations in the federal regime. With regard to toxicity, the court supported the trial judge's observations to the effect that it was not a jurisdictional error to assume the general safety of a federally registered pesticide:

> Common sense dictates that the fact that a federally registered pesticide that has undergone extensive testing must have some probative value. . . . It is important to bear in mind that the Board did not state that a federally registered pesticide could never cause an unreasonable adverse effect.

Indeed, the board showed a willingness to hear site-specific evidence on toxicity and evidence concerning the ability of the permit holder to apply the pesticide safely in conformity with the intent of the registration. With respect to the relevance of alternative approaches to pest control, the court also agreed with the trial judge's reasons:

> Should the Board find an adverse effect (i.e., some risk) it must weigh that adverse effect against the intended benefit. Only by making a comparison of risk and benefit can the Board determine if the anticipated risk is reasonable or unreasonable. Evidence of silvicultural practices will be relevant to measure the extent of the anticipated benefit. Evidence of alternative methods will also be relevant to the issue of reasonableness. If the same benefits could be achieved by an alternative risk-free method then surely the risk method would be considered unreasonable.

---

71   *Environmental Protection and Enhancement Act*, RSA 2000, c E-12, Part 8; *Pesticides Act*, RSQ c P-9.3; *Pesticides Act*, RSO 1990, c P.11 [Ontario *Pesticides Act*]; *Pesticide Control Act*, RSPEI 1988, c P-4; *Pesticides Regulation*, Man Reg 94/88 R; *Pesticides Control Act*, RSNB 2011, c 203; *Pest Control Act*, RSS 1978, c P-7; *Pesticides Control Regulations*, 2012, NLR 26/12.

72   *Canadian Earthcare Society v BC (Environmental Appeal Board)* (1988), 3 CELR (NS) 55 (BCCA).

Failure to address site-specific and application-specific evidence relevant to the reasonableness or unreasonableness of an identifiable risk would be a reviewable error by the decision maker.[73] In subsequent decisions, British Columbia's EAB demonstrated a greater willingness to impose additional controls over the conditions under which pesticides may be used and to explore alternatives to chemical pest control.[74]

The vital matters canvassed in these British Columbia decisions, may now be less relevant in that jurisdiction where the *Pesticide Control Act* has been replaced by the *Integrated Pest Management Act*.[75] The new legislation, in introducing "pesticide-free zones" and "no treatment zones," significantly reduces overall requirements for specific government approvals as a pre-condition of pesticide use in the province. One anticipated consequence of the new arrangements is a reduction in opportunities to ensure public accountability for the manner in which pesticides are used in British Columbia.[76]

Provinces that recognize the continuing risks associated with the accumulation and storage of pesticides may initiate remedial programs to reduce the danger of contamination. Alberta Environment, for example, through Operation Clean Farm, has worked in cooperation with non-governmental organizations over a three-year period to recover obsolete pesticides from the agricultural sector.[77] Other jurisdictions have set up depots to receive unused pesticides or containers from the agricultural setting, and several have introduced programs to reduce pesticide use in crop production.

3) The Municipal Level

For a variety of reasons, municipal initiatives to restrict and regulate the use of pesticides within municipal boundaries have proliferated.[78]

---

73 *Wier v British Columbia (Environmental Appeal Board)* (2003), 8 Admin LR (4th) 71 (BCSC); *Eberhardt v British Columbia (Ministry of Water, Land and Air Protection)* (2004), 5 CELR (3d) 157 (BCEAB).

74 See also *Re Proposed Class Environmental Assessment by the Ministry of Natural Resources for Timber Management on Crown Lands in Ontario* (1990), 4 CELR (NS) 50 (OEAB).

75 SBC 2003, c 58.

76 West Coast Environmental Law, Bill 53, *The Integrated Pest Management Act* (Backgrounder), online: wcel.org/resources/publication/deregulation-backgrounder-bill-53-integrated-pest-management-act.

77 *Annual Report 2004–2005* (Edmonton: Alberta Environment, 2005) at 17.

78 J Swaigen, "The *Hudson* Case: Municipal Powers to Regulate Pesticides Confirmed by Quebec Courts" (2000) 34 CELR (NS) 162.

The general legal foundation for these actions has been confirmed by the Supreme Court of Canada.

Having been licensed provincially, and using federally approved pesticides, a lawn care company challenged a municipal pesticide by-law enacted by the town of Hudson, Quebec. The company argued that such a bylaw was *ultra vires*, beyond the powers of the municipality, and that it was inconsistent with federal and provincial legislation. The SCC upheld the bylaw as a valid exercise of the general power of the municipality to make bylaws "to secure peace, order, good government, health and general welfare in the territory of the municipality."[79] In upholding the validity of Hudson's pesticide regime, the SCC noted that the bylaw regulated but did not prohibit pesticide use, that it was enacted for legitimate purposes, and that courts should exercise caution in holding that elected municipal bodies have exceeded their powers. In connection with the alleged inconsistency between the bylaw and the federal and provincial framework for pesticide management, Justice L'Heureux Dubé stated, "as a general principle, the mere existence of a provincial (or federal) legislation in a given field does not oust municipal prerogatives to regulate the subject matter." She concluded that there was no conflict sufficient to nullify the bylaw; indeed, Quebec's *Pesticide Act* was "meant to coexist with stricter municipal bylaws of the type at issue in this case."[80]

Municipalities have considered several alternative approaches to pesticide regulation. Some focus on the protection of populations considered to be facing the most severe risks, children in particular. Others emphasize the elimination of pesticide use by municipalities themselves. By way of example, the Regional Municipality of Halifax prohibited pesticide application on municipally owned property and within a specified distance of properties occupied by such institutions as schools and hospitals. Except in the case of "permitted pesticides" as designated by the Halifax Regional Council, and in cases where use has been specifically authorized in connection with a danger to human beings over an insect infestation, pesticide applications within the municipality were subject to a prohibition as of April 2003.[81]

Pursuant to By-Law No. 456-2003, the City of Toronto declared that "no person shall apply or cause or permit the application of pesti-

79   114957 Canada Ltée (Spraytech, Société d'arrosage) v Hudson (Town), 2001 SCC 40.
80   In the aftermath of the decision Quebec introduced a new *Pesticide Management Code* which is substantially more protective than its predecessor: *Pesticide Management Code*, RRQ, c P-9.3, r 0.01.
81   Regional Municipality of Halifax, "Pesticide By-law," By-law P-800 Respecting the Regulation of Pesticides, Herbicides and Insecticides.

cides within the boundaries of the City," although this restriction does not apply to pesticides used for disinfecting pools, purifying water, controlling termites or health hazards, and certain other listed applications. Municipal authority to enact the bylaw in question was upheld pursuant to the power set out in section 130 of the Ontario *Municipal Act, 2001:*

> A municipality may regulate matters not specifically provided for by this Act or any other Act for purposes related to the health, safety and well-being of the inhabitants of the municipality.[82]

Provincial legislation in the form of the *Cosmetic Pesticides Ban Act,* and associated regulatory guidance now supersedes local bylaws by prohibiting cosmetic use of pesticides other than in prescribed circumstances.[83]

On the basis of general legislation such as Ontario's or by virtue of municipal bylaws, cosmetic pesticide regulation is now in place in approximately two hundred Canadian communities.

F. INFORMATION ON HAZARDOUS MATERIALS IN THE WORKPLACE AND WORKER HEALTH AND SAFETY LEGISLATION

The development and implementation of a nationwide system of information on hazardous materials in the workplace extended over the better part of the 1980s, largely as a consequence of the technical complexity involved and the constitutional division of relevant responsibilities. In 1982 a federal-provincial task force recommended that a combination of warning labels, data sheets on material safety, and worker-education programs would be required to address hazardous materials in the workplace comprehensively. Consultations involving governments together with representatives of labour and industry resulted in a more refined appreciation of the implementation issues at mid-decade. In 1988 the Workplace Hazardous Materials Information System (WHMIS) came into effect.

---

82 *Croplife Canada v Toronto (City)* (2005), 75 OR (3d) 357 (CA), leave to appeal to SCC refused, [2005] SCCA No 329.

83 *Cosmetic Pesticides Ban Act,* SO 2008, c 11. Now see Ontario *Pesticides Act,* above note 71, s 7.1; and O Reg 63/09.

Through the combined operation of federal and provincial/territorial legislation, WHMIS establishes procedures regarding the disclosure of information concerning the nature and management of hazardous substances in the workplace. Described generally as "controlled products," the materials subject to the WHMIS arrangements are substances designated by regulation under the federal *Hazardous Products Act*[84] within the following categories: compressed gas, flammable and combustible material, corrosive material, and dangerous reactive material.[85] Other potentially harmful materials were expressly excluded from the WHMIS regime on the grounds that they were subject to existing legislation. Section 12 of the *HPA* excludes various materials governed by the *Explosives Act*, the *Food and Drugs Act*, the *Pest Control Products Act*, the *Consumer Product Safety Act*, and the *Nuclear Safety and Control Act*, as well as hazardous waste and tobacco products.

Those who manufacture, process, package, or import or sell controlled products in the course of business (collectively known as suppliers) are required to provide material safety data sheets (MSDSs) and labels. This documentation will disclose prescribed information including the chemical identity and concentration of the controlled products present.[86] Other provisions are intended to respect the legitimate concerns of suppliers and employers regarding confidential business information. This reconciliation between workers' right to know about hazardous materials in the workplace and the confidentiality of certain business data is accomplished through exemption claims heard by the Hazardous Materials Information Review Commission.

Legislation governing workplace health and safety in various sectors and jurisdictions throughout Canada sets out further disclosure requirements and employee "right to know" provisions for the purpose of making MSDS information available.[87] Worker health and safety legislation, supplemented by negotiated agreements, authorizes employees to refuse to work in dangerous conditions, including the presence of environmental hazards.[88] To promote compliance with

84 RSC 1985, c H-3.
85 *Ibid*, s 2 and Sch II.
86 *Ibid*, ss 13 & 14; *Controlled Products Regulations*, SOR/88-66; *Ingredient Disclosure List*, SOR/88-64.
87 For example, in Ontario WHMIS is implemented via the regulation: *Workplace Hazardous Materials Information System (WHMIS)*, RRO 1990, Reg 860 promulgated under the *Occupational Health and Safety Act*, RSO 1990, c O.1. For explanation of the integration of WHMIS within the BC occupational health and safety framework, see, online: www2.worksafebc.com/topics/whmis/legislation. asp.
88 See, for example, *Canada Labour Code*, RSC 1985, c L-2.

regulations governing the workplace, legislation protecting employees from certain forms of reprisal has also been widely enacted. That
is, employees who complain, report, or otherwise act in response to
problems or hazardous situations in the workplace have some statutory means of redress against dismissal or other penalties that might
ensue. In relation to environmental compliance, these "whistleblower"
provisions not only offer workers job security if they seek to protect
themselves from personal risk, but may also have the effect of encouraging those with detailed knowledge of environmental practices in the
workplace to serve the public interest by promoting employer compliance through internal or external reporting.[89] Other attempts to extend
the level of whistleblower protection and to increase the likelihood that
environmental harm will figure more prominently in decisions about
the workplace include Ontario's *Environmental Bill of Rights, 1993*, and
CEPA 1999.[90]

FURTHER READINGS

BOYD, DR, *Unnatural Law: Rethinking Canadian Environmental Law and
Policy* (Vancouver: University of British Columbia, 2003) c 4.1

DOELLE, M, *Canadian Environmental Protection Act and Commentary,
2008 Edition* (Markham, ON: LexisNexis Canada, 2008)

FISHER, E, "Risk and Environmental Law: A Beginner's Guide" in B
Richardson & S Wood, eds, *Environmental Law for Sustainability*
(Portland, OR: Hart Publishing, 2006) c 4

LEISS, W, "The *CEPA* Soap Opera" in William Leiss, *In the Chamber of
Risks: Understanding Risk Controversies* (Montreal: McGill-Queen's
University Press, 2001) c 8

Managing Potentially Toxic Substances in Canada (Ottawa: National
Round Table on the Environment & the Economy, 2001)

MCCLENAGHAN, T, *et al*, "Environmental Standard Setting and Children's Health in Canada: Injecting Precaution into Risk Assessment" (2003) 12 J Envtl L & Prac 245

---

89 *Environmental Protection Act*, RSO 1990, c E.19, s 174(2); *Kraan v Custom Muffler
Ltd*, [1985] 2 OLRB Rep October 1461.
90 SO 1993, c 28; and *CEPA 1999*, above note 15, s 16, respectively.

REPORT OF THE HOUSE OF COMMONS STANDING COMMITTEE ON ENVIRONMENT AND SUSTAINABLE DEVELOPMENT, *It's About Our Health! Towards Pollution Prevention* (Ottawa: Canada Communication Group, 1995)

TRUDEAU, H, "Le rôle du gouvernement fédéral dans la régulation des substances toxiques au Canada" (2009) Revue de droit de l'Université libre de Bruxelles

CHAPTER 14

ENDANGERED SPACES AND SPECIES

A. RATIONALES

Many features of environmental law safeguard human populations from the adverse effects of environmental contamination and deterioration. Other initiatives, however, are specifically designed to protect the environment and its non-human inhabitants from seemingly inexorable human interventions, even where such interventions — a transportation corridor, or a drainage program, for example — might be perceived as "improvements." Along with pollution, developments of this kind impose severe costs on wildlife either by contamination, fragmentation of breeding territories, or destruction of certain types of vital habitat and migration routes. In addition, of course, humans themselves value and benefit from natural spaces for a range of economic, social, and spiritual reasons.

The *Canadian Wilderness Charter*, a document developed under the auspices of the World Wildlife Fund Canada and signed by more than half a million people, constitutes a powerful statement of the rationale for protecting wild and natural spaces. Humankind, the charter reminds us, is but one of millions of species sharing a planet whose future is severely threatened by our activities. Much of the Earth's former wilderness character is already lost, thereby endangering many species and ecosystems, but Canadians still have the opportunity to complete a network of protected areas representing the biological diversity of the country. For their inherent value, for their influence on national identity, and in light of an intrinsic human need for spiritual rekindling and artistic inspiration, Canada's remaining wild spaces should be protected. Protected areas can serve a variety of purposes, including preserving a genetic reservoir of wild plants and animals for future use and appreciation; producing economic benefits from environmentally sensitive tourism; offering opportunities for research and environmental education; and maintaining options for traditional and sustainable use by Aboriginal people.[1]

Very similar themes emerged from international discussions culminating in the *Convention on Biological Diversity (CBD)* adopted at the United Nations Conference on Environment and Development in Rio de Janeiro in 1992. Since Canada was the first industrialized country to ratify the *CBD* and since the Secretariat for the Convention is located in Montreal, it may be worthwhile outlining current strategic goals under the *CBD* to provide a point of reference for related Canadian initiatives.

In 2010, the Parties to the *CBD* adopted a *Strategic Plan for Biodiversity 2011–2020*, with the purpose of inspiring broad-based action in support of biodiversity.[2] The Strategic Plan envisages that, "by 2050, biodiversity is valued, conserved, restored and wisely used, maintaining ecosystem services, sustaining a healthy planet and delivering benefits essential for all people." The Strategic Plan is comprised of five strategic goals and twenty associated targets, collectively known as the Aichi Targets.

The first strategic goal is to address the underlying causes of biodiversity loss by mainstreaming biodiversity throughout government and society. Accordingly, the Parties will work to raise awareness on the values of biodiversity and integrate them into national and local development and poverty reduction strategies and planning processes. It is also hoped to eliminate, phase out, or reform subsidies or comparable incentives that are harmful to biodiversity, while developing and applying positive incentives. A further aim is to ensure that governments, business, and stakeholders implement plans for sustainable production and consumption. Secondly, the CBD Parties seek to reduce direct pressures on biodiversity and to promote sustainable use by halving the rate of loss of all natural habitats, including forests, and significantly reducing degradation and fragmentation; using sustainable practices to manage and harvest fish and invertebrate stocks, aquatic plants, and areas under agriculture, aquaculture, and forestry;

---

1   M Hummel, ed, *Endangered Spaces: The Future for Canada's Wilderness* (Toronto: Key Porter, 1989) at 275.
2   Online: www.cbd.int/doc/strategic-plan/2011-2020/Aichi-Targets-EN.pdf.

reducing pollution to levels that are not detrimental to ecosystem function and biodiversity; and identifying and prioritizing invasive alien species and pathways, controlling or eradicating priority species, and putting measures in place to manage pathways to prevent their introduction and establishment.

A third goal is to improve the status of biodiversity by safeguarding ecosystems, species, and genetic diversity. In order to achieve this objective, the parties seek to conserve at least 17 percent of terrestrial and inland water, and 10 percent of coastal and marine areas; prevent the extinction of known threatened species, and improve their conservation status; maintain the genetic diversity of cultivated plants and farmed and domesticated animals and of wild relatives; and develop, and implement strategies for minimizing genetic losses. Fourth, the Parties propose to enhance the benefits of biodiversity and ecosystem services by restoring and safeguarding ecosystems that provide essential services, including services related to water, public health, livelihoods, and well-being. Related initiatives include enhancing ecosystem resilience and the contribution of biodiversity to carbon stocks through conservation and restoration of at least 15 percent of degraded ecosystems. Implementing the *Nagoya Protocol on Access to Genetic Resources and the Fair and Equitable Sharing of Benefits Arising from their Utilization* represents a further important component of this overall goal.

The final goal is to enhance implementation through participatory planning, knowledge management, and capacity building. Thus, the parties plan to develop, adopt, and begin implementing an effective, participatory, and updated national biodiversity strategies and action plans; respect the traditional knowledge, innovations, and practices of indigenous and local communities relevant for the conservation and sustainable use of biodiversity, and integrate them in the implementation of the *CBD*.

Canadian measures that are generally responsive to biodiversity loss, or more specifically offer potential avenues of protection to spaces and species, are found in many pieces of general legislation at the federal and provincial levels. The *Fisheries Act*, for example, historically prohibited the deposit of deleterious substances into water frequented by fish and the destruction of fish habitat, while environmental assessment procedures may be used to identify developmental threats to natural environments and non-human populations and to propose mitigative measures.[3] As scientific and public understanding of the vul-

---

3   For discussion of revisions to federal fish habitat protection provisions, see Chapter 2, and to environmental assessment, see Chapter 12.

nerability of environmental systems to cumulative and wide-ranging impacts from human activity has increased, however, the search for more comprehensive responses has intensified. This chapter considers a number of other such broad approaches and legal mechanisms intended to safeguard spaces and species, ecosystems, and biodiversity.[4]

B. PROTECTING ENDANGERED SPACES

Conservation lands may include parks and wildlife-management areas or sanctuaries at the national, provincial, and territorial levels, as well as forest and ecological reserves, recreational land reserves, and a variety of special arrangements such as conservation easements and stewardship agreements to preserve private lands in their natural state. The total area protected in Canada, according to Environment Canada, amounted in 2011 to approximately 991,482 km^2 or 9.9 percent of the land base. Under federal jurisdiction, 505,033 km^2 of lands are protected, representing a 47 percent increase since 1990. The extent of protected areas as a percentage of each province in Canada is as follows: Yukon, 11.88 percent; Northwest Territories, 8.93 percent; Nunavut, 9.97 percent; British Columbia, 14.38 percent; Alberta, 12.41 percent; Saskatchewan, 7.98 percent; Manitoba, 10.18 percent; Ontario, 10.21 percent; Quebec, 8.86 percent; New Brunswick, 3.06 percent; Nova Scotia, 8.32 percent; Prince Edward Island, 2.8 percent; Newfoundland, 4.57 percent.[5] An extensive and growing but still incomplete system of land-based and marine parks has been established under the authority of both federal and provincial legislation whose express purposes and administrative provisions appear to signal a significant long-term commitment to environmental protection.[6]

The National Parks of Canada are, by statute, "dedicated to the people of Canada for their benefit, education and enjoyment, subject

---

4 　For commentary on the effectiveness of Canadian performance in relation to biodiversity protection, see OECD Environmental Performance Reviews: Canada (Paris: Organisation for Economic Co-operation and Development, 2004) c 4; S Bocking, ed, Biodiversity in Canada: Ecology, Ideas, and Action (Peterborough, ON: Broadview Press, 2000); D Boyd, Unnatural Law: Rethinking Canadian Environmental Law and Policy (UBC Press, 2003) c 5.

5 　Online: www.ec.gc.ca/indicateurs-indicators/default.asp?lang=en&n=478A1D3D-1; www.ec.gc.ca/indicateurs-indicators/default.asp?lang=en&n=8390800A-1#pa3.

6 　Significant extensions of protected areas coverage were undertaken in connection with Ontario's Living Legacy program. A major expansion of national parks and wildlife areas throughout northern Canada was announced by the federal government in 2007 and has been ongoing.

to . . . [the *Canada National Parks Act*] and the regulations, and the
National Parks shall be maintained and made use of so as to leave them
unimpaired for the enjoyment of future generations."[7] Moreover, the
CNPA reinforces a proposition that had previously served as departmental policy for years by establishing that "maintenance or restoration of ecological integrity, through the protection of natural resources
and natural processes, shall be the first priority of the minister when
considering all aspects of the management of parks."[8] The incorporation of the principle of "ecological integrity" into the federal legislative
framework (as discussed below), raises issues around the standard to
be met and its ultimate enforceability through the process of judicial
review.

Echoing the federal initiative and previous recognition of ecological considerations by Quebec, Nova Scotia, Prince Edward Island, and
Newfoundland and Labrador, Ontario has included within new legislation a statement to the effect that in planning and managing protected
areas, "maintenance of ecological integrity shall be the first priority and
restoration of ecological integrity shall be considered."[9] Nova Scotia's
Beaches Act is another example of protected spaces legislation, devoted
in this case to a particular type of environment: "The beaches of Nova
Scotia are dedicated in perpetuity for the benefit, education and enjoyment of present and future generations of Nova Scotians." Among the
Act's stated purposes are the protection of beaches and associated dune
systems as significant and sensitive environmental and recreational resources; the regulation and enforcement of the full range of land-use
activities on beaches, including aggregate removal, so as to leave them
unimpaired for the benefit and enjoyment of future generations; and
control of recreational and other uses that may cause undesirable environmental effects.[10]

In practice, the interpretation of such provisions and their application has proven to be controversial. Across the country parks vary in
terms of protection from potentially damaging activities and even in

---

7   *Canada National Parks Act*, SC 2000, c 32, s 4(1) [*CNPA*]. See, generally, P Kopas,
    Taking the Air: Ideas and Change in Canada's National Parks (UBC Press 2007).

8   *CNPA*, above note 7, s 8(2). As defined in the Act, ecological integrity with
    respect to a park means a condition that is determined to be characteristic of
    its natural region and likely to persist, including abiotic components and the
    composition and abundance of native species and biological communities, rates
    of change and supporting processes.

9   *Provincial Parks and Conservation Areas Act, 2006*, SO 2006, c 12, s 3.

10 *Beaches Act*, RSNS 1989, c 32. For a discussion of the history and operation of
    the Act, see *Mossman v Nova Scotia (AG)* (1995), 140 NSR (2d) 321 (SC).

terms of the permanence and stability of their boundaries (see table 14.1). They remain subject to considerable developmental pressure from the resource, tourism, and transportation sectors, both within their boundaries and on the periphery.

Table 14.1   Selected Parks and Protected Areas Legislation[11]

Alberta	*Provincial Parks Act*, RSA 2000, c P-35
British Columbia	*Park Act*, RSBC, 1996, c 344
Manitoba	*The Provincial Parks Act*, CCSM c P20
New Brunswick	*Parks Act*, R.S.N.B. 2011, c 202
Newfoundland and Labrador	*Provincial Parks Act*, RSN 1990, c P-32 *Wilderness and Ecological Reserves Act*, RSNL 1990, c W-9
Nova Scotia	*Provincial Parks Act*, RSNS 1989, c 367 *Wilderness Areas Protection Act*, SNS 1998, c 27
Ontario	*Provincial Parks and Conservation Reserves Act*, 2006, SO 2006, c 12
Prince Edward Island	*Recreation Development Act*, RSPEI 1988, c R-8
Quebec	*Parks Act*, RSQ c P-9
Saskatchewan	*The Parks Act*, SS 1986, c P-1.1
Federal	*Canada National Parks Act*, SC 2000, c 32

In the context of a dispute over the expansion of skiing facilities in BC's Cypress Provincial Park, opponents of the increased development sought a judicial declaration to the effect that the dominant purpose of the province's *Park Act* was the preservation and protection of the natural environment of parks.[12] Melnick J, while noting that the provision was not actually applicable to Cypress, analysed a key element of the legislation. Section 53 states that certain parks are "dedicated to the preservation of their natural environments for the inspiration, use, and enjoyment of the public." While acknowledging the importance of preserving the natural environment of those parks designated for such protection, Melnick J noted a legislative intent to foster "recreational values" that were "not necessarily subsumed in the concept of nature conservancy." He concluded, accordingly, that the Act "provides a framework for the creation and preservation of parkland for a variety

---

11   The legislation consolidates the statutory framework in Ontario for wilderness class parks, nature reserve class parks, cultural heritage class parks, natural environment class parks, waterway class parks, and recreational class parks.

12   *Friends of Cypress Provincial Park Society v BC (Minister of Environment, Lands and Parks)* (2000), 33 CELR (NS) 276 (BCSC).

of purposes to serve a broad cross-section of the citizens of British Columbia whose interests are as diverse as its landscape."[13]

One prominent example of an attempt to reconcile the environmental protection dimensions of national parks with development was the subject of the Banff Bow Valley Study. Its report, *At the Crossroads*, formulated recommendations to address the study's principal finding that "[i]f current trends and pressures are allowed to continue, they will threaten the qualities that make Banff a national park" and the conclusion that "the ecological integrity of the Banff-Bow Valley cannot be sustained." The general thrust of the proposed actions responds to the injunction that "[a]d hoc decision making must give way to a more holistic approach, one that puts the Park ahead of human needs and desires." Although legal matters, including the application of federal parks legislation, international conventions and agreements, and an intricate web of local leasing arrangements, were all identified as sources of some support for the vision of the future as proposed by the task force, the overall need for accountable decision making, public participation, and effective use of scientific data remained as continuing challenges.[14] These were among the matters subsequently pursued on a more comprehensive basis by an expert panel appointed in 1998 to advise the minister of Canadian heritage.[15] Although this inquiry devoted particular attention to administrative and planning matters internal to Parks Canada, a number of principles advanced have wider significance. Of special interest in terms of broader legal implications is the suggestion that national parks must be more systematically viewed as elements of ecological networks rather than as "islands" in isolation from the surrounding landscape.

Judicial recognition of the status of environmental values in national-parks management is evident in numerous judgments, including a Federal Court of Appeal decision on the need for environmental assessment of the expansion of skiing facilities at Banff's Sunshine Village. The court's decision calling for an examination of the cumulative impact

13   *Ibid* at 291.
14   Banff-Bow Valley Task Force, *Banff-Bow Valley: At the Crossroads: Summary Report* (Ottawa: Supply & Services, 1996). The emergence of "Riverkeeper" organizations, including one dedicated to oversight of the Bow River valley, is one response to the need for a comprehensive approach to ecological protection, in such cases at the watershed level. For background on the riverkeeper movement, see J Cronin & RF Kennedy Jr, *The Riverkeepers* (New York: Simon & Schuster Touchstone, 1999).
15   "Unimpaired for Future Generations?" *Conserving Ecological Integrity within Canada's National Parks* (Ottawa: Panel on the Ecological Integrity of Canada's National Parks, 2000).

of ongoing development rather than an incremental assessment was forward-looking and appropriate.[16] Development proposals on or affecting parklands continue to generate litigation, often in relation to environmental assessment,[17] and now in relation to expectations surrounding the meaning of ecological integrity as a standard for parks management.

Parks Canada, in connection with its responsibility for national parks, has undertaken significant steps to assess and to maintain or restore ecological integrity within the parks system. "State of the Park" reports will provide information over five-year cycles that will support the evaluation of management actions against benchmarks and objectives. On a system-wide basis Parks Canada anticipates that elements of ecological integrity will show improvement by 2014. An audit report carried out by the Commissioner of the Environment and Sustainable Development, while containing recommendations for improvements, appears generally favourable to the manner in which Parks Canada has begun to pursue ecological integrity on an administrative basis.[18]

In relation to the legal status of ecological integrity, however, doubts have been expressed on the basis of judicial review of a decision of the minister of Canadian heritage to approve winter road construction in Wood Buffalo National Park.[19] As noted above, ecological integrity is referred to as "the first priority" of the minister when considering parks management. The concept of ecological integrity itself is statutorily defined as "a condition that is determined to be characteristic of its natural region and likely to persist, including abiotic components

---

16   *Sunshine Village Corp v Canada (Minister of Canadian Heritage)* (1996), 20 CELR (NS) 171 (FCA), leave to appeal to SCC refused, [1996] SCCA No 498.

17   *Alberta Wilderness Assn v Canada (Minister of Fisheries and Oceans)* (1999), 29 CELR (NS) 21 (FCA); *Bowen v Canada (AG)* (1997), 26 CELR (NS) 11 (FCTD); *Bow Valley Naturalists Society v Canada*, (1999), 32 CELR (NS) 84 (FCTD); *Friends of Point Pleasant Park v Canada (AG)* (2000), 36 CELR (NS) 253 (FCTD); *Society of Friends of Strathcona Park v BC (Minister of Environment, Lands and Parks)* (1999), 31 CELR (NS) 274 (BCSC). Legislative changes in 2012 alter the basis on which federal environmental assessment procedures might be applicable in relation to national parks.

18   *2005 September Report of the Commissioner of the Environment and Sustainable Development* (Ottawa: Office of the Auditor General, 2005) c 2 "Ecological Integrity in Canada's National Parks" [*CESD September Report 2005*]. For specific illustrations of the range of initiatives involved in Parks Canada's ecological integrity work, see *Action on the Ground: Ecological Integrity in Canada's National Parks* (Ottawa: Parks Canada, 2005). An analysis of trends current to 2011 may be found online at: www.ec.gc.ca/indicateurs-indicators/default. asp?lang=en&n=CDE1612B-1.

19   *Canadian Parks and Wilderness Society v Canada (Minister of Canadian Heritage)* (2003), 1 CELR (3d) 20 (FCA).

and the composition and abundance of native species and biological communities, rates of change, and supporting processes."[20] When a national environmental organization challenged the minister's approval of the winter road for failing to meet the statutory standard established by the definition and its designation as "the first priority," the trial court found no evidence that the concept of ecological integrity had even been addressed in the decision-making process. The trial judge further observed that ecological integrity was not, within subsection 8(2), the determinative factor and could be overridden "where impairment of such integrity can be minimized to a degree that the minister concludes is consistent with the maintenance of the Park for the enjoyment of future generations."[21] The Federal Court of Appeal, in upholding the lower court's dismissal of the judicial review application, roughly equated the ecological integrity standard with a screening test for federal environmental assessment. Accordingly, the FCA concluded that the minister's approval of the road was not "patently unreasonable" and therefore a legitimate exercise of the statutory authority under which it was made.[22]

Another doctrine, public trust, has also been invoked in litigation by those seeking to impose an obligation on governmental authorities to safeguard the environmental conditions and integrity of designated parklands. The argument, roughly stated, is that certain statutory provisions establish a trust in park areas for the benefit of the public or some designated class of persons that the government as trustee is under a legally enforceable duty to uphold.

In *Green v R*, a researcher with the Canadian Environmental Law Association unsuccessfully asserted that the provincial government's conduct in relation to Sandbanks Provincial Park was in breach of such a trust.[23] In 1968, Ontario leased some of the sandbanks bordering Lake Ontario to a company that accordingly gained the right to excavate sand. The province subsequently established Sandbanks Provincial Park on adjacent land, thereby prompting Green to argue that by per-

---

20   *CNPA*, above note 7, s 2(1).

21   *Canadian Parks and Wilderness Society v Canada (Minister of Canadian Heritage)* (2001), 212 FTR 1 at paras 52–53 (TD).

22   For commentary and analysis of the decisions, see S Fluker, "'Maintaining Ecological Integrity Is our First Priority'—Policy Rhetoric and Practical Reality in Canada's National Parks? A Case Comment on *Canadian Parks and Wilderness Society v Canada (Minister of Canadian Heritage)*" (2003) 13 J Envtl L & Prac 131; and S Fluker, "Ecological Integrity in Canada's National Parks: The False Promise of Law" (2010) 29 Windsor Rev Legal Soc Issues 89.

23   [1973] 2 OR 396 (HCJ) [*Green*].

mitting excavation to continue on the leased property the province was in breach of certain trust obligations established by the then current *Provincial Parks Act.* Section 2 of that legislation stated that provincial parks are "dedicated to the people of the Province of Ontario . . . for their healthful enjoyment and education, and the provincial parks shall be maintained for the benefit of future generations in accordance with this Act and the regulations."[24]

Although Lerner J resolved the conflict by ruling that Green lacked standing to proceed with the litigation, he addressed the argument that section 2 created a public trust imposing obligations on the provincial government. Lerner J concluded that the elements of a trust were lacking in the circumstances of the case in that the existence of legislative authority to increase, decrease, or close the park meant that the subject matter of the alleged trust was uncertain; nor could the objects or beneficiaries of the trust be ascertained with certainty. In addition, Lerner J found that the wide powers of discretion conferred upon the province to manage parks were inconsistent with the existence of a trust.

The failure of the public-trust argument in *Green* does not preclude its use in other settings where different legislative language has been employed. Indeed, the concept of the public trust was favourably remarked on in the context of a damage claim by municipal authorities against a builder whose operations negligently destroyed a number of mature maple trees within a city road allowance. Writing for a majority of the Ontario Court of Appeal, Lacourcière J stated: "In our judgment, the municipality is, in a broad sense, a trustee of the environment for the benefit of the residents in the area of the road allowance and, indeed for the citizens of the community at large."[25] Public-trust claims remain rare in Canada,[26] although they may ultimately be encouraged by an important decision on fiduciary relationships in which the Supreme Court of Canada rejected the assumption that the nature of fiduciary relationships is exhaustively established by the categories of agent, trustee, partner, director, and so on:

> It is the nature of the relationship, not the specific category of actor involved that gives rise to the fiduciary duty. The categories of fiduciary, like those of negligence, should not be considered closed.[27]

---

24   *Provincial Parks Act*, RSO 1990, c P.34, s 2.
25   *Scarborough (City) v REF Homes Ltd* (1979), 10 CELR 41 at 41–42 (Ont CA).
26   A public trust argument was advanced in *Canadian Parks and Wilderness Society v Wood Buffalo National Park* (1992), 55 FTR 286 (TD), but was not addressed by the court when the parties settled the litigation.
27   *Guerin v R*, [1984] 2 SCR 335 at 384. Nevertheless, it has recently been stated in an environmental decision that "[t]he Defendants cannot be subject to obliga-

It would also appear that judicial acknowledgement of environmental values is more favourable than at the time of the *Green* case when Lerner J dismissed the plaintiff's assessment of the importance of the sandbanks by remarking: "That 'the towering sand dunes . . . constitute . . . a unique ecological, geological and recreational resource . . .' is clearly a statement of opinion as much as a comment that a particular *objet d'art* is good or bad esthetically."[28]

Significantly, some legislation is now explicit in its reference to the existence of a statutory public trust. Thus, the Yukon *Environment Act* designates the government of the Yukon as "the trustee of the public trust," defined as "the collective interest of the people of the Yukon in the quality of the natural environment and the protection of the natural environment for the benefit of present and future generations." The statute formally requires the Yukon government to "conserve the natural environment in accordance with the public trust" subject to the Act and other scheduled enactments.[29] A comparable provision was introduced in the Northwest Territories and has been referred to in judicial proceedings involving wildlife matters, essentially as an indication of the fundamental importance of the northern environment to the people resident there.[30]

Several jurisdictions have used ecological reserves and other comparable designations to safeguard vulnerable sites from development. Typical reasons for such designations were set out in British Columbia's *Ecological Reserves Act*, which identified relevant criteria for selecting areas to be reserved:

(a)   suitable for scientific research and educational purposes associated with studies in productivity and other aspects of the natural environment;

---

tions under a public trust because no such trust exists in Canadian law." *Burns Bog Conservation Society v Canada (Attorney General)*, 2012 FC 1024 at para 39.

28   *Green*, above note 23 at 401.

29   *Environment Act*, RSY 2002, c 76, ss 2 and 38. For discussion, see DWM Waters, "The Role of the Trust in Environmental Protection Law" in DWM Waters, ed, *Equity, Fiduciaries and Trusts* (Toronto: Carswell, 1993) 383. For discussion of the public trust concept in relation to the territorial legislation, see B von Tigerstrom, "The Public Trust Doctrine in Canada" (1998) 7 J Envtl L & Prac 379. For discussion of public trust in relation to resources such as fisheries and forest lands, see S Kidd, "Keeping Public Resources in Public Hands: Advancing the Public Trust Doctrine in Canada" (2006) 16 J Envtl L & Prac 187.

30   *Environmental Rights Act*, RSNWT 1988 (Supp), c 83. See *R v Ram Head Outfitters Ltd*, [1995] NWTJ No 29 (Terr Ct).

(b) that are representative examples of natural ecosystems within the Province;

(c) that serve as examples of ecosystems that have been modified by man and offer an opportunity to study the recovery of the natural ecosystem from modification;

(d) where rare or endangered native plants and animals in their natural habitat may be preserved; and

(e) that contain unique and rare examples of botanical, zoological or geological phenomena.[31]

The Act conferred upon the lieutenant governor in council the power to designate ecological reserves on Crown land and to cancel or amend such reserves once established. Reserves thus created are not subject to further disposition that might be granted under other provincial legislation such as the *Land Act*, the *Forest Act*, the *Mineral Act*, and the *Petroleum and Natural Gas Act*.[32]

Protection of endangered spaces extends beyond the terrestrial landscape to encompass marine areas and wetlands. The creation of marine parks and reserves is a comparatively recent initiative in Canada, and one that may be carried out under several pieces of legislation. The *Oceans Act* confers authority on the federal minister of fisheries and Oceans to lead the development of a system of marine protected areas.[33] These are intended to serve several purposes, including the protection of fisheries resources or habitat (including that for marine mammals); the protection of endangered or threatened marine species or habitat; the protection of unique habitats; the protection of marine areas of high biological diversity or productivity; and the protection of other marine resources. While there have been some delays in the designation of marine protected areas under the *Oceans Act*, and some uncertainty or lack of coordination between Fisheries and Oceans, Parks Canada and the Canadian Wildlife Service in relation to an overall approach, a program to address such limitations was published in

---

31   *Ecological Reserve Act*, RSBC 1996, c 103, s 2.

32   *Ibid.* See also *Protected Natural Areas Act*, SNB 2003, c P-19.01; *Wilderness Areas, Ecological Reserves, Natural Areas and Heritage Rangeland Act*, RSA 2000, c W-9. The Alberta legislation has been extended to provide for "heritage rangeland" designations.

33   *Oceans Act*, SC 1996, c 31, as am by 2002, c 7, s 223; 2003, c 22, s 224(E); 2005, c 29, s 36. See also *Canada National Marine Conservation Areas Act*, SC 2002, c 18; and the *Canada Wildlife Act*, RSC 1985, c W-9, s 4.1. See also Canadian Parks and Wilderness Society, *How deep did Canada dare? Assessing national progress towards marine protection to December 2012* (21 January 2013), online: www.documentcloud.org/documents/560303-cpaws-marine-protection-report.html.

2005.[34] Challenges remain to ensure the coordination and integration of federal and provincial measures.

In relation to wetlands, these have been profoundly affected by land-use practices and policies affecting such matters as drainage, transportation, and urban expansion. Twenty million hectares of Canadian wetlands have been converted to agricultural use. Significant and widespread losses of habitat and ecological functions, notably relating to water quality, have thus already occurred. Some provinces, led by Alberta, Manitoba, Nova Scotia, PEI, and New Brunswick, have begun to introduce various forms of wetland protection. For its part, the federal government has formulated a policy on wetland conservation.[35] This document calls for cooperation with provinces and territories to pursue goals including the maintenance, enhancement, and rehabilitation of wetland functions, and, in relation to federal responsibilities in particular, for no net loss of wetland functions on federal lands and for recognition of those functions in federal planning, management, and decision making. Objectives for further development regarding wetlands conservation, including aspects of the relationship between wetlands and climate change, have been formulated by the North American Wetlands Conservation Council.[36]

C. CONSERVATION MECHANISMS FOR PRIVATE LANDS

Measures to protect sensitive areas in private ownership from disruption and development include conservation easements, related covenants, and other forms of stewardship either initiated by conscientious landholders or promoted more systematically by nature protection and conservation organizations.[37] Such mechanisms may be particularly

---

34 *CESD September Report 2005*, above note 18, c 1 at 15–20; *Canada's Federal Marine Protected Areas Strategy* (June 2005), online: www.dfo-mpo.gc.ca/oceans-habitat/ oceans/mpa-zpm/fedmpa-zpmfed/pdf/mpa_e.pdf. For a detailed illustration of the planning process, see the Regulatory Impact Analysis Statement prepared in connection with proposed *Manicouagan Marine Protected Area Regulations* under the *Oceans Act*, in C Gaz 2006, Vol 140, No 39 (30 September 2006), online: http://publications.gc.ca/gazette/archives/p1/2006/2006-09-30/pdf/g1-14039.pdf.

35 Environment Canada, *The Federal Policy on Wetland Conservation* (Ottawa: Minister of Supply and Services, 1991).

36 Online: www.wetlandscanada.org/pubs.html.

37 The Nature Conservancy of Canada is one important example. See online: www. natureconservancy.ca.

useful in relation to numerous small sites that fulfil vital ecological functions—wetlands, for example.

At common law, certain interests in land might be recognized through easements granted by the owner to an easement holder who would thereby gain a right to use the owner's land in some prescribed manner (a right of way, for example) or to restrict the owner against using the land for some specified purpose. These arrangements were known as positive and negative easements respectively. Covenants between the landowner and another contracting party or parties could also be used to create restrictions on the manner in which land could be used. In principle these mechanisms could be employed to safeguard environmental values, but limitations in transferability and enforceability severely undermined their utility for this purpose.

Statutory reforms in several jurisdictions[38] have alleviated many historic constraints on conservation easements. These often permit conservation easements to be granted to public bodies and to recognized non-governmental conservation organizations. The Ontario legislation now permits a landowner to "grant an easement to or enter into a covenant with a conservation body . . . for the conservation, maintenance, restoration, or enhancement of all or a portion of the land or the wildlife on the land; or . . . for access to the land for these purposes."[39] In addition, the easement or covenant is valid whether or not the conservation body or assignee owns appurtenant land or land capable of being accommodated or benefited by the easement or covenant and regardless of whether the easement or covenant is positive or negative in nature. The easement or covenant is enforceable against the owner of the land and, if registered, against any subsequent owner of the land.[40] Comparable Saskatchewan legislation permits a landowner to grant a conservation easement for the purposes of "protection, enhancement or restoration of natural ecosystems, wildlife habitat or habitat of rare, threatened or endangered plant or animal species; . . . [or] the conservation of soil, air and water quality."[41]

---

38   S Lieberman, "New Game in Town: Conservation Easements and Estate Planning" (1995) 14 E & TJ 315; AJ Kwasniak "Conservation Easements: Pluses and Pitfalls, Generally and for Municipalities," (2009) 46 Alta LR 651; WJ Andrews & D Loukidelis, *Leaving a Living Legacy: Using Conservation Covenants in BC* (Vancouver: West Coast Environmental Law Research Foundation, 1995); A Silver, "Canadian Legislation for Conservation Covenants, Easements and Servitudes" (Ottawa: North American Wetlands Conservation Council, 1995); *Land Title Act*, RSBC 1996, c 250; *Environmental Protection and Enhancement Act*, RSA 2000, c E-12, s 22.

39   *Conservation Land Act*, RSO 1990, c 28, s 3(2).

40   *Ibid*, s 3(6).

41   *The Conservation Easements Act*, SS 1996, c C-27.01, s 4.

Although legislation of this nature enables landowners to pursue statutorily approved conservation objectives with greater confidence that their intentions will not be thwarted by historic common law principles, these arrangements must nonetheless be implemented with care on an individual basis.[42] Their attractions to landowners have been summarized as follows:

- right to continued use of the land after the conservation objectives have been determined;
- significantly less disruption than total disposition of the property in that other elements of control are retained;
- flexibility and adaptability to particular individual circumstances relating to the land and to the interests of the owner; and
- a possible lowering of the tax burden.[43]

Other forms of private-stewardship agreements have been implemented through the efforts of conservation groups across Canada. Voluntary stewardship agreements, both oral and written, and varying in duration and permanence from short-term renewable to multi-year undertakings, have emerged from discussion between conservation interests and landowners. NGOs such as Wildlife Habitat Canada, Ducks Unlimited, and the Nature Conservancy of Canada have devoted extensive effort and resources to wetlands, sometimes leasing and sometimes acquiring property, and sometimes consulting on appropriate land-use practices. In Saskatchewan, a Prairie Pothole Project was designed to elicit the support of agricultural landholders for measures to safeguard waterfowl habitat. Other programs with provincial involvement include the Critical Wildlife Habitat Program in Manitoba, the Watershed Management Fund in Prince Edward Island, and the Ontario Heritage Trust.

D. THE PROTECTION OF ENDANGERED SPECIES

Plant and animal species have been and remain extremely vulnerable to the direct impact of human activities on their populations or

---

42   For a case study on the tools (including conservation covenants) available to safeguard environmental values on private lands, see M. Campbell, "Tools for the Protection of Ecologically Significant Private Lands in Ontario: A Case Study of Marcy's Woods" (2006) 17 J Envtl L & Prac 47.

43   Lieberman, above note 38 at 316.

habitat and to the indirect, cumulative, and unintended consequences of human behaviour as well. In addition to such threats as hunting and capture whether for consumption, ornament, commerce, or other purposes and to the demolition of habitat for agricultural use, urban expansion, or transportation, species have been adversely affected by pollution and the release of toxic substances. New threats—whose ultimate impacts remain imperfectly understood—include the introduction of invasive species, the release of genetically-modified competitors, and climate change. The loss of individual species furthers the loss of planetary biodiversity whose value has recently been articulated in the preamble to Ontario legislation:

> Biological diversity is among the great treasures of our planet. It has ecological, social, economic, cultural and intrinsic value. Biological diversity makes many essential contributions to human life, including foods, clothing and medicines, and is an important part of sustainable social and economic development.[44]

Many observers also find the destruction of other forms of life on the planet to be deeply disturbing from an ethical perspective. For this and other reasons legal measures have been introduced and proposed to safeguard endangered species and in some instances to endeavor to restore their numbers. Protective measures are also in place in relation to livestock, domestic, and exotic animals.

At the international level, the importance of species preservation has been a recurring focus of concern. Since 1975 the *Convention on International Trade in Endangered Species of Wild Flora and Fauna* (*CITES*) has been one of the more prominent international legal initiatives directly affecting the development of species protection measures within Canada and approximately 180 other parties to the convention.[45] With the support of national management and scientific authorities as well as an international secretariat, *CITES* protects wildlife by regulating international trade in designated species. Three categories of species are set out in the convention. First, subject to "exceptional circumstances" outside the commercial context, *CITES* prohibits trade in species that are threatened with extinction. Second, export permits are required for species that are not yet threatened but that might face pressures towards extinction in the absence of effective regulation. A third category comprises species identified by individual *CITES* mem-

---

44 *Endangered Species Act, 2007*, SO 2007, c 6.
45 For a discussion of other international agreements dealing with species and habitat protection, see M Bowman, P Davies, & C Redgwell, eds, *Lyster's International Wildlife Law*, 2d ed. (Cambridge UP, 2010).

bers as protected under their own domestic regulatory regimes. Exports of such species from the listing state are subject to a system of export permits and to the presentation by importers of satisfactory documentation concerning origin.

Canada originally implemented *CITES* through the *Export and Import Permits Act*,[46] which established a permit program to control exports of listed goods and the *Game Export Act*.[47] The sentencing of a young man who entered a plea of guilty to a charge of attempting to export four falcon eggs in contravention of the legislation was the occasion for a moving analysis of the situation by Mr Justice Bourassa of the Territorial Court of the Northwest Territories. Bourassa J began by rejecting the view that this is an offence where there is no real victim and no real impact on the community. The victim, he argued, "is the community of Frobisher Bay, in fact, the community of the Northwest Territories, and indeed, the whole world." By contributing to a further decline of an endangered species of bird, the accused exacerbated a serious situation:

> Here in the Northwest Territories, wildlife is an essential feature of life, and not only that, it is a treasured resource to be conserved, husbanded, protected and fostered, so it can continue to provide sustenance for the body and for the spirit in future ages as it has in past ages. The placing of the gyrfalcon on the export permit control list is precisely for that purpose, to allow the community through its legislation to conserve and protect that species of wildlife.[48]

Subsequent legislation, the *Wild Animal and Plant Protection and Regulation of International and Interprovincial Trade Act*, replaced the previous game-export legislation.[49] The new legislation is designed to conform to *CITES* while providing for federal-provincial cooperation to regulate interprovincial as well as international trade in designated plants and animals. Several key prohibitions have been formulated:

> 6. (1) No person shall import into Canada any animal or plant that was taken, or any animal or plant, or any part or derivative of an animal or plant, that was possessed, distributed or transported in contravention of any law of any foreign state.
>
> (2) Subject to the regulations, no person shall, except under and in accordance with a permit issued pursuant to subsection 10(1) im-

---

46   RSC 1985, c E-19.
47   RSC 1985, c G-1.
48   *Krey v R* (1982), 12 CELR 105 (NWT Terr Ct).
49   SC 1992, c 52 [*WAPPRITA*]; *Wild Animal and Plant Trade Regulations* SOR/96-263.

port into Canada or export from Canada any animal or plant, or any part or derivative of an animal or plant.

(3) Subject to the regulations, no person shall, except under and in accordance with a permit issued pursuant to subsection 10(1), transport from one province to another province any animal or plant, or any part or derivative of an animal or plant.

Moreover, the legislation requires importers, exporters, and transporters to maintain prescribed documentation and makes possession of illegally imported plants and animals an offence.

Regulations implementing *WAPPRITA* establish rules applicable to importation, exportation, and interprovincial transport while providing certain exemptions. In prosecutions to date it is not uncommon to combine charges under *WAPPRITA* with related charges under provincial or territorial wildlife legislation.

While restrictions on inter-jurisdictional trade offered one means of protection for species facing pressures associated with their commercial value and marketability, it has long been evident that more comprehensive measures were required to address a far broader range of threats to habitat, for example, and that the rationales for such measures might also be quite diverse. Thus, the World Conservation Strategy (1980) identified the "preservation of genetic diversity" as one of its principal objectives, while the World Commission on Environment and Development described protection of species and their ecosystems as "an indispensable prerequisite for sustainable development."[50] Parties contracting to the *Convention on Biological Diversity* acknowledged "the intrinsic value of biological diversity and of the ecological, genetic, social, economic, scientific, educational, cultural, recreational, and aesthetic values of biological diversity and its components"[51] and agreed that, "as far as possible and as appropriate" each nation should "[d]evelop or maintain necessary legislation and/or other regulatory provisions for the protection of threatened species and populations."[52]

Within Canada, intergovernmental discussion of general wildlife matters takes place under the auspices of the Wildlife Ministers Council of Canada. Within this framework, agreement was reached in 1996 on a National Accord for the Protection of Species at Risk, a document in which the signatory jurisdictions undertook "to prevent species in

---

50 World Commission on Environment and Development, *Our Common Future* (Oxford UP, 1987) at 166.
51 *Convention on Biological Diversity*, 5 June 1992, 1760 UNTS 79, (1992) 31 ILM 818, preamble.
52 *Ibid*, art 8(k).

Canada from becoming extinct as a consequence of human activity" as well as "to establish complementary legislation and programs that provide for effective protection."

Effective protection will ultimately be subject to assessment against the actual performance record of species protection measures that are put in place. On the nature of appropriate measures, however, there is some basic agreement. Legislation should provide a suitable mechanism for identifying and officially designating endangered species according to their degree of vulnerability. Direct harm to designated species should be prohibited and the habitat required for their survival should be protected, in each case with a suitable set of incentives, penalties, and enforcement mechanisms. Procedures accompanied by adequate financial support should be in place to promote the recovery of endangered species in a timely manner.[53]

Several provinces enacted new legislation or amended existing arrangements subsequent to the intergovernmental accord. Manitoba's *Endangered Species Act* addresses some of the concerns typically raised in connection with such initiatives: What is the status of species protection in relation to other statutory provisions? Is habitat safeguarded in any way? The Manitoba legislation identified an important consideration in environmental law by indicating that the *MESA* provisions will apply in cases of conflict with other legislation, "unless the other Act expressly provides that the other Act prevails."[54] The Act also authorizes regulations relating to habitat[55] and prohibits the disturbance and destruction of the habitat of an endangered, a threatened, or an extirpated species that has been reintroduced.[56] On the other hand, developments may be exempted from the provision of the *Endangered Species* legislation where the minister is satisfied either that the protection and

---

53 D Boyd, *Unnatural Law: Rethinking Canadian Environmental Law and Policy* (Vancouver: UBC Press, 2003) at 190–92.

54 *The Endangered Species Act*, CCSM c.E111, s 2(2) [*MESA*]; *Endangered Species Act, 2007*, SO 2007, c 6; *Endangered Species Act*, SNB 1996, c E-9.101 [*NBESA*]; *Endangered Species Act*, SNS 1998, c 11 [*NSESA*]; *An Act Respecting Threatened or Vulnerable Species*, RSQ c E-12.01 [*Que TVSA*]. In provinces lacking statutory protection for endangered species as such, analogous provisions may sometimes be found in wildlife legislation. See, for example, *Wildlife Act General Regulation*, BC Reg 340/82. Other BC initiatives regarding endangered species were associated with the *Forest Management Code* (now see, for example, *Forest and Range Practices Act*, SBC 2002, s 149.1 on general wildlife measures), or administered through the Conservation Data Centre at the Ministry of Sustainable Resource Management; *Wildlife Act*, SS 1998, c W-13.12, Part V.

55 *MESA*, above note 54, s 9(1)(a).

56 *Ibid*, s 10(1).

preservation of the species or habitat is assured, or that appropriate measures will be established to minimize the impact of the development on protected species and their habitats.

Another approach to the habitat issue appears in Nova Scotia legislation.[57] That province's *Endangered Species Act*, adopted in 1998, distinguishes between the dwelling places and the core habitat of an endangered or threatened species. In contrast with specific dwelling places such as a nest or den, core habitat for an endangered or threatened species encompasses areas that are essential for long-term survival and recovery. While interference, destruction, and disturbance of dwelling places is subject to a general prohibition, core habitat must first be designated by the minister before it will enjoy statutory protection. Core habitat will not be designated for a threatened or endangered species until a recovery plan has been prepared. Thus, while protection may be extended to habitat, that process is subject to potentially significant delays.

On a national basis, significant shortfalls remain between the number of species understood on the basis of scientific assessment to be threatened or vulnerable to extinction and the number of species designated for protection under provincial endangered species or wildlife legislation.[58] The contribution of federal legislation to the overall framework for species protection in Canada is therefore of great importance.

E. FEDERAL SPECIES AT RISK LEGISLATION

Canada's first bird sanctuary was established at Last Mountain Lake in 1887. A noticeable decline in the population of migratory bird species

---

57   *NSESA*, above note 54 .
58   The shortfall in Ontario has been the subject of repeated comment. See *Annual Report 2002–2003: Thinking beyond the Near and Now* (Toronto: Environmental Commissioner of Ontario, 2003) at 134–38; *Annual Report 2004–2005: Planning Our Landscape* (Toronto: Environmental Commissioner of Ontario, 2005) at 148–52. The *Endangered Species Act, 2007*, above note 44, offers the possibility of substantially strengthening the provincial regime on the basis of scientific listing and automatic habitat protection. However, to the extent that courts view ministerial decision making as an exercise of balancing social and economic benefits against the protection of species at risk, there is a strong tendency to show continued deference: *Sierra Club Canada v Ontario (Ministry of Natural Resources)*, 2011 ONSC 4655. See also *Wildlife Act*, RSBC 1996, c 488; *Forest Practices Code of British Columbia*, RSBC 1996, c 159; *Forest and Range Practices Act*, SBC 2002, c 69; *Wildlife Act*, RSA 2000, c W-10; *Wildlife Act*, SS 1998, c W-13.12; *Wildlife Habitat Protection Act*, SS 1983–84, c W-13.2; *Que TVSA*, above note 54; *NBESA*, above note 54.

then spurred federal legislative action nearly a century ago when Canada, in conjunction with the United States, enacted legislation in 1917 to implement a *Migratory Birds Convention* agreed upon the previous year. In 1994, the original statute was replaced by the *Migratory Birds Convention Act, 1994.* This statute provides for a licensing and permit scheme within the context of a general prohibition against possession of migratory birds or commercial transactions involving them.[59] Alongside severe fines for contravention, persons convicted under the *Migratory Birds Convention Act, 1994* are potentially subject to court orders requiring remedial action, community service, and other alternative forms of punishment.[60] In the case of certain offences prescribed by regulation, ticketing with a maximum fine of $1000 is established as an enforcement option.[61] Other federal legislation, the *Canada Wildlife Act*, provides for the designation of national wildlife areas and for other measures related to wildlife research, conservation, and interpretation.[62] The existing federal measures were widely judged to be inadequate in relation to the requirements for national legislation highlighted by the international *Convention on Biological Diversity.*[63]

New legislation, the *Species at Risk Act (SARA)* represents a federal initiative to complement provincial and territorial measures to promote the protection and recovery of endangered species.[64] Many of its provisions were also conceived to enhance other supportive partnerships with governments, Aboriginal communities, conservation organizations, and individuals, or to promote voluntary activity relating to species protection.

The stated purposes of *SARA* are threefold. First, to prevent Canadian wildlife species from becoming extinct or extirpated; second, to provide for the recovery of species that are extirpated, endangered or threatened; and, finally, to provide for the management of species of special concern so as to prevent them from becoming endangered or threatened.[65] A narrower expression of the intent of the legislation as

---

59   *Migratory Birds Convention Act, 1994*, SC 1994, c 22.
60   *Ibid*, ss 13 and 16. For discussion of the interaction of the *Migratory Birds Convention Act, ibid*, provincial fish and game regulation and bylaws under the *Indian Act*, see *R v Blackbird* (2005), 74 OR (3d) 241 (CA).
61   *Migratory Birds Convention Act, 1994*, above note 59, s 19. In June 2008, federal *Migratory Bird Regulations* making it an offence to disturb or destroy the nest of a migratory bird without a permit were held to be constitutional in New Brunswick Provincial Court: *R v JD Irving Ltd* (2008) 37 CELR (3d) 200 (NB Prov Ct).
62   *Wildlife Act*, RSC 1985, c W-9.
63   *Convention on Biological Diversity*, above note 51.
64   *Species at Risk Act*, SC 2002, c 29 [*SARA*].
65   *Ibid*, s 6.

formulated by the Commissioner of Environment and Sustainable Development describes its essential scope of operation: "The purpose of the Act is to protect and recover species considered to be at risk that are found on federal lands or under federal jurisdiction and to protect their critical habitat."[66] The categories of risk—extinct, extirpated, endangered, and threatened—as well as the manner in which this status is determined and the responses then available are central elements of the federal act.

SARA formally constitutes the Committee on the Status of Endangered Wildlife in Canada, (COSEWIC), whose members bring scientific expertise from such fields as conservation biology or genetics, or traditional Aboriginal knowledge of wildlife conservation to the assessment of the status of wildlife species considered to be at risk.[67] This assessment involves classifying such species according to the categories noted above, or determining that insufficient information is available to make the determination, or that the species is not at risk. *SARA* explains the classifications as follows:

> A species is **extirpated** if it no longer exists in the wild in Canada, but exists elsewhere in the wild.
>
> A species is **endangered** if it is facing imminent extirpation or extinction.
>
> A species is **threatened** if it is likely to become an endangered species if nothing is done to reverse the factors leading to its extirpation or extinction.
>
> A species is of **special concern** if it may become a threatened or endangered species because of a combination of biological characteristics and identified threats.[68]

COSEWIC's status assessment reports, including the reasons for the assessment, are included on a public registry provided for under *SARA*.[69] A further designation beyond the expert assessment of COSEWIC is required, however, before a species will be included on the List of Wildlife Species at Risk. This crucial determination is made by the Governor in Council or cabinet with reference to recommendations from the federal minister of the environment.[70] Only species "listed" in this way are eligible for the protective measures available under *SARA*.

---

66   *CESD September Report 2005*, above note 18, ch 8 and 12.
67   *SARA*, above note 64, ss 14–16.
68   *Ibid*, s 2.
69   *Ibid*, s 120. See online: www.sararegistry.gc.ca.
70   *Ibid*, s 27.

When the initial listing decisions under *SARA* were made in 2004, some species assessed as being at risk by COSEWIC were not recommended for listing by the minister, and some species recommended for listing by the minister were not listed by cabinet. Guidelines to suggest criteria for decision making with regard to listing have been under development, but early decisions indicated that socio-economic considerations which are not part of the COSEWIC status assessment influenced the outcome in several cases including a ministerial recommendation against listing Cultus Lake and Sakinaw Lake sockeye salmon.[71]

Table 14.2 Canadian Species at Risk, November 2012

Taxon	Extinct	Extirpated	Endangered	Threatened	Special Concern	Totals
Mammals	3	2	23	17	29	74
Birds	3	2	29	27	20	81
Reptiles	0	4	18	11	9	42
Amphibians	0	2	10	5	6	23
Fishes	7	3	50	40	49	149
Arthropods	0	4	31	5	6	46
Molluscs	1	2	19	3	7	32
Vascular Plants	0	3	94	47	43	187
Mosses	1	1	8	3	4	17
Lichens	0	0	5	3	6	14
Totals	15	23	287	161	179	665

Source: online: www.cosewic.gc.ca/eng/sct0/rpt/csar_e_2012.pdf

By way of protective measures, section 32 prohibits killing, harming, harassing, capturing, or taking "an individual of a wildlife species that is listed as an extirpated species, an endangered species, or a threatened species." Section 33 would prohibit the destruction of the "residence" of species at risk.

These safeguards are subject to significant limitations, however. In particular, the protections apply in the first instance only to federal lands — national parks, military bases, and Indian reserves, for example. That is, the general prohibitions against harming listed species and their residences do not apply to those species on provincial lands unless a further designation is made by the Governor in Council extending the

---

71   *CESD September Report 2005*, above note 18, cc 8 and 14.

prohibitions to provincial lands after it has been determined that provincial laws do not effectively protect the species or their residences.[72] Moreover, as observers have critically noted, the concept of "residence" is of limited scope. Residence for purposes of *SARA* means a specific dwelling place, such as a den, nest, or other similar area, place or structure, that is occupied or habitually occupied by one or more individuals during all or part of their life cycles.[73] The residence of a species is therefore far more restricted in scope than its habitat.

SARA calls for the preparation of recovery strategies for extirpated, endangered or threatened species, assuming that such a strategy would be "technically and biologically feasible."[74] While the requirement for recovery strategies in the interests of listed species has been welcomed, particularly because these may extend protection to critical habitat, observers note that implementation of recovery strategies in the form of action plans calls for a substantial and ongoing financial commitment.[75]

Governmental decisions under *SARA* have been subject to judicial review on a number of occasions. For example, in connection with the identification of critical habitat under section 41(1)(c) as an element of a recovery strategy for a listed species, the competent minister is required to proceed to identify as much critical habitat as possible using the "best available information" at the time. There is no discretion to delay on policy grounds such as the expectation that information may change over time.[76] It has also been determined that the critical habitat of a species must offer a defined geographic area capable of being located on a map and must also provide the physical and biological features required by the listed species for its life processes and survival.[77] The significance of addressing both of these dimensions of critical habitat in a recovery strategy was illustrated with reference to killer whales in a recent decision of the Federal Court of Appeal.[78]

---

72 *SARA*, above note 64, s 34. The prohibitions do apply automatically in the case of migratory birds and aquatic species.

73 Provisions for the protection of "critical habitat" are included elsewhere in the legislation where such habitat is identified in a recovery plan or action strategy for a listed species. See *SARA*, *ibid*, ss 57–64.

74 *Ibid*, ss 37–40.

75 For a survey of reservations that have been expressed about the effectiveness of *SARA*, see DL Vanderzwaag & JA Hutchings, "Canada's Marine Species at Risk: Science and Law at the Helm, But a Sea of Uncertainties" (2005) 36 Ocean Devel & and Int'l L 219 at 224–37.

76 *Alberta Wilderness Assn v Canada (Minister of the Environment)*, 2009 FC 710.

77 *Environmental Defence Canada v Canada (Minister of Fisheries and Oceans)*, 2009 FC 878.

78 *Georgia Strait Alliance v Canada (Minister of Fisheries and Oceans)*, 2012 FCA 40.

The minister of fisheries and oceans, as competent minister in the case of aquatic species, was responsible for developing a recovery strategy for two populations of killer whales following designation of the southern population (85 individuals) and the northern population (205 individuals) as endangered and threatened, respectively. The minister produced a Killer Whales Protection Statement that addressed only the geophysical aspects of critical habitat, prompting the Federal Court of Appeal to underscore the limitations and shortcomings of this restrictive understanding of critical habitat:

> The difficulty in defining critical habitat in terms of geophysical attributes was that some of the most important elements of the critical habitat which had been identified in the recovery strategy were left without protection. The recovery strategy had indeed identified acoustic degradation, chemical and biological contamination and diminished prey availability as key components of the critical habitat of killer whales. Yet the Killer Whales Protection Statement did not consider these components as parts of "critical habitat" for the purposes of the protection order under the SARA. Rather the Killer Whales Protection Statement treated these components as "ecosystem features" to be dealt with through "legislative and policy tools", and not under the SARA.[79]

In the same case, the Federal Court of Appeal clarified conditions governing the use of a protection statement in contrast with a protection order under *SARA*. As the court explained, the legislation set out two options for protecting the critical habitat of the killer whales under the recovery strategy:

> That protection could be achieved either through a protection order made by the Minister under subsections 58(1) and (4) or through a statement by the Minister setting out how the critical habitat or portions of it, as the case may be, would be legally protected under an Act of Parliament.[80]

The minister, as indicated, proceeded by means of a protection statement in which he identified sections of the *Fisheries Act* as sources of protection for the critical habitat of killer whales which could be substituted for a protection order under section 58 of *SARA*. The inadequacy of the designated *Fisheries Act* provisions to meet *SARA* requirements

---

79   *Ibid* at para 32.
80   *Ibid* at para 30.

for legal protection of critical habitat was emphatically underscored by the court:

> Ministerial discretion does not legally protect critical habitat within the meaning of section 58 of the *Species at Risk Act*, and it was unlawful for the Minister to have cited provisions of the *Fisheries Act* in the Killer Whales Protection Statement where such provisions are subject to ministerial discretion.[81]

In a submission to the Commission for Environmental Cooperation, the Center for Biological Diversity has asserted that Canada has failed to effectively enforce *SARA* as a result of its failure to list the polar bear as a threatened or endangered species.[82]

In addition to these proceedings challenging and clarifying the exercise of governmental decision-making powers under *SARA*, prosecutions for offences under the act have been successfully initiated against private parties. For example, a BC boat operator who accelerated towards two orcas that had come to the surface in the vicinity of his boat was convicted and fined for unlawfully harassing a threatened species.[83]

F. ANIMAL WELFARE

Animal welfare law enhances the study of environmental law by extending our awareness of the well-being of non-human species. [84] Indeed it is widely argued that ethical obligations extend to non-human creatures who are in their own right deserving of such considerations as respect and dignity as well as essential security and care.[85] In this regard it may be noted that the preamble to Ontario's *Provincial Animal Welfare Act, 2008*, reads in part: "The people of Ontario and their gov-

---

81 *Ibid* at para 152.

82 Commission for Environmental Cooperation, Submissions on Enforcement Matters, SEM-11-003 (Protection of Polar Bears) (5 December 2011), online: www.cec.org/Page.asp?PageID=2001&ContentID=25143&SiteNodeID=250.

83 "First species at risk conviction a warning to other BC whale watchers," *Campbell River Courier Islander* (10 January 2013).

84 L Bisgould, *Animals and the Law* (Toronto: Irwin Law, 2011); DS Favre, *Animal Law: Welfare, Interests, and Rights* (New York: Aspen Publishers, 2008); E Hughes, *Animal Welfare Law in a Canadian Context*, 3d ed (Edmonton: University of Alberta, 2006).

85 TL Beauchamp & RG Frey, eds, *The Oxford Handbook of Animal Ethics* (Oxford UP, 2011); A Taylor, *Animals and Ethics: An Overview of the Philosophical Debate*, 3d ed (Peterborough ON: Broadview Press, 2009); SJ Armstrong & RG Botzler, eds, *The Animal Ethics Reader*, 2d ed (London: Routledge, 2008).

ernment: Believe that how we treat animals in Ontario helps define our humanity, morality, and compassion as a society."[86]

In addition to provisions found in Canada's *Criminal Code*, jurisdictions across Canada have enacted statutes intended generally to promote the welfare of animals.

- Alberta: *Animal Protection Act*, RSA 2000, c A-41.
- British Columbia: *Prevention of Cruelty to Animals Act*, RSBC 1996, c 372.
- Manitoba: *The Animal Care Act*, CCSM c A84.
- New Brunswick: *Society for the Prevention of Cruelty to Animals Act*, RSNB 1973, c S-12.
- Newfoundland: *Animal Health and Protection Act*, SNL 2010, c A-9.1.
- Northwest Territories: *Dog Act*, RSNWT 1988, c D-7.
- Nova Scotia: *Animal Protection Act*, SNS 2008, c 33.
- Nunavut: *Dog Act*, RSNWT (Nu) 1988, c D-7.
- Ontario: *Ontario Society for the Prevention of Cruelty to Animals Act*, RSO 1990, c O.36.
- Prince Edward Island: *Animal Health and Protection Act*, RSPEI 1988, c A-11.1.
- Quebec: *Animal Health Protection Act*, RSQ c P-42.
- Saskatchewan: *Animal Protection Act, 1999*, SS 1999, c A-21.1.
- Yukon: *Animal Protection Act*, RSY 2002, c 6.

Various prohibitions or regulatory provisions have also been enacted with respect to animals that pose a risk to the health and safety of people. It is an offence, for example, to import, possess, breed, release, or transport exotic or "non-indigenous" wildlife. Provincial legislation provides exceptions in the form of licences to permit individuals to possess exotic wildlife for the purposes of zoological display, educational or scientific research, and animal training for the filming of commercials or movies. The issuance of such permits is usually conditional on the applicant satisfying the government that the exotic animal will be adequately cared for while in captivity. For example, an individual who is granted a captive wildlife licence in Saskatchewan is required to:

(a) keep a fresh and adequate water supply available at all times;
(b) provide a fresh, nutritive, uncontaminated and adequate food supply at least once daily;
(c) keep the enclosure sanitary and in an attractive and presentable condition;
(d) clean the enclosure regularly as required;

---

86   SO 2008, c 16, Preamble.

(e) clean the bathing pool and change or filter the water in the bathing pool regularly as required; and

(f) keep the wildlife in a humane manner.[87]

Animal welfare legislation seeks to prevent cruelty to animals, ordinarily by a prohibition against causing an animal to be in distress. Alberta legislation, for example, indicates that:

an animal is in distress if it is

(a) deprived of adequate shelter, ventilation, space, food, water or veterinary care or reasonable protection from injurious heat or cold,

(b) injured, sick, in pain or suffering, or

(c) abused or subjected to undue hardship, privation or neglect.[88]

With reference to commercial contexts, other legislation places restrictions on game keeping and hunting, or on the manner in which animals may be trapped for fur or other commercial purposes. In May 1999, Canada ratified the *Agreement on International Humane Trapping Standards between the European Community, Canada and the Russian Federation*[89] (AIHTS). The agreement sets out trap performance requirements for trapping nineteen wild animal species, twelve of which are found in Canada. In accordance with the requirements under the AIHTS, Canada has established a national trap certification process that is recognized and administered by all provinces and territories.[90]

In the context of farming, provincial animal protection legislation protects farm animals during most activities.[91] The animal protection legislation defines "animal" very broadly (i.e., any animal that is not a human), and it prohibits a person from causing distress to an animal under his or her possession or ownership. For example, in *R v Bernier*, a commercial beef farmer was charged in a nine-count information under Manitoba's *Animal Care Act* for failing to provide adequate medical attention for, inflicting harm to, and failing to provide an adequate source of food and water for his herd of cows.[92]

Readers will be aware from their own experience of public controversies associated with the broad debate around the welfare of animals.

---

87   *Captive Wildlife Regulations*, RRS, c W-13.1, Reg 13, s 23.

88   *Animal Protection Act*, RSA 2000, c A-41, s 1(2).

89   Official Journal of the European Communities (14 February 1998) L 42, online: www.fur.ca/files/AIHTS.pdf.

90   For Government of Canada information on the agreement, see online: www.registrelep-sararegistry.gc.ca/document/default_e.cfm?documentID=84.

91   Online: www.inspection.gc.ca/animals/terrestrial-animals/humane-transport/provincial-and-territorial-legislation/eng/1358482954113/1358483058784.

92   2012 MBPC 36.

Examples have involved the confinement in zoos or aquaria of animals or marine mammals.[93] Considerable care is taken by the operators of these facilities to respect codes of ethics,[94] or to adhere to standards.[95] Statutory initiatives to strengthen safeguards and standards of protection are being considered in several jurisdictions.

Experimentation with animals is also controversial and subject to regulation and monitoring. For example, the Canadian Council on Animal Care (CCAC) acts as a quasi-regulatory body and sets standards on animal care and use in science that apply across Canada. CCAC has issued specific guideline documents related to farm animals, fish, and wildlife.[96]

FURTHER READINGS

BANKES, N, "Protecting Listed Aquatic Species under the Federal *Species at Risk Act*: The Implications for Provincial Water Management and Provincial Water Rights" (2012) 24 J Envtl L & Prac 19

BEAZLEY, K, & R BOARDMAN, *Politics of the Wild: Canada and Endangered Species* (Toronto: Oxford University Press, 2001)

BENIDICKSON, J, "Canada: Protected Areas Law and Policy" in Barbara Lausche, *Guidelines for Protected Areas Legislation* (IUCN Environmental Policy and Law Paper No 81) (IUCN, 2011)

DOELLE, M, "The Quiet Invasion: Legal and Policy Responses to Aquatic Invasive Species in North America" (2003) 18 International Journal of Marine and Coastal Law 261

ENVIRONMENTAL COMMISSIONER OF ONTARIO, *Redefining Conservation: Annual Report 2009–2010*, Part 3 "Conserving Our Biodiversity"

ENVIRONMENTAL COMMISSIONER OF ONTARIO, *Engaging Solutions: Annual Report 2010–2011*, Part 3 "Biodiversity Matters"

---

93 *Reece v Edmonton (City)*, 2011 ABCA 238.
94 *Code of Professional Ethics* (Ottawa: Canada's Accredited Zoos and Aquariums, 2011), online: www.caza.ca/documents/document_Ethics.pdf.
95 *CAZA Animal Care and Housing Manual* (Ottawa: Canada's Accredited Zoos and Aquariums, 2008), online: www.caza.ca/documents/manual_AnimalCare Housing.pdf; Alberta Zoo Standards Committee, *Government of Alberta Standards for Zoos in Alberta* (Calgary: Government of Alberta, 2005), online: srd. alberta.ca/fishwildlife/zoostandards/documents/Alberta_Govt_Standards_for_ Zoos_in_Alberta_Sept2008.pdf.
96 Canadian Council on Animal Care, "CCAC Guidelines," online: www.ccac.ca/ en_/standards/guidelines.

FINDLAY, CS, *et al*, "Species Listing under Canada's *Species At Risk Act*" (2009) 23:6 Conservation Biology 1609

FLUKER, S, & J STACEY, "The Basics of Species at Risk Legislation in Alberta" (2012) 50:1 Alta L Rev 95.

HUNT, C, "The Public Trust Doctrine in Canada" in J Swaigen, ed, *Environmental Rights in Canada* (Toronto: Butterworths, 1981)

KILLAN, GF, *Protected Spaces: A History of Ontario's Provincial Parks System* (Toronto: Dundurn Press, 1993)

LEIBERMAN, S, "New Game in Town: Conservation Easements and Estate Planning" (1995) 14 E & TJ 309

PASSELAC-ROSS, M, *Overview of Provincial Wildlife Laws*, Wildlife Law Paper No 3 (Calgary: Canadian Institute of Resources Law, 2006)

SWAIGEN, J, "Parks Legislation in Canada: A Comparison of the New *Canada National Parks Act* and Ontario's Existing *Provincial Parks Act*" (2000) 10 J Envtl L & Prac 223

VANDERZWAAG, D, & JA Hutchings, "Canada's Marine Species at Risk: Science and Law at the Helm, but a Sea of Uncertainties" (2005) 36 Ocean Devel & Int'l L 219

WALTON, JH, *Blake's Canadian Law of Endangered Species*, loose-leaf (Toronto: Carswell, 2007–)

WATERS, DWM, "The Role of the Trust in Environmental Protection Law" in DWM Waters, ed, *Equity, Fiduciaries and Trusts* (Toronto: Carswell, 1993)

CHAPTER 15

ENVIRONMENTAL LAW
AND THE CITIZEN

The importance of individual commitment to environmental protection cannot by overemphasized. As Mr. Justice Gonthier of the Supreme Court of Canada remarked, "[e]veryone is aware that individually and collectively, we are responsible for preserving the natural environment,"[1] and legislation is replete with such observations as "all persons should be responsible for the consequences to the environment of their actions,"[2] or with references to "the shared responsibility of all . . . citizens for ensuring the protection, enhancement and wise use of the environment through individual actions."[3] The foundation for these responsibilities is more than exhortation, for responsibilities are conceptually integrated with environmental rights:

> Since the correlative of rights is responsibility, if we have these rights we also have the responsibility to respect those rights in others and must be prepared for constraints on our own conduct. So there is a notion of duty or responsibility, in addition to the notion of entitlement.[4]

How, apart from liability under pollution laws and other general environmental legislation, law promotes and facilitates environmentally responsible individual action is considered in this chapter primarily

1 *R v Canadian Pacific Ltd*, [1995] 2 SCR 1028 at 1075.
2 *Environment Act*, SY 1991, c 5, s 5(2)(e).
3 *Environmental Protection and Enhancement Act*, SA 1992, c E-13.3, s 2(f) *[AEPEA]*.
4 EL Hughes & D Iyalomhe, "Substantive Environmental Rights in Canada" (1998–99) 30 Ottawa L Rev 240.

with reference to the automobile, household waste, and energy efficiency, and the Environmental Choice program for consumers.

A. THE AUTOMOBILE

In 1994 at least one member of almost two-thirds of Canadian households commuted to work; for nearly 80 percent of these households, the motor vehicle was the preferred mode of travel, and the overall situation was very much the same in 2006.[5] Many and varied environmental effects of the automobile demonstrate linkages between individual behaviour and environmental quality. The equally varied responses demonstrate the complexity and the persistence of the challenge of reducing the environmental impact of a way of life.

In terms of impact, now intimately associated with greenhouse gas emissions, automobile traffic makes continuing demands on land-use priorities, leading to the destruction of agricultural and other rural lands and in general undermining environmental amenities.

In responding to the environmental issues raised by automobile use, Canadian governments utilize an array of instruments and incentives. Attempts to address the problem of automobile traffic volume have included improved public-transit services, dedicated lanes to favour multipassenger vehicles, and, on occasion, tax measures designed to promote alternative forms of transport such as bicycles. However, in the early 1990s the only province to see an increase in public-transit use by commuters was British Columbia, where the light-rail transit system was expanded on the lower mainland.[6] In some settings we are now seeing toll charges on designated routes or surcharges for travel during rush hour. Although planning and urban-design principles are gradually being reassessed with a view to reducing actual needs for transport, courts have emphasized the conventional utility of highway corridors. Thus, in *St. Pierre v Ontario (Minister of Transportation & Communications)*, when plaintiffs, rural landowners whose retirement residence was adversely affected by the construction of a highway nearby, brought a nuisance claim, McIntyre J. remarked:

---

5   *Households and the Environment, 1994* (Ottawa: Statistics Canada, 1995) at 14–15 [*Households, 1994*]; *Households and the Environment, 2006* (Ottawa: Statistics Canada, 2007) at 26 [*Households, 2006*].

6   *Households, 1994*, above note 5 at 15.

In the balancing process inherent in the law of nuisance, their utility [highways] for the public good far outweighs the disruption and injury which is visited upon some adjoining lands.[7]

The issue of automobile fuels, once predominantly associated with concern about energy shortages and pricing, is also the subject of renewed interest in relation to vehicle-emission standards, since these have been seriously implicated in the threat of global warming from greenhouse gases.

Like other provinces, British Columbia requires sellers and operators of designated types or classes of motor vehicle to have pollution-control devices installed according to regulatory specifications.[8] The province subsequently instituted annual inspection and certification of exhaust emissions as a precondition of the licence-renewal process for designated classes of motor vehicles in certain parts of the province, notably Vancouver and the Fraser Valley.[9] In southern Ontario, in a comparable program known as Drive Clean, approximately 88 percent of light duty vehicles passed the initial emissions assessment.[10]

British Columbia has also been at the forefront of Canadian efforts to accelerate the introduction of cleaner-technology vehicles on provincial roads. In 1992, the *Motor Vehicle Emissions Reduction Regulation*[11] made low-emission exhaust standards formulated by California's Air Resources Board applicable to all vehicles sold in British Columbia as of 2001. The regulation also called for the creation of an advisory committee on cleaner technology to promote the use of hybrid electric vehicles and vehicles meeting California's low-emission standards.

The statutory foundations of fleet-wide emissions requirements were subsequently reviewed in the context of BC Bill 39-2008, the *Greenhouse Gas Reduction (Vehicle Emission Standards) Act*. A further provincial initiative in BC set out to promote emissions reduction through an incentive program designed to reduce the number of vehicles pre-dating 1988, when catalytic converters were first used on a comprehensive basis. British Columbia's AirCare program, the first in the country, provides comprehensive analysis of testing results and associated benefits.

---

7 *St Pierre v Ontario (Minister of Transportation & Communications)*, [1987] 1 SCR 906 at 916.

8 *Motor Vehicle Act*, RSBC 1996, c 318, s 47.

9 *Ibid*, s 50; *Emission Inspection Exemption Regulation*, BC Reg 320/92. See, generally, AirCare: The Vehicle Emissions Testing Program for Vancouver and the Fraser Valley, online: www.aircare.ca.

10 See online: www.ene.gov.on.ca/environment/en/category/drive_clean/index.htm.

11 BC Reg 517/95. Now see *Exhaust Emission Standards Regulation*, BC Reg 274/2000.

AirCare reported a 31 percent reduction in vehicle emissions for the period 1992–2006.[12]

Fuel-emission standards were strengthened significantly during the 1980s (lead was virtually eliminated[13]) although some anomalies remain. There has been less progress in relation to greenhouse gases originating in automobile use although attention is shifting towards this problem. Federal legislation also authorized the regulation of vehicle fuel-consumption standards, but until recently the power remained dormant.[14] Other measures have been instituted to promote oil recycling as a means of reducing the amount of used oil dumped in garages and yards across the country.[15]

Even after its useful life has come to an end, the conventional automobile presents environmental challenges and risks. The 1990 tire fire at Hagersville, Ontario, showed the hazardous implications of an accumulation of used tires that are ordinarily treated or classified as waste and brought within the overall regulatory framework for waste handling.[16]

Tire taxes have been introduced in several jurisdictions as a possible means of directing remedial resources at a specific problem.[17] In 1995 Manitoba designated motor vehicle tires under provisions of the *Waste Reduction and Prevention Act*[18] and provided for a Tire Stewardship Board with responsibility for establishing and administering a

12   Online: www.aircare.ca.
13   *Gasoline Regulations*, SOR/90-247. For further developments in relation to planned fuel-emission standards, see *Canada Gazette* (17 February 2001).
14   *Motor Vehicle Fuel Consumption Standards Act*, RSC 1985, c M-9, s 3. The 2012 federal budget proposed changes to the vehicle fuel consumption testing requirements to provide for closer alignment with those in the United States. See the *Jobs, Growth and Long-term Prosperity Act*, SC 2012, c 19, ss 25–28.
15   Hon R Grier, *Speaking Notes for Official Launch of Used Oil Depot Network* (21 September 1992).
16   Considerable litigation resulted from the Hagarsville incident: see *Ontario (AG) v Tyre King Tyre Recycling Ltd* (1992), 9 OR (3d) 318 (Gen Div); *Pilot Insurance Co v Tyre King Tyre Recycling Ltd* (1992), 8 OR (3d) 236 (Gen Div); *Re Straza* (1992), 9 CELR (NS) 314 (OEAB). See, generally, RRO 1990, Reg 347, s 2(1)(9); and *Baldwin Rubber Recycler and Stephen Sager v Ontario (Ministry of the Environment)*, [2001] OERTD No 21.
17   *Retail Sales Tax Amendment Act, 1989 (No 2)*, SO 1989, c 38, s 3; *Environment Tax Act*, SPEI 1991, c 9. The BC Tire Stewardship Plan operates pursuant to the *Recycling Regulation*, BC Reg 449/2004. The Multi-Materials Stewardship Board of Newfoundland and Labrador embarked upon a scrap tire management program in 2001.
18   CCSM c W40.

scrap tire waste-reduction and prevention program (WRAP).[19] Levies of $2.80 on each new tire are directed to a fund that will finance the scrap tire WRAP program and associated expenditures including research and education initiatives.[20] Ontario launched a Used Tires Program in 2009 to manage all the used tires generated annually and to address the cleanup of existing tire stockpiles. Industry stewards (identified as brand owners and first importers) are required to fund the cost of the Ontario Tire Stewardship.[21]

Other automobile components such as air-conditioning units present a noteworthy post-consumer threat to the ozone layer as CFCs from cooling units leak out into the atmosphere. With respect to the challenge of CFCs and related chemicals, while the automobile represents only one element of the problem, significant efforts are under way to reduce or eliminate the use and release of these chemicals into the atmosphere. Steps taken in Ontario and British Columbia, among other provinces, to regulate automobile air-conditioning, servicing, and disposal practices, and eventually to eliminate designated chemicals from new vehicles, illustrate alternative means of achieving these objectives.[22] More generally, the automobile CFC process illustrates the way in which global concerns addressed internationally by means of conventions and protocols have begun to have a direct impact on the operations of manufacturers, service personnel, and consumers.

B. THE HOME ENVIRONMENT

Initiatives directed at environmental problems emerging from residential settings often combine financial incentives with regulation and other inducements to lessen the cumulative environmental impact of contemporary lifestyles. While the most comprehensive reductions in residential environmental impacts will ultimately result from col-

---

19   *Tire Stewardship Regulation, 2006*, Man Reg 222/2006. See also *Scrap Tire Management Regulations*, RRS, c E-10.2, Reg 9; and *Tire Designation Regulation*, Alta Reg 95/2004.

20   An earlier BC initiative along similar lines was successfully challenged on the grounds that it had been implemented on the basis of policy rather than by means of a regulation-making power that had been provided within the *Waste Management Act* for this purpose. See *Valley Rubber Resources Inc v British Columbia (Minister of Environment, Lands and Parks)*, [2001] BCJ No 629 (SC).

21   *Used Tires*, O Reg 84/03 (made under the *Waste Diversion Act, 2002*, SO 2002, c 6).

22   *Ozone Depleting Substances and Other Halocarbons Regulation*, BC Reg 387/99; *Ozone Depleting Substances and Other Halocarbons Regulation*, Man Reg 178/2005.

lective planning and land-use decisions to reduce urban sprawl and the associated burden of infrastructure requirements, and energy use, especially for transportation, the design of individual homes is also an important influence. Energy Solutions Alberta in association with Climate Change Central, a public-private partnership, offers information and advice to homeowners or prospective purchasers on a wide range of energy-saving and pollution-reducing innovations. These run from solar housing projects through transportation options to advice on detergents and Christmas lights.[23] Residential construction is itself a major contributor to the waste burden. Thus, some jurisdictions have taken steps to recover costs associated with the disposal of such materials as construction and demolition waste.[24]

Some measures to lessen residential environmental impacts are directed toward individual behaviour while others address the characteristics of household products and appliances at the point of manufacture and distribution.

The importance of waste reduction for sustainable development is suggested by primary statistics. Based on 2002 data, the residential, commercial, and non-hazardous industrial waste streams, which together constitute Canada's municipal garbage, amounted to 30.4 million metric tonnes.[25] As more graphically stated by *Regeneration: Toronto's Waterfront and the Sustainable City*, "every year, homes, institutions, industries and commercial establishments in the GTA [Greater Toronto Area] produce 4.5 million tonnes (5 million tons) of garbage—enough to fill six SkyDomes to the roof."[26] Another perspective highlighting the enormous environmental importance of certain forms of waste reduction is indicated by a commentary on the benefits of recycling aluminum soft drink cans:

> First, recycling these containers conserves very large amounts of energy and raw materials. Second, the extraction and processing of the raw materials needed to make new cans release large quantities of pollutants and greenhouse gases. In 2003, the World Watch Institute estimated that making 1 million tonnes of aluminum cans from virgin materials requires 4.95 million tonnes of bauxite ore and the

---

23 Online: www.climatechangecentral.com.

24 See for example, *Quebec's Regulation respecting the charges payable for the disposal of residual materials*, RRQ, c Q-2, r 43.

25 M Cameron et al, *Human Activity and the Environment: Feature Article: Solid Waste in Canada* (Ottawa: Statistics Canada, 2005).

26 Royal Commission on the Future of the Toronto Waterfront, *Regeneration: Toronto's Waterfront and the Sustainable City: Final Report* (Toronto: Queen's Printer, 1991) at 28.

energy equivalent of 35 million barrels of crude oil. Recycling the cans, in comparison, saves all of the bauxite and more than 75 per cent of the energy, and avoids production of about 75 per cent of the pollutants. Recycling just one aluminum can saves enough electricity to run a laptop computer for 4 hours.[27]

Various elements of the household component of the waste stream invite different treatment and responses. For example, significant efforts are now made to encourage the redirection of organic materials to composting either on a residential basis or at community composting facilities. By 2006, the national average participation in composting had risen to 27 percent, a figure that encapsulates a wide range from 70 percent participation in Halifax down to below 10 percent in Quebec City.[28]

Perhaps the most visible symbol of environmental responsibility at the individual level are blue box recycling programs, implemented on an experimental basis in Kitchener, Ontario, in 1981 and subsequently introduced in other communities in various jurisdictions across Canada.[29] The original curbside recycling programs have become increasingly sophisticated. Once confined to private residences in urban settings, they have been introduced to multi-unit apartment complexes and in a growing number of rural communities. Once operated on the assumption of voluntary participation, they are now occasionally implemented as mandatory programs. Once restricted to a limited range of recyclable materials including newsprint, glass, and tin cans, they have diversified to accept a wider range of recyclables. Once premised on the hope that markets for recycled material would emerge on the basis of reliable supply, the programs have subsequently attempted to address structural obstacles to the creation of markets. All these developments have taken place in the context of an ongoing debate about the relationship among reduction, reuse, and recycling as long-term strategies to deal with waste. In Alberta, a recycling fund was established to administer waste minimization and recycling programs and to encourage related educational and research activities.[30] To promote recycling, regulations made blue box management systems compulsory

---

27   *Annual Report, 2003–2004: Choosing Our Legacy* (Toronto: Environmental Commissioner of Ontario, 2004) Part 4, "Ministry Environmental Decisions" at 81.
28   *Households, 2006* above note 5 at 19–20.
29   For background information on the development and introduction of recycling programs and the optional design features available, see VW MacLaren, "Waste Management: Current Crisis and Future Challenge" in B Mitchell, ed, *Resource Management and Development: Addressing Conflict and Uncertainty* (Toronto: Oxford UP, 1991) 38.
30   *AEPEA*, above note 3, s 171.

in designated Ontario municipalities. Additional measures to promote composting and the diversion of household and yard waste from landfill were implemented simultaneously.[31]

Despite high participation levels (especially in relation to paper recycling), blue box programs have encountered some criticism. The need for supplementary financial support for recycling where markets are not readily available or where prices remain below collection costs has presented challenges. Manitoba, under the Manitoba Product Stewardship Plan, arranged funding by means of a levy on newspapers and on beverage containers (other than dairy product containers and containers to which a deposit-refund scheme applies.)[32] In Ontario, where refillable bottles have been heavily displaced by cans and plastic containers, the industry contributed direct financial support to the Blue Box program. Pursuant to the *Waste Diversion Act*, companies responsible for paper and packaging in the consumer marketplace ("stewards") are expected to finance half the net cost of the municipal Blue Box waste diversion program.[33]

Another focus has been on an actual reduction in the level of curbside deposits. Thus, proposals to charge for waste collection have emerged in some settings. These arrangements typically require the purchase of a tag or sticker which must be affixed to garbage bags set out for collection, or perhaps the use of specially marked bags. The arrangements may provide that all household waste be accompanied by confirmation of payment, or the system may permit a base level of one or more bags to be collected from each household before charges apply. In Peterborough, Ontario, a proposal for user fees was advanced in part to provide an incentive for the separation of recyclables, and in part to ensure more appropriate revenue contributions from users. Although this plan was defeated in a municipal referendum, amendments to the *Municipal Act* later confirmed the authority of municipalities to charge user fees in lieu of property rates for services.[34] User-pay approaches

31   O Reg 101/94. See also *Environmental Management Act*, SBC 2003, c 53, Part 3 "Municipal Waste Management," requiring municipal waste-management plans, including provisions for recycling.

32   *Waste Reduction and Prevention Act*, above note 18; *Multi-Material Stewardship (Interim Measures) Regulation*, Man Reg 39/95 (repealed by Man Reg 35/2011).

33   *Waste Diversion Act*, above note 21, s 25(5); O Reg 273/02; online: www.bottlebill. org/legislation/canada/ontario.htm; and www.stewardshipontario.ca. A comparable arrangement respecting the apportionment of recycling costs exists in Quebec where Eco Entreprises Quebec, on behalf of the container and packaging industries, contributes to municipal associations representing the municipal operators of curbside recycling programs.

34   Now see *Municipal Act, 2001*, SO 2001, c 25, Part XII, "Fees and Charges."

have been introduced in several other communities. The city of Edmonton introduced an elaborate curbside collection program as early as 1989 to provide for the pickup of about a dozen separate categories of household waste, and began to explore user-pay alternatives.[35]

Despite refinement and extension, the effectiveness as well as the cost of the blue box or curbside approach have been questioned, particularly in comparison with deposit/refund systems to promote reuse. The latter approach adds a direct economic incentive to reinforce the essentially voluntary underpinnings of curbside recycling. On the basis of effectiveness, that is, recovery rates, western Canadian provinces resisted pressure from soft drink manufacturers to replace their established deposit/refund systems with curbside recycling. Instead, modifications to these systems were examined with a view to reducing the inequities and inconvenience associated with the chain of relationships among bottlers, distributors, retailers, and consumers.[36] In Nova Scotia, a deposit-refund scheme for beverage containers involving a series of payments linking distributors, retailers, and consumers was challenged on the grounds that it constituted an indirect tax that was outside the constitutional jurisdiction of the province. The Nova Scotia Court of Appeal concluded that the arrangement was within the powers of the provincial legislature to enact as it was merely ancillary to a valid regulatory scheme.[37] Several individual initiatives addressed the use and disposal of corrosive, toxic, flammable, and reactive consumer products that collectively constitute household hazardous waste (HHW). British Columbia's Waste Reduction Commission, for example, formulated a discussion paper on HHW strategy that reviewed both consumer-based and producer-based approaches to the problem. On the consumer side, the strategy identified several alternative approaches to collection and deposit arrangements, but it placed greater emphasis on the principle of product stewardship, which may be promoted through taxes, deposit/refund systems, or industry levies reinforced through regulation. Yet, in a conclusion similar to that reached in most

---

35 MacLaren, above note 29 at 41. For further information on innovations in Edmonton, see City of Edmonton, "History of Waste Management in Edmonton," online: www.edmonton.ca/for_residents/garbage_recycling/history-of-waste-management-in-edmonton.aspx.

36 For background discussion, see Recycling Council of British Columbia, "Recap: E-Newsletter for Members of the Recycling Council of British Columbia," online: rcbc.bc.ca/node/624. Current arrangements are found in the *Recycling Regulation*, above note 17. See also New Brunswick's *Beverage Containers Act*, RSNB 2011, c 121.

37 *Cape Breton Beverages v Nova Scotia (AG)* (1997), 24 CELR (NS) 319 (NSCA).

other jurisdictions where the threats posed by HHW have been carefully examined, British Columbia's discussion paper argued that

> HHW is, first and foremost, a problem of *source reduction or product/material substitution* . . . . The primary challenge is to increase source reduction and product/material substitution in order to reduce the amount of material entering the HHW stream.[38]

In British Columbia the brand-owners and sellers of consumer paint products (whether the coatings are latex, oil, or solvent-based) are responsible for ensuring that an approved post-consumer paint-stewardship program is in place.[39] Such stewardship programs provide for the collection, transportation, and final treatment of post-consumer paint and are expected to incorporate pollution-prevention principles by moving progressively from treatment or containment to recovery of energy, recycling, or reuse. Similar initiatives were subsequently introduced in relation to solvents, pesticides, gasoline, and pharmaceuticals in British Columbia.[40] Saskatchewan amended *The Environmental Management and Protection Act* to provide for comparable product-management programs.[41]

So called e-wastes associated with electronic devices pose distinctive and increasing challenges. To reduce the volume of these materials finding their way to landfills, the Canadian Council of Ministers of the Environment (CCME) has formulated Canada-Wide Principles for Electronics Stewardship and targeted responses have been contemplated. Alberta, for example, has introduced fees on computers and televisions sold in the province. These charges help to offset costs that must be borne somehow in relation to collecting, transporting, and recycling the metal and chemical components of modern consumer technology.[42] While televisions and computers may be the most readily imagined examples of e-waste, the category extends to other audio-visual equip-

---

38 British Columbia, Ministry of Environment, Lands and Parks, Toxic Reduction Branch, Environmental Protection Division, *Household Hazardous Waste Strategy* (Discussion Paper) (March 1993) at 6.

39 *Recycling Regulation*, above note 17. For its part, the federal government has moved to reduce the initial presence of hazardous substances such as lead and mercury in products entering the home environment. See *Surface Coating Materials Regulation*, SOR/2005-109.

40 *Recycling Regulation*, above note 17.

41 *The Environmental Management and Protection Act, 2002*, SS 2002, c E-10.21, ss 81(1)(aa)(iii)–(viii).

42 Alberta's environmental fees have been applicable to televisions and computers since 1 February 2005 under a program administered by the Alberta Recycling Management Authority. See online: www.albertarecycling.ca.

ment, telecommunications devices, a range of products associated with sports and leisure pursuits, as well as numerous tools, navigational instruments and so on. An emerging focus of concern is the environmental impact of pharmaceuticals and a wide range of personal care products. These have been associated with abnormalities in aquatic species and initiatives have been introduced to reduce the volume of unused products entering the municipal waste stream en route to land fill or simply being flushed away in the course of household cleaning.[43]

There are indications that a broader approach to waste diversion for a wider range of products in the form of "extended producer responsibility" (EPR) schemes is gaining support. Following a discussion paper prepared under the *Waste Diversion Act, From Waste to Worth: The Role of Waste Diversion in the Green Economy*, Ontario initiated steps towards EPR in relation to a series of sectors.[44] More generally, the CCME published a Canada-wide Action Plan for Extended Producer Responsibility in 2009. The plan outlines a set of guiding principles applicable to questions of design and implementation as well as in relation to environmental goals with the hope that "environmental benefits are maximized while economic dislocations are minimized."[45]

Both the federal and provincial governments have enacted legislation to foster more efficient use of energy. At the national level, the *Energy Efficiency Act* provides for standard-setting, testing, research, and promotional initiatives to encourage the efficient use of energy and the use of alternative energy sources. Those involved in the manufacture, importation, sale, or leasing of energy-using products are required to ensure that such products comply with prescribed standards and labelling requirements.[46] In a 2012 report, the federal Office of Energy Efficiency indicated that some 600,000 homes across the country were saving about $400 million in energy costs each year as a result of retrofitting. The *National Energy Code of Canada for Buildings* (2011) or equivalent

---

43 *Annual Report 2004–2005: Planning Our Landscape* (Toronto: Environmental Commissioner of Ontario, 2005) at 179–85.

44 Ontario, Ministry of the Environment, *From Waste to Worth: The Role of Waste Diversion in the Green Economy: Minister's Report on the Waste Diversion Act 2002 Review* (October 2009), online: www.dsa.ca/fileBin/mediaLibrary/WDA_Report. pdf. See also, *Waste Diversion Act, 2002*, above note 21; and *Stewardship Ontario Regulation*, O Reg 33/08.

45 Canadian Council of Ministers of the Environment, *Canada-Wide Action Plan for Extended Producer Responsibility* (29 October 2009) at 10.

46 *Energy Efficiency Act*, SC 1992, c 36; and *Energy Efficiency Regulations*, SOR/94-651. Amendments proposed in 2007 were designed to facilitate the phasing out of most uses of incandescent lighting by 2012 and to strengthen packaging requirements to enhance consumer understanding of included information.

measures is now being implemented in a number of provinces and a revised code designed to promote continuous improvement in the energy performance of Canadian buildings is under consideration.[47]

Residential appliances and equipment have been an important focus of attention at the provincial level. Ontario's *Energy Efficiency Act* specifically identified central air conditioners, clothes dryers, clothes washers, dishwashers, freezers, furnaces, heat pumps, ovens, ranges, refrigerators, room air conditioners, pool heaters, and water heaters as appliances to which provincial energy-efficiency standards would apply.[48] Quebec more generally defined "appliance" as "any new household, commercial, industrial or institutional electrical or hydrocarbon-fuelled appliance."[49] Long ago, the House of Commons Standing Committee on Environment and Sustainable Development clearly envisaged an even broader effort, arguing that "energy efficiency should be more important in Canada than in other countries, and must be our first priority."[50]

C. GREEN MARKETING AND ENVIRONMENTAL CHOICE

Next we consider the position of the citizen as consumer, one illustration of the potential of pricing and markets to promote environmental benefits.[51] David Cohen, in examining arguments that are used to support the privatization of environmental protection through market-based incentives, identifies an underlying assumption that is directly relevant to the issue of green consumerism:

> Using markets to deliver environmental quality assumes that there is a substantial number of individuals who are demanding improve-

---

47   Canada, Energy and Mines Ministers' Conference, *Moving Forward on Energy Efficiency in Canada: Achieving Results to 2020 and Beyond* (Ottawa: Government of Canada, 2012) online: oee.nrcan.gc.ca/sites/oee.nrcan.gc.ca/files/files/pdf/EMC_Report_e.pdf.

48   *Energy Efficiency Act*, RSO 1990, c E.17, repealed 9 September 2009: see SO 2009, c 12, Sched A, ss 18(2) and 19.

49   *An Act Respecting the Energy Efficiency of Electrical or Hydrocarbon-Fuelled Appliances*, RSQ c.E-1.2, s 1. This Act has been replaced by *An Act Respecting Energy Efficiency and Innovation*, RSQ c E-1.3. Other provincial legislation includes the *Energy Efficiency Act*, RSBC 1996, c 114; the *Energy-efficient Appliances Act*, SNS 1991, c 2; and *the Energy Efficiency Act*, RSNB 2011, c 149.

50   Canada, House of Commons, Standing Committee on Environment, *Out of Balance: The Risks of Irreversible Climate Change* (Ottawa: Queen's Printer, 1991) at 27.

51   See Chapter 17.

ments in their local and global environments, and who will express that demand in their economic decisions. The vast untapped demand for environmental benefits can be harnessed to the dynamically efficient and creative engine of industry for the benefit of us all.[52]

Viewing the issue directly from the perspective of environmental quality, Cohen explains:

> The decision to privatize environmental regulation, thereby using the market to deliver environmental benefits, recognizes that through all of our personal, professional, and corporate decisions we are continuously creating and transforming the environment. The use of markets to deliver environmental benefits recognizes that consumers are environmental planners.[53]

There are some indications to suggest that environmental consumerism is a potentially robust phenomenon. In the food sector, the demand for certified organic items has grown substantially. And, in relation to consumer electronic goods, by 2005, according to a Pollara survey, 88 percent of Canadians were prepared to pay more for such goods if they were more energy efficient, or generally less wastefully produced, or were produced using recycled materials.[54] Major retailers in other sectors have responded with initiatives intended to satisfy the expectations of more environmentally-conscious shoppers. In the service sector as well, programs are emerging to advise users of hotel or marina facilities, for example, that their environmental concerns are being addressed.[55] Apart from the theoretical base and these somewhat anecdotal illustrations, the policy-making challenge in employing market mechanisms to enhance environmental protection raises a number of issues around information, the reliability of that information, and mechanisms for communicating it to potential purchasers of goods and services. Consumers can be well meaning and wrong, just as one can be incapable of acting on a latent disposition to contribute to a better environment (even at some personal cost or sacrifice) because of unavailable or unreliable information. Regulated standards relating to disclosure or product-per-

52   DS Cohen, "The Regulation of Green Advertising: The State, the Market and the Environmental Good" (1991) 25 UBC L Rev at 228, n 10.
53   *Ibid* at 230.
54   A Macey, *Retail Sales of Certified Organic Food Products, in Canada, in 2006* (Truro, Nova Scotia: Organic Agriculture Centre of Canada, 2007), online: www.ota.com/pics/documents/RetailSalesOrganic_Canada2006.pdf.
55   The Canadian hotel industry has developed a "Green Leaf" eco-rating program. Marina operators are involved in a comparable initiative. See online: www. boatingontario.ca/CleanMarine/Facts.aspx.

formance characteristics and approved-use and disposal practices were introduced to overcome some of these types of deficiencies. It has also been argued, however, that the proliferation of unverifiable claims by producers calls for even more stringent regulation in order to ensure the integrity of the green marketplace.[56]

The Environmental Choice[57] initiative was announced in 1988 and dubbed by one observer a variation on the "good housekeeping seals of approval."[58] Following identification of environmental considerations relevant to particular product categories and the formulation of performance guidelines, time-limited licences to use the "ecologo" were issued to applicants whose products complied with the established standards. The relevant criteria were not without controversy as commentators point variously to the importance of production considerations, characteristics associated with actual use, and concerns around ultimate disposal, noting that these are often difficult to determine, and perhaps even more difficult to compare. Even if relevant information on alternative products and alternative production processes has been developed, it is typically in the hands of private manufacturers who, for reasons of competitive advantage and on the basis of their research investment, will be reluctant to place it into general circulation.[59] Once certified or approved, licensees pay fees and submit to ongoing monitoring on the assumption that the logo will contribute to sales by attracting environmentally sensitive consumers. Purchasers presumably enjoy environmental satisfaction and are relieved of the otherwise burdensome tasks of searching for and assessing information.

The range of products and services certified under the Environmental Choice program was limited at the outset. Initial categories in-

---

56 Louis-Philippe Lampron, "L'encadrement juridique de la publicité écologique fausse ou trompeuse au Canada : une nécessité pour la réalisation du potentiel de la consommation écologique?" (2004-2005) 35 RDUS 449.

57 For general information on the original framework of the Environmental Choice program, see *Environmental Choice Program: Certification Overview* (Ottawa: Environment Canada, 2001).

58 M Rankin, "Economic Incentives for Environmental Protection: Some Canadian Approaches" (1991) 1 J Envtl L & Prac 256. These programs are by no means confined to the Canadian market. See, for an international survey, the US EPA study *Environmental Labelling Issues, Policies and Practices Worldwide* (Washington, DC: Environmental Protection Agency, 1998).

59 For a brief survey of issues associated with environmental standard-setting for labelling programs, see K. Harrison, "Promoting Environmental Protection Through Eco-Labelling: An Evaluation of Canada's Environmental Choice Program" in K Webb, ed, *Voluntary Codes: Private Governance, the Public Interest and Innovation* (Ottawa: Carleton University, 2004) 279–82.

cluded re-refined motor oil; insulation made from recycled wood-based cellulose fibre; products made from recycled plastic; reduced-pollution water-based paints; fine paper made from recycled paper; newsprint made from recycled paper; reduced-pollution solvent-based paints; reusable cloth diapers; residential composters; ethanol-blended gasoline; reusable shopping bags; water conserving devices; and rechargeable batteries. The range of products has continued to expand, and alternative forms of certification emerged more recently when administration of the eco-labelling program was placed in the hands of an environmental marketing firm.[60]

One subject of particular significance in light of market growth is the use of the descriptor "organic." Controls on the use of the term were initially absent, allowing producers to self-declare. This era was followed by a more generalized set of characteristics developed by producer associations with a view to standardizing the concept to a greater degree. Most recently, the Canadian Food Inspection Agency put forward a proposed regulatory framework to deal with continuing uncertainties through the creation of a "Canada organic" standard.[61] The federal government subsequently enacted Organic Products Regulations under the *Canada Agricultural Products Act*.[62] Pursuant to subsection 13(1) of the regulations:

A certification body shall certify an agricultural product as organic if it determines, after verification, that:

(*a*) in the case of a multi-ingredient product, at least 70% of its contents are organic and its composition complies with the requirements set out in CAN/CGSB 32.310 [*Organic Production Systems—General Principles and Management Standards*];

(*b*) the substances used in the production and processing of the agricultural product are those set out in, and used in the manner described in, CAN/CGSB 32.311 [*Organic Production Systems—Permitted Substances List*]; and

(*c*) the production and processing methods used and the control mechanisms in place comply with the requirements set out in

---

60   Online: www.ecologo.org/en/certifiedgreenproducts.
61   Canadian Food Inspection Agency, *Organic Products Regulation*, Canada Gazette Part I (2 September 2006). For additional information, see "Organic Production Systems—General Principles and Management Standards," online: www.tpsgc-pwgsc.gc.ca/ongc-cgsb/programme-program/normes-standards/internet/bio-org/documents/032-0310-2008-eng.pdf.
62   *Canada Agricultural Products Act*, RSC 1985, c 20 (4th Supp); and *Organic Products Regulations, 2009*, SOR/2009-176.

CAN/CGSB 32.310 and with the general principles respecting organic production set out in that standard.

For its part, the government of British Columbia has established authority to control the manner and circumstances in which environmental labels or certification may be used.[63]

The initiatives noted in this chapter are merely representative of ways in which modifications in individual behaviour—induced through informal mechanisms and education, or encouraged by changes in the legal framework—have significant potential to lessen environmental damage and reduce high levels of personal resource consumption.

FURTHER READINGS

BARTENSTEIN, K, & S Lavallée, "L'écolabel est-il un outil du protectionnisme vert?" (2003) 44 C de D 361

COHEN, D, "Procedural Fairness and Incentive Programs: Reflections on the Environmental Choice Program" (1993) 31 Alta L Rev 544

DOELLE, M, "IT Waste Management in Canada: From Cost Recovery to Resource Conservation?" (2006) 5 CJLT 59

HAGEN, PE, "Product-based Environmental Regulations: Europe Sets the Pace" (2006) 6 Sustainable Development Law and Policy 63

Households and the Environment 1994 (Ottawa: Statistics Canada, 1995)

MACLAREN, VW, "Individualized Waste Management: Integrated Approaches" in B Mitchell, ed, Resource and Environmental Management in Canada, 3d ed (Don Mills, ON: Oxford UP, 2004) 371

URMETZER, P, et al, "Solutions to Environmental Problems: The Case of Automobile Pollution" (1999) 25 Canadian Public Policy

WEBB, K, ed, Voluntary Codes: Private Governance, the Public Interest and Innovation (Ottawa: Carleton Research Unit for Innovation, Science and Environment, Carleton University, 2004)

---

63   Environmental Management Act, above note 31, s 118.

CHAPTER 16

CONSULTATION, ALTERNATIVE DISPUTE RESOLUTION, AND VOLUNTARY MEASURES

Interest in innovative mechanisms for managing environmental conflicts has been stimulated by distinctive features of environmental decision making, notably those related to the element of uncertainty, and by the limitations of conventional forms of adjudication. Court-based proceedings, either civil or criminal, in which legal adversaries endeavour to persuade decision makers, who often lack environmental or scientific experience, that a particular standard of proof of controversial and uncertain scientific hypotheses has or has not been met, are both costly and slow. The scope for participation by interested parties who are not immediately affected by the matters in question is typically constrained by rules of standing, and the comparatively narrow range of remedial powers traditionally available to judicial decision makers has often frustrated the design of appropriate solutions. Administrative decision making by officials, boards, and tribunals is typically more flexible, but it often remains cumbersome and unsatisfying as well as being vulnerable to the complexities of judicial review. Further pressures for new approaches derive from financial constraints that severely restrict the ability of governments to pursue traditional enforcement strategies culminating in prosecution.

Several procedures associated with new forms of participation, or even "social learning" have been seen as increasingly attractive. Such approaches "emphasizing dialogue, mutual learning, and the continual evolution of ideas" are considered well-suited to "circumstances characterized by high uncertainty," for only arrangements of this type "enable individuals, organizations and communities to construct legitimate end points, identify appropriate technologies for reaching those end points, and navigate through the complexities of human-nature interactions."[1]

In the context of disputes, several mechanisms under the umbrella of alternative dispute resolution (ADR) have become quite common. Negotiation between or among interested parties, though certainly not a recent innovation, and mediation involving a disinterested third party are prominent examples. In addition, experiments with other mechanisms such as round tables, co-management councils, and commissions have been used to avoid conflicts or to minimize their scope and consequences.

A. CONSULTATIVE PROCEDURES AND THE ROUND TABLE MOVEMENT

As discussed elsewhere in this text, environmental assessment processes, environmental bills of rights, intervenor status, standing rules, and so on facilitate public participation especially in relation to specific projects or development initiatives.[2] But as a National Task Force on Environment and Economy emphasized some twenty-five years ago, the participatory aspirations of constituencies such as business, labour, Aboriginal peoples, and environmentalists extend beyond the project level to include an interest in the fundamental policy-making and planning processes that determine the framework for more concrete initiatives. The task force recommended that senior decision makers from these diverse groups be involved in a new process of consultations known as "round tables." It explained that

> [t]his process must involve individuals who exercise influence over policy and planning decisions and who can bring information and different views to the debate. The process should be designed to work towards consensus and to exert direct influence on policy and deci-

---

1 A Diduck, "Incorporating Participatory Approaches and Social Learning" in B Mitchell, ed, *Resource and Environmental Management in Canada*, 3d ed (Don Mills, ON: Oxford UP, 2004) at 498.

2 For information on public participation in connection with federal environmental assessment procedures under the *Canadian Environmental Assessment Act, 2012*, SC 2012, c 19, s 52, see "Public Participation," online: www.ceaa-acee.gc.ca/default.asp?lang=En&n=8A52D8E4-1.

sion makers at the highest levels of government, industry, and non-government organizations.[3]

On the basis of deliberations concerning environment-economy issues, task force members concluded that round tables—each of which would include environment, resource, and economic development ministers—should make recommendations "directly to the First Ministers of their respective jurisdictions."[4]

Endorsement by a national task force whose membership included cabinet ministers from seven jurisdictions contributed to the rapid adoption of the proposal. Round tables, however, were not implemented on a uniform basis across Canada, and some early observers doubted the ability of these new institutions as originally constituted to remedy the deficiencies that inspired their creation:

> [O]nly a few of the Round Tables are structured, composed, and mandated in such a way that they could reasonably be expected to legitimize the environmental policy process through enhanced representation and participation of non-corporate actors in the process of environmental policy formulation and implementation.[5]

Supporters emphasized the contribution of consensus-building and the benefits of the exchange of ideas, as well as the possibility of furthering mid-stream transformation of outlook without having to wait for intergenerational changes in leadership. Indeed, in announcing the membership of the National Round Table on the Environment and the Economy (NRTEE), Prime Minister Mulroney anticipated that "this new organization will help us all re-think how we make decisions, personally and within institutions, that affect our common environment."[6]

In 1993 legislative measures were taken to formalize the status of the National Round Table. As expressed in the statute, the Round Table's role was to be that of catalyst in identifying, explaining, and promoting the principles and practices of sustainable development. This was to be accomplished on the basis of research and advice to governments, business sectors, and the public.[7]

---

3   *Report of the National Task Force on Environment and Economy* (Downsview, ON: Canadian Council of Resource and Environment Ministers, 1987) at 10.
4   *Ibid.*
5   M Howlett, "The Round Table Experience: Representation and Legitimacy in Canadian Environmental Policy-Making" (1990) 97 Queen's Quarterly 580 at 588.
6   Prime Minister's Office, Release, "Membership of National Round Table on Environment and Economy Announced" (28 March 1989).
7   *National Round Table on the Environment and the Economy Act*, SC 1993, c 31, s 4.

The NRTEE developed its mandate imaginatively and comprehensively over roughly twenty years. Among projects of particular interest was a collaborative initiative with Statistics Canada on environmental and sustainable development indicators. NRTEE anticipated that such indicators have the potential to assist environmental policy making in the same way that economic indicators contribute to economic and fiscal management.[8]

The introduction of multi-stakeholder forums such as the NRTEE involves structural changes in participation. These bodies accommodate a greater range of interests and to some degree even suggest a transformation in philosophical attitudes towards a policy-making process in which the state no longer serves as the exclusive representative of environmental interests; instead, environmental groups and individuals would assume direct involvement.[9] Despite its pioneering accomplishments, the NRTEE was eliminated in 2013 as a cost-saving measure and on the assumption by government that other organizations would be able to fulfill its role.

B. ALTERNATIVE DISPUTE RESOLUTION PROCEDURES

Processes of alternative dispute resolution, notably negotiation and mediation, are now regularly employed to assist in the resolution of environmental disputes. Possibilities for negotiation exist throughout the environmental regime, some more and some less attractive, depending on the perspective of the observer. Negotiations are common in relation to the formulation and issuance of licences, approvals, or administrative orders.[10] This appears to some as a desirable means of providing for effective consultation and of ensuring flexibility and responsiveness in decisions that might otherwise be rigid and inappropriate. On

---

8   *Environment and Sustainable Development Indicators for Canada* (Ottawa: NRTEE, 2003). Other areas in which the NRTEE has pursued collaborative and consultative initiatives include brownfields redevelopment, Aboriginal interests in resource development, sustainable transportation, and regional environmental governance of the boreal forest.

9   G Hoberg, "Governing the Environment: Comparing Canada and the United States" in K Banting, G Hoberg, & R Simeon, eds, *Degrees of Freedom: Canada and the United States in a Changing World* (Montreal: McGill-Queen's UP, 1997) at 341.

10 For recent examples from BC, see online: www.wcel.org/our-work/environmental-dispute-resolution-fund.

the other hand, there are those who caution that bargaining between regulators and industry may constitute an abdication on the part of the former and an effort at manipulation on the part of the latter. In the context of non-compliance with the possibility of prosecution under contemplation, further negotiations are likely concerning remedial measures and the form of administrative orders.

Negotiations about environmental matters take place in settings other than licensing and prosecutorial confrontations. For example, a process approximating what is known in the US context as negotiated rule-making was utilized in the original development of regulations under the *Canadian Environmental Assessment Act.* Representatives of several federal departments, provincial governments, and various industry associations, public-interest organizations, and Aboriginal groups deliberated extensively in connection with the development of a set of regulations known as the Law List, the Inclusion List, the Exclusion List, and the Comprehensive Study List.[11] In addition, negotiation has contributed to the resolution of specific controversies in relation to environmental assessment. Thus, Ontario's EAB relied upon negotiations between the proponent and public-interest interveners in the formulation of many of the terms and conditions that emerged from the province's Timber Management Class Environmental Assessment.[12]

A mediation exercise conducted in British Columbia serves to illustrate numerous procedural aspects of ADR in an environmental context. The Sandspit Small Craft Harbour mediation was set up in 1992 to respond to concerns about the environmental impact of a proposed harbour for recreational boaters provided for under the Canada–British Columbia South Moresby Agreement. The matter was of interest to several federal departments, two BC ministries, and various parties on the Haida Gwaii/Queen Charlotte Islands. On the basis of initial terms of reference prepared by federal officials in consultation with a range of interested parties, the principal parties themselves subsequently formulated ground rules for the mediation.

As described in the ground rules, the objective of the mediation was to identify an acceptable way to provide Sandspit with small-craft harbour facilities pursuant to the South Moresby Agreement and to do so in a manner consistent with the principles of sustainable development and with the federal Environmental Assessment and Review Process. The potentially relevant options were broadly defined to encompass

---

11   These arrangements have been replaced by amendments to the federal environmental assessment regime, as discussed in Chapter 12.

12   Ontario Environmental Assessment Board, *Reasons for Decision, Class Environmental Assessment* (EA–87–02) (20 April 1994).

mitigation and/or compensation for fish and bird habitat, the possible relocation of the harbour to alternative sites, and alternative harbour designs. The parties agreed to operate on a consensus basis and to establish smaller working groups to address procedural and substantive issues as they arose.

Parties, at their own expense, were entitled to use appropriate experts. To preserve flexibility, and to encourage exploration of the options, the parties agreed "that any specific offers or statements made during the proceedings are not to be used by any other participant to attempt to bind any other party or person in any other forum including pending or future administrative procedures or litigation." The mediator, in addition to substantive contributions, was responsible for documenting discussions and for developing the text of any agreement as it was reached. From the fact that consensus was ultimately reached on an environmentally acceptable site and design for the harbour, observers have concluded that the process was successful.[13]

In some cases the use of alternative dispute resolution is based on general discretionary authority, but it is increasingly common to see formal statutory reference to ADR schemes.[14] One of the more elaborate provisions is found in the Nova Scotia legislation, which authorizes the minister of the environment to use conciliation, negotiation, mediation, or arbitration in the resolution of either procedural or substantive conflicts concerning disputes about various certificates and approvals under the statute, or concerning responsibility for rehabilitating a contaminated site.[15]

Given the wide range of settings in which ADR processes are now being employed—from the development of regulations to issues resolution in environmental assessment and the determination of terms and conditions in the licensing context—several legal matters must be considered. What basis of authority exists for the use of ADR and what restrictions are inherent in that authority? It may be necessary to determine who, as a matter of law, is entitled to participate in ADR proceedings, especially when these are used to replace other mechanisms. In what respects can official decision makers commit themselves in advance to the substantive outcome of ADR without misusing their discretion through fettering

---

13   J Mathers, *Sandspit Small Craft Harbour Mediation Process: A Review and Evaluation* (Ottawa: Supply & Services, 1995).

14   *Canadian Environmental Assessment Act*, SC 1992, c 37, s 30; *Environment Act*, CCSM c E125, s 3(3); *An Act to Amend the Environmental Protection Act*, RSNWT 1988 (Supp), c 117, s 4; *Environmental Assessment Act*, SBC 2002, c 43, s 27(3)(f); *Environmental Assessment Act*, RSO 1990, c E.18, as am by SO 1996, c 27, s 3.

15   *Environment Act*, SNS 1994-95, c 1, s 14.

or dictation? And to what degree or through what mechanisms can agreements be made enforceable on behalf of participants or by third parties whose interests may have been affected by the outcome?[16]

In the case of Aboriginal consultations as constitutionally-mandated, judicial guidance provides some indication of the essential requirements that must be met. A constitutional duty to consult arises as the SCC concluded in *Haida Nation v British Columbia (Minister of Forests)* "when the Crown has knowledge, real or constructive, of the potential existence of the Aboriginal right or title and contemplates conduct that might adversely affect it."[17] A more elaborate analysis of the question "when does the duty to consult arise?" was provided in *Rio Tinto Alcan Inc v Carrier Sekani Tribal Council* where the courts set out a three-part test.[18] Firstly, knowledge by the Crown of a credible claim to land or resources, even if unproven, will trigger the duty to consult, where — secondly — there is Crown conduct or a decision to be taken with a potential for adverse impact on the claim or right in question. The claimant must further demonstrate "a causal relationship between the proposed government conduct or decision and a potential for adverse impacts on pending Aboriginal claims or rights."[19]

What is required to satisfy the duty to consult varies with the circumstances. "The richness of the required consultation increases with the strength of the *prima facie* Aboriginal claim and the seriousness of the impact on the underlying Aboriginal or treaty right."[20] Courts have considered, for example, how existing treaty arrangements would affect consultation arrangements and have observed that where a treaty has been concluded, "[i]f a process of consultation has been established in the treaty, the scope of the duty to consult will be shaped by its provisions."[21] Where a decision-making tribunal has explicitly or implicitly received powers to consult and possesses associated remedial powers, its procedures may fulfil the requirements.[22]

---

16   For an introduction to some of these questions, see D Brach *et al*, "Overcoming the Barriers to Environmental Dispute Resolution in Canada" (2002) 81 Can Bar Rev 396 at 410–14.

17   2004 SCC 73 at para 35.

18   2010 SCC 43 at paras 31–50 [*Rio Tinto Alcan*].

19   *Ibid* at para 45.

20   *Ibid* at para 36.

21   *Beckman v Little Salmon/ Carmacks First Nation*, 2010 SCC 53 at para 67.

22   *Rio Tinto Alcan*, above note 18. For a very detailed account of an extended process of consultation concerning water management and Aboriginal property rights, see *Halalt First Nation v British Columbia (Minister of Environment)*, 2012 BCCA 472. For the case of a municipality as the decision-making tribunal, see *Neskonlith Indian Band v Salmon Arm*, 2012 BCCA 379.

Considerations of this nature have, in some circumstances, encouraged the introduction of joint management arrangements intended to provide on an ongoing basis for participation in operational decisions affecting environment and resources.

C. CO-MANAGEMENT INSTITUTIONS

Co-management has been described as "power-sharing in the exercise of resource management between a government agency and a community or organization of stakeholders."[23] Co-management institutions, highly variable in their design, present opportunities for greater levels of direct citizen involvement in environmental decision making. Comprehensive co-management regimes may encompass a full range of resource-management functions including habitat protection, long-range planning, and even enforcement practices.

Although not restricted to situations involving native communities, co-management arrangements have been particularly attractive where Aboriginal uses of fish and wildlife or other natural resources are involved.[24] The basis for evaluation of co-management in Canada remains fairly limited, but positive results have been anticipated on the basis of American experience: "The legal rights of tribes to protect habitat eventually led environmentalists and recreational fishermen to ally with them in the struggle to protect fish habitat, and a strong lobby which could no longer be identified on racial lines was created."[25] Yet, in Canada, co-management mechanisms involving Aboriginal participation have been more readily implemented in areas far removed from centres of population. Arrangements concerning fish and wildlife management under the *Inuvialuit Final Agreement* and institutions to facilitate Aboriginal participation in certain land-use decisions under the *James Bay and Northern Quebec Agreement* are prime examples.[26]

---

23   EW Pinkerton, "Overcoming Barriers to the Exercise of Co-management Rights" in M Ross & JO Saunders, eds, *Growing Demands on a Shrinking Heritage: Managing Resource-Use Conflicts* (Calgary: Canadian Institute of Resources Law, 1992) 276 at 277. See also Diduck, above note 1 at 519–21.

24   *Wale v British Columbia (AG)*, [1991] 1 SCR 62.

25   E Pinkerton, "Introduction: Attaining Better Fisheries Management through Co-Management — Prospects, Problems, and Propositions" in E Pinkerton, ed, *Co-Operative Management of Local Fisheries* (Vancouver: University of British Columbia Press, 1989) at 12.

26   *The Western Arctic Claim: The Inuvialuit Final Agreement* (Ottawa: Indian Affairs and Northern Development, 1984); *James Bay and Northern Quebec Native Claims Settlement Act*, SC 1976–77, c 32; *An Act Approving the Agreement*

In 1992 British Columbia appointed a commissioner of resources and environment (CORE) with responsibility for advising cabinet "in an independent manner on land use and related resource and environmental issues in British Columbia and on the need for legislation, policies and practices respecting these issues."[27] The mandate encompassed the development and monitoring of regional land-use planning, community-based participatory processes concerning land use, resources, and environmental management, and a related dispute-resolution system.[28]

In a public report entitled *Land Use Strategy for British Columbia*, the commissioner recommended shared decision making involving representatives of government and affected interests, while in a *Draft Land Use Charter* for the province he urged the use of processes to "promote decision-making through the building of consensus amongst diverse perspectives and stakeholders." Although influential in promoting many apparently promising initiatives, CORE was abolished in 1996.[29]

D. VOLUNTARY MEASURES

Environmental protection measures in Canada have historically relied on government intervention in the form of command and control regulation. However, the importance of supplementary and alternative approaches, particularly of a preventive nature, and implemented on a voluntary basis, is now widely—if not universally—accepted.

Voluntary environmental protection measures by industry may be implemented with or without government participation, assistance, and consent, and with or without the involvement of other interested parties. Thus, although the federal government established a National Office of Pollution Prevention in 1991 to promote voluntary efforts to reduce the use and emission of pollutants, programs can be initiated without the involvement of the office. They may be adopted at the level of individual companies with comparatively localized objectives, or they may be developed in relation to the needs and capacity of an entire

---

Concerning James Bay and Northern Québec, SQ 1976, c 46. For the suggestion that environmental protection requirements may be derived from Aboriginal resource rights, see LM Collins and M Murtha, "Indigenous Environmental Rights in Canada: The Right to Conservation Implicit in Aboriginal Rights to Hunt, Fish, and Trap" (2010) 47 Alta LR 959.

27 *Commissioner on Resources and Environment Act*, RSBC 1996, c 59, s 3(1).

28 *Ibid*, s 4(2).

29 For an assessment by a prominent participant in the CORE process, see S Owen, "Land Use Planning in the Nineties: CORE Lessons" (1998) 25 Environments 14.

industry or sector with much broader implications. Moreover, despite their voluntary nature originating in the consent of parties to them, voluntary measures can be designed to promote compliance through sanctions or financial and other penalties.[30]

Depending on the manner in which they are implemented, voluntary agreements may offer a range of potential attractions to participants. From the perspective of government, voluntary measures have the potential to enhance overall environmental performance with lower expenditures in financial and human resources terms. Insofar as government acknowledges the limitations and deficiencies of the command and control model, voluntary initiatives permit a more collaborative relationship with industry and may facilitate accelerated environmental improvement in comparison with more cumbersome and inflexible regulations. To the extent that voluntary measures are established for industry groups or industrial sectors, some of the burden of monitoring performance and encouraging backsliders may be assumed by industry associations rather than public officials.

For its part, industry may find voluntary measures attractive ways to forestall regulations that are often perceived as rigid and insufficiently tailored to the requirements and opportunities available to individual businesses depending on their particular geographical and competitive setting. Opportunities to improve operational efficiency without lowering environmental performance are felt to be more readily available where industry has some scope to determine voluntarily the manner in which it will fulfil social, including environmental, obligations. In addition, public relations advantages may accrue to businesses and industries that can demonstrate a genuine commitment to the environment, particularly one that is independent of official coercion and perhaps produces beneficial results faster than or in excess of regulatory timetables.

The voluntary nature of participation in such arrangements does not mean they are without legal consequences or implications. The leading analysts of linkages between law and voluntary codes in Canada have provided an inventory of possible relationships, including the following observations:

- Voluntary standards can be referentially incorporated in law, with or without the approval of the initiators of the voluntary standard;

---

30   See, for example, *Environmental Code of Practice for Underground Storage Tank Systems Containing Petroleum Products and Allied Petroleum Products*, 1993 edition (Ottawa: Canadian Council of Ministers of the Environment, National Task Force on Storage Tanks, 1993), online: www.ccme.ca/assets/pdf/pn_1055_e.pdf.

- Voluntary code initiatives may elaborate on and refine the generality of legislative requirements;
- Voluntary initiatives may be explicitly created pursuant to legislative instruments;
- Governments may support the development of voluntary initiatives that have extraterritorial application when it might be difficult to directly legislate these non-domestic operations;
- Non-compliance with voluntary standards can be a factor used by judges in determining liability, compliance with voluntary standards can aid firms in avoiding penal liability or reducing penalties, and the terms of voluntary programs can be judicially imposed on firms as part of sentencing;
- Consumers or affected members of a community may be able to use the commitments made in voluntary initiatives in legal actions to assist in establishing liability against individual firms and against those who develop voluntary standards;
- Disciplinary actions by code administrators against participating firms may be undertaken through contractual actions;
- The fairness of disciplinary actions taken by code administrators toward participating firms may be reviewed by the courts and, if found wanting, the actions can be overturned.[31]

The nature of voluntary initiatives is illustrated in the following examples.

1) Environmental Performance Agreements

Environment Canada's National Office of Pollution Prevention undertook to develop environmental performance agreements with individual companies, industrial sectors, other departments of the federal government, and provincial and territorial agencies.[32] Such agreements have been described as "a complement, a precursor or an alternative to regulations." In developing guidelines for EPAs, Environment Canada identified four general principles: effectiveness, credibility, accountability, and efficiency. Design criteria were formulated in order to ensure overall compliance with those principles:

---

31 K Webb & A Morrison, "The Law and Voluntary Codes" in K Webb, ed, *Voluntary Codes: Private Governance, the Public Interest and Innovation* (Ottawa: Carleton Research Unit for Innovation, Science and Environment, Carleton University, 2004) 97 at 98–99.

32 *Policy Framework for Environmental Performance Agreements* (Ottawa: Environment Canada, 2001).

- clear objectives and measurable results;
- clearly defined roles and responsibilities;
- provision for consultation;
- public reporting;
- incentives and consequences;
- verification of results;
- a regulatory backstop;
- continuous improvement.

Roughly a dozen agreements have been completed within this framework, while five are currently in effect.[33]

2) ARET

Beginning in the early 1990s, a program known as ARET (Accelerated Reduction/Elimination of Toxics) encouraged voluntary action on the part of industrial users of toxic substances in order to reduce or eliminate toxics. The ARET committee was constituted as a stakeholders' group including representatives from health and professional bodies and government along with eight industry associations. After screening some 2000 substances and grouping them on the basis of persistence, bioaccumulation, and toxicity criteria, the committee designated some for virtual elimination after a 90 percent reduction from 1993 levels by 2000. Others were targeted for a 50 percent reduction in emissions by the same year.

Significant emission reductions were achieved by the participants who constitute approximately 70 percent of the members of ARET's sectoral stakeholder associations.[34] Despite the accomplishments attributable to the ARET initiative, overall assessments have been mixed.[35]

3) Responsible Care

Responsible Care, a set of initiatives of the Canadian Chemical Producers' Association and subsequently adopted on a much wider international

---

33   Online: www.ec.gc.ca/epe-epa/default.asp?lang=En&n=0D8C879E-1.

34   Environment Canada, Health Canada, & Industry Canada, *Environmental Leaders 1: Voluntary Commitments to Action on Toxics through ARET: Accelerated Reduction/Elimination of Toxics* (Hull: ARET Secretariat, 1995). For critical comment on the ARET initiative, see DL VanNijnattan, "The ARET Challenge" in R Gibson, ed, *Voluntary Initiatives: The New Politics of Corporate Greening* (Peterborough, ON: Broadview Press, 1999) at 93–100.

35   DL VanNijnattan & E Darier, "Voluntary Instruments" in W Leiss, ed, *In the Chamber of Risks: Understanding Risk Controversies* (Montreal: McGill-Queen's UP, 2001) at 221.

basis,[36] was designed to demonstrate at a sectoral level that the industry is capable on a voluntary basis of implementing effective measures for managing chemicals, chemical products, and processes. CCPA members agreed to guiding principles that underlie the program and that require each to

- ensure that its operations do not present an unacceptable level of risk to employees, customers, the public, or the environment;
- provide relevant information on the hazards of chemicals to its customers, urging them to use and dispose of products in a safe manner, and make such information available to the public on request;
- make Responsible Care an early and integral part of the planning process leading to new products, processes, or plants;
- increase the emphasis on the understanding of existing products and their uses and ensure that a high level of understanding of new products and their potential hazards is achieved prior to and throughout commercial development;
- comply with all legal requirements that affect its operations and products;
- be responsive and sensitive to legitimate community concerns; and
- work actively with and assist governments and selected organizations to foster and encourage equitable and attainable standards.[37]

In addition, codes of practice have been formulated in relation to such issues as community awareness and emergency response; research and development; manufacturing; transportation; distribution; and hazardous-waste management. Reported results suggest that substantial advances were made at the outset. In particular, on the basis of aggregated member-company data, the CCPA reported a 50 percent reduction in chemical emissions between 1992 and 1996 and a decline in the frequency and severity of transportation incidents. The Responsible Care initiative was also associated with benefits to participating companies including anticipated insurance-premium reductions, a reduction in the potential for legal claims, lower workers' compensation costs, and reduced delays in permit-application proceedings.[38]

---

36   International Council of Chemical Associations, see online: www.icca-chem.org/en/Home/Responsible-care.
37   *Responsible Care: A Total Commitment* (Ottawa: Canadian Chemical Producers' Association, 1992).
38   *Does Responsible Care Pay? A Primer on the Unexpected Benefits of the Initiative* (Ottawa: Canadian Chemical Producers' Association, 1996). For an overview of the evolution and effectiveness of the program, see J Moffett & F Bregha, "Responsible Care" in Gibson, ed, *Voluntary Initiatives*, above note 34 at 69.

Responsible Care has been credited with certain direct accomplishments in the sense that the health and safety records of participating firms had improved while several categories of emissions to the environment were measurably decreased. In addition, the mere existence of the program is understood to have served indirectly to elevate the expected levels of performance of those seeking to demonstrate that they had exceeded the common law's negligence standard or that they had, in the context of a regulatory prosecution, demonstrated due diligence. The significance of this experience raised interesting policy questions: "To what extent should resource strapped government enforcement officials use membership in Responsible Care as the basis for placing a CCPA company low on their list of inspection priorities? Is it valid to assume that a Responsible Care company will always comply with environmental regulations?"[39] As the authors of a comprehensive assessment of the program reported in response to this inquiry:

> Even its strongest proponents do not argue that participation in Responsible Care is a guarantee of compliance. Instead, proponents argue, Responsible Care certification means that companies will more likely *want* to be in compliance. Thus, they say, a Responsible Care company will less likely be systematically non-compliant, and will more likely be willing to take remedial measures without a threat of prosecution if it inadvertently falls out of compliance. In short, it is argued, government enforcement officials should treat Responsible Care companies differently from other companies by emphasizing a compliance-promotion approach versus a stricter enforcement approach.[40]

4) Environmental Management Systems, ISO 14000 and Certification

The International Standards Association (ISO), a Geneva-based federation of standards bodies, is recognized for its work in the formulation of technical product and design standards applicable in a range of contexts.

The ISO 14000 series establishes environmental standards in two general categories, generally in the form of guidelines rather than as prescriptive specifications. In relation to management systems and organization evaluation, standards addressing environmental manage-

---

39   J Moffet, F Bregha, & MJ Middelkoop, "Responsible Care: A Case Study of a Voluntary Environmental Initiative" in Webb, ed, *Voluntary Codes*, above note 31, 177 at 188.

40   *Ibid* at 189.

ment systems, environmental auditing, environmental site assessments, and environmental performance evaluation have been formulated. In relation to product evaluation, the ISO 14000 series includes guidelines on environmental labelling and life-cycle product assessment, as well as a document dealing with terms and conditions relevant to self-declared environmental claims.

Related initiatives include ISO 20121, a management standard for event sustainability. ISO 20121 was utilized, for example, in connection with the 2012 Olympic Games in London, England, but offers guidance to event organizers at all scales on factors relevant to environmental, social, and economic sustainability.

A general description of the nature of the ISO 14000 series may be helpful in understanding its scope and intent:

> The standards are "systems" standards, not legal standards and are intended to harmonize, not invent standards. They are designed to help organizations manage their environmental obligations such as compliance with legal requirements; the standards do not supplant nor do they add to existing legal requirements. They do not tell organizations how to run their businesses but rather define management processes to be followed to control the impact an organization will have on the environment. The organization identifies what environmental impacts are acceptable within the legal framework.

Nonetheless, it is of interest to note that Canadian courts, on sentencing a corporation convicted of an environmental violation, have occasionally ordered the company to obtain certification pursuant to ISO 14001, the Environmental Management Systems Specification.[41]

The prevalence of environmental management system initiatives has produced assessment and commentary designed to enhance their effectiveness. The Commission for Environmetal Cooperation, for example, in a guidance document on improving environmental performance and compliance identified the following essential elements of an EMS:[42]

(a) The EMS should be based upon a documented and clearly communicated policy.

(b) The EMS should provide a means to identify, explain, and communicate all environmental requirements and voluntary under-

---

41 *R v Prospec Chemicals Ltd* (1996), 19 CELR (NS) 178 (Alta Prov Ct); see also *R v Calgary* (2000), 35 CELR (NS) 253 (Alta Prov Ct).

42 *Improving Environmental Performance and Compliance: 10 Elements of Effective Environmental Management Systems* (Montreal: Commission for Environmental Cooperation, 2000).

takings to all employees, on-site service providers, and contractors, whose work could affect the organization's ability to meet those requirements and undertakings.

(c) The EMS should establish specific objectives and targets for:

1) Achieving and maintaining compliance with environmental compliance.

2) Environmental performance demonstrating continuous improvement in regulated and non-regulated areas.

3) Pollution prevention that emphasizes source reduction.

4) Sharing information with external stakeholders on environmental performance against all EMS objectives and targets.

(d) Sufficient personnel and resources should be provided to meet the objectives and targets of the EMS.

(e) The EMS should identify and provide for the planning and management of all the organization's operations and activities with a view to achieving the EMS objectives and targets.

(f) The organization should establish and maintain documented procedures for preventing, detecting, investigating, promptly initiating corrective action, and reporting (both internally and externally, in accordance with applicable laws) any occurrence that may affect the organization's ability to achieve the EMS objectives and targets.

(g) The EMS should establish procedures to ensure that all personnel whose job responsibilities affect the ability to achieve the EMS objectives and targets have been trained and are capable of carrying out their responsibilities.

(h) The EMS should describe how these elements will be integrated into the organization's overall decision making and planning.

(i) The EMS should establish procedures to ensure maintenance of appropriate documentation relating to its objectives and targets and should also ensure that those records will be adequate for subsequent evaluation and improvement of the operation of the EMS.

(j) The EMS should require periodic, documented, and objective auditing of the organization's performance in achieving the objectives and targets.

In certain sectors, with forestry a leading example, independent third party certification procedures to assess the sustainability of operations have achieved widespread acceptance, typically in conjunction with mechanisms to ensure stakeholder participation.[43]

---

43   GT Rhone, D Clarke, & K Webb, "Two Voluntary Approaches to Sustainable Forestry Practices" in Webb, ed, *Voluntary Codes*, above note 31 at 249; B Cashore,

In British Columbia, for example, a coalition of forest industry operators, environmental organizations, and coastal First Nations concluded the Great Bear Rainforest Agreements in 2006 within a supportive planning framework advanced by the provincial government. The agreement endorsed ecosystem-based management and First Nations land management planning, all for eventual reconciliation and integration into British Columbia's Central Coast Land and Resource Management Plan.[44]

On a broader scale, and initially without government involvement, nearly two dozen forest companies concluded the Canadian Boreal Forest Agreement in 2010 with a number of environmental organizations and charitable foundations. The agreement calls for a range of efforts to accelerate completion of a representative network of protected areas within the boreal region; support protective measures for boreal species at risk with an immediate priority on caribou; introduce sustainable forest management practices consistent with ecosystem management principles; enhance forest sector prosperity, including the well-being of dependent communities; promote marketplace recognition for the environmental performance of participating forest industry organizations. For their part, the forest companies immediately suspended logging across roughly 29 million hectares of licensed timber lands covering caribou habitat. Correspondingly, the participating environmental organizations undertook to suspend campaigns against the forest industry participants aimed at discouraging sales of their forest products and ownership of company shares.[45] Some delays have subsequently been experienced in securing government approval for more detailed forest management arrangements necessary to confirm implementation.[46]

G Auld, & D Newsom, *Governing Through Markets: Forest Certification and the Emergence of Non-State Authority* (New Haven, CT: Yale University School of Forestry and Environmental Studies, 2003), online: www.yale.edu/forestcertification/pdfs/2003/03_modified_auld_newsom.pdf.

44 M Howlett, J Rayner, & C Tollefson, "From Government to Governance in Forest Planning? Lessons from the Case of the British Columbia Great Bear Rainforest Initiative" (2009) 11(5–6) Forest Policy and Economics 383.

45 *The Canadian Boreal Forest Agreement*, 18 May 2010, online: canadianborealforestagreement.com/media-kit/Boreal-Agreement-Full.pdf.

46 H Scoffield, "Red tape threatens delicate logging truce in Ontario" *The Globe and Mail* (10 February 2013), online: www.theglobeandmail.com/news/national/red-tape-threatens-delicate-logging-truce-in-ontario/article8434734. See also, B Jang, "Greenpeace backs down from Resolute accusations" *The Globe and Mail* (20 March 2013).

E. CONCLUSION

The proliferation of voluntary and alternative forms of decision making and performance setting may facilitate elaboration of the environmental management framework. Notwithstanding the enthusiasm with which these developments were initially embraced in some quarters, certain criticisms and reservations have been voiced. These often concern the relationship between the new approaches and the prior regime to which they are described as alternatives. That prior regime, comprised of legislative, regulatory, and administrative rules and procedures, embodies or is subject to a number of fundamental public law values: opportunities for participation, the accountability of decision makers, review mechanisms of an administrative or judicial nature, formal monitoring and reporting procedures, and so on. The maintenance of these valued attributes is at some risk in the context of new forms of environmental governance and decision making unless steps are taken to ensure their continuation.[47] It is therefore unsurprising that in its assessment of the federal government's initial approach to climate change, an approach heavily reliant upon voluntary action, the Commissioner of the Environment and Sustainable Development emphasized the fundamental importance of good management, notably the need for overall governance and accountability. The CESD emphasized, in particular, that those involved should clearly understand and agree to their roles and responsibilities. Results-based targets and timetables will facilitate implementation and monitoring which in turn may identify necessary adjustments.[48]

---

47   K Beattie, "Fairness, Openness and Self-Regulation: An Examination of Administrative Law Values and the Use of Voluntary and Self-Regulatory Measures for Environmental Protection" (2001) 14 Can J Admin L & Prac 1; AR Lucas, "Voluntary Initiatives for Greenhouse Gas Reduction: The Legal Implications" (2000) 10 J Envtl L & Prac 89. See also, *2000 May Report of the Commissioner of the Environment and Sustainable Development* (Ottawa: Office of the Auditor General, 2000), online: www.oag-bvg.gc.ca/internet/English/parl_cesd_200005_08_e_11235.html.

48   *2006 September Report of the Commissioner of the Environment and Sustainable Development* (Ottawa: Office of the Auditor General, 2006) at 25, online: www. oag-bvg.gc.ca/internet/English/parl_cesd_200609_e_936.html.

FURTHER READINGS

BAETZ, MC, & AB TANGUAY, "'Damned if You Do and Damned if You Don't': Government and the Conundrum of Consultation in the Environmental Sector" (1998) 41 Canadian Public Administration 395

BEATTIE, K, "Fairness, Openness and Self-Regulation: An Examination of Administrative Law Values and the Use of Voluntary and Self-Regulatory Measures for Environmental Protection" (2001) 14 Can J Admin L & Prac 1

DOELLE, M, & AJ SINCLAIR, "Mediation in Environmental Assessments in Canada: Unfulfilled Promise?" (2010) 33 Dal LJ 117

GIBSON, RB, ed, *Voluntary Initiatives: The New Politics of Corporate Greening* (Peterborough, ON: Broadview Press, 1999)

KIRTON, J, & M TREBILCOCK, *Hard Choices, Soft Law: Voluntary Standards in Global Trade, Environment and Social Governance* (Ashgate, 2004)

KRAHN, PK, "Enforcement versus Voluntary Compliance: An Examination of the Strategic Enforcement Initiatives Implemented by the Pacific and Yukon Regional Office of Environment Canada, 1983–1998" in *5th INECE Conference Proceedings*, vol 1 (Washington, DC: INECE Secretariat, 1998) 25

LUCAS, AR, "Voluntary Initiatives for Greenhouse Gas Reduction: The Legal Implications" (2000) 10 J Envtl L & Prac 89

MOFFET, J, & F BREGHA, "An Overview of Issues with Respect to Voluntary Environmental Agreements" (1998) 8 J Envtl L & Prac 63

PARDY, B, "Asking the Dog to Guard the Puppy Chow: Three Objections to Environmental Voluntarism" (2003) 12 J Envtl L & Prac 129

PINKERTON, E, ed, *Co-operative Management of Local Fisheries: New Directions for Improved Management and Community Development* (Vancouver: UBC Press, 1989)

ROUNTHWAITE, HI, "Alternative Dispute Resolution in Environmental Law: Uses, Limitations and Potential" in E Hughes, AR Lucas, & WA Tilleman, eds, *Environmental Law and Policy*, 3d ed (Toronto: Emond Montgomery, 2003) c 14

TOLLEFSON, C, F Gale, & D Haley, *Setting the Standard: Certification, Governance, and the Forest Stewardship Council* (Vancouver: UBC Press, 2008)

WEBB, K, ed, *Voluntary Codes: Private Governance, the Public Interest and Innovation* (Ottawa: Carleton Research Unit for Innovation, Science and Environment, Carleton University, 2004)

WINFIELD, M, "Alternative Service Delivery in the Natural Resources Sector: An Examination of Ontario's Forestry Compliance Self-Inspection System" (2005) 48 Canadian Public Administration 552

CHAPTER 17

ECONOMIC INSTRUMENTS

Economic instruments, another of the more recently prominent approaches to environmental protection, take a variety of forms. Not all of the economic incentives currently in place or under consideration are particularly innovative, even though efforts to appreciate the environmental implications of their operation have intensified in recent years. Nor is the focus entirely on initiatives that are explicitly directed at improving environmental conditions, for the environmentally-adverse impacts of other policy measures is of equal significance. A simple example is subsidies to the agriculture, energy, transportation, and industrial sectors which have encouraged waste, pollution, and excessive natural resource consumption.[1] Although this is an important matter, it will not receive much attention here.

After discussing the general attractions of economic instruments and market mechanisms from an environmental perspective, as well as noting some of the reservations that are expressed about them, this chapter describes non-tax instruments, tax incentives, and public funds dedicated to the environment. The chapter concludes with reference to insurance and financial institutions in light of their potential to use economic incentives in the interests of environmental protection.

---

1   *Improving the Environment through Reducing Subsidies* (Paris: OECD, 1998); *Environmentally Harmful Subsidies: Challenges for Reform* (Paris: OECD, 2005); *Subsidy Reform and Sustainable Development: Economic, Environmental and Social Aspects* (Paris: OECD, 2006).

A. SOME BASIC PROS AND CONS

Proponents of economic incentives anticipate that environmentally appropriate behaviour can be encouraged if the environmental costs of various activities are recognized, and then appropriately valued and allocated. Certain elements of the legal regime can already be seen as consistent with an economic approach to regulation. For example, statutory arrangements assigning financial liability for cleanup costs and other expenses to "persons responsible" for the damages express the general intention that the burden of compensation for environmental losses should be borne by those who stand to benefit from the activity that resulted in the damage. As the Supreme Court of Canada remarked in *Imperial Oil*, the polluter-pays principle "assigns polluters the responsibility for remedying contamination for which they are responsible and imposes on them the direct and immediate costs of pollution."[2] In this regard, profit-stripping provisions are expected to eliminate the financial attraction of disregarding environmental protection requirements. Legal implementation of the polluter-pays principle is also often assumed to create incentives for preventive measures and alternative approaches that serve to avoid environmental harm in the first place. Such an observation might be made in connection with the following provision from Newfoundland legislation:

> Where pollution occurs and the person or municipal authority that the minister considers responsible for the occurrence of the pollution fails to do the things that the minister considers are appropriate to prevent, control, eliminate or ameliorate the pollution, the minister may take appropriate action to prevent, control, eliminate or ameliorate the pollution and the costs incurred by the minister in taking that action are a debt due the Crown and are recoverable from the person or municipal authority that the minister considers responsible for the occurrence of the pollution.[3]

Principles that direct the court to consider both use values and non-use values as aspects of environmental damage that serve as "aggravating factors" in the context of sentencing also underscore economic consequences.[4]

---

2   *Imperial Oil v Quebec*, [2003] 2 SCR 624 at 642.
3   *Environment Act*, SN 1995, c E-13.1, s 21. Now see *Environmental Protection Act*, SNL 2002, c E-14.2.
4   *Canadian Environmental Protection Act, 1999*, SC 1999, c 33, s 287.1 [*CEPA 1999*].

Although there are certain satisfactions in requiring those who pollute to assume the costs of the damage they have caused, prevention is more attractive. In general, advocates of economic instruments expect not only that harm to the environment will be less likely when those benefiting from the harmful activity must assume the costs, but that society's overall costs of achieving a given level of environmental protection will be lower because of a more efficient distribution among polluters of the costs of meeting that standard. It is also anticipated that appropriately designed economic incentives will promote the development of innovative means to safeguard and improve environmental quality on an ongoing basis.

A number of potential advantages have been claimed for economic instruments over traditional command and control regulation in achieving a given level of environmental protection.[5] First, insofar as they recognize and respond to the fact that pollution-abatement costs will vary among different sources of the same contaminant, economic instruments permit a specified level of environmental protection to be attained at lower cost than uniform emission standards applied under regulatory supervision. Secondly, economic instruments may provide greater ongoing incentives than regulation for polluters to design and implement more efficient processes and technology: if polluters are held responsible for cleaning up the environmental damage they cause, then being able to do so more cheaply saves them money. Finally, these instruments may accelerate progress towards environmental improvement, assuming either that more environmental protection may be realized for the same expenditure or, alternatively, that the operational flexibility they permit will allow for more stringent environmental targets in the first place. It is also claimed that economic instruments reduce the administrative burden and may more readily accommodate growth and the entry of new firms than the established regulatory approach.[6]

---

5   Environment Canada, *Economic Instruments for Environmental Protection* (Discussion paper) (Ottawa: Supply & Services, 1992); Stratos Inc, *Economic Instruments for Environmental Protection and Conservation: Lessons for Canada* (2003); National Round Table on the Environment and the Economy, *Economic Instruments for Long-term Reductions in Energy-based Carbon Emissions* (2005), online: collectionscanada.gc.ca/webarchives2/20130322202211/http://nrtee-trnee.ca/wp-content/uploads/2011/06/Energy-Based-Carbon-Emissions-FullReport-eng.pdf; *Marbek Resource Consultants, Analysis of Economic Instruments for Water Conservation* (November 2005), online: http://ccme.ca/assets/pdf/ei_marbek_final_rpt_e.pdf.

6   Environment Canada, *Economic Instruments for Environmental Protection*, above note 5 at 14–15.

Other factors contributing to the attractiveness of economic instruments and incentives include greater appreciation of the competitive position of Canadian businesses in international markets, and a general concern to address the public debt and deficit situation through lowered public expenditures, including enforcement expenditures, and greater regulatory efficiency.

Notwithstanding the attractive features of economic incentives, their adoption has been resisted, certainly as a complete replacement for more traditional regulatory and enforcement practices. Some observers are reluctant to entrust government with responsibility for setting appropriate total emission and quality levels and for maintaining them through market-oriented mechanisms. Others claim that cost-benefit calculations associated with economic incentives could lead to the imposition of environmental burdens on minorities of some kind. Still more fundamental objections revolve around the assertion that no one should be able simply to buy the right to undertake activities that are inherently bad. And, from a practical perspective, critics charge that the tools of economic analysis currently available to us remain wholly inadequate to the task of assigning satisfactory values to the environment and its constituent elements. There are also critics who argue from the perspective of the rule of law that consistent application of legal standards is the desirable norm, both as a matter of fairness and in light of the need for governments as well as potential polluters to be held accountable for their actions.

B. CANADIAN EXPERIENCE WITH ECONOMIC INSTRUMENTS

The range of economic instruments is sometimes described as encompassing tax-based and non-tax-based mechanisms. Both are discussed in this section along with public funds dedicated to environmental programs.

1) Non-tax Instruments

On the non-tax side, economic instruments might include deposit and refund schemes such as those associated with consumer use of beverage containers, batteries, and so on.[7] User charges, that is, payments directly associated with the costs of resource use, waste management,

---

7   See, for example, *Beverage Containers Act*, RSNB 2011, c 121.

or environmental damage arising from the discharge of pollution, have also been proposed.

New Brunswick's beverage container legislation is typical of deposit and refund regimes designed to encourage reuse of containers with resulting environmental savings from the perspective of reduced use of materials, reduced consumption of energy in container production, decreased demand on land fill facilities and so on. The legislation sets out requirements for distributors of beverages to establish arrangements for receiving used containers, or redeeming them from consumers, and subsequently for refilling or recycling them. The deposit and refund level itself is provided for within the legislative framework. Thus, the deposit and refund level is prescribed by regulation, and consumers are statutorily required to pay this amount.[8]

National efforts to promote water conservation through pricing have been encouraged for a quarter century in the aftermath of a valuable inquiry into water policy. *Currents of Change*, the report of the *Inquiry on Federal Water Policy*, made a major contribution simply by broadening awareness of the implications of pricing on the consumption of water, a highly valuable natural resource that is essential in domestic as well as industrial and institutional settings. The water inquiry identified several benefits anticipated from water pricing:

It will create incentives to avoid waste and to use water efficiently, thus contributing to water conservation.

By reducing the water needed and the waste disposal capacity, it will reduce infrastructure costs.

The resulting lower demand will reduce environmental pressures on water resources.

By demonstrating users' willingness to pay for water, prices help allocate supplies among uses and users so that the highest value is generated from limited resources.

Pricing will generate revenue to cover the cost of water supply and waste disposal systems.

Suitable pricing can ensure that the cost of water services is equitably borne by the beneficiaries according to the benefits they receive.[9]

---

8   *Ibid*, ss 4, 5, and 7(1).
9   PH Pearse et al, *Currents of Change: Final Report, Inquiry of Federal Water Policy* (Ottawa: Supply and Services Canada, 1985) at 98–99.

In the aftermath of the report, more and more users who had become accustomed to receiving the benefits of water and related services at no charge or at nominal expense, are finding that their water usage is being measured through metering devices. On a national basis, between 1991 and 2009, the percentage of residential water consumers whose consumption is metered increased from 51.5 percent to 72 percent. The results strongly indicate that metering significantly lessens water consumption in comparison with use by customers who are on a flat rate and whose charges are not varied on the basis of volume consumed.[10] The next challenge, currently underway, is to refine the relationship between pricing clean water and the costs of supply.[11] Under Ontario's *Sustainable Water and Sewage Systems Act*, the full cost of providing water services was described as including "the source protection costs, operating costs, financing costs, renewal and replacement costs and improvement costs associated with extracting, treating or distributing water to the public and such other costs as may be specified by regulation."[12]

Statutory authorization for economic instruments is apparent elsewhere. Thus, Manitoba's *Environment Act* anticipates the sale of emission rights for designated pollutants by authorizing the lieutenant governor in council to market units of allowable emission of specific pollutants, in accordance with the regulations. Such arrangements must be consistent with established environmental quality objectives. Resulting revenues may be held in trust by the provincial minister of finance as an environmental contingency fund, to be used at the request of the minister of the environment in cases of environmental emergency.[13] Alberta's *Environmental Protection and Enhancement Act* authorizes the use of economic and financial instruments and market-based approaches such as emission trading, incentives, subsidies, and emission, effluent- and waste-disposal fees as well as differential levies "for the purposes of protecting the environment, achieving environmental quality goals in a cost effective manner and providing methods of financing programs and other measures for environmental purposes."[14]

---

10 Environment Canada, *Residential Water Use Indicator*, online: www.ec.gc.ca/indicateurs-indicators/default.asp?lang=en&n=7E808512-1.

11 M Sproule-Jones, "User Fees" in AM Maslove, ed, *Taxes as Instruments of Public Policy* (Toronto: University of Toronto Press, 1994) at 19–23. For details on the Walkerton inquiry, see Dennis O'Connor (Commissioner), *Report of the Walkerton Inquiry* (Toronto: Ministry of the Attorney General, 2002).

12 *Sustainable Water and Sewage Systems Act*, SO 2002, c 29, s 3(7). This legislation was repealed in December 2012.

13 *The Environment Act*, CCSM c E125, s 45.

14 *Environmental Protection and Enhancement Act*, RSA 2000, c E-12, s 13.

Nova Scotia legislation contemplates research on and the eventual adoption of an even broader array of economic and market-based approaches including tradeable emission and effluent permits; offsetting environmental costs and benefits; user charges; resource pricing and physical-resource accounts; deposit-refund systems; emission, effluent- and waste-disposal fees; product charges; charges on inputs or materials; tax incentives and tax differentiation; subsidies, loans, and grants.[15]

Tradeable emission permits that may be exchanged within a market of users (and sometimes even of non-users) are increasingly important examples of non-tax economic instruments. The particular attraction of tradeable permits (assuming an adequate number of participating purchasers) lies in their potential to control aggregate emissions of designated contaminants through the operation of market forces rather than the decisions of regulators.[16] Canada's use of such economic instruments remains limited when set against the use that has been made of similar mechanisms in other jurisdictions. But some sophisticated applications have been examined as part of an effort to provide environmentally beneficial economic incentives to industry and encouragement for individual Canadians to incorporate environmental considerations into the decisions they make as consumers. Significant studies have been carried out, including those for the CCME on emissions trading,[17] for the province of Alberta on air pollution,[18] and for the International Joint Commission on toxic substances in the Great Lakes.[19]

While international discussions about the appropriate design and development of emissions trading regimes continue in the post-Kyoto Protocol context as a response to climate change from greenhouse gas emissions, a number of organizations have begun to acquire emission rights in private transactions. This activity is providing experience that

---

15   Environment Act, SNS 1994–95, c 1, s 15 [NSEA]; see also Environment Act, RSY 2002, c 76, s 57 [YEA]; CEPA 1999, above note 4, ss 322–27.

16   K Hoey & AJ Roman, "The Regulatory Framework" in G Thompson, ML Mc-Connell, & LB Huestis, eds, Environmental Law and Business in Canada (Aurora, ON: Canada Law Book, 1993) at 59–64.

17   Canadian Council of Ministers of the Environment, Emission Trading Working Group, Emission Trading: A Discussion Paper (Winnipeg: Emission Trading Working Group, 1992). Ontario adopted an emissions trading regulation for the energy sector in October 2001: O Reg 397/01.

18   For background, see Market-based Approaches to Managing Air Emissions in Alberta (Discussion paper) (Cambridge, MA: National Economic Research Associates, 1991). For implementation, see Emissions Trading Regulation, Alta Reg 33/2006.

19   Economic Instruments for the Virtual Elimination of Persistent Toxic Substances in the Great Lakes Basin (Windsor: International Joint Commission, 1994).

has been likened to the early development of negotiable instruments preceding legislation on bills of exchange. It is being carried out on the assumption that the public environmental goals of emission trading regimes will eventually mesh with the private interests of rights holders, and that the vital issue of monitoring and verifying actual emissions will be satisfactorily addressed.[20]

Economic instruments have also been employed to promote the protection and restoration of biodiversity in Canada on the basis of incentives to safeguard riparian lands, or to re-establish wetlands, to manage farms and forests with a view to increased carbon storage, among other examples.[21]

2) Tax Incentives and Allowances

Taxes are popularly perceived as revenue-generating devices for governments; however, they can also serve to promote changes in behaviour, including behaviour intended to reduce environmental damage. Specific uses of taxation regimes to promote environmental quality are thus the subject of increased attention.[22]

Environmental taxes may be applied to industrial inputs, that is, on resources consumed during production, on pollution emissions discharged into the environment, or on waste. Taxes can also be applied at the point of consumption by individual purchasers. In each case, levels of taxation must be carefully monitored to reduce the risk of unwanted distortions and side effects.

One widely discussed possibility is the carbon tax, contemplated for its potential to lower the rate of production of carbon dioxide, a major greenhouse gas contributor to global warming. In principle such a tax could be applied to fossil-fuel energy inputs based on the proportion of carbon in their composition. Coal, a high carbon-content fuel, would be subject to a higher level of taxation per unit of energy potential than a comparatively low carbon-content fuel such as natural

---

20   AJ Black, "Emission Trading and the Negotiation of Pollution Credits" 225 *Energy Economist (Financial Times)* (July 2000) at 14–18. At meetings in Montreal (2005) and Nairobi (2006), parties to the Kyoto Protocol continued to discuss the operation and future administration of GHG emissions trading schemes. See Chapter 19.

21   A Kenny, S Elgie, & D Sawyer, *Advancing the Economics of Ecosystems and Biodiversity in Canada: A Survey of Economic Instruments for the Conservation & Protection of Biodiversity* (Background Paper) (Ottawa: Sustainable Prosperity, University of Ottawa, 2011), online: www.sustainableprosperity.ca/article1431.

22   N Olewiler and S Bowman, "Environmental Taxation" in H Kerr, K McKenzie, & J Mintz, eds, *Tax Policy in Canada* (Toronto: Canadian Tax Foundation, 2012).

gas. Analysts see some potential for a carefully designed carbon tax to provide the economic incentive necessary to induce energy users to lower their use of fossil fuels or to reorient their consumption from high to low carbon-content fuel sources. Apart from the concerns of different aspects of the energy sector, most governments have also been preoccupied with the impact of carbon taxes on the competitive position of their domestic industries if other jurisdictions fail to implement similar measures.[23]

One operational initiative along these lines has been introduced by the province of Quebec.[24] Here it is proposed to charge the producers or importers of coal, gas, and oil on the basis of their carbon dioxide emissions with the proceeds constituting an annual duty payable to a new provincial Green Fund intended to achieve compliance with Kyoto goals of GHG reductions. The provincial government has encouraged the producers and importers to absorb this additional charge, but the possibility that costs might be passed on to consumers is not foreclosed. Either way, GHG emitters would contribute financially to costs associated with efforts to address climate change either by reducing GHG emissions or through adaptation measures.

Tax-based instruments also include incentives in the form of eligibility for expense deductions or other inducements to stimulate particular forms of investment. One example of a tax-based incentive to investment is the availability under the federal *Income Tax Act* of accelerated depreciation write-offs for eligible pollution-control equipment. The legislation permits those who have incurred capital expenditures for the acquisition of pollution-control equipment to set off these costs against business income more rapidly than would otherwise be permissible.[25] At the provincial level, a sales-tax rebate on pollution-abatement equipment provided a comparable stimulus. In Ontario, tax measures on automobiles with high fuel consumption may promote greater awareness of the environmental consequences of vehicle choice.[26] The overall tax regime applicable to a particular business or undertaking may vary significantly as between one industry and an-

---

23 *Report of the Ontario Fair Tax Commission: Fair Taxation in a Changing World* (Toronto: University of Toronto Press, 1993) at 559–63; TJ Courchene & JR Allan, eds, *Canada: The State of the Federation 2009 Carbon Pricing and Environmental Federalism* (Montreal: McGill-Queen's UP, 2010).

24 *An Act Respecting the Implementation of the Quebec Energy Strategy*, SQ 2006, c 46. For discussion of related initiatives from other provinces, see Chapter 19.

25 *Income Tax Regulations*, CRC, c 945, Sch II, Classes 24 and 27.

26 See *Retail Sales Tax Act*, RSO 1990, c R.31, s. 4, as am by SO 1992, c 13, s 2, 1997, c 19, s 22.

other, depending upon location, the nature of assets utilized in production or operations — including land, equipment, technology, and so on — as well as the business structure involved. In the forest sector, for example, tax treatment of the resource itself, of machinery utilized in harvesting, transport and production, as well as expenditures on supporting infrastructure, and even research must all be considered.[27]

Apart from environmental tax measures as such, general provisions concerning allowable expense deductions affect the ultimate cost of environmental compliance by business. That is, in the absence of explicit treatment of environmental costs, basic principles of business income taxation serve to determine the deductibility of environmental expenditures, including ordinary costs to avoid pollution, specific expenditures required to obtain and maintain necessary approvals, costs incurred through compliance with administrative orders, remedial work following the cessation of operations, or even penalty costs imposed for non-compliance.[28] Mining reclamation trusts and environmental trusts dedicated to waste disposal and other environmental restoration obligations have the effect of advancing the timing of the deduction of expenses in connection with reclamation work.

Economic incentives (or disincentives) are also highly relevant in the context of municipal property tax assessment. In a pair of Alberta property tax cases, the provincial assessment appeal board and the Edmonton Court of Revision reduced property taxes on contaminated lands to reflect lower market values. The two companies involved had been responsible themselves for the practices that resulted in pollution and, accordingly, lower land values. Although both companies were persuaded by public pressure to pay taxes at the original assessment level, commentators took the occasion to urge a more appropriate reconciliation of property taxes with the goals of environmental policy.[29]

---

27 For a valuable review of these and other relevant factors, see N. Chalifour, "Encouraging the Transition to Sustainable Forestry in Canada with Ecological Fiscal Reform — Potential and Pitfalls" (2004) 14 J Envtl L & Prac 253 at 268–82.

28 RJ MacKnight, "Taxation: Environmental Cost Write-Offs" in D Estrin, ed, *Business Guide to Environmental Law* (Toronto: Carswell, 1992) c 5. In response to public concern that fines, including environmental fines or penalties, might be eligible deductions from otherwise taxable business income as indicated by the Supreme Court of Canada in *65302 British Columbia Ltd v Canada*, [1999] 3 SCR 804, the *Income Tax Act* was amended in the course of implementing the 23 March 2004 federal budget. See *A second Act to implement certain provisions of the budget tabled in Parliament on March 23, 2004*, SC 2005, c 19, s 16.

29 EJ Sidnell, "Property Assessment of Contaminated Land in Alberta" (1993) 3 J Envtl L & Prac 231.

3) Public Spending and Environmentally Dedicated Funds

The historic reluctance of Canadian governments to link specific revenue sources, taxes in particular, with expenditure programs is gradually being overcome to some degree in relation to environment and sustainability measures. The so-called tire tax levied in 1989 on new tire purchases in Ontario and dedicated to research issues and the disposal challenge was a small-scale example until its repeal in 1993. In the same province, conservation measures such as energy audits and retrofits are now supported in part by an assessment on energy consumers.[30]

Alberta established a fund for environmental protection and enhancement that is also available for environmental emergencies.[31] As well, the province has a Recycling Fund, which in addition to any gifts or donations, is based on surcharges on designated material and may be used to support waste minimization and recycling programs along with research, education, and development activities in the same areas.[32] British Columbia operates a Waste Management Trust Fund to finance the cleanup of waste-management facilities that were inadequately closed and for the long-term care of other such facilities.[33] The same province provided for a Sustainable Environment Fund in 1990.[34] Revenues for the fund are derived in part from fines and penalties under provincial environmental legislation and from approvals fees under the *Environmental Management Act* (previously the *Waste Management Act.*) British Columbia also established a Forest Renewal Fund in 1994, a resource-oriented initiative similar in some respects to Ontario's Forestry Futures Trust.[35] In Manitoba a dedicated fund exists to support environmental innovation[36] while in Nova Scotia an environmental trust administered by the provincial Round Table was established to support environmental research, management, and conservation.[37]

---

30   *Assessments for Ministry of Energy and Infrastructure Conservation and Renewable Energy Program Costs*, O Reg 66/10.

31   *Environmental Protection and Enhancement Act*, RSA 2000, c E-12, s 30, as am by SA 2003, c 2, s 1(24), SA 2004, c 7, s 19, SA 2006, c 23, ss 27 and 31 [*AEPEA*].

32   *AEPEA, ibid*, s 171; see also *YEA*, above note 15, s 108.

33   *Environmental Management Act*, SBC 2003, c 53, s 136.

34   *Sustainable Environment Fund Act*, RSBC 1996, c 445.

35   *Crown Forest Sustainability Act, 1994*, SO 1994, c 25, s.51.

36   *The Sustainable Development Act*, CCSM c S270, s 17.

37   *NSEA*, above note 15, s 28. See also *Environmental Trust Fund Act*, RSNB 2011, c 151.

C. OTHER ECONOMIC INCENTIVES

1) Insurance

Insurance against environmental liabilities may be required as a matter of law either by statute[38] or pursuant to the terms of an environmental approval, or perhaps as a contractual precondition for borrowing funds or leasing property. Where not required in any of these senses it may nonetheless be considered prudent on the part of those undertaking activities that entail risk of environmental harm to safeguard themselves against certain forms of potential liabilities to the extent that appropriate insurance coverage is available. Insofar as insurance policies spread or reallocate risks and thus in some respects have the potential to alter incentives for preventive care or to facilitate or to impede certain forms of activity, they fall generally within the realm of economic instruments relevant to environmental protection.

Three important advantages have been identified in a greater level of insurance industry involvement in managing environmental risk. First, loss prevention would help to replace reactive management as the primary basis for decision making. Second, insurers would not only consider the nature and potential scope of physical risks inherent in whatever particular activity is under consideration, but they might also be expected to investigate the track records and past performance of their prospective insurees. Finally, to the extent that environmental decision making by government bodies has embodied political considerations, the influence of these factors would likely be lessened.[39]

Many design features of liability insurance can, in principle, be used to induce insured parties to take accident-avoidance measures, including measures to reduce the likelihood of environmental damages from industrial operations. Adjustments in the size of the insured's deductible, variations in premium levels and their specific relationship to risk, restrictions on repeat claimants, the elimination of coverage for certain activities or forms of damage, and duties to report or submit to inspections can all be used for this purpose. It is also possible to im-

---

38   *AEPEA*, above note 31, s 84; for Ontario statutes requiring insurance see D Estrin & J Swaigen, *Environment on Trial* (Toronto: Emond Montgomery, 1993) at 130; *Pesticides Act*, RSO 1990, c P.11. For discussion, see BJ Richardson, "Mandating Environmental Liability Insurance" (2002) 12 Duke Envtl L & Pol'y F 293.

39   LA Reynolds, "New Directions for Environmental Impairment Liability Insurance in Canada" (1996) 6 J Envtl L & Prac 89.

agine insurers requiring, as a condition of insurability, that appropriate risk management systems be maintained.

Insurance coverage specifically designed for environmental risk and pollution is comparatively recent, although comprehensive general-liability policies (CGL) traditionally fulfilled this function. The costs and availability of environmental pollution-insurance coverage have been influenced by changes in general-liability coverage arrangements. In some respects, however, the general changes, such as higher deductibles, increased premiums, and a shift from "occurrence-based" claims towards "claims made" policies, were brought about by considerations that were most prevalent in the environmental context, notably the insurer's risk of pollution-damage claims arising years after comparatively modest premiums had been received.[40]

Particular difficulties have arisen in predicting the likelihood and severity of claims involving toxic substances. Scientific uncertainty, including uncertainty about the synergistic effect of chemicals that have been mixed together in waste deposits, is a significant factor here. Moreover, the pathways followed by hazardous contamination as it migrates from storage facilities into neighbouring properties and enters underground water supplies are difficult to anticipate. Disasters, sporadic in occurrence and by definition catastrophic in proportions, defy prediction. The extended latency period between exposure to a toxic substance and manifestation of disease symptoms caused by exposure is a further complicating factor.[41]

During the 1960s and 1970s, claims for environmental liabilities were made under the general wording of comprehensive commercial-liability policies.[42] Under one CGL policy in common use at the time environmental claims began to arise frequently, insurers undertook to "pay on behalf of the Insured all sums which the Insured shall become legally obligated to pay as damages because of property damage caused by accident."[43] Uncertainty with respect to the nature of "accident" led some insurers to replace this concept with the idea of "occurrence," defined as "an accident, including continuous or repeated exposure to

---

40 KS Abraham, *Distributing Risk: Insurance, Legal Theory, and Public Policy* (New Haven, CT: Yale UP, 1986); *Final Report of the Ontario Task Force on Insurance* (Toronto: Ministry of Financial Institutions, 1986).

41 *Ontario Task Force on Insurance, ibid* at 45–49.

42 From about 1986, comprehensive general-liability policies have been known as Commercial General Liability. For recent discussion of CGL coverage, see *Demarco v 997366 Ontario Ltd*, 2012 ONSC 2076.

43 MD Faieta, "Liability Insurance for Environmental Contamination in Ontario" (1991) 2 CILR 125 at 129.

conditions which results in bodily injury or property damage neither expected nor intended from the standpoint of the insured." Yet this language also failed to resolve the issue of whether certain forms of polluting activity were "occurrences" within the terms of the policy or were instead the consequence of the insured's normal operations. Other controversial questions arose in connection with the scope of damages, as policyholders sometimes sought to recover expenditures on preventive measures designed to contain pollutants or costs incurred on the basis of administrative orders requiring extensive cleanup programs.

In response to the size and frequency of claims made by policyholders whose interpretations of the contract were often sympathetically viewed by the courts, insurers sought to reduce their own financial risks by including some form of environmental or pollution-liability exclusion clause. Such clauses were intended to restrict coverage to pollution incidents that could be considered "sudden and accidental" rather than the result of general business operations. One such clause, dating from the mid-1970s, stated:

> It is agreed that this policy does not apply to bodily injury or property damage arising out of the discharge, dispersal, release, or escape of smoke, vapours, soot, fumes, acids, alkalis, toxic chemicals, liquids or gases, waste materials, or other irritants, contaminants, or pollutants into or upon land, the atmosphere or any water of any description no matter where located or how contained, or into any watercourse, drainage, or sewage system, but this exclusion does not apply if such discharge, dispersal, release, or escape is sudden and accidental.[44]

Other exclusion clauses were introduced, including clauses intended to address insurance industry concerns with judicial interpretation of "sudden and accidental." One such clause, known as an "absolute" pollution liability exclusion became the standard in both the United States and Canada by about 1986. When residents of an apartment complex claimed compensation for injury from exposure to carbon monoxide attributed to a faulty furnace, the insurer argued that an "absolute" pollution liability exclusion in the building owner's policy barred coverage for such damages. Following a review of the history of "absolute" pollution clauses and consideration of divergent lines of

---

44   Aspects of a clause along these lines were considered in *Ontario v Kansa General Insurance Co* (1994), 17 OR (3d) 38 (CA), leave to appeal to SCC refused (1994), 19 OR (3d) xvi (note) (SCC).

interpretation in US and Canadian cases, Borins JA formulated his assessment in the context of insurance law generally and of pollution:

> When the full panoply of insurance contract construction tools is brought to bear on the pollution exclusion, defective maintenance of a furnace giving rise to carbon monoxide poisoning, like related business torts such as temporarily strong odours produced by floor resurfacing or painting, fail the common sense test for determining what is "pollution." These represent claims long covered by CGL insurance policies. To apply an exclusion intended to bar coverage for claims arising from environmental pollution to carbon monoxide poisoning from a faulty furnace, is to deny the history of the exclusion, the purpose of CGL insurance, and the reasonable expectations of policy-holders in acquiring the insurance . . . . Based on the coverage provided by a CGL policy, a reasonable policy-holder would expect that the policy insured the very risk that occurred in this case. A reasonable policy-holder would, therefore, have understood the clause to exclude coverage for damage caused by certain forms of industrial pollution, but not damages caused by the leakage of carbon monoxide from a faulty furnace. In my view, the policy provisions should be construed to give effect to the purpose for which the policy was acquired.[45]

Apart from distinctive situations along the lines apparent in this case, the effect of the "absolute" pollution liability exclusion clauses, sharply increased premiums, and higher deductibles, was that by the early 1980s environmental pollution coverage had more or less disappeared or was not considered to be affordable.[46]

A limited pollution-liability policy (LPL) may now be obtained as a special endorsement to the CGL policy. The LPL coverage was introduced in 1985 with the support of an association of insurers and re-insurers known as the Pollution Liability Association, which offers reinsurance for certain pollution incidents, frequently those associated with manufacturing, farming, and dry-cleaning operations. Where the risks appear especially hazardous, measures may be taken to have the

---

45 *Zurich Insurance Company v 686234 Ontario Limited* (2002), 62 OR (3d) 447 at 462–63 (CA). See also *Boliden Ltd v Liberty Mutual Insurance Co*, [2008] OJ No 1438 (CA); *Dave's K & K Sandblasting (1998) Ltd v Aviva Insurance Co of Canada* (2007), 30 CELR (3d) 74 (BCSC); and *ING Insurance Co of Canada v Miracle (cob Mohawk Imperial Sales)*, 2011 ONCA 321.

46 *Ontario Task Force on Insurance*, above note 40.

insured respond to the concerns, or the association may introduce a policy surcharge.[47]

The LPL contains several provisions that illustrate the relationship between compliance with environmental regulations and the availability of protection for the insured. In addition to the fact that coverage is not provided in connection with waste-management operations, transportation services, nuclear facilities, "war, invasion, act of foreign enemy, hostilities . . . or any other act of deliberate destruction or property, or terrorism," there are several notable general exclusions. Thus, the insurance does not apply to claims arising out of a pollution incident that "results from or is attributable to a failure to comply with any applicable statute, regulation, ordinance, directive, or order relating to the protection of the environment and promulgated by any governmental body, provided that failure to comply is a wilful or deliberate act or omission of any insured." Nor does coverage extend to

> "cleanup costs" caused by a "pollution incident" if any insured is convicted of an offence under any applicable statute or regulation, relating to the protection of the environment and promulgated by any governmental body, as a result of any insured's failure to comply with a legal duty to report the "pollution incident" to a governmental body or to take remedial steps after the "pollution incident."

Other general exclusions address pollution incidents determined to be "expected or intended from the standpoint of any insured."

In *Pilot Insurance Co v Tyre King Tyre Recycling Ltd*,[48] several aspects of the PLA policy were judicially considered in the aftermath of the Hagersville tire fire of February 1990. Tyre King managed a storage compound containing approximately fourteen million used tires in three piles surrounded by exterior walls of interwoven tires. When a group of teenagers set fire to tires in the compound, nearly all of the tires were consumed over a two-week period and some 60,000 litres of oil and other contaminants entered the environment. When compensation claims arose, the insurer advanced several arguments in an attempt to avoid responsibility under the PLA policy for defending the action or for indemnifying Tyre King in the event that damages were awarded.

In response to the insurer's assertion that the fire was not "unexpected or unintentional," Jarvis J indicated that the intent of third parties such as the vandals had no bearing on the provision in the

---

47   *Faieta*, above note 43. For judicial consideration of an LPL policy, see *Harvey Oil Ltd v Lombard General Insurance*, [2003] NJ No 273 (SC), aff'd [2004] NJ No 47 (CA).
48   (1992), 8 OR (3d) 236 (Gen Div).

insurance contract. Nor could possibly negligent conduct on Tyre King's part support an allegation that the company intended the conflagration and its consequences. The court also dismissed Pilot's argument that no pollution incident was involved because pollutants were not discharged from a structure or container by determining that the interwoven tire wall itself constituted a structure in that it was a thing "which is constructed." In addition, Jarvis J rejected the suggestion that the teenagers' conduct constituted an "act of 'deliberate destruction of property'" within the meaning of the contract. The judge indicated that the conduct excluded must be similar in kind to other elements listed in the war-risk exclusion. Finally, when the insurer claimed an exclusion on the ground that the damage was "expected or intended from the standpoint of the insured," Jarvis J commented as follows:

> It is notorious that some handlers of pollutants do so in a careless manner, without regard for the safety of others. A court might well find that such actions were so careless that the resulting injury or property damage was "expected or intended" and that coverage would therefore not be available to indemnify such an insured. I think it likely that such conduct was intended to be caught by this exclusion. However, the exclusion clearly does not apply to intentional acts of third parties. The acts of vandals are not covered.[49]

Although also subject to significant exclusions, and available only on a claims-made basis, another type of policy known as environmental impairment insurance may offer appropriate coverage in some circumstances. Environmental impairment rather than accidents or pollution incidents is the subject of protection, with environmental impairment defined as bodily injury; property damage; interference with or diminution of any environmental right or amenity protected by law; liability to clean up outside the premises of the insured arising out of any and all emissions, discharges, dispersals, disposal, seepages, releases, or escapes of any liquids, solids, gaseous, or thermal irritants into or upon land, the atmosphere, or any watercourse or body of water; or generations of smells, noises, vibrations, light, electricity, radiations, changes in temperature, or any other sensory phenomenon but not fire or explosion.

2) Financial Institutions and Environmental Monitoring

As previously discussed, there are circumstances in which those other than the actual operators of polluting businesses have been held legally

---

49   *Ibid* at 241.

responsible for cleaning up contaminated lands or for other costs associated with environmental protection (see Chapters 7, 11). Lenders and those acting on their behalf such as trustees and receivers have experienced losses that have encouraged some critics of the lender-liability provisions to label such statutes as "deep-pocket" statutes in contrast to more widely accepted polluter-pays legislation. Even where those advancing funds do not face direct environmental costs, they are increasingly aware that the value of their security may be undermined if environmental charges and liabilities threaten a borrower's solvency.

The Canadian Bankers Association, among others, predicted the implications for financing:

> [e]nvironmentally risky borrowers will find it difficult, or perhaps impossible, to make credit arrangements, whether from a bank or any other lender. Since additional investigations will be required to alleviate lenders' environmental concerns and an increased risk premium will be built into the cost of borrowing to cover possible loan losses arising from environmental liability, all borrowers will pay increased costs to obtain funds.[50]

Although unable to quantify the impact on Canadian financial markets, the CBA reported "an increasing number of instances" where member banks refused to advance certain forms of credit on the basis of the risk of environmental liability. As regular participants or "repeat players" in business development, major lending institutions moved quickly along the learning curve to introduce environmentally specific loan documentation and to require environmental audits.[51] In addition to purely domestic initiatives, a number of major Canadian financial institutions have adopted the Equator Principles, a set of international criteria or benchmark practices intended to manage social and environmental risk in project financing.[52]

Some lament the loss of specific economic activity in those cases where lenders, having investigated the nature of the environmental

---

50   *Sustainable Capital: The Effect of Environmental Liability in Canada on Borrowers, Lenders, and Investors* (Toronto, Canadian Bankers Association, 1991) at 3–4.

51   For a general guide to environmental concerns from a banker's perspective, see *Your Business, Your Bank and the Environment: An Overview of How Banks Address Environmental Risk in the Credit Review Process* (Toronto: Canadian Bankers' Association, 2000). For further discussion, see "Banks and the Environment," online: www.cba.ca/en/component/content/category/62-banks-and-the-environment.

52   Online: www.equator-principles.com/index.php/about-ep/the-eps. For discussion, see BJ Richardson, *Socially Responsible Investment Law: Regulating the Unseen Polluters* (Oxford UP, 2008) at 411–420.

risk and the applicant's capacity to manage it, decline to advance funds. On the other hand, systematic pre-screening stimulated by a broader assessment of risk and financial viability strikes many as highly desirable in the general interest of environmental protection and accident avoidance. It is a mechanism, in other words, integrating environmental considerations directly into economic decision making. As such, the systemic concern of financial institutions with environmental liability in commercial and real estate transactions significantly increases the likelihood that environmental factors will be integrated to some degree into business planning on a comprehensive basis.

D. CONCLUSION

The introduction of a variety of economic instruments for environmental protection raises questions about the relationship between such initiatives and more traditional forms of regulation. Economic instruments remain anathema to some, while certain advocates enthusiastically appear to anticipate the dismantling of governmental controls in the environmental field. It is more likely that economic and regulatory approaches will coexist indefinitely. Bruce Doern has described one perspective on the challenge of identifying the appropriate interrelationship:

> It calls for a more sensible pairing of functions for those aspects of environmental policy that only the state can do well—setting standards in a democratic way and ensuring overall compliance—with those that only markets can do well—doing it at least cost, through the use of competitive technologies and price signals, by choices made at the firm or micro-organizational level.[53]

Canada was the subject of a general assessment of national environmental performance conducted by the OECD in which it was argued that increased use of economic instruments should be treated as a "matter of urgency." The study identified a series of constraints which, in the authors' view, had impeded more general adoption of such tools:

> Industry is concerned about day-to-day competitive pressures, especially in relation to cost competitiveness with the U.S. It has difficulty understanding how to implement new instruments such as trading. Within governments, economic agencies have supported economic

---

53   GB Doern, "Regulations and Market Approaches: The Essential Environmental Partnership" in GB Doern, ed, *Getting It Green: Case Studies in Canadian Environmental Regulation* (Toronto: CD Howe Institute, 1990) 1 at 2.

instruments in principle, but resisted specific proposals for targeted
incentives on allocative efficiency grounds. The public is wary of new
fees and charges, and of the allocation of "rights to pollute." There
is a general resistance to external pressure to change consumption
patterns. Small but influential groups have blocked some proposals.[54]

In recent years, however, there is mounting evidence of increased appreciation of the important contribution that economic instruments
and incentives can make to both environmental protection and economic competitiveness.[55]

FURTHER READINGS

AFFOLDER, NA, "Rethinking Environmental Contracting" (2010) 21
    J Envtl L & Prac 155

CHALIFOUR, N, "Encouraging the Transition to Sustainable Forestry in
    Canada with Ecological Fiscal Reform" (2004) 14 J Envtl L & Prac
    253

CHALIFOUR, N, MA Grau-Ruiz, & E Traversa, "Multi-level Governance:
    The Implications of Legal Competences to Collect, Administer
    and Regulate Environmental Tax Instruments" in JE Milne & MS
    Andersen, eds, *Handbook of Research on Environmental Taxation*
    (Cheltenham, UK: Edward Elgar Publishing, 2012)

CHALIFOUR, N, & A Taylor, "Stimulating the Use of Renewable Energy
    in the Canadian Residential Sector With Economic Instruments"
    in J Cottrell *et al*, eds, *Critical Issues in Environmental Taxation:
    International and Comparative Perspectives*, vol VI (Oxford: Oxford
    UP, 2009)

DOERN, GB, "Regulations and Market Approaches: The Essential En-
    vironmental Partnership" in GB Doern, ed, *Getting It Green: Case
    Studies in Canadian Environmental Regulation* (Toronto: CD Howe
    Institute, 1990)

DOLDEN, EA, "The Comprehensive General Liability Policy: Re-
    sponding to Modern Business Risks" (1991) 2 CILR 11

DUFF, DG, "Tax Policy and Global Warming" (2003) 51 Can Tax J
    2063

---

54   *OECD Environmental Performance Reviews: Canada* (OECD, Paris, 2004) at 124–25.
55   See, generally, research associated with the Sustainable Prosperity network, on-
     line: www.sustainableprosperity.ca/Home+EN.

GRANDBOIS, M, "Entre la déréglementation et la surréglementation : le droit québécois de l'environnement" (1999) 78 Can Bar Rev 111

JUTLAH, RS, "Economic Instruments and Environmental Policy in Canada" (1999) 8 J Envtl L & Prac 323

REYNOLDS, LA, "New Directions for Environmental Impairment Liability Insurance in Canada" (1996) 6 J Envtl L & Prac 89

RICHARDSON, BJ, "Financing Environmental Change: A New Role for Canadian Environmental Law" (2004) 49 McGill LJ 145

———, Socially Responsible Investment Law: Regulating the Unseen Polluters (Oxford University Press, 2008)

SARGENT, JH, "The Economics of Energy and the Environment: The Potential Role of Market-based Instruments" (2002) 28 Can-USLJ 499

SWAIGEN, JZ, Compensation of Pollution Victims in Canada (Study prepared for the Economic Council of Canada) (Ottawa: Supply & Services, 1981)

TEITELBAUM, MS, & LJ BRABANDER, "Environmental Insurance Coverage Issues: Will US Developments Filter into the Canadian Courts?" (2003) 21 Can J Ins L 57

VALIANTE, M, "Privatization and Environmental Governance" in Albert Breton et al, eds, Governing the Environment: Salient Institutional Issues (Cheltenham, UK: Edward Elgar Publishing, 2009)

WEERSINK, AJ, et al, "Economic Instruments and Environmental Policy in Agriculture" (1998) 24 Can Pub Pol'y 309

CHAPTER 18

ENVIRONMENTAL REPORTING AND INFORMATION SOURCES

A. INTRODUCTION

Under the auspices of the Economic Commission for Europe an agreement was reached at Aarhus, Denmark, in 1998 concerning access to information, public participation in decision making and access to justice in environmental matters. In this context, the Aarhus Convention formally defined "environmental information" as any information, in whatever form, relating to:

(a) The state of elements of the environment, such as air and atmosphere, water, soil, landscape, and natural sites, biological diversity and its components, including genetically modified organisms, and the interaction among these elements;

(b) Factors such as substances, energy, noise, and radiation, and activities or measures, including administrative measures, environmental agreements, policies, legislation, plans, and programmes, affecting or likely to affect the elements of the environment within the scope of subparagraph (a) above, and cost-benefit and other economic analyses and assumptions used in environmental decision-making;

(c) The state of human health and safety, conditions of human life, cultural sites and built structures, inasmuch as they are or may be affected by the state of the elements of the environment or,

388

through these elements, by the factors, activities, or measures referred to in subparagraph (b) above.[1]

Although Canadian environmental law has not yet provided an all-encompassing approach to information nor formally recognized the significance of its availability along the lines set out in the Aarhus Convention, the rationales for making information more widely available are equally applicable to environmental information. Freedom of information legislation has been introduced across the country and aspects of its contribution to democracy have been recognized by the Supreme Court of Canada:

> Access to information legislation . . . helps to ensure first, that citizens have the information required to participate meaningfully in the democratic process, and secondly, that politicians and bureaucrats remain accountable to the citizenry.[2]

In addition to arguments oriented around democracy, that is, to claims around informed public decision making, the availability of environmental information facilitates individualized decision making, as citizens may, to a greater or lesser extent depending on the circumstances, make choices about the environmental risks to which they or their families should be exposed. An initiative of the National Round Table on the Environment and the Economy (NRTEE) and the minister of finance to promote a new set of environmental and sustainable development indicators (ESDI) was specifically intended to advance understanding of the overall progress of Canadian society in ways that are largely overlooked by current measures such as gross domestic product:

> The Minister of Finance instigated the ESDI Initiative because of widespread agreement . . . that the national-level, macroeconomic indicators currently in use to judge a society's success provide only part of the information needed: they exclude many of the factors on which we depend for continued development as a society, particularly the services provided by a clean environment and by our education system. Moreover, macroeconomic indicators emphasize current income rather than wealth, but it is the latter that is the basis for generating income in the future. By neglecting the needs of future

---

1   *Convention on Access to Information, Public Participation in Decision-Making and Access to Justice in Environmental Matters*, 25 June 1998, 2161 UNTS 447, art 2 (adopted at Aarhus, Denmark; entered into force 30 October 2001).

2   *Dagg v Canada (Minister of Finance)*, [1997] 2 SCR 403 at para 61.

generations, macroeconomic indicators ignore the main concern of sustainable development.[3]

The Commissioner of the Environment and Sustainable Development recently illustrated a number of concrete settings in which environmental information is essential to effective action and decision making:

- *Health professionals.* Public health officials are concerned about short-term environmental impacts, such as poor air quality and the need to issue smog advisories. They are also concerned about long-term health effects, such as the presence of toxic substances in the environment and human bodies.
- *Planners.* Municipal engineers responsible for designing flood control systems need to know the maximum height to which water levels could rise. When they set premiums, insurance companies need accurate information about current and future environmental risks. If they lack sound information, they pay a real financial cost.
- *Emergency responders.* When an earthquake or a major industrial accident occurs, it is vital to know without delay exactly where it occurred and how severe it is; armed with accurate and timely information, responders can deliver rapid and targeted assistance. Magnetic disturbances caused by solar flares induce electric currents in long conductors, such as power lines and pipelines, and can lead to power system outages or pipeline corrosion. Monitoring information can help emergency managers predict and respond to such events.
- *Resource managers.* Farmers need to know the short-term weather — for example, to help them decide when to harvest their crops. They also rely on information about long-term climate trends — for example, when deciding how to respond to declining water supplies. Mining companies in the North need to know whether changes in permafrost and the extent of sea ice will affect their access to resources.
- *Industries.* Wind power developers need reliable information about wind patterns and bird migration routes to plan their facilities. Major industries need to monitor their own environmental effects to ensure that they comply with regulations. For example, the National Pollutant Release Inventory requires many businesses in Canada to measure and report how much pollution they release into the environment from their facilities.[4]

---

3 *Environment and Sustainable Development Indicators for Canada* (Ottawa: NRTEE, 2003) at 9.

4 *2011 December Report of the Commissioner of the Environment and Sustainable Development* (Ottawa: Office of the Auditor General, 2011) c 5 "A Study of Environmental Monitoring" at para 5.10 [*2011 December Report*].

B. STATE OF THE ENVIRONMENT REPORTS

Attempts to meet the challenge of describing the state of the environment at the global and national levels have become more common since the publication in 1987 of the WCED report, *Our Common Future*.[5] A prototype report on Canada's state of the environment was published in 1986, using fifteen terrestrial ecozones and four aquatic ecosystems for organizational purposes. This approach, it was explained,

> allows characteristics of the environment to be compared within ecosystems over time and between one ecozone and another at any one time. It also makes possible, for the first time, an examination of an ecosystem based not on a general description and subjective interpretation, but on quantitative data of physical, biological, and dynamic response characteristics. Thus the extent and seriousness of potential or actual environmental change, or the amount and condition of a specific natural resource and its relation to other resources, may be identified in a way not previously possible.[6]

In subsequent editions, those responsible for preparing the report refined the presentation of data, and facilitated access to the document by publishing it as a CD-ROM and on the Internet. As of 2004, the challenge set out by the NRTEE in its environment and sustainable development initiative has been at least partially met on the basis of a new data series, Canadian Environmental Sustainability Indicators, a collaborative project involving Environment Canada, Health Canada and Statistics Canada.[7]

The concept of state of the environment reporting arranged along jurisdictional lines has been adopted in legislation in several provinces and territories.[8] Government reporting obligations differ somewhat in terms of the frequency of report-publication and in terms of the required scope or coverage of the reports. Yukon legislation is most explicit in relation to the purposes of state of the environment reporting

---

5   From a global perspective, see the *Millennium Ecosystem Assessment* (2005).

6   Environment Canada, *State of the Environment Report for Canada* by PB Bird & DJ Rapport (Ottawa: Supply & Services, 1986) at viii.

7   *Canadian Environmental Sustainability Indicators, 2005* (Ottawa: Statistics Canada, 2005). Now see Canadian Environmental Sustainability Indicators (CESI) online: www.ec.gc.ca/indicateurs-indicators.

8   *The Environment Act*, SM 1987–88, c 26, s 4; *Environment Act*, SNS 1994–95, c 1, s 16 [*NSEA*]; *Environmental Protection and Enhancement Act*, SA 1992, c E–13.3, s 15 [*AEPEA*].

and with regard to content requirements. In the words of the statute, the Yukon State of the Environment report is intended to "provide early warning and analysis of potential problems for the environment; . . . to allow the public to monitor progress toward the achievement of the objectives of this Act; and . . . to provide baseline information for environmental planning, assessment and regulation."[9] In addition to baseline information on the environment, the Yukon report is required to establish indicators of impairment or improvement and to analyse changes in the indicators as these emerge over time. The report is further expected to identify emerging environmental problems, particularly any that involve long-term and cumulative effects.[10] In Nunavut, the federal government's failure to implement a program of ecosystem and socio-economic monitoring as provided for in the Nunavut Land Claims Agreement was the subject of a successful claim for damages by the Inuit community.[11]

Other forms of environmental reporting requirements have frequently been established for individual departments or in connection with specific pieces of legislation. The federal minister of the environment, for example, must report annually on the administration and enforcement of CEPA 1999[12] while Natural Resources Canada is under a statutory duty to report annually on the state of Canada's forests. Canada's Fisheries Act provides for the creation of additional data sources. Specifically, the responsible minister is required to report annually "on the administration and enforcement of the provisions . . . relating to fish habitat protection and pollution prevention."[13]

Considerable public attention has also been directed towards environmental monitoring programs in connection with significant resource developments, with oil sands projects in northern Alberta as a prominent example.[14] In the case of the oil sands, scientific criticism arising from the presence of toxic releases found in the waters of the Athabasca River followed by the work of an expert advisory panel in 2010 led to a joint Canada–Alberta program for integrated environ-

---

9   Environment Act, RSY 2002, c 76, s 47.

10   Ibid.

11   Nunavut Tunngavik Inc v Canada (Attorney General), 2012 NUCJ 11.

12   Canadian Environmental Protection Act, 1999, SC 1999, c 33, s 342 [CEPA 1999].

13   Fisheries Act, RSC 1985, c F-14, s 42.1(1) [FA]. See also Wild Animal and Plant Protection and Regulation of International and Interprovincial Trade Act, SC 1992, c 52, s 28.

14   For discussion and illustration of the characteristics of effective environmental monitoring programs, see 2011 December Report, above note 4, c 5, "A Study of Environmental Monitoring."

mental monitoring. The joint monitoring arrangements are intended to provide consolidated and comprehensive information on air quality, water quantity and quality, aquatic ecosystem health, wildlife toxicology, and terrestrial biodiversity and habitat.[15]

Certain designated federal departments have prepared sustainable-development strategies for presentation to the House of Commons. These were originally due by 15 December 1997 and are to be updated at least every three years. To monitor and report on departmental progress towards sustainable development, the office of the federal commissioner of the environment and sustainable development (CESD) was established to work with the auditor general of Canada, whose responsibilities were extended to include bringing to the attention of the House of Commons any cases where "money has been expended without due regard to the environmental effects of those expenditures in the context of sustainable development."[16] In this regard, the CESD undertook a review and assessment of departmental progress towards meeting commitments set out in earlier sustainable development strategies.[17]

Statistics Canada's survey of consumer behaviour in relation to the environment, *Households and their Environment*, is intermittently updated. This reference provides information concerning consumption and conservation of water, energy use and home heating, gasoline powered equipment use, pesticide and fertilizer use, recycling, composting and waste disposal practices, air and water quality, and transportation decisions.

C. CORPORATE INFORMATION

As noted in the previous discussions of environmental regulation (Chapter 6) and corporate environmental obligations (Chapter 9), businesses will frequently be required by legislation, governance principles, or under the terms and conditions of operating permits and licences to file information and reports on the environmental dimensions of their operations. Separate reporting obligations apply in the case of spills. Other specialized pieces of legislation also impose reporting and disclosure obligations.

---

15   "Joint Canada-Alberta Implementation Plan for Oil Sands Monitoring" (19 October 2012), online: www.ec.gc.ca/scitech/default.asp?lang=En&n=B403B932-1.

16   *Auditor General Act*, RSC 1985, c A–17, s 7(1)(f).

17   *2006 September Report of the Commissioner of the Environment and Sustainable Development*, (Ottawa: Office of the Auditor General, 2006) c 4, "Sustainable Development Strategies."

Included in this inventory of new or refined sources of information are disclosure requirements relating to the workplace or the transportation of dangerous goods, and notice provisions applicable to other regulatory initiatives. In some jurisdictions, vendors of real estate may be required to file information concerning the condition of their property. In addition, those convicted of offences under the *Fisheries Act* may, for a three-year period following conviction, be ordered to report on their activities.[18] At the municipal level, a Toronto bylaw on *Environmental Reporting and Disclosure* (Toronto bylaw 1293-2008) requires certain businesses operating in the city to monitor and report annually on their usage of designated substances.

The increasingly widespread practice of undertaking an environmental audit or self-evaluation (see Chapter 9) has resulted in a further source of information on business operations and environmental compliance. The existence of such detailed information raises questions about access and about the uses to which such information may be put.

Some environmental legislation addresses the release on request of environmental information in the possession of government. Information to be disclosed may include documentation received from licence or permit applicants, emission-monitoring results, and reports provided by those operating under approvals or orders. Although the disclosure provisions generally provide for confidentiality in certain specified circumstances, the presumption of public access to requested environmental information seems firmly established.[19] Under *CEPA 1999*, for example, apart from certain specific exceptions, the minister may disclose information where:

(a)   the disclosure is in the interest of public health, public safety, or the protection of the environment; and

(b)   the public interest in the disclosure clearly outweighs in importance

  (i)   any material financial loss or prejudice to the competitive position of the person who provided the information or on whose behalf it was provided, and

  (ii)   any damage to the privacy, reputation or human dignity of any individual that may result from the disclosure.[20]

---

18   *FA*, above note 13.

19   *AEPEA*, above note 8, s 33; *Environmental Rights Act*, RSNWT 1988 (Supp), c 83, s 3; *Freedom of Information and Protection of Privacy Act*, RSO 1990, c F.31, s 18; *Municipal Freedom of Information and Protection of Privacy Act*, RSO 1990, c M.56. See also Bill 48, *An Act to Provide a Charter of Environmental Rights and Responsibilities*, 2d Sess, 22nd Leg, Saskatchewan, 1992, cl 9.

20   *CEPA 1999*, above note 12, s 315(1). See, generally, ss 313–21.

Notwithstanding a widely acknowledged presumption in favour of disclosure of information held in public hands, data and documentary materials are not always forthcoming and their release may be contested.[21]

A further challenge to the issue of disclosure of information is the complexity of identifying relevant environmental information, assuming its availability. One partial response is the creation of an environmental registry, or a central listing of decisions and instruments concerning environmental operations in a given jurisdiction. Modern technology greatly facilitates access to such databases. Nova Scotia legislation now provides for a registry along these lines, as do the *OEBR* and *CEPA 1999*.[22]

In some jurisdictions, the long-standing difficulty of lack of public information concerning the compliance status of industry has been at least partially addressed. In 1990, for example, the British Columbia government began systematic reporting of non-compliance in relation to waste-management permits and more general "pollution concerns." Environmental charges laid by provincial officials were also included.

D. THE NATIONAL POLLUTANTS RELEASE INVENTORY

A national inventory of releases of pollutants (NPRI) established under the legislative authority of *CEPA 1999* provides published information on releases to the environment of a wide range of substances.[23] Fulfilment of the information-gathering requirements associated with the NPRI, including substances deposited to tailings impoundment areas contributes to the overall statutory goals of protecting Canadians against health and environmental hazards.[24]

In 1993, its first year of operation, the NPRI collected data on 178 substances that were released to air, land, or water or that were transferred off-site in the form of waste. The selection was initially based on a review of the United States Toxic Release Inventory and the Can-

---

21 LM Collins, JV De Marco, & AD Levy, "Accessing Environmental Information in Ontario: A Legislative Comment on Ontario's *Freedom of Information and Protection of Privacy Act*" (2004) 13 J Envtl L & Prac 267.

22 *NSEA*, above note 8, s 10; *Environmental Bill of Rights, 1993*, SO 1993, c 28; *CEPA 1999*, above note 12, s 12.

23 *CEPA 1999*, *ibid*, ss 46–50. These provisions shore up the statutory basis for information requests from industry in comparison with the *CEPA* era. See *IPSCO v Canada (Minister of Environment)* (2000), 33 CELR (NS) 223 (Sask QB).

24 *Great Lakes United v Canada (Minister of the Environment)*, 2009 FC 408.

adian Chemical Producers' Association National Emissions Reduction Masterplan.

NPRI provides information relating to approximately 300 substances released at 8000 reporting facilities in Canada. The information base is expected to assist in further environmental protection by identifying priorities, permitting progress to be monitored, stimulating voluntary efforts to reduce releases, and generally supporting regulatory programs.[25] The Canadian Institute for Environmental Law and Policy, the Canadian Environmental Law Association, and the Canadian Environmental Defence Fund provide location-specific information on pollutant releases in cooperation with a US organization, Environmental Defense.[26]

FURTHER READINGS

Canadian Environmental Directory 1996/97, 6th ed (Toronto: Canadian Almanac & Directory Publishing Co, 1996)

Environmental Performance Reviews: Canada (Paris: OECD, 2004)

ESTRIN, D, & J SWAIGEN, EDS, *Environment on Trial*, 3d ed (Toronto: Emond Montgomery, 1993) appendix

Public Access to Government-held Information (Montreal: Commission for Environmental Cooperation, 2003)

Taking Stock: 2004 North American Pollutant Releases and Transfers (Montreal: Commission for Environmental Cooperation, 2007)

---

25 For a general commentary on NPRI data and trends, see online: www.ec.gc.ca/inrp-npri/default.asp?lang=En&n=F98AFAE7-1#X-201302081512532.

26 Online: www.pollutionwatch.org.

CHAPTER 19

CLIMATE CHANGE: CANADIAN LEGAL AND POLICY RESPONSES

The causes and consequences of climate change, as discussed in connection with the international legal context for Canadian environmental law, now command attention at all levels of government and throughout society for the range and complexity of challenges they present. Even as it has become increasingly urgent to endeavour to mitigate the factors and processes that contribute to ongoing climate change, simultaneous efforts are essential to facilitate adaptation to the impact and effects of climate change that are already underway. Following a brief review of climate change information, notably the work of the Intergovernmental Panel on Climate Change (IPCC), this chapter surveys recent Canadian responses at the federal level, in intergovernmental settings, in a number of provinces, and within the municipal context.

A. CAUSES AND CONSEQUENCES

For the benefit of policy-makers, experts from the physical sciences associated with the IPCC summarized their current understanding of the contribution of human activity to changing atmospheric conditions:

> Global atmospheric concentrations of carbon dioxide, methane and nitrous oxide have increased markedly as a result of human activities since 1750 and now far exceed pre-industrial values . . . . The global increases in carbon dioxide concentration are due primarily to fossil

fuel use and land-use change, while those of methane and nitrous oxide are primarily due to agriculture.[1]

In the view of the same IPCC assessors, "warming of the climate system is unequivocal, as is now evident from observations or increases in global average air and ocean temperatures, widespread melting of snow and ice, and rising global average sea level."[2]

Long-term changes in climate have been observed at the continental and regional bases and on the ocean basin level as well. These observations include significant increases in Arctic temperatures and changes in ice conditions, pronounced alteration in precipitation levels, shifting wind patterns as well as weather extremes such as droughts, heavy precipitation, heat waves, and more intense tropical cyclones. IPCC scientists have concluded that "most of the observed increase in globally averaged temperatures since the mid-twentieth century is *very likely* due to the observed increase in anthropogenic greenhouse gas concentrations."[3] Projections based on modelling support the expectation that

> [c]ontinued greenhouse gas emissions at or above current rates would cause further warming and induce many changes in the global climate system during the 21st century that would very likely be larger than those observed during the 20th century.[4]

Examinations of climate change and its anticipated sectoral impacts on agriculture, forestry, and fisheries, for example, have also been conducted from the Canadian perspective.[5] On a broad scale, ecosystems and habitat are transformed by climate change with disruptive implications for biodiversity and dependent human populations. Regionally-focused studies, including studies of the Canadian Arctic, the Prairies and the Great Lakes have pursued the inquiry in more detail.[6] The latter have often identified potential social, economic, and health conse-

---

1   Intergovernmental Panel on Climate Change, *Climate Change 2007: The Physical Science Basis—Summary for Policymakers* (Cambridge: Cambridge University Press, 2007) at 2, online: www.ipcc.ch/pdf/assessment-report/ar4/wg1/ar4-wg1-spm.pdf. The results of updated research are anticipated in 2013.
2   *Ibid* at 4.
3   *Ibid* at 8 [emphasis in original].
4   *Ibid* at 10.
5   *Climate Change Impacts and Adaptation: A Canadian Perspective* (Ottawa: Climate Change Impacts and Adaptation Program, 2004).
6   GW Kling *et al*, *Confronting Climate Change in the Great Lakes Region: Impacts on Our Communities and Ecosystems* (Cambridge, MA: Union of Concerned Scientists, 2003); S Nickels *et al*, *Unikkaaqatigiit—Putting the Human Face on Climate Change: Perspectives from Inuit in Canada* (Ottawa: Inuit Tapiriit Kanatami, 2006). For additional information on a regional basis, including teaching ma-

quences of continuing climate change. Health-related implications of climate change—both direct and indirect—have been explained along the following lines:

> Climate change can affect health *directly* as a result of exposure to climatic extremes (e.g. high temperatures causing dehydration and heat stroke) or sudden, intense changes in the environment (e.g. tornadoes causing injury). While direct pathways such as these often result in immediate health impacts, in some cases the impacts are not apparent until years of prolonged environmental exposure (e.g. ultraviolet (UV) radiation and skin cancer).
>
> Health can also be affected *indirectly* as a result of climate-induced changes in biological and geochemical systems, for instance by creating conditions favourable for disease (e.g. warmer, wetter weather favours the life cycle of mosquitoes, influencing the spread of the West Nile virus). Climate change can also indirectly have an impact through economic and social systems, for example through loss of employment or property after a natural disaster resulting in stress and other illnesses. These indirect pathways generally result in longer-term health impacts.
>
> Virtually all aspects of life, from food production and water management, and energy production and consumption, to storm sewer, drainage and sanitation systems, and housing and health infrastructures, including disease surveillance and control, are designed for a specific climate. Health risks arise when any one of these systems fails or becomes compromised—as they may in a changing climate.[7]

Increasingly severe threats posed by the continuing process of climate change have encouraged many jurisdictions to take steps intended to reduce the emission of greenhouse gases,[8] while economic studies have indicated the virtue of prompt action rather than delay. One of the most prominent of these, known as the Stern Review, after the au-

---

terials, see online: www.nrcan.gc.ca/earth-sciences/climate-change/community-adaptation/poster/623.

7   K-L Clarke, "Health in a Changing Climate" Health Policy Research Bulletin, Issue 11 (2005), online: www.hc-sc.gc.ca/sr-sr/pubs/hpr-rpms/bull/2005-climat/index-eng.php.

8   For valuable and influential overviews of climate change and policy options, see T Flannery, *The Weather Makers: How We Are Changing the Climate and What It Means for Life on Earth* (Toronto: HarperTrophyCanada, 2007); and G Monbiot, *Heat: How to Stop the Planet from Burning* (Scarborough, ON: Doubleday, 2006). Important legislative developments in other jurisdictions include the Australian *Energy Efficiency Opportunities Act* (2006) and California's *Global Warming Solutions Act* (2006).

thor of the report, Sir Nicholas Stern of the United Kingdom, utilized a number of techniques to analyse the economic costs of climate change.[9]

Evidence accumulated by the Stern Review supports, in the view of its author, "a simple conclusion," namely that "the benefits of strong and early action far outweigh the economic costs of not acting."[10] The report estimated that the long-term costs and risks of inaction in relation to climate change "will be equivalent to losing at least 5 percent of global GDP each year, now and forever,"[11] whereas the costs of acting now to reduce greenhouse gas emissions in order to avoid the worst climate change impacts "can be limited to around 1 percent of global GDP each year."[12] It is unnecessary and inappropriate, the study insisted, to imagine conflict between economic development and measures to avert climate change.[13]

By way of policy prescription, Stern highlights the importance of increased energy efficiency, changes in demand, and the adoption of clean power, heat and transport technologies. The Stern Review characterizes climate change as the greatest market failure in history and identifies three core ingredients of an effective global response:

> The first is the pricing of carbon, implemented through tax, trading or regulation. The second is policy to support innovation and the deployment of low-carbon technologies. And the third is action to remove barriers to energy efficiency, and to inform, educate and persuade individuals about what they can do to respond to climate change.[14]

These objectives provide a valuable framework within which to outline steps that have been taken to address climate change within the Canadian context. It might also be added that implementation of effective climate change policy within each jurisdiction should be carried out in a manner that is consistent with principles of good governance and the rule of law.

Canada's lamentable national failure to respond effectively to emission reduction commitments assumed under the Kyoto Protocol 1997 has significantly increased the challenge of adjustment that lies ahead. As an Annex I Party to the UN *Framework Convention on Climate*

---

9   N Stern, *The Economics of Climate Change: The Stern Review* (Cambridge: Cambridge UP, 2007).

10   *Ibid* at vi.

11   *Ibid*.

12   *Ibid*.

13   *Ibid* at viii.

14   *Ibid* at viii.

Change, Canada is required to submit a national inventory of anthropogenic sources and sinks of greenhouse gases. The *National Inventory
Report 1990–2010: Information on Greenhouse Gas Sources and Sinks in
Canada* was updated for 2010.[15] In 2010, Canadian emissions were 17
percent above 1990 levels. This overall statistic reflects fifteen years of
steady emissions increases followed by a period of fluctuation between
2005 and 2008. Emissions fell steeply in 2009 and somewhat stabilized
for the latest reporting year, 2010. Trends in the past decade are widely
attributed to an overall shift in the economy towards service sector
activity accompanied by significantly lower growth rates in Canadian
industry and manufacturing.

On a geographic basis, the province of Alberta produced the largest
amount of greenhouse gas emissions in 2010, representing 34 percent
of national emissions, and also has had the largest increase since 1990.
Ontario accounted for a quarter of national greenhouse gas emissions
in 2010.

In sectoral terms, stationary energy (fuel combustion for heat, manufacturing, construction and so on) accounted for 46 percent of GHG
emissions in 2009. Passenger and freight transportation represented
27 percent of emissions. Agriculture and industrial processes, including mineral, chemical, and metal production were responsible
for 8 percent and 7 percent respectively. Emissions attributed to solid
waste and waste water management constituted 3 percent of the national total, while 9 percent of 2009 emissions were associated with
so-called fugitive sources. This latter category encompasses intentional and unintentional emissions from fossil fuel production, processing, transmission, storage, and delivery.[16]

B. FEDERAL CLIMATE CHANGE INITIATIVES

Notwithstanding Canada's withdrawal from the Kyoto Protocol as described in Chapter 4, it remains worthwhile to review the evolution of
the federal government's response to climate change against the international backdrop. The federal government remains within the Frame-

---

15 *National Inventory Report 1990–2010: Information on Greenhouse Gas Sources and
Sinks in Canada* (Ottawa: Environment Canada, 2012).

16 *Reality Check: The State of Climate Progress in Canada* (Ottawa: National Roundtable on the Environment and Economy, 2012) at 37, online: collectionscanada.
gc.ca/webarchives2/20130322165457/http://nrtee-trnee.ca/wp-content/uploads/
2012/06/reality-check-report-eng.pdf.

work Convention on Climate Change (FCCC) and within that context has expressed its support for the Durban Platform which established a working group to develop a new legal mechanism by 2015 that would be applicable to all Parties to the FCCC.

Since 1997, the date of the Kyoto negotiations setting out emissions reductions targets to be achieved during the 2008-2012 period by industrialized nations subject to the terms agreed, several climate change plans have been produced at the federal level. The *Government of Canada Action Plan 2000 on Climate Change*[17] was followed in 2002 by the *Climate Change Plan for Canada*[18] which in its turn gave way to *Project Green—Moving Forward on Climate Change: A Plan for Honouring Our Kyoto Commitment*[19] in 2005, the year in which the underlying international agreement came into legal force. In general terms, this sequence of proposals, accompanied by public funding announcements, relied heavily upon voluntary emission reduction measures. These were to be adopted on a sectoral basis, and by individual Canadians. The utility and appropriateness of economic incentives to promote behavioural transformation eventually received some acknowledgement: *Project Green* emphasized the role of large final emitters (LFEs) in the mining, oil and gas, manufacturing and thermal electricity sectors, and anticipated a combination of regulations and tradable emissions credits and other incentive programs to encourage compliance.[20]

These initiatives overall were evaluated by the House of Commons Standing Committee on Environment and Sustainable Development as *ad hoc* in nature, lacking strategic coherence, and generally devoid of an accountability framework. As assessed by the Commissioner of the Environment and Sustainable Development, progress was sporadic. No effective governance structure was established for the management of climate change activity at the federal level, and in the case of the most prominent voluntary agreement—an arrangement with the automotive industry—no provision was made to verify the model, data, or results to be employed in measuring progress.[21]

---

17   Online: publications.gc.ca/collections/Collection/M-22-135-2000E.pdf.

18   Online: dsp-psd.pwgsc.gc.ca/Collection/En56-183-2002E.pdf.

19   *Project Green—Moving Forward on Climate Change: A Plan for Honouring Our Kyoto Commitment* (Ottawa: Environment Canada, 2005).

20   To facilitate regulation of greenhouse gas emissions, carbon dioxide, methane, nitrous oxide, hydrofluorocarbons, perfluorocarbons, and sulfur hexafluoride were listed, upon assessment, as toxic substances under section 64 of the *Canadian Environmental Protection Act, 1999*, SC 1999, c 33 [*CEPA 1999*]. See C Gaz 2005.II.2568.

21   *2006 September Report of the Commissioner of the Environment and Sustainable Development* (Ottawa: Office of the Auditor General, 2006) c 1 "Managing the

A private member's bill, Bill C-288, *An Act to ensure Canada meets its global climate change obligations under the Kyoto Protocol* was enacted at the close of the parliamentary session in June 2007.[22] This legislation was intended by its proponents to encourage Canadian compliance with commitments under the Kyoto Protocol. Although repealed in 2012, the *Kyoto Protocol Implementation Act* helped to provide some structure to federal government planning for climate change.[23] Going forward, the Conservative government's plan to regulate GHGs, together with other air pollutants, was embodied in *Turning the Corner: An Action Plan to Reduce Greenhouse Gases and Air Pollution.*[24] *Turning the Corner* confirmed energy efficiency measures related to fuel consumption standards for vehicles to apply effective the 2011 model year, and called for the elimination of most incandescent lighting by 2012. *Turning the Corner* was not intended to address Canada's Kyoto commitment of a 6 percent GHG reduction from 1990 levels by 2012. Instead, a new *Regulatory Framework for Air Emissions* was proposed with the intention of reducing GHG emissions 20 percent from 2006 levels by 2020.[25] It is anticipated that these reductions will be realized on the basis of regulations applicable to large final emitters (LFEs): fossil-fuel electricity generation, oil and gas, forest products, smelting and refining, iron and steel, iron-ore pelletizing, potash, lime, and chemical production, and cement. The proposal calls for emission intensity targets rather than absolute reductions and will apply on a differential basis to existing and new facilities. The operational implications of this approach were explained by Environment Canada as follows:

> The April 2007 framework set an initial required reduction of 18% percent from 2006 emission-intensity levels in 2010 for existing facilities. Every year thereafter, a 2% continuous improvement in emission intensity would be required. By 2015, therefore, an emission-intensity reduction of 26% from 2006 levels would be required, with a further

---

Federal Approach to Climate Change," online: www.oag-bvg.gc.ca/internet/docs/c20060901ce.pdf.

22 *Kyoto Protocol Implementation Act*, SC 2007, c 30.

23 The legislation was repealed by the *Jobs, Growth and Long-term Prosperity Act*, SC 2012, c 19, s 699. For assessment of the *Kyoto Protocol Implementation Act*, see *2012 Spring Report of the Commissioner of the Environment and Sustainable Development* (Ottawa: Office of the Auditor General, 2012) c 1, "Kyoto Protocol Implementation Act," online: www.oag-bvg.gc.ca/internet/English/parl_cesd_201205_01_e_36773.html.

24 Introduced 26 April 2007, online: publications.gc.ca/collections/collection_2009/ec/En88-2-2008E.pdf.

25 Environment Canada, *Regulatory Framework for Air Emissions*, introduced 26 April 2008, online: www.ec.gc.ca/doc/media/m_124/toc_eng.htm.

reduction to 33% by 2020. The emission-intensity approach ties the emission reduction targets to production. This allows emission reductions to be achieved while accommodating economic growth.

New facilities, which are those whose first year of operation is 2004 or later, would be granted a three-year commissioning period before they would face an emission-intensity reduction target. After the third year, new facilities would be required to improve their emission intensity each year by 2%. A cleaner fuel standard would be applied, thereby setting the target as if they were using the designated fuel. A flexible approach would be taken in special cases where the equipment or technology used in a new plant facilitates carbon capture and storage or otherwise offers a significant and imminent potential for emission reductions.

The purpose of this policy is to provide an incentive for new facilities to choose cleaner fuels or to invest in the technology needed for carbon capture and storage or in other less emission-intensive technologies.

For both existing and new facilities, fixed process emissions, which are emissions tied to production and for which there is no alternative reduction technology, would receive a 0% target in the regulations. In other words, for these types of emissions, there is no way, with current technology, for them to be reduced except by shutting down production.[26]

Three options were set out to allow regulated sectors to achieve their target objectives: actual reductions in emissions intensity; financial contributions to a technology fund payable at an initial rate of $15 per tonne on excess emissions of CO_2; or the purchase of emission credits generated for exchange within Canada, or derived from domestic "offsets," or associated with international mechanisms established under the Kyoto Protocol.[27]

Additional measures to promote carbon capture and storage at oil sands facilities and to eliminate coal-fired energy production were announced in March 2008 as refinements to the *Regulatory Framework*.

On a longer horizon, the *Regulatory Framework* called for further emission reductions to be achieved by mid-century. In response to a

---

26   *Ibid* at para 2.1.
27   See M Doelle, "Global Carbon Trading and Climate Change Mitigation in Canada: Options for the Use of the Kyoto Mechanisms" in S Bernstein *et al*, eds, *A Globally Integrated Climate Policy for Canada* (Toronto: University of Toronto Press, 2008) 189.

formal request for guidance in achieving longer-term GHG emission reductions, ultimately in the order of a 45 percent to 60 percent reduction from 2003 levels by 2050, the NRTEE set out the following recommendations:

> Implement a strong, clear, consistent and certain GHG emission price signal across the entire Canadian economy as soon as possible in order to successfully shift Canada to a lower GHG emissions pathway, achieve the targeted reductions for 2020 and 2050, avoid higher emission prices that a delay would entail, and reduce cumulative emissions released to the atmosphere.
>
> Institute a market-based policy that takes the form of an emission tax or a cap-and-trade system or a combination of the two.
>
> Develop complementary regulatory policies, in conjunction with the emission price signal, to address sectors of the Canadian economy that do not respond effectively to such a price signal or where market failures exist. [28]

Several attempts have been made through litigation to accelerate decision making or to promote compliance. In the spring of 2007, the environmental NGO Friends of the Earth commenced litigation in order to compel the federal minister of the environment to take action in response to national greenhouse gas emissions. The application for judicial review, which was eventually declared to be non-justiciable, asserted that the minister failed to comply with requirements set out in the *Kyoto Protocol Implementation Act*. [29] Resort to the courts in Canada for judicial enforcement of climate change response roughly parallels litigation in other jurisdictions including Australia and the United States where judicial decisions confirmed and reinforced the existence of administrative authority to take action to assess and control greenhouse gas emissions. [30] Thus, a federal permit associated with an oil sands development in Alberta was determined to be invalid because the environ-

---

28 *Getting to 2050: Canada's Transition to a Low-emission Future* (Ottawa: National Round Table on the Environment and the Economy, 2007) at 49.

29 *Friends of the Earth v Canada (Governor in Council)*, 2008 FC 1183, aff'd 2009 FCA 297, leave to appeal to SCC refused, [2009] SCCA 497.

30 In *Massachusetts v EPA* (2 April 2007) case no 05-1120 (US Supreme Court), the Court required the agency to include CO_2 emissions in its regulatory work (online: www.supremecourtus.gov/opinions/06pdf/05-1120.pdf). The Land and Environment Court of New South Wales, Australia decided on 29 November 2006 that an environmental assessment prepared by the Centennial Coal company did not adequately account for greenhouse gas emissions that would result from coal produced by the proposed Anvil Hill mine if approved. See *Gray v The Minister of Planning and Ors*, [2006] NSWLEC 720.

mental assessment report on which it was based failed to address greenhouse gas emissions in an adequate manner.[31] In addition, a petition was addressed to the Inter-American Commission on Human Rights from representatives of the Inuit Circumpolar Conference who sought relief—ultimately without success—from the United States for the adverse consequences of climate change on their health and livelihoods.[32]

Climate change initiatives at the federal level currently revolve around an overall emissions reduction target that was re-formulated in the context of international negotiations, notably the Copenhagen Accord and subsequent Cancun agreements, that is, 607 million tonnes, or 17 percent below 2005 levels by 2020. In addition to measures directed towards short-term climate pollutants such as black carbon, the government will continue with sector-based regulations that will be harmonized where appropriate with corresponding arrangements in the United States. Transport sector regulations applicable to light and heavy-duty vehicles and regulations applicable to coal-fired electricity generating facilities have been formulated. In the case of the latter, for example, the regulations address several considerations. Firstly, the regulation establishes a performance standard for the intensity of CO_2 emissions from regulated facilities, subject to exceptions based on the substitution of units and for temporary exemptions in relation to emergencies and units integrated with carbon capture and storage systems. The regulations also set out requirements for reporting, submitting, recording, and retaining information. In addition, rules are provided for determining the intensity of CO_2 emissions from regulated units.[33] Comparable regulations are currently being formulated for application in the oil and gas sectors.

Commentators have noted the importance of integration or coordination with climate change response measures that have also continued to evolve at the provincial level across Canada.[34]

---

31 *Pembina Institute for Appropriate Development v Canada (AG)*, [2008] FCJ No 324; *and Imperial Oil Resources Ventures v Canada (Minister of Fisheries and Oceans)*, 2008 FC 598.

32 S Watt-Cloutier, *Petition to the Inter American Commission on Human Rights Seeking Relief from Violations Resulting from Global Warming Caused by Acts and Omissions of the United States* (7 December 2005).

33 *Reduction of Carbon Dioxide Emissions from Coal-Fired Generation of Electricity Regulations*, SOR/2012-167.

34 D Sawyer, D Beugin, & P Gass, *Regulating Carbon Emissions in Canada: Canadian Carbon Policy Year in Review and Emerging Trends, 2012* (International Institute for Sustainable Development Policy Brief, February 2013), online: www.iisd.org/pdf/2012/regulating_carbon_canadian_policy.pdf.

C. PROVINCIAL RESPONSES TO CLIMATE CHANGE

In Alberta, initiatives associated with greenhouse gas emissions and climate change have been underway in the aftermath of a 2002 report, *Albertans and Climate Change: Taking Action*[35] which encouraged progress towards mandatory reporting by large industrial emitters in the province. Subsequently, legislation in the form of the *Climate Change and Emissions Management Act*[36] provided for a provincial emission target aimed at a reduction of specified gas emissions relative to GDP to 50 percent of 1990 levels or less. The legislation also allowed sectoral arrangements to facilitate achievement of that target, among other technical matters.[37] Gas emitters were a particular focus of early regulation, and efforts to ensure consistency with anticipated federal regulations are already underway.

It is notable that the approach taken by Alberta addresses *emission intensity* relative to the overall level of economic activity in the province. This focus on emission intensity—now also reflected in federal regulation—may reduce the rate of growth in greenhouse gas emissions, but is not directed at the more fundamental question of reducing the total level of such emissions. Accordingly, Alberta's intensity-based approach has been criticized for failing to rigorously address the urgent need for lower overall emissions.

Like Alberta, Nova Scotia enacted legislation, the *Environmental Goals and Sustainable Prosperity Act*, to establish a provincial framework on climate change.[38] This statutory landmark establishes a wide range of environmental and economic goals. Those provisions most directly linked to climate change and greenhouse gas emissions included the adoption of emission standards for greenhouse gases and pollutants from new vehicles by 2010. Targets for emissions of nitrogen oxides and greenhouse gases were also proposed. The legislation set out the further objective of meeting 18.5 percent of the province's electricity needs from renewable sources by 2013.[39]

Quebec's initial response to climate change dating from 1995 took the form of an essentially voluntary action plan to encourage the stabil-

35   Online: environment.gov.ab.ca/info/library/6123.pdf.
36   *Climate Change and Emissions Management Act*, SA 2003, c C-16.7. Now see *Climate Change and Emissions Management Amendment Act*, SA 2007, c 4, online: environment.gov.ab.ca/info/library/6123.pdf.
37   *Climate Change and Emissions Management Act*, above note 36, ss 3 & 4.
38   *Environmental Goals and Sustainable Prosperity Act*, SNS 2007, c 7.
39   *Ibid*, s 4.

ization of greenhouse gas emissions in keeping with the general goals of the *Framework Convention on Climate Change.*[40] Following Kyoto, a somewhat more ambitious action plan was introduced in 2000 and replaced by a third formulation, *Quebec and Climate Change: A Challenge for the Future, 2006–2012.*[41] This program, comprised of some two dozen sectorally-oriented actions, was expected to reduce emissions of greenhouse gases by 10 megatons of CO_2 or equivalent gases by 2012, bringing overall emissions to approximately 1.5 percent below 1990 levels. Four guiding principles underpinned the design of the Quebec plan:

1) Assuming our responsibilities in our fields of jurisdiction
2) Economic efficiency to preserve the competitiveness of Quebec's companies
3) Complementarity of interventions in such manner as to maximize the positive impacts
4) The participation of all members of Quebec society: citizens, companies, municipalities and public institutions.[42]

A new climate change action program for the period 2013–2020 was announced in 2012 with the objective of reducing greenhouse gas emissions to 20 percent below 1990 levels by 2020, primarily as a result of initiatives in the transportation, building, and industrial sectors.[43]

Early Ontario policy initiatives included proposals to replace coal-fired electricity generation with cleaner sources of power and renewable supplies, as well as demand reduction measures. Other steps involved the introduction of ethanol to gasoline,[44] and financial encouragement to the automobile sector to pursue significantly increased fuel efficiency. In 2008, Ontario and Quebec agreed to more vigorous joint action and have begun to explore participation in the Western Climate Initiative, discussed below in connection with British Columbia's climate change policy.

Early statutory proposals intended to strengthen the formal framework for advancing emissions reductions in the province were unsuccessful.[45] Subsequently, however, legislative arrangements have been implemented to facilitate emissions trading and to require reporting on

---

40 Online: www.mddep.gouv.qc.ca/changements/inter_en.htm.
41 Online: www.mddep.gouv.qc.ca/changements/plan_action/2006-2012_en.pdf.
42 *Ibid* at 19.
43 Online at: www.mddefp.gouv.qc.ca/changements/plan_action/pacc2020-en.pdf.
44 Ontario, Ministry of the Environment, News Release, "Ontario Makes Progress on Climate Change" (16 February 2005).
45 Bill 179, *Ontario Climate Change Act, 2006*; Bill 200, *Ontario Climate Change Act, 2007*.

greenhouse gas emissions.[46] These initiatives have been accompanied by a series of discussion papers and policy proposals.[47] Shortly after finalization of federal regulations concerning coal-fired electricity producers, Ontario announced its intention to phase out all coal-fired thermal electricity production in the southern region of the province. In a 2012 assessment, the Environmental Commissioner of Ontario identified the energy sector as a central element of further progress towards provincial GHG reduction targets:

> Ontario's greatest opportunity to decarbonize its economy and achieve its target of 150 Mt by 2020—and the much more challenging total emission level of 35 Mt by 2050—lies in its low-carbon electricity supply. If the province succeeds in increasing and improving this supply, it can be used as a substitute for fossil fuels in other sectors, such as transportation and industry, which continue to be major sources of GHGs.[48]

In the Speech from the Throne, 13 February 2007, British Columbia outlined three key initiatives on climate change. The provincial government expressed its intention to set a target to reduce greenhouse gas emissions by 33 percent below current levels by 2020, to set new tailpipe emissions standards for all new vehicles sold in BC, and to identify practical options for making the Government of BC carbon neutral by 2010.[49] Subsequently, British Columbia announced its participation in the Climate Registry, a greenhouse gas database and reporting system operating in jurisdictions whose cumulative population exceeds 200 million. The registry will allow members to track progress in emissions reduction. In collaboration with California, the province has also undertaken to cap greenhouse gas emissions, such that, by 2020, levels would be reduced to at least 1990 levels. The two Pacific coast jurisdictions also work together to reduce greenhouse gases from the transportation sector by adopting a low carbon fuel standard and greenhouse gas tailpipe emissions. Additional elements of the 31 May Memorandum

---

46 *Environmental Protection Amendment Act (Greenhouse Gas Emissions Trading)*, 2009, SO 2009, c 27; *Greenhouse Gas Emissions Reporting Regulation*, O Reg 452/09.

47 Ontario, Moving *Forward: A Greenhouse Gas Cap-and-Trade System for Ontario* (June 2009); Ontario, Ministry of the Environment, *Greenhouse Gas Emissions Reductions in Ontario: A Discussion Paper* (January 2013), online: www.downloads. ene.gov.on.ca/envision/env_reg/er/documents/2013/011-7940.pdf.

48 Environment Commissioner of Ontario, "Opportunities," online: www.ecoissues. ca/index.php/GHG12_Opportunities.

49 British Columbia, *Speech from the Throne* (13 February 2007).

of Understanding involve aggressive clean and renewable energy poli-cies, and a "Hydrogen Highway" linking BC and California.[50]

British Columbia's February 2008 budget announced the introduc-tion of a carbon tax to take effect in July 2008. The tax, initially set at $10 per tonne of CO_2, has increase annually in increments of $5 to $30 in July 2012. Upon introduction, it applied to gasoline, diesel fuel, natural gas, home-heating fuel, propane, and coal. The measure is intended to be "revenue neutral," in that income tax reductions cor-responding to the value of the new tax will be made. The province also introduced legislation, including the *Greenhouse Gas Reduction (Cap and Trade) Act*, to permit trading under a hard cap within the frame-work of the Western Climate Initiative.[51]

British Columbia was the first Canadian province to join the Western Climate Initiative (WCI), a multi-jurisdictional consortium launched by the US states of California, Washington, New Mexico, Oregon, and Arizona in February 2007. One central objective of the WCI is the creation of a versatile regional carbon-trading mechanism to encourage an efficient and effective market-based approach to green-house gas emissions reduction.[52]

In July 2008, the WCI announced a recommended design for a cap-and-trade emissions reduction program which was further refined in 2010.[53] In contrast with regulatory measures oriented around emis-sions intensity standards, the WCI trading program is grounded upon an aggregate regional cap, representing a level of total regional emis-sions which will progressively decline over the course of successive three-year compliance periods. Methodology for apportioning allow-ances amongst participating jurisdictions within the capped aggregate regional emissions level is incorporated within the framework. Partici-pating governments are responsible for the distribution of allowances within their own jurisdictions, having regard to such considerations as consumer impacts, worker and industrial transition requirements,

---

50   Online: www2.news.gov.bc.ca/news_releases_2005-2009/2007OTP0075-000704-Attachment1.pdf.

51   *Greenhouse Gas Reduction (Cap and Trade) Act*, SBC 2008, c 32. See also *Green-house Gas Reduction (Renewable and Low Carbon Fuel Requirements) Act*, SBC 2008, c 16; *Greenhouse Gas Reduction (Vehicle Emissions Standards) Act*, SBC 2008, c 21 (not yet in force).

52   See, generally, CJ Kneteman, "Building an Effective North American Emissions Trading System: Key Considerations and Canada's Role" (2010) 20 J Envtl L & Prac 127.

53   Western Climate Initiative, "Design for the WCI Regional Program" (July 2010), online: www.westernclimateinitiative.org/the-wci-cap-and-trade-program/program-design.

adaptation to climate change impacts, recognition of early reduction efforts, and so on. The WCI cap-and-trade program applies initially (2012) to facilities or entities in electricity generation, industry, and commerce with an emission threshold of 25,000 metric tons of CO_2. Coverage will be extended in the second compliance period (2015) to smaller facilities and transportation.

The WCI cap-and-trade framework anticipates the use of offsets whereby regulated facilities that do not meet their reduction targets directly from internal operations may purchase substitute credits from other eligible activities, including use of the Kyoto Protocol's Clean Development Mechanism and Joint Implementation arrangements. As explained by the WCI, offsets are emission reduction projects undertaken to address emissions not included in a cap-and-trade program. An offset mechanism enables covered entities to offset their own emissions by purchasing emission reduction credits generated through projects that address emissions not covered by the cap. Participants in the WCI cap-and-trade mechanism have also recognized the significance of other policies in meeting greenhouse gas-reduction targets and are exploring ways to integrate such other policies, including BC's carbon tax, with the cap-and-trade system.[54]

Saskatchewan's Energy and Climate Change Plan, as announced in 2007, was underpinned by a frank acknowledgement of the impacts of climate change on provincial forests, on the prairie landscape and on the availability of fresh water within the jurisdiction. The program highlighted five elements known as "emissions reductions wedges":

- Conservation and efficiency measures by industry, business and homeowners;
- Carbon dioxide capture and storage measures in Saskatchewan's oil and gas industry and in the province's electricity sector;
- Increased use of renewable energy, including wind, solar power and hydrogen, and further development of Saskatchewan's ethanol and biodiesel resources;
- Reduction of methane and other emissions in the oil and gas industry, and methane and nitrous oxide emissions in the agriculture industry; and
- Creation of more natural carbon sinks in Saskatchewan's forests and soils.[55]

---

54   For details in the program design, see online: www.westernclimateinitiative.org/
designing-the-program.

55   Saskatchewan, News Release, "New Plan Attacks Climate Change in Saskatchewan" (14 June 2007).

Following a change in government, a new set of principles was articulated to guide provincial climate change legislation. These included:

1. *Flexibility*: Ability to accommodate emerging legislative and regulatory regimes in Canada, the US and internationally;
2. *Saskatchewan First*: Retain carbon emission payments in Saskatchewan to support investments in real GHG reductions to meet provincial GHG reduction targets;
3. *Competitiveness*: Maintain the competitiveness of Saskatchewan industries, including emission-intensive trade exposed sectors, to support sustained economic growth;
4. *Simplicity*: Administrative efficiency, simplicity and certainty for regulated industries; and,
5. *Collaboration*: A cooperative framework for program implementation between government, industry and other stakeholders.

Legislation, *An Act Respecting the Management and Reduction of Greenhouse Gases and Adaptation to Climate Change*, was enacted in 2010 but at the time of writing is not yet in force.[56]

D. MUNICIPAL ACTION

For their part, Canadian municipalities have also moved to address the climate change concerns of their constituents. They have acted, often in advance of provincial or federal guidance, in areas of responsibility available to them. In relation to transportation, for example, specific legal measures have included the creation of dedicated multi-passenger lanes. In the construction field, we have seen stricter regulation of building in flood plains or other vulnerable areas. Some communities have begun to deal either through guidelines or bylaws with idling vehicles. Other municipal programs seek to encourage residential, commercial and industrial renovation to enhance heating and cooling efficiency. Some Canadian municipalities have also demonstrated initiative in relation to the energy use and emissions of their own fleets of vehicles, and in relation to emergency preparedness.

Overall, municipal action in Canada has been stimulated and encouraged since 1998 through a program known as Partners for Climate Protection. Approximately 220 Canadian municipalities now partici-

---

56   Saskatchewan, Ministry of Environment, "Participant Background Materials: Consultations on the Climate Change Regulations" (March 2010), online: www.environment.gov.sk.ca/adx/aspx/adxgetmedia.aspx?MediaID=3210&Filename=Summary%20of%20Climate%20Change%20Regulations.pdf.

pate in this network, which is associated with international counter-parts around the world.[57] Municipal efforts are now widespread and can merely be illustrated here.[58]

In 2003, Vancouver's city council sought expert guidance on the challenges of climate change at the municipal level. Recommendations from the Cool Vancouver Taskforce culminated in two sets of climate change goals. The first set of objectives targeted municipal operations with a *Corporate Climate Change Action Plan*. The second set of goals, embodied in a *Community Climate Change Action Plan*, was oriented towards citizens and residents.

Approved by Council on 15 March 2005, the fundamental goal of the *Corporate Climate Change Action Plan*[59] is for Vancouver to reduce GHG emissions from its own facilities and operations by 20 percent of 1990 levels by 2010. The corporate plan rests on eight fundamental priorities:

1. Energy efficient retro-fits for facilities
2. Green design for new and replacement civic buildings
3. Green energy and sustainable dense development
4. Active and public transportation
5. Fuel-efficient fleets and fleet management
6. Energy efficient street/park lighting and traffic control signals
7. Corporate waste reduction and landfill gas utilization
8. Educating people to curb energy demands

Approved at the same time as the corporate plan, the *Community Climate Change Action Plan*[60] sought to engage residents in efforts to reduce their own GHG emissions 6 percent from 1990 levels by 2012 on the basis of six priority initiatives:

1. Home renovations for energy efficiency
2. Energy efficient retro-fits for institutional facilities
3. Energy efficient retro-fits for large commercial buildings
4. Bio-diesel fuel blends
5. Efficient driver training and anti-idling

---

57   Federation of Canadian Municipalities, "Partners for Climate Protection," on-line: www.fcm.ca/home/programs/partners-for-climate-protection.htm.

58   BJ Richardson, ed, *Local Climate Change Law: Environmental Regulation in Cities and Other Localities* (Edward Elgar Publishing: Cheltenham, 2012). The Federa-tion of Canadian Municipalities has provided extensive guidance on climate change issues through webinars. See online: www.fcm.ca/home/events/past-webinars-and-workshops.htm.

59   See City of Vancouver, *Greenest City: 2020 Action Plan*, online: vancouver.ca/files/cov/Greenest-city-action-plan.pdf.

60   City of Vancouver, "Climate Change Adaptation Strategy" (28 June 2012), on-line: www.cakex.org/sites/default/files/documents/rr1.pdf.

6.   Transportation alternatives

In Halifax, the *SMART Community Action Guide to Climate Change and Emergency Preparedness* dates from September 2006.[61] The guide combines encouragement to reduce GHG emissions with discussion of adaptation to the effects of climate change. Thus, it highlights recent weather disruptions, such as ice storms, torrential rains and flooding, and advises residents on how to adapt and protect themselves from such occurrences. It then encourages behaviour that reduces GHG emissions by drawing the connection between adverse weather phenomena and GHG emissions.

Quebec City provides an additional example, indeed one predating the Vancouver and Halifax initiatives. In 2004, Quebec adopted a *Plan de réduction des émissions de gaz à effet de serre*.[62] The initiative aimed to reduce municipal GHG emissions by 60,000 tonnes by 2010. By 2005, just one year after the adoption of the policy, the city had reached 75 percent of its objective, in that 46,000 tonnes of GHG emissions had already been eliminated by measures directed at four key sectors:

1)   waste and recycling,
2)   motorized equipment and transportation,
3)   municipal installations, and
4)   other sectors of intervention.

The City of Quebec's plan emphasizes that substantial savings can be expected from reducing GHG emissions. Specifically, the plan estimated that emissions reductions during the initial phase could produce savings of approximately $15,527,000 that could be reinvested in the local economy.

E. CLIMATE CHANGE ADAPTATION

Alongside initiatives intended to reduce GHG emissions and thereby lessen or *mitigate* the impact of human activity on the atmosphere, it is now necessary to take steps to *adapt* a wide range of operations and infrastructure to the effects of climate change. Adaptation challenges will vary with regional circumstances. Thus, the impact of heat in large urban centres such as Toronto may pose particular risks from

---

61   *Community Action Plan for Climate Change*, available on the Halifax Regional Municipality website, online: www.halifax.ca/climate/index.html.
62   *Plan d'action* (2005), online: www.ville.quebec.qc.ca/publications/docs_ville/gaz_serre.pdf.

the perspective of public health. In northern Canada, melting permafrost threatens to destabilize transportation and other infrastructure. In British Columbia milder temperatures have already undermined the effect of cold weather to control populations of mountain pine beetles, while the Prairies may now be exposed to more prolonged periods of devastating drought. Financial arrangements such as disaster relief, crop insurance or income stabilization funds constitute elements of an adaptation program, as do initiatives such as the National Disaster Mitigation Strategy formulated under the leadership of Public Safety and Emergency Preparedness Canada.[63]

Once again, the Stern Review provides useful general guidance about the range of measures likely to be highly relevant in adapting to the local and regional effects of climate change.

> Adaptation to climate change—that is, taking steps to build resilience and minimize costs—is essential. It is no longer possible to prevent the climate change that will take place over the next two to three decades, but it is still possible to protect our societies and economies from its impacts to some extent—for example, by providing better information, improved planning and more climate-resilient crops and infrastructure.[64]

Governments at all levels will be called upon to support adaptation measures, ranging from the possibility of strengthened water-rationing programs in the municipal context, through provincial land-use controls intended to reduce the vulnerability of buildings and their inhabitants to natural disasters. All Canadian provinces have indicated their intention to address adaptation, while several jurisdictions have recently published adaptation strategies:

- British Columbia, *Preparing for Climate Change: British Columbia's Adaptation Strategy* (2010)
- Ontario, *Climate Ready: Ontario's Adaptation Strategy and Action Plan, 2011–2014* (2011)
- Quebec, *2013–2020 Government Strategy for Climate Change Adaptation* (2012)
- Nunavut, Yukon and Northwest Territories, *Pan-Territorial Adaptation Strategy: Moving Forward on Climate Change Adaptation in Canada's North* (2011)

---

63   *2006 September Report of the Commissioner of the Environment and Sustainable Development*, above note 21, c 2 "Adapting to the Impacts of Climate Change" at 4–5.

64   Stern, above note 9 at vii.

At the federal level, climate modelling and research are expected to receive increased attention. Natural Resources Canada is currently overseeing two programs along these lines, the *Climate Impacts and Adaptation Program*, and a second initiative on *Reducing Canada's Vulnerability to Climate Change.*

FURTHER READING

Agenda for Climate Action (Arlington, VA: Pew Center on Global Climate Change, 2006)

BANKES, N, "The Legal and Regulatory Issues Associated with Carbon Capture and Storage in Arctic States" (2012) 6 Carbon and Climate Law Review 21

BERNSTEIN, S, *et al*, eds, *A Globally Integrated Climate Policy for Canada* (Toronto: University of Toronto Press, 2008)

BOTHE, M, & E Rehbinder, *Climate Change Policy* (Utrecht: Eleven International, 2005)

BRUNÉE, J, M DOELLE, & L RAJAMANI, eds, *Promoting Compliance in an Evolving Climate Regime* (Cambridge UP, 2011)

BURTON, I, *et al*, *Adaptation Policy Framework for Climate Change: Developing Policies, Strategies, Measures* (Cambridge: Cambridge UP, 2005)

COURCHENE, TJ, & JR ALLAN, *Carbon Pricing and Environmental Federalism* (McGill-Queen's UP, 2010)

DOELLE, M, *From Hot Air to Action?: Climate Change, Compliance and the Future of International Environmental Law* (Toronto: Thomson/ Carswell, 2005)

FREESTONE, D, & C STRECK, *Legal Aspects of Carbon Trading: Kyoto, Copenhagen and Beyond* (Oxford UP, 2009)

HAITES, E, *Harmonisation between National and International Tradeable Permit Schemes* (Paris: OECD, 2003), online: www.oecd.org/ dataoecd/11/63/2957623.pdf

HOLMES, M, *et al*, *All Over the Map 2012: A Comparison of Provincial Climate Change Plans* (David Suzuki Foundation, March 2012)

INTERGOVERNMENTAL PANEL ON CLIMATE CHANGE, *Climate Change 2007: the Physical Science Basis, Summary for Policy Makers* (Cambridge: Cambridge UP, 2007), online: www.ipcc.ch/publications_

and_data/publications_ipcc_fourth_assessment_report_wg1_report_the_physical_science_basis.htm

LANTZ, V, & J RUGGERI, eds, *The Kyoto Protocol and Environmental Policy in Atlantic Canada* (Fredericton, NB: Policy Studies Centre, University of New Brunswick, 2003)

MAHONY, D, ed, *Climate Change Law in Canada* (Toronto: Canada Law Book, 2011)

MEADOWS, T, & AR LUCAS, "Alberta Climate Change Law and Policy" in D. Mahony, ed, *The Law of Climate Change in Canada* (Toronto: Canada Law Book, 2010)

MEADOWS, T, & T Crossman, "A Tale of Two Provinces: Imposing Greenhouse Gas Emissions Constraints Through Law and Policy in Alberta and British Columbia" (2010) 47 Alta L Rev 421

PAEHLKE, RC, *Some Like It Cold: The Politics of Climate Change in Canada* (Toronto: Between the Lines, 2008)

Reality Check: The State of Climate Progress in Canada (Ottawa: National Roundtable on Environment and Economy, 2012)

SAWYER, D, D BEUGIN, & P GASS, *Canadian Carbon Policy Year in Review and Emerging Trends, 2012* (IISD Policy Brief, February 2013)

SIMPSON, J, M JACCARD, & N RIVERS, *Hot Air: Meeting Canada's Climate Change Challenge* (Toronto: McClelland & Stewart, 2007)

STERN, N, *The Economics of Climate Change: The Stern Review* (Cambridge: Cambridge University Press, 2007)

TRUDEAU, H, & S LALONDE, "La mise en oeuvre du Protocole de Kyoto au Canada: concertation ou coercitation?" (2004) 34 RGD 141

CONCLUSION

Not long ago, the agility of pre-robotic, pre-mutant, and pre-digital cartoon characters such as rabbits and roadrunners was constantly being tested at the brink of disaster, notably in proximity to terrifying cliffs. As they approached the edge of a daunting precipice, some of these colourful creatures would attempt—with mixed and limited success—to screech to a halt; others seemed capable of launching themselves into the air and then, with an incredible reversal of spinning feet, defying gravity to return to the safety of the ledge. An assessment of the adequacy and prospects for the contemporary environmental protection regime is likely to be influenced by metaphor: do we still have a little traction to work with on the ledge, or have we already gone over the brink? Those readers whose imaginations require the stimulus of further drama and suspense, may factor in the destabilizing effects of climate change: anyone hoping to screech to a halt or return to the safety of the ledge after overshooting the mark must now remember that the ledge itself is crumbling.

To present the situation less abstractly, it is helpful to note conclusions from the OECD's 2012 report *Environmental Outlook to 2050: The Consequences of Inaction*. This study, in projecting significant population and economic growth to the mid–twenty-first century highlights severe environmental threats in terms of water availability, adverse public health impacts, disruptive climate change, and biodiversity loss. In the OECD's assessment, "progress on an incremental, piecemeal, business-as-usual basis in the coming decades will not be enough."[1]

---

1   *OECD Environmental Outlook to 2050: The Consequences of Inaction* (OECD Pub-

In these circumstances, to contemplate a future for environmental law—even in general terms—is something of a cause for celebration. It is also to acknowledge defeat. This paradox derives from sharply divergent perceptions of the efficacy of law as a response to environmental problems. For those who anticipated ecological apocalypse, mere survival must constitute something of a success, while from the perspective of those who have championed one legal innovation after another as *the* magic answer, the continuation of struggle against environmental degradation will be something of a setback. But so it will be, a future much like the past in which a wide range of instruments will be employed against an equally wide range of multifaceted problems in a complicated and dynamic context.

The first of the contextual elements is the continuation of environmental crises and resource depletion. Arctic ice cover is retreating rapidly; the collapse of fish stocks on a global basis is predicted; increasing average temperatures around the world threaten irreversible and accelerating transformation of planetary climate control systems. Despite significant advances in Canada, including some progress in terms of the rehabilitation of particular sites and ecosystems, there can be no illusion about general success in bringing severe threats of continuing environmental risk under control. Old bad habits die hard, and it is only realistic to anticipate new indications of significant environmental deterioration, further toxic and industrial accidents, and ongoing resource depletion.

The economic context will also continue to affect environmental regimes. One effect of the combined impact of habitual deficits and accumulated debt, trade liberalization, and international competition has been longstanding pressure to relieve "regulatory burdens." To some degree this has been attempted through the downloading of environmental responsibilities to local governments. Several jurisdictions have also witnessed severe reductions in public expenditures for environmental research, monitoring, and enforcement, although the pattern may now be reversing.

There has also been evidence of a tendency to consider harmonization measures in order to mitigate the potential—if poorly documented—impact of so-called "pollution havens" on domestic investment and employment. International legal developments relating to the environment are another continuing influence, an increasing one,

lishing, 2012) at 19, online: www.oecd.org/environment/indicators-modelling-outlooks/oecdenvironmentaloutlookto2050theconsequencesofinaction.htm.

perhaps, as compliance and enforcement mechanisms become a focus of attention.

Federalism and *Charter* considerations also remain highly relevant in litigation and to the design and effectiveness of the overall Canadian environmental regime. The *Charter's* influence on the environmental regime to date has been indirect. By formalizing the procedural protections applicable in the context of investigation and prosecutions, the *Charter* may have increased the cost and complexity of the enforcement process. On the other hand, this situation has probably helped to redirect attention to other and perhaps more efficient means of promoting compliance and environmental protection.

Lawyers can no longer remain as professionally isolated from scientific and ecological considerations as they have often been in the past, for resource use and management decisions require continuing reassessment from the perspective of health and environmental consequences. Cooperative problem-solving and alternative dispute-resolution approaches in the environmental context present additional opportunities and challenges for the corporate bar, government lawyers, and public-interest counsel alike. New institutions need to be designed and managed, while those participating in business and environmental policy-making will require the assistance of counsel with strategic planning skills. These requirements for a more informed scientific understanding and for more sophisticated approaches to dispute resolution are examples of ways in which members of the legal profession are being asked to grapple with the implications of sustainability as an emerging environmental norm and a contending economic paradigm.

An extended commentary on the status of sustainability cannot be attempted here, but it can at least be noted that statutory affirmations have proliferated. Corporate and institutional endorsements—though sometimes cautious and qualified—have been commonplace. Moreover, numerous sustainable-development research centres have been established. However, while the conceptual foundations are gradually being laid, the utility of sustainability as an enforceable legal standard remains to be determined. And, regrettably, the notion of sustainability seems as yet poorly connected to the challenge of global population growth.

The precautionary approach also offers great promise. As an antidote to an unfortunate pattern of underestimating the severity of environmental risks and overestimating our capacity to respond, it is long overdue. But, again, an uphill battle is in store for its advocates. And, in some of its most recent Canadian statutory formulation as "erring on the side of caution," the justiciability of this principle appears challenging indeed.

If the developments described in this volume in relation to toxics, environmental assessment, economic incentives, and the extension of responsibility have anything in common, it is perhaps to be found in the potential now in place for systematic preventive action rather than the more *ad hoc* remedial impact of earlier initiatives. By moving towards the consideration of policy, planning, and cumulative impact, environmental assessment procedures might become better able to identify the underlying causes of environmental damage. By identifying specific toxics for rigorous controls—or in some cases "virtual elimination"—government can more effectively direct administrative resources towards preventing harm. And by extending liability to financial institutions that facilitate economic activity, government and the courts will sensitize these institutions to the campaign for environmental quality. More broadly, economic incentives require strengthening through effective environmental valuation and the unwinding of harmful subsidies. Measures taken to highlight the personal responsibility of directors and officers, to expand opportunities for public participation in environmental decision making, and to mitigate the adverse consequences of consumer behaviour are further important dimensions of the Canadian environmental law regime on whose success the well-being of future generations depends. For some time we have been doing better, but we are not yet doing well enough.

WEBSITES

Alberta Department of Environment: www.environment.alberta.ca

Arctic Council: www.arctic-council.org/index.php/en

British Columbia Ministry of Environment: www.gov.bc.ca/env

Canadian Council of Ministers of the Environment: www.ccme.ca
Canadian Environmental Assessment Agency: www.ceaa.gc.ca
Canadian Environmental Law Association: www.cela.ca
Canadian Parks and Wilderness Society: www.cpaws.org
Canadian Water and Wastewater Association: www.cwwa.ca
Commission for Environmental Cooperation: www.cec.org
Commissioner of the Environment and Sustainable Development:
    www.oag-bvg.gc.ca
Committee on the Status of Endangered Wildlife in Canada:
    www.cosewic.gc.ca
Convention on Biological Diversity: www.cbd.int
Convention on International Trade in Endangered Species:
    www.cites.org

Environment Canada: www.ec.gc.ca
Environmental Commissioner of Ontario: www.eco.on.ca
Environmental Law Centre (Alberta): www.elc.ab.ca

Federation of Canadian Municipalities: www.fcm.ca
Intergovernmental Panel on Climate Change: www.ipcc.ch
International Institute for Sustainable Development: www.iisd.org

International Joint Commission: www.ijc.org
International Union for Conservation of Nature: www.iucn.org

Manitoba Department of Conservation: www.gov.mb.ca/conservation

National Pollutants Release Inventory: www.ec.gc.ca/inrp-npri/
Nature Conservancy of Canada: www.natureconservancy.ca
New Brunswick Department of Environment: www2.gnb.ca/content/
gnb/en/departments/elg.html
Newfoundland and Labrador Department of Environment:
www.env.gov.nl.ca/env
Nova Scotia Department of Environment: www.gov.ns.ca/nse
Nunavut Department of Environment: env.gov.nu.ca

Ontario Ministry of the Environment: www.ene.gov.on.ca/environment

Prince Edward Island Department of Environment, Labour and Justice:
www.gov.pe.ca/environment

Quebec Department of Environment: www.mddep.gouv.qc.ca/
index_en.asp

Saskatchewan Department of Environment and Resource Management:
www.environment.gov.sk.ca
Sustainable Prosperity: www.sustainableprosperity.ca

United Nations Environment Program: www.unep.org

West Coast Environmental Law Association: www.wcel.org
World Conservation Union: www.iucn.org
World Wildlife Fund Canada: www.wwf.ca

Yukon Department of Environment: www.env.gov.yk.ca

TABLE OF CASES

INDEX

ABOUT THE AUTHOR

Jamie Benidickson, Faculty of Law, University of Ottawa, teaches Environmental Law, Administrative Law, Water Law, and Legal History. He is the author of *The Culture of Flushing: A Social and Legal History of Sewage* (UBC Press, 2007). His previous publications include *The Temagami Experience: Recreation, Resources and Aboriginal Rights in the Northern Ontario Wilderness* (University of Toronto Press, 1989), *Getting the Green Light: Environmental Regulation and Investment in Canada* (C.D. Howe Institute, 1994), and *Idleness, Water, and A Canoe: Reflections on Paddling for Pleasure* (University of Toronto Press, 1997). In 2004 he was appointed Director of the IUCN Academy of Environmental Law.